THE CHURCH OF ENGLAND

A PORTRAIT

Michael De-la-Noy

SIMON & SCHUSTER

LONDON · SYDNEY · NEW YORK · TOKYO · SINGAPORE · TORONTO

First published in Great Britain by
Simon & Schuster Ltd in 1993
This paperback edition first published by Simon & Schuster Ltd 1994
A Paramount Communications Company

Simon and Schuster Ltd
West Garden Place
Kendal Street
London W2 2AQ

Simon & Schuster of Australia Pty Ltd
Sydney

A CIP catalogue record for this book is
available from the British Library
ISBN 0–671–71292–6

Phototypeset in 11/13 Trump Medieval by
Intype, London

Printed and bound in Great Britain by
Butler & Tanner Ltd, London and Frome

A [illegible] *or:*

Michael De-la-Noy was educated at Bedford School. From 1962 to 1965 he was Religious Editor of Prism Publications and from 1965 to 1967 he represented the diocese of London in the House of Laity of the Church Assembly, serving at the same time as a member of the Steering Committee on Liturgical Revision. From 1967 to 1970 he was press officer to the archbishop of Canterbury, Dr Michael Ramsey, and assistant information officer in the Church Information Office.

Since then he has established a literary reputation as the biographer of Elgar, Denton Welch and Edward Sackville-West; his other books include histories of the Honours System, the Samaritans, Windsor Castle and Oxford. In 1990 he published a personal and affectionate account of his former employer, *Michael Ramsey: A Portrait*.

Also by Michael De-la-Noy

Before the Storm (poems)

A Child's Life of Christ

Young Once Only: A Study of Boys on Probation

A Day in the Life of God

Elgar: The Man

Denton Welch: The Making of a Writer

The Honours System

Acting as Friends: The Story of the Samaritans

Eddy: The Life of Edward Sackville-West

Michael Ramsey: A Portrait

Windsor Castle: Past and Present

Exploring Oxford

Edited

The Fields of Praise: An Anthology of Religious Poetry

The Journals of Denton Welch

The Collected Short Writings of Denton Welch

For my cousin
Gordon Johnson
in gratitude for his generous encouragement

Contents

An Introduction

THE CHOICE in 1991 of an unknown and untried bishop, George Carey, as archbishop of Canterbury has proved to be the most controversial appointment to the throne of St Augustine this century, an event speedily followed in November 1992 by a vote in the General Synod in favour of legislation allowing women to be ordained into the Church of England as priests – the most divisive ecclesiastical decision made in this country in four and a half centuries. No matter how successful the Archbishop is in persuading clergy and laity opposed to women priests to remain in the Church of England, or how many Anglicans eventually seek reception into the Church of Rome, the face of the Church of England has already been changed for ever; by mid–1993 there were 150 women deacons in charge of parishes. And from a liturgical point of view, with much of the spiritual mystique of High Church services abandoned and many evangelical services bearing no recognisable relationship to Anglican worship as it has been known since the Reformation, the Church of England has undergone, in the past decade, a transformation that has distressed faithful worshippers and shocked well-wishers alike.

This was the background against which I set out to write a reasonably objective pen portrait of the contemporary Church of England. But it soon developed into a self-portrait, for those I met – bishops, parish clergy, laity, monks and nuns, chaplains and those engaged in social work – largely speak for themselves, sometimes very amusingly, often very movingly. But an entirely objective book about the Church of England would be virtually impossible; for one thing, there is no objectively archetypal Anglican about whom to write. How could there be in a Church that contains biblical fundamentalists and charismatic Anglo-Catholics, believers in transubstantiation and even – the founder of the Samaritans, an Anglican clergyman, is one – in reincarnation? Hence it should not be assumed that the team rector, for example, whose footsteps I dog in Chapter One is intended to be archetypical. It may come as a surprise to some that he is as hospitable as he is, or drinks so much; others may wonder why he doesn't drink more! Generally speaking, my descent upon vicarages and monasteries, hospitals and prisons has been more or less by chance, but I do believe that in all of those people whose words and actions – sometimes extremely bizarre – I have recorded there resides an essence of Anglicanism.

Keeping abreast of certain developments in the Church of England has, however, presented a far greater problem than merely trying to paint its atmosphere, for events on a number of fronts are moving ahead almost on a daily basis; the future of the theological colleges, the method of appointment of senior clergy like deans and suffragan bishops, and the consequences of the decision (not even ratified by Parliament by the time the book was due to go into production) to ordain women to the priesthood are obvious examples, and I have simply tried to keep the text as up to date as possible.

Two things have struck me in particular: a tendency on the part of social commentators with no serious criteria of success, few of whom ever darken the Church's doors, to regard the Church of England as having, in some ill-defined and generalised manner, 'failed'; and a view held by traditionalists that the Church has been betrayed into the hands of ordained atheists. These people seem to long for a return to some kind of mythical golden age, when the Church was supposedly secure in its faith and its buildings were correspondingly packed to the rafters. It was not, of course, too difficult to fill churches when Parliament made churchgoing compulsory (although many did stay away), and church attendance has frequently been as much a social activity as a religious observance, a Sunday morning's stroll from one three-hour City sermon to the next providing an entertaining eighteenth-century pastime between rising and dining. Again, if a church with a seating capacity of 200 serves a population of 20,000 it may well fill up on Sunday; if twenty churches serve the same population they will probably look pretty empty.

Deciding whether or not the Church has 'failed' raises the question, what is 'the Church'? I happen to believe that the Church's liturgy is in a chaotic state of free fall, and, worse, that nobody in authority cares. At the same time it is quite obvious that in recent years the Church has rediscovered a social gospel that places it in the forefront of agencies struggling to alleviate poverty and injustice. Of course not every parish priest or member of the laity cares about the poor and the homeless, but although, like everyone else, I have met my fair share of unpalatable Christians, in the course of my research I have met many more who make me feel ashamed not to share their faith or goodness. Certainly so far as the Church's social gospel is concerned, the work of someone like Canon Paul Oestreicher, director of international ministry at Coventry Cathedral, makes nonsense of any general assertion that the Church of England has become spiritually – or as a catalyst for good – a spent force. In October 1992 a feeling of public revulsion swept the country when the government precipitately announced plans to close thirty-one coal mines. I cannot remember a previous occasion when so many bishops (on this occasion the Archbishop of York and the Bishops of Durham, Birmingham, Blackburn, Derby, Lichfield, Sheffield, Southwark, Southwell, Wakefield, Sherwood, Shrewsbury, Stafford and Tewkesbury) moved so swiftly to condemn a government in such forthright terms – again making nonsense of the often-heard general criticism that the bishops never give a lead.

In a basically impressionistic book intended for the general reader I have decided to resist any temptation to proffer erudite definitions of ecclesiastical terminology. Anyone trying to write about the Church of England should take heed of the example set by Paul Welsby, the style of whose concise and lucid handbook *How the Church of England Works*[1] cannot, surely, be improved upon. Nevertheless I do realise there are people who do not know the difference between a deacon and a deaconess, a suffragen bishop and a diocesan bishop, what duties fall to an archdeacon, what a faculty is or why some Anglicans practise auricular confession while others are content to receive a general absolution, and for their benefit I have felt it right to provide some basic explanations. I hope that those who already know, and in particular those who know a great deal more than I do, will bear with me.

I should also explain that while this is a book exclusively about the Church of England, I feel that constantly to spell out the full name would be tedious, and I hope members of Christian denominations other than the Church of England will forgive the occasions when I abbreviate and merely refer to 'the Church'. In the case of complementary terms like priest and clergyman, Father and Mister, Mass and holy communion, I have given the liturgical expressions used by the people I am writing about, so that the choice in effect is theirs.

When I began to assemble a list of names to acknowledge I found it would have filled several pages; indeed, I have been overwhelmed by offers of help with research, and by a willingness to be interviewed, and after twenty years away from the centre of Church affairs I have been surprised to discover a friendliness and openness within many areas of the Church of England which did not exist in my day. A failure to answer a letter or thank one for presents still seems to be endemic to Anglican clerics, and there are still certain key establishment figures who suffer from professional paranoia, but there are also bishops who look up times of trains and meet you at the station, chaplains and parish priests who lay on a delicious lunch, and plenty of exceedingly vulnerable men and women in the Church with an enviable moral courage. Those throughout the book who have agreed to be named and to have remarks attributed to them will of course be readily identifiable, and for their great kindness in cooperating I am most grateful. I must emphasise that in every case where an interviewee is identified, permission to be interviewed on an attributable basis has been given, and that all quotations are verbatim.

There are many other people – staff at Church House, for instance – who have no cause to be identified but who have been liberal with help of every kind, and clergy and laity in parishes I visited almost at random who I have thought best and fairest to cloak in anonymity; to all these people, too, I extend heartfelt thanks.

Carol O'Brien, editorial director of Simon & Schuster, has provided much constructive criticism and stimulating encouragement, and Ingrid von Essen has proved a most valuable and conscientious copy editor. Any errors of fact or judgement, however, remain my own. I especially appreciate Lord Runcie's generosity in responding in unlooked-for detail to questions he may well have found painful. And for finding time to give me a lengthy interview, despite a schedule of engagements which might legitimately see importunate authors relegated low on his order of priorities, I am greatly indebted to the Archbishop of Canterbury.

Lines from 'Little Gidding' by T. S. Eliot are reproduced by kind permission of Mrs Valerie Eliot.

Michael De-la-Noy
The Feast Day of the Martyrs of the Serapeum, 1993

ONE

Roughly Knowing What to Do

It was a warm sunny day when I arrived at the rectory, and the garden was full of white blossom. The weather was not the only surprise; the rectory was spacious, spotless and well furnished, a fact that seemed to embarrass the team rector, as the incumbent turned out to be. He confessed that for the first time in thirty years he was better off than any of his parishioners, many of whom had a dozen children and no car.

He showed me into his study, after re-locking the front door, and apologised for making instant coffee. On the telephone I had been promised a 'cream slice', but that, not in the least to my regret, never appeared at all, and I later discovered that 'a cup of coffee and a slice of cream cake' was one of his favourite expressions.

The team rector was rather handsome in a clerical sort of way, and was dressed in a dark suit with a dog collar. He was extremely easy to get along with, laughed a lot but not too much, and talked well and without affectation. He was funny about certain people we both knew – a bishop in particular – but was not in the least uncharitable. There was nothing parsonical about him, but he was unmistakably a 'man of the cloth'. I instantly felt, having more or less drawn his name out of a hat, that I had struck extremely lucky.

It was an hour before we got around to the purpose of my visit, to plan whether it would be possible for me to dog his footsteps while he did whatever it is that Church of England vicars and rectors do. A rector, in years past, was a parish priest who received his tithes (corn, wood, pigs, milk and so on) in full. A vicar looked after a parish on behalf of some cathedral or monastery which had appropriated the greater tithes (corn or wood). Today there is no practical difference between rectors and vicars. A team rector heads a group of churches each with its own vicar.

'I don't think you can come on a bereavement visit,' he said, and I said I quite understood that. Neither, I assured him, did I expect to be present when he was hearing confession. He roared with laughter. By this time we had moved to the sitting room upstairs, which contained a colour television and two brand-new settees, and it seemed to be the atmosphere on the first floor that triggered his embarrassment about being relatively so wealthy. He justified himself (quite needlessly) by explaining that he *had* lived for six years in a mud hut while working as a missionary. At least three telephone calls had been intercepted by the answerphone since I had arrived, and he went off to investigate whether they were important.

When he returned we discussed whether the parish was to be identified. My own view remained strongly that anonymity for the parish and the clergy was right, and that is what I have decided upon. He seemed quite keen that it should be named, though he had recently fallen foul of his local newspaper's idea of a 'good story', which had resulted in a headmaster demanding his resignation. The rector had written in his parish newsletter, 'The reason for all anti-social behaviour is lack of education and lack of jobs.' The local newspaper had inserted the word 'this' between 'all' and 'anti-social', and ran a story claiming the rector had said that better education would have prevented local riots. In his parish newsletter he had not even used the word 'riot'.

However, Father Wright's team ministry is confronted by deprivation on a large scale. Boys of twelve are experimenting with drugs. A parishioner's uncle had gone to prison the previous week for incest. Families of ten are living in two-bedroom accommodation. 'Me sister got banged up last night,' a young unmarried mother remarks with a cheerful grin. Houses and cars have been set alight, youngsters have attacked the fire brigade, and instant retribution was being meted out without reference to the law. Eventually a policeman arrived to patrol the main housing estate on foot.

After reading anthropology at university, Fr Wright trained for the ministry at an Anglo-Catholic theological college, and four years before my visit, after a quarter of a century as a celibate priest, he got married. I was introduced in the hall to his daughter, a pretty baby about to be wheeled out for a walk by her nanny, a young woman from the estate, Fr Wright's wife having returned to a lucrative job in advertising. More clergy wives than ever before find it necessary, or desirable, to go out to work.

Fr Wright is much concerned about money. His parishioners are poor people whom he regards as belonging to a new, hidden 'underclass', in many cases emotionally unstable and almost impossible to educate, with children of ten completely out of parental control. His own fortunate circumstances make it 'very difficult for me to tell them to give more to the Church. Why should they?' But he is worried about the general level of support for the Church by the Church. In his diocese alms-giving is less than £3 a head per week. At his sung Mass on Sunday the average congregation is 150, drawn from a population of 10,000. Through the collection plate and planned giving, in April 1992 they produced about £700. Assuming there are 100 adults in the congregation, that came to £1.75 per adult per week – the cost of a pint of beer.

The parish had been vacant for two years when Fr Wright, who was then working in another diocese, was rung up in 1987 by the bishop and offered the team ministry. The rectory was derelict and vandalised, and Mrs Wright spent some of her own money enhancing the rooms. 'Before I was married I would not have spent so much money,' says her husband, with some feeling. 'You can't take the decorations with you.' Not all the houses in the parish are that small compared to the rectory, for many had been built as the nucleus of a garden city, in the days before the Second World War when it was widely believed that given the opportunity, working-class people would take to gardening, which indeed many did. Few go in for horticulture on the estate now. Most of the gardens are knee-deep in debris, and graffiti is sprayed on walls. What the council omitted to include on the estate when they expanded it with third-rate housing after the war was a pub, a leisure centre, a medical centre, a library or even any shops.

More and more 'problem' families were tipped on the estate as though it was a rubbish dump. The people had nothing to do and nowhere to do it, and today 30 per cent of potentially employable inhabitants are out of work. When a young girl was murdered the council rushed in with lorryloads of double glazing and pebbledash. The rectory escaped the pebbledash but it did benefit from a free hand-out of double glazing.

I called for Fr Wright a few days later, and he drove me to a pub, where he had arranged for all the team to meet me for lunch before their weekly staff meeting. 'I don't think it looks good for a pub to be seen full of clergy,' he said as we entered, by way of explanation for his open-necked shirt. But the curate and one of the team vicars had their dog collars on; the other team vicar had taken his off, leaving his grey stock open at the neck. It was a hot day, but he seemed uncomfortable in a dog collar anyway; he put it on in the car park as we were leaving (perhaps in case he encountered a road accident on the way back) but took it off again as soon as we were in the rectory.

They all called each other Father, except for Fr Wright, who called his team by their Christian names. As it turned out, all three churches in the team were firmly in the catholic tradition, which made for a lack of choice in churchmanship for a combined population of 20,000, the two smaller churches serving about 5,000 people each. Fr Wright had inherited a team when he arrived, all of whom had since moved on, and the present trio had been hand-picked by himself. They were all quite different but seemed to get on extremely well.

'There was no communication within the team when I first arrived,' Fr Wright told me while the others were at the bar negotiating glasses of beer and cider and plates of what looked like curry. 'Communication in a team ministry is quite simply vital.' Fr Wright and I had a ploughman's, and he drank Coca-Cola.

Father John, who was already at the bar when we arrived, had deep-set blue eyes and well-mannered hair. He was thirty (born the year the rector was ordained) and was much more attractive than he probably realised. He told me he had wanted to be a priest from the age of eight, and was agreeably surprised when he was accepted for training at the age of twenty-four; all he had done before was one year as a primary-school teacher, but he had coped with a good deal of family bereavement, and this, it seems, had impressed the selection conference. He came from a totally nonclerical family (as many ordinands do today) and his family had opposed his plans for ordination. He spoke less than the others, and seemed more guarded.

Father Damien, the vicar who kept discarding his dog collar, turned out to be an accentless Canadian of thirty-seven. He had a trim black beard and wore denims. He wore a ring on his wedding finger, but he was unmarried, as were the other two. He was alert and amusing, very relaxed and lively. The curate, Father Peter, had been ordained two years and was thirty-four; previously he had worked for British Telecom where, he maintained, he had gained 'valuable managerial skills'. He was short and slightly corpulent, his teeth were not too well arranged and he was losing his hair. The overall effect was Trollopean. I could imagine him at school as as youthful but fully fledged eccentric.

The rector wore sandals but the other three all wore black shoes with laces. They may have been old-fashioned in dress and behaviour but, I guessed, liberal in their attitudes towards life. Interestingly enough, they had been spending part of their time at staff meetings discussing a book of sermons by the new evangelical Archbishop of Canterbury, whom Fr Wright referred to as their employer, and they thought quite highly of them.

The lay reader normally took minutes at the staff meeting – 'He's very discreet and would never repeat anything in the parish' – but he could not be there on this occasion. Fr Wright produced tea and coffee in the rectory dining room, but the others insisted on lolling comfortably in the study, where fat Filofaxes and diaries appeared. There was not much of an agenda and to an outsider it appeared pretty incomprehensible, but *they* all knew what they were talking about, making arrangements for conducting an almost ceaseless round of services while dashing off to do all sorts of other things. The list of parish organisations was prodigious: choirboys' club, Brownies, Women's Fellowship, Tenants' Association, even a

Photo Friends' Camera Club. 'Can you cover my Low Mass on such and such a day?' was banded round the room. They discussed plans for a pilgrimage to the cathedral. They discussed a confirmation, to be conducted by the diocesan bishop. 'Just to remind you, Father, on Friday I'm with the Boy's Brigade camp.'

'By the way,' said Fr Wright, 'I had a saga on Monday,' and they all groaned, for it was about a long-running rumpus over a lunch club, the ins and outs of which would have filled several editions of the parish newsletter. During this discussion they almost got heated, Fr Wright addressing the curate at one stage as 'my dear chap'. He believed very strongly that the clergy had failed to support this venture. Fr Damien confessed it bored him to death. 'It's become very personal,' said Fr John. I had no idea what they were talking about.

The telephone rang, and they started talking about the merits of answerphones. It was then reported that the minibus needed £150 spending on it, which they had not got. 'The engine is very good. We'd better scrap it for whatever we can get.'

Next we heard about some itinerant clergyman of dubious credentials who had snatched a funeral from under their noses. 'He is extremely sincere and has a beautiful smile, and does his homework very well,' said Fr Wright. 'He had been to visit the man when he was dying, but he hovers over the undertakers like a vulture.' Apparently Fr Wright had managed to snatch the funeral back. 'That's the fourth week I shan't be at Rotary.'

There was talk of a wedding rehearsal, and of plans for Ascension Day. ('If you could bring your own white vestments,' Fr Damien pleaded. 'For evensong, just alb and stole, because the church is terribly hot.') Someone had a convent Mass 'for the nutty nuns'. Someone else had a singing group which clashed with a meeting of the Parochial Church Council, and at the end of the day he did not seem to have a free evening all week. One tends to forget what unsocial hours the clergy work, and how clergy wives constantly have their homes invaded. 'What I really resent,' Mrs Wright told me, 'is when they don't wipe their feet.' After an hour Fr John and the curate left for some other engagement. A school governors' meeting, perhaps, or was it to organise the playschool group, or the Thursday Club, or the Good Companions, or just to polish the silver?

Two parishioners greeted Fr Wright as we stood outside the rectory. 'Would you like to see the church?' he asked, and a hunt for the key ensued. He described the building as Odeon Gothic. It is lit by dormer windows, but he insisted on flood-lighting it too. 'It looks better with the lights on.' The smell of incense hung in the air. Fr Wright genuflected as he passed the Lady Chapel, where the Sacrament was reserved,[1] and we inspected a filthy dirty sixteenth-century painting which seemed incongruous in a modern church. No one knows where it came from. 'I expect it's worth a few thousand,' said Fr Wright. He gave me his and Fr John's parish magazines (Fr Damien doesn't believe in parish magazines so he doesn't have one) and invited me to join a lunch two days later for local leaders in the community.

I thought I was early, but already at half past twelve an assortment of community leaders were tucking into paté, French bread, cheese and fruit. Orange juice and red and white wine were also on offer. About twenty-five people had turned up, including the mayor. 'Sometimes we even have the local MP,' Fr Wright told me. 'He's terribly right-wing, and we're all left-wing, it's very funny.' I wondered whether the towering police officers (there were two of them, both members of their parochial church councils) were left-wing too, and rather doubted it. One told me he would have found it very difficult, over the years, to have coped as a police officer had he not been a Christian, and he claimed to have let some hundreds of local lads off with a caution before taking them in front of the magistrates when they reoffended.

There was a young black trainee youth worker; otherwise everyone was white, and what one might term lower-middle-class – all save perhaps a headmistress, who had an educated voice and a streaming cold. There was a chaplain from the polytechnic, a parks superintendent, town councillors and representatives from community associations. 'There are not many parish priests who lay on this sort of thing,' an appreciative funeral director told me.

There was a debate about whether to hold the post-lunch discussion in the garden (it was another very hot day) or in the house; those in favour of remaining cool indoors won, and with the doors dividing the rector's study and the dining room opened up, and an overflow into the hallway, somehow everyone got seated. A young woman tried to whip up enthusiasm for the provision of a 'motorbike project', obviously a good idea in a perfect world, for many of the parish youngsters were at present riding motorcycles full tilt across private property, but the cost of funding such a scheme – the provision of proper supervision, for example – and the overcoming of objections to the noise created, not to mention the difficulty of finding adequate space, seemed daunting.

The second speaker was from a drugs-prevention team funded by the Home Office. He was clearly a professional, and had come with a clear-cut suggestion. Should the parish want his organisation to come in, he could provide a youth worker at a cost of £15,000 a year, possibly paid for out of the confiscated assets of convicted drug dealers. Finally, one of the police officers briefly introduced the main topic for the next lunch, the setting-up of a neighbour mediation project to try to take the heat out of disputes before they got out of hand. Already, he said, he was opening a surgery in the parish hall two nights a week, to advise people on crime prevention, and the police division was going to foot the bill. Both this and the drugs-prevention scheme sounded feasible and potentially useful.

'The Church can't do much,' Fr Wright told me, 'but these lunches are something we can do.'

'Thank you for your hospitality,' said the headmistress, from behind her handkerchief. 'We always enjoy coming here.'

Fr Wright told them the date of the next lunch, and reminded them there was a basket by the front door if they felt like making a contribution. Like Buddhists, Church of England clergy always seem to have a begging bowl at the ready.

It was the feast of St Augustine of Canterbury, and half a dozen of us had gathered in the Lady Chapel for a 7 p.m. Mass. 'The server has just telephoned to say he's feeling a *little* weary!' Fr Wright explained with a wan smile as he lit the candles himself, still wearing a suit. 'And the lay reader is away. And the curate's in camp with the Boys' Brigade.' He reappeared in a gold-embroidered chasuble and preached a little homily, relating the mission of St Augustine to knocking on doors, which was what we were about to do.

Back in the rectory, nine laity in all, mostly elderly ladies but with two youngish men among them, were preparing for their monthly sortie into the parish. Parish visiting was once the exclusive preserve of the parish priest, and even now people sometimes seem affronted if he does not call in person. Others see a clerical collar through the window and bolt under the sideboard. 'It's like the Forth Bridge,' Fr Wright explained. 'We start at one end and then go round again.' But in five years he had not yet covered his entire parish once. The strategy was to take one road at a time, with seven or eight houses allocated to each pair of visitors. One jovial man, recently declared redundant, volunteered to do a round on his own, and I went with the team rector. My task was to carry copies of the parish newsletter (many of the people we called on pretended they read a neighbour's) and a leaflet explaining that the Church was the only organisation which told you the purpose of life and the only organisation which existed for the sake of those who do not belong to it.

Fr Wright had printed invitations to the next 10 a.m. Sunday Mass, and these he distributed rather like At Home cards. His opening gambit was, 'Are you a member of the Church of England?' Most looked a bit sheepish and then said they were. 'When did you last come to St Anne's?' One old boy said he had been twice in twenty years.

Two little girls attached themselves to us as escorts. They knew Fr Wright and were very informative about who was in and who was out, who was deaf and so on. Large numbers of enormously fat women could be seen sitting in their gardens. There were fewer rottweilers than I had been led to expect but a lot of friendly cats.

'I was just admiring your garden, Mr Hamilton,' said

Fr Wright to a man with his sprinkler on. He had taken everybody's names from the electoral register, but he had warned the others to be careful, since not all were married. 'All the people in this street will be remembered at Mass on Sunday,' he told everyone as he handed out their invitation card. 'Thank you,' they said, in a dutiful sort of way. There was no hostility, but no great enthusiasm, except from one dear old lady who wanted us to go in for refreshments.

Someone claimed allegiance to St Anne's because her son had been married there. A young father opened the door and Fr Wright said, 'Of course I know you're Church of England,' because he had baptised the man's son a few months before. But I had the strong impression it would be a long time before he saw father or son again. One man said, No, he wasn't C of E but his wife was, seeming somehow to be placating the vicar while hiding behind his wife's skirts. A curtain was drawn apart by a child, and you could imagine her screaming out, 'It's the vicar, Mum!' Her mother half opened the door and seemed suspicious. And why not? The lives of these people are full of unexpected callers, some come to collect debts, some to pay off old scores.

'It was a nicer road than I expected,' said Fr Wright as we regained the car. On returning to the rectory one evening he had run into a fight; one youth, being beaten up, had practically fallen in front of his car, and as Fr Wright slowed down he had the door kicked. Break-ins to the church have been too numerous to catalogue.

Back at the rectory there was some sighing over a nearby charismatic church of no particular denomination which apparently attracts a congregation of 900. 'They like certainty, you see!' said Fr Wright, with his characteristic cheerfulness. 'We done fifteen houses but we still didn't do no good,' one of the returning laymen reported. Someone had encountered an elderly lady whose husband had died and who wanted the clergy to call. 'An awful family, terrible people' was the verdict on one household. An 'unmarried mum' with three children between four and eight had also wanted a visit from the clergy, to discuss having her offspring baptised. Someone else, when asked if they were Church of England, had said, 'I'm nothing,' and had closed the door. It certainly sounded, during the debriefing, as if the others had been given a rougher ride than Fr Wright; I suspect deference had been paid to his collar. One pair of visitors had been interviewed by a boy of ten, 'only interested in football, so we made no headway there', and another house they called at had been empty and boarded up.

I thought Fr Wright had been brisk, well versed in his opening gambit, just sufficiently probing ('Have you any children?') but sometimes a bit nervous, and not too sorry to scarper over the steps into the next garden. His plan was not to convert or inconvenience, merely to remind parishioners of the presence of their parish church, and perhaps to ferret out whether a second, in-depth, visit would be appreciated. During the debriefing he made a note of houses to return to. In essence it had been an exercise in going out to look for the one lost sheep, except that here, as in every parish in England today, those lost outnumber those safely grazing by about fifty to one.

Mrs Wright produced coffee (let us hope the Church Commissioners have shares in a coffee plantation somewhere), and everyone said compline. A task many clergy dread above all others, and which some funk entirely, had been faithfully performed and was over for another month.

Before I left, although it was half past nine and neither he nor his wife had yet eaten, Fr Wright sat me down with a large glass of white wine.

When I arrived at the local railway station to attend a monthly meeting of the District Church Council, three seventeen-year-olds, presumably bored out of their minds, were systematically, in broad daylight, kicking the station to pieces.

Mrs Wright unlocked the front door and let me in, then disappeared upstairs again. The council came trooping across from the church, having attended a Mass prior to the meeting. 'Oh, we offer them up all the time!' Fr Wright joked. He sat behind an enormous desk in his study, with the council secretary at his side, ready to scribble minutes. There were eleven members present (two had sent apologies for absence), five women and six men, not one of them under forty-five. Coffee and tea were distributed.

Under Matters Arising someone reported that a damaged plaque had been 'fitted up, by yours truly'. Under Correspondence there had been 'the usual bundle of appeals'. The first report was presented by the treasurer. He ran through the income and expenditure accounts for the month, which included an item for £96.17 on repairs to a motor mower used for cutting grass in the Memorial Garden, and £33 spent on repairs to a window in the sanctuary broken by burglars. (In one Midlands diocese theft and vandalism rose from 19 cases in 1980 to 140 in 1991, and 80 per cent of parish churches are now locked during the day.) The parish had met its quota to the diocese, a sum of £1,028. Income included fees of £89 for weddings, and £2.50 paid by the Boys' Brigade, who had broken another window. Covenants, Planned Giving and Collections had come to £827.97. The treasurer said he had written two letters to the council about poll tax on the church hall, and he did not intend paying the tax until he got a reply. There had been an expenditure of £177.70 over income, and he was hoping 'for some good results' from the summer fête, due to be held in a fortnight's time.

Someone reported there had been very few bookings for the hall; they were interviewing for a new caretaker. Then Fr Wright gave his report, which was a way of keeping the council abreast of a new scheme in the diocese for financing parish quotas, and about the state of the minibus and the lunch club. He said if the parish had to pay its own way there would be just one priest to look after 20,000 people; money was being 'poured in', which was why the Church of England, like the Roman Catholics, remained on the ground while the Baptists and Methodists, who did have to pay their own way, had pulled out.

As Fr Damien had now been ordained ten years, he was going home to Canada on a three-month sabbatical, and his services would be taken by a Canadian archdeacon doing a swop. I wondered if the archdeacon knew what sort of area he was going to spend his holiday in. Pastoral duties in Fr Damien's parish would be undertaken by the curate. 'And just to remind you about the Christmas Day lunch for the isolated and elderly,' said Fr Wright. It was 2 June.

Any Other Business developed into a long discussion about

hymns. 'We've become a bit predictable about the hymns we sing,' someone said from the depth of a settee. 'Could we enlarge our range a bit?' He was told there was difficulty in motivating adult members of the choir. The treasurer said they were getting music, like everything else, on the cheap, for it appeared that the organist was paid practically nothing. Fr Wright said, 'If there is a new hymn that people don't know they will only complain about it.' Someone who had lost his voice croaked that it was time girls were admitted to the choir, a move which, he thought, 'might swell the congregation'. The rector thanked him 'for an interesting extra ingredient'.

The meeting broke up after an hour and a quarter. It had been conducted with brisk efficiency but without denying anyone the chance to chip in. There seemed complete harmony and a genuine interest on everyone's part in the agenda. By far the majority of time had been taken up talking about money. Had I been in the chair I should speedily have become as bored as the boys at the railway station, and I wondered how an intelligent, highly qualified man in his early fifties could endure it. Most of Fr Wright's school friends were probably running an industrial complex or a public relations firm. But Fr Wright seemed in his element – patient, courteous and committed to his job. At half past nine he waved me goodbye as cheerfully as ever.

The telephone rang as I was leaving for London. 'John Wright here. In this morning's post a funeral's come in for Thursday, if you'd like to come. It's a good one, a big local family.'

'How gruesome you sound,' I said. 'Yes, I'd love to.'

The service had been arranged, by the undertakers, for one o'clock, at a local cemetery; not the most convenient hour. 'The undertaker is almost always the first point of contact,' Fr Wright explained. 'Most people are totally ignorant what to do. The undertaker asks if they would like a C of E burial, and unless they have any strong objection they just say yes. I go round to see them, to find out as much as I can about the person who's died so that I can make the funeral as personal as possible. Nine times out of ten I've never met them. I always ask if the family would like me to visit again after the funeral, and I actually get adult confirmation candidates as a result. I regard funerals as a major pastoral opportunity. They get interested in the Church, and I always tell them the dead person will be remembered at the main Sunday service, and usually everyone comes.'

My train was delayed so I grabbed a taxi. I need not have bothered. When I arrived at the rectory at half past twelve, Fr Wright was drinking coffee. 'Would you like a gin?' he asked. I settled for orange juice. Then he took a long telephone call. ('Did you say I had someone with me?' he had asked the part-time parish secretary. She had, but he took the call all the same.) As the minutes ticked by, Fr Wright began to explain his usual panic symptoms about being late or going to the wrong cemetery – 'which *has* happened before now. Nobody minds if you're late for a wedding, they think that's a joke, but they never forgive you if you're late for a funeral.' At last we drove off, with Fr Wright pretending – or was he? – that he was unsure of the way. By now I was the one who was feeling anxious.

'It's rather embarrassing,' he explained. 'When I went to see the family, who all talked at once, I realised the widow was a tea lady at a local school where I'm a governor. She had been doing naughty things and I was on a committee that had to discipline her. I spend a lot of time in schools, helping children to read. Most of them are illiterate. But it's all sorted out now.'

We arrived at the dreary little municipal chapel ten minutes ahead of schedule. There were only two mourners waiting, and a man in charge, to whom Fr Wright, who now slipped into a cassock, plain cotta and purple stole, was very pleasant. The man kept darting behind a curtain to adjust 'Abide with Me'. There was a Calor gas stove in the middle of the floor, two artificial candles on the altar and two narrow rows of seats facing inwards. The paint was indescribably awful. There were no flowers. Apparently the deceased was called Harry, he was fifty-seven, and he had smoked and drunk himself to death. 'I've found out one or two nice things to say about him,' Fr Wright had told me before we left.

The cortege arrived, three hired cars and five private vehicles. Two dozen people, more or less in black, trooped into the chapel, all looking extremely uncomfortable. One woman had on a skirt which just about covered her thighs. The men were distinctly sinister, and managed to seem not only unchurched but dispossessed. Six sons acted as pallbearers. One looked Cypriot. 'Probably a throwback,' Fr Wright suggested afterwards.

'Will you all stand,' he said as he preceded the coffin. The undertaker wore a frock coat and top hat. No wonder this Mafia-style send-off was going to set Vera and her family back at least £1,000, £29 of which would go to Fr Wright, who would send it on to the diocese. Everyone had sat on the south side, for some reason, and one enormously fat woman had positioned herself behind the altar and was busy with a fan.

The opening sentences were practically drowned by the man behind the curtain, who had now found some suitable organ music to play. No one knew any of the responses. 'They just about recognise Psalm 121 and the Lord's Prayer,' Fr Wright had warned me. There was a reading from the Wisdom of Solomon, and then the address. Fr Wright spoke about how we all faced death, the absolutely certain thing about the life we shared being the certainty of our own death. We tended to be frightened of death as if life and death were opposites, but death was part of the whole human experience. There were no final farewells, only au revoirs. Harry had gone a little ahead.

At last he got round to the virtues of the late lamented. He had been a devoted husband, a good father (the word 'good' sounded to me a bit restrained) and 'very good' with his thirteen grandchildren, none of whom appeared to have turned up. He had also been very keen on deep-sea angling. After his last heart attack he had built bookshelves for others, and when in hospital he had asked to see his beloved dog Rover. Rover had been allowed into the ward and had licked his hand. By this time there was not a dry eye in the house. I kept my own eyes fixed on a broken pane of glass and wondered if anyone would ever get around to replacing it.

Out we marched to the committal, Fr Wright leading the way in his own car, pretending not to know where the newly dug grave was located. I half believed him. When we stopped to get out he got back in again, said, 'I've forgotten my hat,' and reached for a biretta on the back seat. 'It keeps my hair out of my eyes.'

The undertaker in his frock coat scattered the earth. Fr Wright gave a final blessing, crossing himself with his biretta, and went over to speak to Vera. Back at the car he was looking pleased. 'She says the whole family's coming to church on Sunday when Harry is remembered, and I told her I'd call again in a week or two. Let the dust settle.'

As we drove off he asked, 'Would you like a peppermint?'

I told him I thought he had conducted the service extremely well. 'Oh, do you think so? I never get any feedback.'

'The first glass of wine will be free,' Fr Wright told the congregation of some 250, assembled for a confirmation service at 7.30 in the evening. Having the candidates he had prepared confirmed was the climax to some of his most important pastoral work. 'There will,' he added, 'be a compulsory voluntary charge for any other glasses.' This was in preparation for the bunfight in the church hall afterwards. More jokes followed. 'This doesn't apply to the clergy. They will pay £1.'

Two dozen men, women and children were seated in the sanctuary. In the context of a sung Eucharist, six of them were to be baptised as well. The youngest was a boy of ten, the oldest, Fr Wright's mother-in-law, 'who had just not got around to being confirmed before', her daughter explained afterwards. The bishop later told me he would confirm even younger than ten these days. He had once confirmed three generations at one go, and this evening he was due to confirm a mother and her three children. He made a scurrying manoeuvre from the vestry to the west door, where he joined a skeleton choir and the clergy, who included two neighbouring priests each presenting one candidate. Then he entered the nave in a cloud of incense.

Preaching to the candidates at right angles to the congregation, and therefore almost inaudibly, the bishop said we were all born self-centred, and one of the vital things to do as we grew up was to put Jesus in the centre. 'Remember all your life long,' he said, 'that Jesus loves you, cares for you and always wants to be with you.' So saying, he anointed with the oil of chrism, and baptised and confirmed. The service lasted an hour and twenty minutes. Then Mrs Wright made a dash to the hall to grab a sandwich for herself before the parish descended. Glasses of red and white wine were poured out but I saw no money changing hands. The bishop went on to the platform to be photographed with each of the candidates. Afterwards he mingled in an absent-minded sort of way with friends and family.

'Oh dear, it's been one of those days,' said one of the visiting clergy. 'Births, deaths and marriages, even a divorce. On top of everything my secretary told me she's two months pregnant and her husband's left her.' The young man he had prepared for confirmation had only recently been released from a psychiatric hospital. 'There was a nasty moment when I thought he might make a run for it, but we gave him a tranquilliser.'

Before long the team rector swept his bishop off to the rectory, where his lordship collapsed on a settee and the rector opened a bottle of champagne. I had been told the bishop had a phenomenal memory. 'You interviewed me in 1974,' he reminded me. (He had not known that he was going to meet me that evening.) We were joined by his chaplain, who had to forgo all but one glass of champagne because he was driving that night, having acted, with great dignity and aplomb, as master of ceremonies at the Eucharist; the chauffeur had recently renegotiated his hours of work. Other clergy drifted in. So too did Fr Wright's brother-in-law, with whom the bishop shook hands without getting up.

Almost inevitably the conversation got around to the ordination of women. 'I would vote for the ordination of women tomorrow,' said the bishop, 'if the rest of the Church wished for it.' It transpired he meant the Church worldwide. 'There is no ecumenical consent,' he explained. He told some amusing stories about Michael Ramsey (archbishop of Canterbury 1961–74) and listened politely if somewhat distantly while ecclesiastical anecdotes were retailed by others.

The bishop said he conducted about twenty-five confirmations a year, varying in size from a handful of candidates to large numbers at public schools, but he commented on the decrease in public school candidates for ordination. 'I suppose it has to do with materialism,' he said. 'They go into more lucrative professions now.'

All the clergy called the bishop Father, except when Fr Wright introduced his brother-in-law, when he called him 'my Lord'. The bishop seemed in no hurry to leave, and more Champagne appeared, but not the rector's wife, who was holding a hen party in the kitchen. Eventually the bishop tore himself away, without shaking hands with the other guests. In the hall there was some gossip about a diocesan pastoral matter, and then Fr Wright said, 'Thank you for coming, Father,' and kissed the bishop's ring. The bishop hardly seemed to notice. All he said in the car, having kindly offered to give me a lift, was how odd it was to see a fountain playing in a square so late at night. There had been a vague search for the flag 'which we use when we want the police to hurry things along', but on this occasion there was little traffic, and the chaplain drove with studied care.

As I stood on the pavement, the bishop, who had that evening performed perhaps the most crucial function of his ministry (only ordination could compare), waggled two fingers in farewell through the closed window, and drove home to his private prayers.

Last year it had poured with rain, but this year the parish fête, held on the green, was blessed with what the weather forecasters call warm weather. It was sweltering. Fr Wright had on a pale-grey lightweight suit. The mayor looked elegant in green, sporting her chain of office. She declared the proceedings open very swiftly, mentioning support from local shops and also that she understood there had been 'a few hiccups'. It turned out the bandmaster had been stricken the night before with an attack of diabetes, and that no one had bothered to check on the arrival of the swings, booked six months before. This was a good example of the vicar being let down by the laity. Fr Wright was not best pleased.

Piles of old clothing were rummaged through, as were second-hand paperbacks. There was rhubarb on sale, home-made marmalade, bric-a-brac, and cakes that by eleven o'clock were in danger of melting in the sun. Parishioners and their neighbours mulled over the stalls in a desultory way. As I left, the curate, with his head stuck through the stocks, was being pelted with sponges soaked in cold water. Would anyone but an Anglican cleric endure such indignity?

Unlike the curate, I was in hot water in the evening. Fr Wright wanted to know why I had disappeared instead of going round the stalls with the mayor and back to the rectory for drinks. He brushed aside my lame excuses and said, 'I expect you hated it as much as I did.' They were due to hold an inquest on the proceedings at eight o'clock. 'I shall pray before that,' he said.

I said I thought he sounded in need of a drink.

'I've had one,' he said.

I asked if I could come to see him with a list of things I wanted to talk about, and was promptly invited to lunch. This began with two glasses of sherry while Mrs Wright, who had come back to the rectory in her own lunch hour, prepared the meal: salmon, new potatoes and salad, strawberries and ice cream and eight different cheeses. Fr Wright vanished to the kitchen to decant a bottle of Chardonnay; when he went out later for the strawberries he returned with half a bottle of red wine left over from the previous night, and later still he offered me port. He had suggested a 'working lunch', to end at 2.30 p.m. It was four o'clock when I left.

I asked him first of all to describe a more or less typical day. For example, what time did he get up?

'About seven. That's when the alarm goes off. But because I've now got a little baby, at the age of fifty-four, when most people have grandchildren, sometimes I get woken up at five o'clock, so I must admit I am feeling tired. But normally I get up at seven to be in church for morning prayer and meditation at eight. I receive communion every day because I regard the Eucharist as the expression of my priestly ministry. But no more essential than the office and the meditation. In fact, I would say the meditation was more important.

'When I say meditation, it's really more in the tradition of the Orthodox Church, of silence and waiting on God, rather than any specific meditation on a Gospel passage, or visualising oneself into an event in the life of Christ. So the kind of contemplation I'm particularly into at the moment is the school of thought concerned about acquiring bodily and mental stillness, becoming aware of the spirit of God within us. I believe we are literally temples of the Holy Spirit, and that within us God is there. He's speaking to us all the time. I use a short prayer as a focus for the mind, to stop it wandering.'

How did his meditation affect the rest of his day?

'Most of us go around feeling slightly tense and anxious, as though we were about to be attacked at any moment. This is not a good state to be in, and by cultivating physical stillness, and then starting to become mentally still, God gives us an inner sense of tranquillity, peace and joy. That, I believe, you can take with you through the day.'

Then he had breakfast?

'I have a cup of coffee. That's breakfast. And on Mondays I have a day off. In the past I would go away for the day but now my day off is the day I look after the baby. So I'm at home all day. I let the answerphone take all the messages, and I don't necessarily go to the door when the bell rings. I feel slightly guilty about that, but I'm hardening myself. Generally speaking people don't understand that the vicar has a day off.

'On a normal day I rough out letters for the secretary to answer, or I dictate on a tape recorder. There might well be a funeral at half past ten or eleven. But generally speaking I tend to devote the morning to administration and the preparation of sermons. I try to keep abreast of things I am interested in. Every time I go into the loo I read something. I read the *Church Times* and *Theology*, and I do a daily Bible study. The lectionary keeps me focused on what I should be thinking about. And I read a certain amount of popular science. I see no conflict between religion and science.'

How well had his theological college prepared him for the work of a parish priest?

'I think that's a very difficult question because one doesn't know how formed one was. I was enormously impressed by my principal's spirituality, by him as a person. He really did dominate the college, and I had a great devotion to him. So it was a sad experience to find that he had feet of clay. But I think that was part of my growing up.'

Had he made any financial sacrifices to be a parish priest?

'No, I wouldn't think so. I'm living in the biggest house in the parish with a great deal more comfort than the majority of people here. We've spent a lot of money on the decorations, because it's my wife's first house and she wants to make it nice. But we do entertain a lot. And I justify the house in that way, because I'm in the justification business!'

How, in terms of the financial cost of running the parish, and the effort put into it, did he equate 150 at the parish Mass out of a population of 10,000?

'Very difficult. In a well-to-do parish I think you'd do rather better, because going to church still tends to be a middle-class phenomenon. I would say the majority of ordinands who trained with me were from a working-class background and as a result of their university education every single one of them became middle-class. And there is a danger of the vicar imposing a middle-class lifestyle on working-class parishes. We do a lot of entertaining here. We give them sherry parties and cheese and wine, and invite them to dinner. But they don't ask us back, it's not their style or tradition. It's the way we can say, "Well done, thank you for decorating the hall." After the fête we had all the committee members back for drinks and eats. So it's a kind of oiling of the wheels all the time. We do it because we want to do it, and we enjoy it. But it costs a lot, of course.'

Did he take any interest in Church politics?

'Vaguely interested. I'm quite entertained by gossip, and I will avidly pass on gossip! But I have no ambition to be in the General Synod, though I am on the diocesan synod. But it's not my scene at all. My vocation is to be a parish priest.'

So if he received a letter offering him a bishopric or an archdeaconry, what would he do?

'I'd look at it. That's the least you can do. I don't think it's very polite not to do that. As far as being an archdeacon's concerned, inspecting drains and silver, well, I'm sure there *are* people cut out for that!'

Did he think, as the Archbishop of Canterbury has suggested, that the clergy should be assessed on a regular basis?

'The problem is, the clergy can do as much or as little as they like, and they know there is very, very little accountability. And they can only be got rid of if they've embezzled the funds or gone off with the organist's wife. So they can be mad or bad and still get away with it. There is no accountability or appraisal, and yes, I think there should be in some way. There's no caring for the clergy, either. In a team we do it to each other.'

What about the parish priest who is not in a team, who cares for him?

'That's a good question. Nobody.'

Was he good at looking after people?

'I would say I'm average. Probably not good enough.'

What part of his job did he find the hardest?

'The social side. Jumble sales. Fêtes. But one has to pretend to rather enjoy them.' As an apparent non sequitur he added, 'I believe that the heart of the Christian faith is about our relationship with God and what we are supposed to be on this earth. We are unique thoughts in the mind of God.'

How did he convey intellectual and theological ideas to parishioners not all of whom were as intelligent or educated as he?

'By analogy. Christ could speak in the most simple terms possible about the profoundest truths, and it is possible to emulate that. I have had people on the staff here who have talked gobbledygook, absolutely unbelievable convoluted language, but it is possible to put the profoundest truths into simple expressions. And that's what I aim to do. I do not believe that Christ, who is the human face of God, required all those who follow him to have a university degree in order to understand. I think we do understand naturally, if we can get it across in the right way.

'What I like most about my job is its variety. And the space it gives me in which to think, to read and to be alone. I could have been alone all this time we've been together. Afternoons are a particularly good time for being alone. Thursdays I go to Rotary. When I was invited to be a Rotarian I said yes because I can use them. I can divert funds from the Rotary Club here, which I do, unashamedly, into our community café, into our minibus. They love to do things for deprived areas. But I have to go along and talk to them and crack jokes. And I hate it. I honestly have to get tanked up to endure the social side – or I have to keep completely off it.'

Did he ever get very discouraged?

There was a long pause. 'I suppose I get depressed. I get

mood swings. I have had a breakdown. When I came back from Africa I hadn't had a proper holiday, I didn't think I needed one. Also I found a whole revolution had taken place in the Church since I'd been away, the new liturgy and so on, and I found all that dreadful. In Africa the churches had been absolutely crammed, and we had no liturgical reform at all. So I began to feel dizzy spells, and inexplicable anxiety getting to an unmanageable state. Eventually I went to a doctor and I was prescribed drugs supposed to stop agitation, and I was told I must have a holiday, so a bishop I knew well took me off to Crete. After eight months I felt better. From time to time I had a reversion to a sense of impending doom, that kind of feeling of inexplicable tension and anxiety, but it hasn't really recurred in a ferocious form since I got married.

'At one time when I felt it coming on I would have hit the bottle rather heavily. What I would do now would be to stay clear of the bottle. At one time I was very much into whisky and gin. I'm much more into wine now. What I do find is, if I start to overindulge, hit the bottle too hard, then those anxiety states begin to reassert themselves. I find it very difficult to leave a bag of crisps alone, but I can now leave a bottle unfinished on the shelf. I give up alcohol for the whole of Lent, always. And I feel a lot better for it.'

Had his depression ever led to a loss of faith?

'No, I don't think so. What I would say, though, is that when a depression comes in from the east over the Dogger Bank one's horizons close in, and life becomes grim. The joy and light of living goes out of the window. And maybe guilt is a powerful ingredient in the depression. I'm sure that everyone is burdened with guilt of one sort or another, and one has to cope with it and learn how to live with it and how to disperse it, to neutralise it, really. If I allow depression to paralyse me it gets worse. If I can compel myself to go out and see people who are very lonely or need help of one sort or another, then it disperses. It is hard to do but I find inevitably it works, even though it's the last thing you feel like doing. This is why I say that my job is the most wonderful one, really, because in helping others you're helping yourself.

'One reason for wanting to be ordained was that my early childhood was fairly traumatic and sad. My mother was killed in the Blitz. I don't know if I've mentioned that to you. My earliest childhood memories are of the Blitz. On this particular night she didn't want to go down to the air-raid shelter, and we went to bed upstairs. And I woke up to find the ceiling had gone, and my mother was killed, downstairs, underneath all the rubble. I was eventually rescued by air-raid wardens. My father was on the aircraft carrier *Illustrious* in the Mediterranean at the time, so I was taken into care by relations in Devon. Life became very hellish because I couldn't understand what was going on. I was four and a half when my mother was killed, I went to boarding school at the age of five, and I was asking questions about the meaning of life and suffering from a fairly early age.'

Was there anything that he would sooner be doing?

'I don't think there is. I have gradually grown into the job as I understand it, starting off very gauche and not really knowing what it was all about. Now I feel I roughly know what it's about! And I roughly know what to do.'

If he were to die in harness and one of his team were to preach at his funeral, what would he most like him to say?

'It's an onwards and upwards path, so I'd like him to say, "he died climbing"!'

TWO

By Law Established

WITHIN 200 years of the death of Christ there were native Christians in Britain, converted either by Roman soldiers who had themselves become Christians or by traders from Gaul (perhaps by both). Bishops from Britain attended the Council of Arles in 314 and the Council of Rimini in 359, and long before St Augustine's arrival in 597, to spread the gospel and establish an English hierarchy, the blood of at least three English martyrs had been shed. The best remembered was a Roman soldier called Alban; his memorial is one of England's great abbey churches. (St Albans Abbey was founded, by Offa the Terrible, in 793.) Its aristocratic twelfth-century Benedictine monks, recent archaeological excavations have revealed, lived the life of wealthy gourmets. And before Augustine – who was to become the first archbishop of Canterbury – had landed in Kent, there were already three bishops in England recognised by Rome; at London, York and probably Lincoln.[1] Following Augustine's success in converting King Ethelbert of Kent (he was already married to a Christian), he turned to the more demanding task of exerting his authority, and by implication that of the pope by whom Augustine had been sent, over the Celtic bishops in the West Country. But they refused to acknowledge the authority of Rome, and came to regard Augustine of Canterbury himself as an insensitive interloper; he in turn wrote off the Celts as uncooperative and recalcitrant. The seeds of much petty squabbling, which so disfigures Church history, had been sown at an early date.

In 627 one of Augustine's companions, Paulinus, was consecrated bishop of York (it is from the year of his consecration that the foundation of the present diocese is dated), and in 735 the see became an archdiocese. But it was not until 1072, at Windsor Castle, that the supremacy of the archbishopric of Canterbury over that of York was settled, the pope deciding to clinch the matter in the fourteenth century by designating York Primate of England, Canterbury Primate of All England.[2] George Carey, installed in April 1991, is the 103rd archbishop of Canterbury. John Habgood, appointed in 1983, is the 95th archbishop of York and the longest-serving diocesan bishop; he was consecrated bishop of Durham in 1973.

It is worth noting that in recent times currency has been given in print to the fiction that diocesan bishops of the Church of England are elected. They are only 'elected', in a purely technical sense, by the cathedral chapter after being nominated by the prime minister and appointed by the sovereign. In effect, the cathedral chapter is told to elect them.

Whether the Church of England as such correctly dates its foundation from the arrival of St Augustine or from Henry VIII's proclamation of the royal supremacy in 1534 is a matter of opinion. In Magna Carta (1215) the Church in England is referred to as '*Ecclesia Anglicana*', and Anglicans who believe that at the Reformation the Church of England retained its catholic orders and sacraments naturally regard St Augustine as their essential link with the past. Those who hold that the Church of England is a creation of the sixteenth century would assert that Magna Carta was referring to the Church in a territorial, not a confessional, sense, and that in severing relations with Rome that branch of the Church later known as the Church of England rendered invalid the episcopal orders of bishops henceforth consecrated without authority from the pope: they believe the Church of England is merely a Protestant sect. And Roman Catholics are officially reinforced in this opinion by Leo XIII's somewhat tardy papal encyclical of 1896, *Apostolicae Curae*, which declared Anglican orders invalid, although it may be asked upon whose finger Pope Paul VI thought he was slipping an episcopal ring when in 1966, in Rome, he gave his own to the 100th archbishop of Canterbury, Michael Ramsey. Not to a layman in fancy dress, surely.

The Church of England claims to be both Protestant and

Catholic: Protestant because at the Reformation it reformed itself in protest against corruptions like the plurality of bishoprics and the absence from their dioceses of many of the bishops themselves, the accumulation of vast monastic wealth and the loose morals of the clergy (Cardinal Wolsey fathered two illegitimate children and acquired in one year three bishoprics and 500 servants); Catholic because at the same time it retained all the essential links, through the creeds, Scripture, the sacraments and its ministerial orders, with the one Holy Catholic and Apostolic Church. Today, despite the best endeavours of Pope Leo, the Church of England is a Church with which Rome is in dialogue, and while it is surely true to say that the break with Rome had as much to do with Henry VIII's desire for a divorce from Katherine of Aragon as with any zealous desire for reform, what emerged in the second half of the sixteenth century was a truly national Church.[3] Since the Second Act of Supremacy, enacted under Elizabeth I in 1559, the Church of England has been known as a Church 'by law established', although what that really means has never been precisely defined; like the British Constitution itself, the established nature of the Church of England has more or less evolved by custom, and nowhere is the Church of England's right to exist, as opposed to its mode of operation, enshrined in legislation. But for better or worse it is the fact of establishment that gives to the Church of England, in its relations at home with the state and abroad with the Anglican Communion, its unique flavour, influence and privileges.

The Established Church in England came about as much through political necessity as through any preference on the part of the English for Protestant forms of worship, and had it not been for the sagacity of Elizabeth I it might not have come about at all. During the preceding reigns of her brother and sister, England had rocked between Protestantism and Catholicism with appalling extremes of violence. Edward VI prayed to be delivered 'from the Bishop of Rome and all his detestable enormities'; in 1555, under the Catholic Mary I, the bishops of London and Worcester, and a year later the archbishop of Canterbury, were burned at the stake.[4] One consequence of what became known as the Elizabethan Settlement was the adoption by the sovereign of the title Supreme Governor of the Church of England,[5] and the Settlement itself was born not only of a political and social desire for religious tolerance but out of a need to define the status and authority of a national Church. State and Church now became so entwined that attendance at public worship was declared compulsory, and by 1568 the Queen's birthday was being celebrated as a holy day of obligation. Already the archbishop of Canterbury had assumed the prerogative of crowning the sovereign – although in the case of Elizabeth herself the bishop of Carlisle had to be recruited, the see of Canterbury being vacant and the archbishop of York and the bishop of Durham pleading conscience and old age. It was not, however, until 1701, in the wake of Stuart pretensions to the throne and hence the threat of a resurgence of Catholic interference in government, that the knot was finally tied between Church and Crown; under the Act of Settlement it was spelled out that in future the monarch must be a Protestant. So at her coronation Elizabeth II, like all her Hanoverian ancestors, was obliged to swear to 'maintain the Protestant Reformed Religion established by law'.

There seem to be two strands to establishment: the strictly practical one by which, among other things, diocesan bishops and cathedral deans are appointed by the Crown, in other words, the political aspects of establishment; and the more nebulous strand, that vague sense in which the national Church is at the service of everyone, no matter what their formal allegiance, and serves the whole country, not just one religious segment of it. Liturgical revision and the appointment of bishops are the most contentious issues (the ordination of women to the priesthood could become another) over which Parliament and the Church of England have engaged in conflict this century. A glance at the time span involved in the Church of England's efforts to revise its liturgy without incurring rebuffs from Parliament, and to achieve a considerable, though not yet a final, say in the appointment of diocesan bishops, gives some indication of the snail's pace at which an evolutionary rather than a revolutionary Church tends to progress. 'A perusal of the records of the Church for the last 100 years makes depressing reading,'

Eric Kemp, now Bishop of Chichester, wrote in 1961, 'for the same problems have been discussed again and again at intervals of a generation, conclusions have been reached but rarely translated into effect.'[6]

In 1928 the bishop of Durham, Herbert Hensley Henson, was converted to the cause of disestablishment by Parliament's rejection for the second time in two years of the Revised Prayer Book; and Parliament's actions, together with Henson's reactions, influenced the attitude to the established nature of the Church for two generations. In 1950 the archbishop of York, Cyril Garbett, wrote, 'Under the totally changed conditions of our time, it is impossible to justify by any appeal to the Scriptures the arrangement by which a Christian society can be to a large extent controlled and governed by those who do not belong to it, who may be uninterested and ignorant of its worship and teaching, and who may even be bitterly hostile to it'.[7] Eleven years later his successor at York, Michael Ramsey, was translated to Canterbury, and in his enthronement sermon he too pleaded for 'a greater freedom in the ordering and in the urgent revising of our forms of worship'. This he managed to achieve, thirteen and a half years later, on his last day in office, which also happened to be his seventieth birthday, when he introduced into the House of Lords the Worship and Doctrine Measure permitting, among other things, parochial church councils and incumbents to make a joint decision about the use of forms of services as alternatives to the Book of Common Prayer.

There was a four-hour debate in the Lords, with plenty of evidence of Parliament's continued reluctance to relinquish its hold over ecclesiastical affairs. When the measure went to the Commons for approval three weeks later, only support from the Labour benches prevented a potentially lethal clash between Parliament and the General Synod, for a substantial number of Conservatives spoke against the measure. 'A sort of gibberish' was how one Tory member described the new services over which scholars and liturgical experts had expended years of effort. At times the debate became extremely heated, and although there was no question of abolishing or banning the Book of Common Prayer, many who were roused to expound its virtues were not noted for their regular attendance in church, a fact which would have caused no concern to Enoch Powell. He told the House that every Member of Parliament, whether or not they were a member of the Church of England, had the responsibility of regulating the worship and doctrine of the Established Church. In fact, the rights which were at last about to pass from Parliament to the General Synod in the matter of revising the liturgy were such as had not been enjoyed by the Church since the time of Henry VIII. The Queen had just given her assent to the measure when Ramsey went to Buckingham Palace for a farewell lunch. He told the Queen that his last hours as archbishop had been spent steering the legislation through the House of Lords. 'I shouldn't have mentioned it,' he used to say. 'I shouldn't have mentioned it. Her face went all governessy.'

Like so many of his own and previous generations, Ramsey had also wanted the Church to have a greater say in the appointment of diocesan bishops, but he had to wait until 1977, by which time he had been retired three years, to witness the establishment of the Crown Appointments Commission. Ramsey's initiatives, based upon an almost total lack of interest in the establishment ('It would not be a grief to me to wake up and find that the English Establishment was no more' he wrote in *Canterbury Pilgrim*[8] in 1974), have come to set their seal on the modern Church of England, but for many radicals it has not been enough, which is why they speak of the Church being locked into money and buildings; they feel that its evangelistic mission has been hindered by the need to think first and foremost about the maintenance of its colossal plant, particularly its churches and cathedrals. A report called *The Deployment and Payment of the Clergy*, commissioned in 1964 from the sociologist Leslie Paul, proposed a coherent plan for redistributing the clergy to match shifts in population. Had its recommendations been put into effect it would have enabled bishops to exercise much more intelligent control over the positioning of parish clergy, for it advocated abolition of the ancient parson's freehold – a right he enjoys to remain in a living (unless unfrocked for grossly improper behaviour) until retirement. Opposition to the Paul Report was led by Gerald Ellison, bishop of Chester, who believed that its proposals would radically alter the character of the Church of England – which was precisely what they were intended to do. His reward was the see of London. 'Who can tell,' Paul Welsby asks in his authoritative history of those years, 'what the course of the Church of England might have been if it had had the will and the vision possessed by some of those it dubbed radicals.'[9]

One may smile at the notion of every Member of Parliament, atheists and Roman Catholics included, having the responsibility of regulating the worship and doctrine of the Established Church, but they certainly have the right, and it remains a right which could easily lead to disestablishment, for there is little doubt that the Church would never again tolerate the kind of interference in its internal affairs that it suffered in 1927 and 1928. Members of both Houses of Parliament may huff and puff, but if any major Synod legislation – for the ordination of women, for example – was rejected by Parliament there would be uproar. Meanwhile, Parliament retains a kind of religious watchdog in the form of the Ecclesiastical Committee. This consists of thirty members, half nominated from the Lords by the Lord Chancellor, half from the Commons by the Speaker. Its duty is to look at measures sent to it by the Legislative Committee of the General Synod to make sure they 'contain nothing that affects adversely the constitutional rights of the citizen' and to report to Parliament 'on their expediency'.

There has been intermittent talk of disestablishment ever since Parliament first declined to sanction use of the Revised Prayer Book in 1927, but there has never, until the separation in 1992 of the Prince and Princess of Wales, been any real interest in the subject evinced by the press or public. And indeed, there have been advocates of disestablishment only among a small minority of radicals in the Church itself. What it would entail constitutionally would be abolition of the coronation oath relating to the Church of England, the monarch relinquishing the right to appoint deans and bishops, and hence a severance of the prime minister's relations with the Crown Appointments Commission; and hence, also, no further need for the sovereign to be Supreme Governor.[10] The

Church of England would in turn relinquish the twenty-six seats in the House of Lords at present automatically allocated to the twenty-six most senior diocesan bishops, which would strike some as a serious diminution of national influence; on the other hand, those bishops who have to travel from Chester or Salisbury for a week at a stretch, to read prayers, might find the loss of one more episcopal chore a relief. On the positive side, the Church would exercise total control over the appointment of diocesan bishops and would be free to legislate in the General Synod without the need to seek parliamentary approval.

What I have called the nebulous strand of establishment, the unofficial connection between the Church and the country, continues to commend itself strongly to the Church at large. 'I am quite clear and confident that the Church of England best serves the nation by being established,' the Archbishop of Canterbury told me. And if an entrant to the establishment from the working class, like Dr Carey, is so enamoured of the trappings of Church-State links, there must still be plenty of mileage in the idea and little incentive for radicals to voice objections. 'I believe,' said Dr Carey, talking to me eighteen months after taking his own seat in the House of Lords, 'that if we were disestablished it would be a statement that this country is turning its back on the Christian religion. Establishment demonstrates the civic dimension of the faith. To be disestablished would make us much more of a sect. By having bishops in the House of Lords it gives us a voice at the very heart and structure of our nation, and enables us to stand alongside the homeless and defenceless. I don't want to lose that. But of course, if the time ever came for the Church to be disestablished we would still get on with our job. We would still want to be available for everybody, but it would be a little more difficult to do.'

It is not only the socially mobile who tend to embrace the system to which they owe their elevation; former radicals, as they grow older, have a tendency to swing in favour of the status quo. Lord Beaumont of Whitley, a politician as well as a priest, who was deeply involved in advocating reform in the 1960s, says, 'I am now a complete convert to the establishment of the Church of England, because on the parochial level it is so useful. It gives the Church of England a persona, and it gives to the parish priest a place in the community, the acknowledged right to call on anyone at any time. By comparison with the Church of England, all other Churches of the Anglican Communion are sects. Establishment may not be rational but we are not a rational country, we are a deeply traditional country, and having an Established Church rather suits the English.'

But there is an obvious dichotomy between the pomp and circumstance of establishment and the reality of the Established Church's life at grass roots. When the clergy rode to hounds it would have been natural for them to support reactionary interests, so many of which are manifest in the countryside, and it has taken the Church of England a long time to live down the jibe that it is the Tory Party at prayer. But by far the majority of the clergy work today in towns and cities, and a majority of socially active parish clergy and theologians are today left-wing. If you run a shelter for the homeless you are obviously more likely to vote Labour than Conservative, and this publicly visible shift to the left in the political allegiance of individual members of the Church has simply reflected the Church's rapidly growing concern about Third World poverty, sexual inequality, homelessness and commercial exploitation. Although Church leaders who are themselves members of the establishment still cherish their state connections, not since the witness in slum parishes of late-Victorian Anglo-Catholic clergy has the Church of England been so keenly aware of its responsibility to preach and practise the social gospel. For this sea change the least establishment-orientated archbishop of modern times, Michael Ramsey, himself a disciple of William Temple and F. D. Maurice, was to a considerable extent responsible.

Even if there is little stomach among the hierarchy for disestablishment, the separation of the Prince and Princess of Wales, and the reasonable assumption that they will eventually divorce, perhaps by the year 1995, gives both Church and Crown an opportunity they may regret not making the most of to look at the mutual advantages to them both of an amicable parting of the ways. The sort of questions that have been raised are whether, if divorced, Prince Charles could, or would wish to, be crowned, whether he could act as Supreme Governor of the Church of England, whether indeed he would ever succeed to the throne. These thorny issues need to be separated into what is possible and what might be deemed desirable. Divorce in itself would be no bar to the throne, nor indeed to the Prince's assumption of the role of Supreme Governor of the Church; Henry VIII separated from two wives, George I was divorced before succeeding to the throne, and on his accession George IV was separated. The constitutional duties of Supreme Governor merely entail formally ratifying appointments of deans and diocesan bishops, and now that the Church of England is quite happy for divorced and remarried clergy to remain in holy orders (one such is actually provost of a cathedral), there can be no impediment (indeed, there has not been in the past) to a divorced Supreme Governor, a layman, signing bits of paper; at least he is not called upon to celebrate holy communion.

Likewise, the coronation service is not dependent upon the marital status of the sovereign, but if Prince Charles, as a separated or divorced monarch, decided he would prefer to dispense with a coronation service, the taxpayer might give three cheers. The prime minister's blithe assertion to the House of Commons that separation was no impediment to the Princess of Wales being crowned may, in theory, be true but in practice it raises the prospect of a pretty bizarre spectacle, and my guess is that if at the time of his accession Prince Charles was still separated, he would decide to forgo a coronation service. If, however, by that time he had contracted another, not morganatic, marriage, a coronation might be regarded as seemly, depending on public sentiment. Under the Royal Marriages Act of 1772, remarriage for the Prince, as he is over twenty-five, would depend upon the consent of Parliament, and a morganatic marriage either as Prince of Wales or as king would require an act of Parliament. There is no provision in English law for a morganatic marriage, and unless the Prince's intended second wife was even more tarnished by scandal than the Prince himself, which in the circumstances seems highly unlikely, there could these days be little purpose in resorting to one more subterfuge.[11]

In the past, kings of England have behaved, in a moral sense, far more reprehensibly than the Prince of Wales. No one ever kept count of Charles II's brood of illegitimate children; William IV had ten bastards when he came to the throne, all of whom moved into Windsor Castle with him; Charles II, James II, William III, George I, George II, George IV and Edward VII all had mistresses; and James I and William III were not, to put it mildly, entirely heterosexual. Today we live in a sickeningly hypocritical age, and the more the populace romp around, the more upright they expect the royal family to remain. The Prince of Wales is, in the strict sense, a highly moral man, and if he were to feel simply uncomfortable, as a separated or divorced sovereign, in the role of Supreme Governor, it would be felt by many as a golden opportunity to sever formal links between the Crown (i.e. Parliament) and the Church, links upon which at the end of the day neither depends for its *raison d'être,* and which as far as the Church is concerned are of dubious moral and theological standing. Disestablishment would also render it unnecessary for the sovereign to be a member of the Church of England, and would permit Anglican clergy to stand for Parliament. It may be a fiction that the sovereign actually appoints bishops, but under the present arrangements these appointments are seen as quite literally Crown appointments and, because they pass through Downing Street, as political appointments too – which indeed they are. The argument for retaining the present system, explained in detail in Chapter Three, is that the prime minister is entitled to some say in the de facto creation of peers spiritual, destined, most of them, to sit and vote in the House of Lords. But the Church of England may have to relinquish its allotted seats in the unelected, and hence undemocratic, second chamber of Parliament as part of the price for retaining the credibility of a future monarch whose marriage has come adrift. No other religious denomination is accorded this privilege, nor do they suffer as a result.

A former bishop of Guildford, preaching some thirty years ago in London, said that trying to define the Church of England was rather like chasing a lightly poached egg on a piece of toast. One can, in fact, quite easily draw up a list of theoretical beliefs and practices that characterise the Church of England, but when a cross-section of Anglicans come to define their beliefs you might be forgiven for wondering if they all belong to the same Church. Essentially, however, the Church of England, together with the worldwide Anglican Communion, claims affinity with the bulk of Catholic Christendom by virtue of its threefold ordained ministry of deacons, priests and bishops, all of whom are ordained and consecrated by bishops who themselves believe the validity of their orders derive from the Apostles. What also defines or identifies the Church of England is generally held to be belief in the Creeds, adherence to the Scriptures, and the administration of baptism and confirmation. There are five other sacraments the Church of England holds in common with the Church of Rome: ordination, absolution, holy communion, holy matrimony and unction (a blessing with consecrated oil, administered to the sick or dying).

What differentiates the three orders of ministry, quite apart from any legal, pastoral or administrative tasks they may be assigned, is the sacraments they may administer. Confirmation and ordination may only be administered by a bishop (and only bishops can consecrate other bishops). No deacon is permitted to celebrate holy communion, give absolution or administer unction, and deacons are allowed to officiate at weddings only with the consent of their incumbent (the vicar or rector), and then only for 'exceptional reasons'. The laity can administer baptism in extremis.

When no university teaching post could be obtained unless a don was in holy orders, someone like Lewis Carroll, who was really the Rev Charles Dodgson, was obliged to be ordained deacon; but with no vocation to the priesthood (Dodgson was a mathematician) he would remain a deacon all his life, and was known as a perpetual deacon. Today a deacon is normally ordained to the priesthood (made priest, or priested) within a year, and during that year he will be training under an experienced parish priest as a curate, strictly speaking, as an assistant curate, for the parish priest is really the curate; it is to the parish priest that the diocesan bishop commits an area of his diocese for the cure (i.e. care) of souls. Since women have been admitted to the diaconate there has been a common misapprehension that a female deacon is a deaconess. Having said that, what exactly a deaconess used to be is far from clear. The office of deaconess, instituted by the laying-on of hands by a bishop, was certainly in existence in the third century, became obsolete in the Middle Ages, but was revived in 1861, and the Order of Deaconess was formally established some sixty years later. Her role, status and duties remained in some doubt, however; William Temple, archbishop of Canterbury from 1942 to 1945, used to describe a deaconess as 'a woman minister, not a female deacon', but the duties she undertook in a parish were identical to those of a male deacon. Once it was made possible for women to be ordained deacon, admission of new applicants to the Order of Deaconess ceased, and only a few deaconesses, who do not wish for the opportunity to become deacon or priest, remain.

Peculiar to the Church of England is a former clerical bugbear, subscription to the Thirty-Nine Articles, a set of doctrinal formulae drawn up in an attempt to define the dogmatic position of the Church of England in relation to the controversies of the sixteenth century. The first draft of the Articles (Elizabeth I herself had a hand in drawing them up) was accepted in 1563. Article 6, for example, declares that Holy Scripture 'containeth all things necessary to Salvation'; Article 8 states that the Creeds are to be accepted because they may be proved by Scripture. Opponents of the ordination of women to the priesthood may be relieved to recall that Article 21 declares General Councils 'to be not of themselves infallible'. With what the *Oxford Dictionary of the Christian Church* describes as 'masterly ambiguity' Article 17 discusses the highly controversial question of predestination. For 400 years, every time a clergyman was inducted to a new living he had to read every Article and assent to each one, many a tender conscience being stretched as a result. And it was not only the parish clergy who were compelled to go through this rigmarole. Until 1854 it was not possible to teach at Oxford without assenting to the Thirty-Nine Articles. But in 1975 the General Synod more or less laid the Articles to rest, deciding that in future the clergy need only 'affirm and declare their belief in the faith which is revealed in the Holy Scriptures and set forth in the catholic creeds and to which the historic formularies of the Church of England bear witness'.

The desire of the pragmatic Elizabeth I to hold together in a common faith men and women of good will who defined their personal beliefs very differently, a desire clearly echoed by the Synod as recently as 1975, was always thought to be typical of that comprehensiveness and catholicity said to be one of the great virtues of the Church of England. And it was held up as evidence that far from being some sort of fundamentalist sect, the Church of England was essentially an intellectual Church, its intellectualism much bolstered through its roots in university life. This is one reason why periodic attempts to demythologise the image of God as a benign old gentleman robed in white and sitting on a cloud have been so readily absorbed by those prepared to trust the intellectual credibility of the Church's thinkers. However, in recent years one can detect in the Church, as in society at large, a rise in fundamentalism, a growing intolerance which is throwing out of balance what at heart has always been a conservative organisation, whose radicals, as in most walks of life, are politely tolerated until they are put out to grass. And because, for all its intellectual exploration and former acceptance of eccentrics and mavericks, the Church of England is perceived by the public to be conservative and therefore a symbol of stability in an otherwise uncertain and ever changing world, the more unorthodox its conduct or pronouncements, the more open it becomes to vilification. But so many cries of 'Crisis!' have now been heard, both from within and without, that they are virtually ignored by those who have responsibility for the day-to-day running of affairs.[12]

In 1973 Trevor Beeson published a book called *The Church of England in Crisis*.[13] He is now a dean and a fully paid-up member of the establishment. There being no copyright in a title, A. N. Wilson and others later produced a book called *The Church in Crisis*. 'People have been saying that the Church of England would die for generations,' Patrick Miller, a former canon of Southwark who is now in secular employment, said on Radio Four in 1991. 'I've got a shelf full of books talking about the crisis in the Church, it ain't going to last, it's going to die any time.'[14] Those who judge success by the numbers who receive communion on Sunday or the numbers offering themselves for ordination and, scanning the statistics, convince themselves the Church is on a slide to oblivion, have indeed been saying this for years. But like the Second Coming, predicted by the earliest Christians for about the year AD 40, the demise of the Church is now well behind schedule. And this is in spite of ever advancing secularisation and the withdrawal of very considerable gratuitous support. Can anyone today imagine the director-general of the BBC declaring that the corporation 'bases its policy upon a positive attitude towards Christian values', the 'whole preponderant weight of its programmes' being directed to that end? That was what Sir William Haley announced in 1948. In the direct aftermath of the war, the BBC actually saw it as part of its God-given task to lead non-churchgoers 'to see Christian commitment as involving active membership of a congregation'. For the Church of England, the BBC acted as a propaganda machine, and any mention on the air of atheism was greeted with howls of hatred. During Haley's regime, no fewer than three church services were broadcast every Sunday, together with *Sunday Half-Hour* and an *Epilogue*. There was a daily service, inaugurated in 1928 and now the BBC's longest-running programme, another daily slot called *Lift Up Your Hearts*, and religious broadcasts to schools and the armed forces. Prayers were even incorporated into *Children's Hour*. It was quite simply assumed that everyone listening was a Christian (and a member of the Church of England), and that if they were not, and they knew what was good for them, they soon would be.

Today the advent of an acknowledged pluralist society holds no terrors for those who have never known anything else, and even acceptance of the word 'crisis' has undergone a reversal. Far from lamenting any possible crisis in Church affairs, young and enthusiastic ordinands will tell you that if the Church is not in crisis then it jolly well ought to be; to be in a perpetual state of crisis, they feel, is the Church's natural calling so long as it strives to serve an unrepentant and as yet unsalvaged world. Many clergy of an older generation, those who were advocating radical reforms in the 1960s, saw their mission as in some way to rescue the Church from organisational incompetence and to lead the Church itself into the promised land. What they did not appreciate is that neither reforms nor reformers recruit churchgoers, only charismatic clergy do that – and I use the word charismatic in its old-fashioned sense of 'magnetic appeal, charm or power of an individual', the sense in which the word was used before it was hijacked by hand-wavers.

Those who maintain that the Church is going down the plughole will point to statistics to prove their case, and there is of course no escaping statistics, although one may wish to deny them; that is to say, many statistics are meaningless and others are open to a variety of interpretations.[15] Supposing it were true that on account of misplaced missionary zeal or poor planning, in the 1950s the Church built too many new buildings, so that today some are redundant, does the closing of redundant plant mean the Church has failed in any definitive sense? Failed at finance or administration, perhaps. If the conversion of the Jews is officially off the agenda (and rightly so), and humanists perversely decide to stick to their own set of moral values, perhaps in assessing success or failure the Church would do best to concentrate on the spiritual lives of those who do opt to join it, although there can be no ultimate criteria for measuring that. What seems self-evidently true is that the Church is not for everyone and therefore cannot account itself a failure if not everybody joins; and if it slumped to just two members, who is to say that was not part of God's plan for starting up again from scratch?

It is tempting as well to suggest that figures for church attendance are no measure of Christian commitment, but so long as the Church maintains buildings and trains clergy it does seem rather pointless if a Christian congregation does not exist to take advantage of those facilities. It is also probably a Christian duty to take part in the joint worship of the local community. About 1.2 million Anglicans in Britain do just that on a normal Sunday.[16] Between 1960 and 1970 there was a 19 per cent decline in church attendance, but between 1986 and 1991 attendance at church by adults remained steady, some 920,000 receiving communion on a weekly basis, and 1,549,200 on Easter Sunday 1990. There has been a dramatic decline in confirmations, down by 39 per cent over the past decade, the figure now hovering around 60,000 per annum, but this could reflect a falling-away of discipline rather than of Christians; many clergy give communion to parishioners they know perfectly well are not confirmed. Between 1978 and 1989 infant baptisms fell from 38 per cent of live births to 29 per cent, so that in 1988 about 233,000 people were baptised into the Church of England, of whom 189,200 were infants; but these figures coincide with a period when increasing numbers of clergy have been refusing to baptise children of non-believers. By contrast, since 1986 baptisms of people over the age of thirteen have been holding steady.

If there ever was a golden age for the Church of England it may perhaps have been during the nineteenth century, with the Oxford Movement reviving catholic worship, new dioceses being created[17] and hundreds of new churches being built: in the first decade of the century twenty-eight new Anglican churches went up; between 1841 and 1845 the number was 401, and in 1866–70, 427. Yet in 1874 Victoria told Disraeli the Church was tottering, and few if any of these new Victorian buildings were ever filled to capacity. The 1851 religious census revealed that even then less than 50 per cent of the population were at worship on a Sunday, at a time when many like to imagine that every parlour maid and bootboy went to matins. In 1845 Friedrich Engels had reported, 'All the writers of the bourgeoisie are unanimous on this point, that the workers are not religious, and do not attend church.' Even though 7,261,032 in church in 1851 out of a population of 17,927,609 might be thought pretty good today, the missing millions were almost all of them nominally Christians, and 'Church of England' at that. Today there are probably 5.5 million baptised Roman Catholics in England, not to mention the second-largest Jewish community in Europe, 300,000 Hindus, 500,000 Sikhs and one million Muslims.

Even if not every adult goes to church, apparently 60 per cent of them watch a religious television programme, and, according to a recent survey by the European Values Group, 54 per cent of Britons claim to be 'religious'. Seventy-one per cent say they believe in God. So why are they all not in church? Peter Byrne, lecturer in the philosophy of religion at King's College, London, suggested to Diana Hinds of the *Independent* in December 1991 that 'Christian symbolism – the cross, the Passion, the Trinity – no longer moves people in the same way.' He might have added that in the Middle Ages people went to church to keep warm and, as often as not, because they believed in God. Today, whatever people may tell those who interview them for surveys, the vast majority do not believe in God; they say they do because to admit to being an atheist is not yet socially acceptable, and may even be hard to admit to oneself. They also hedge their bets. But if most of the time you do not truly believe in God, why go to church? Talk of boring sermons is just an excuse. Another, perfectly healthy, reason for a decline in church attendance is that it is no longer a social duty (matins at the Guards Chapel may be an exception); conversely, all those who are in church are there because they want to be. As one parish priest told me, 'Everyone who comes to my church does so because he or she is a Christian who wants to follow the way of Christ. They may not be very clear what that is, they may thoroughly disagree with some of the ways I suggest it is, but no one is there because it is the done thing to do. No one at all.'

'Figures don't worry me. Not at all,' says Lord Beaumont (who was born in 1928 and ordained in 1956). 'There are two problems. One is the growing proportion of very fundamentalist evangelicals, and it is a problem because they are anti-intellectual. The other is the problem as to how between them the Church and the State are going to educate children. Most of them haven't the faintest idea what the Christian religion is about. Religious education has a very low priority on virtually everyone's list, and to a large extent it is taught by non-Christians, although there are an awful lot of Christians about.' Official church membership may be gauged by the numbers on the Parish electoral rolls: 1,605,500 in 1991, out of a population of 48,058,000, perhaps half of whom are children and 7 or 8 million are members of other faiths. A crucial point about the Church of England is that its influence in public life is out of all proportion to its numerical strength.

A former archbishop of Canterbury, Lord Runcie, has referred to the Church of England as 'the focus of vague religious expectations on the part of the great majority of the English people',[18] and one reason it is possible for the Church to fulfil those expectations is that, in theory at any rate, every square inch of the land falls within an Anglican parish.

Within the parish structure, figures for church membership or attendance bear little relation to actual pastoral work undertaken, most of it a good deal less vague than the expectations it sets out to meet. Every parishioner, nominally Christian or otherwise, can call upon the local church for baptism, marriage and burial, and who can say that a parish priest who conducts two or three funerals a week is of less use to the bereaved whom he may never have met before (and may never meet again) than he is to his regular Sunday morning communicants? There are no statistics for the numbers of prisoners counselled and comforted by prison chaplains, for men and women prayed with before they enter the operating theatre, for the destitute who are given food and shelter for the night, for the old and sick who are visited at home, for confessions heard.

Many clergy really want to be some sort of ordained social workers, rushing round doing good and being needed. But those roles are now undertaken by trained social workers or Samaritans. Many of the disaffected clergy have spent a minimum amount of time in prayer, even in some cases ignoring the daily office, and now bitterly complain about lack of preferment.

In 1991 there were 10,375 full-time male clergy paid for by the Church Commissioners, a fall of 678 in eleven years, but that drop was almost precisely made up by having 674 women deacons in stipendary posts by 1991, although they cannot celebrate holy communion. A fall in ordinations to the priesthood has, however, been fairly dramatic. Whether this matters depends to some extent on how the Church plans to maintain its existing plant – its parish churches, cathedrals, diocesan offices, boards, councils and chaplaincies – and on how it plans to deploy its new women priests once they are ordained. In 1963, 636 men were ordained.Ten years later that figure had plummeted to 373. It has been spasmodically better since: 451 in 1988, 390 in 1989, but only 359 in 1990. However, between 1988 and 1990, 338 women were ordained deacon, 121 of them in 1990. Ordinations to the diaconate for 1990 therefore totalled 480, a figure which compares very favourably with recent trends, especially as those women deacons can expect, if they wish, to be priested.

What must give cause for some concern are the numbers of candidates attending selection conferences and the percentage of those attending being recommended for training. In 1986, 727 candidates attended a selection conference, of whom 363 were recommended for training. By 1990 the numbers attending were down to 545, of whom only 264 were deemed acceptable. However, in 1991, 575 men attended a selection conference, of whom 325 were recommended for training, 274 of them for the stipendiary ministry. And in 1991, 240 women attended conferences, of whom 123 were recommended, 85 for the stipendiary ministry. The total number of men and women (815) attending selection conferences in 1991 in order to test their vocation to the ordained ministry was, by a small margin, the highest number for four years. And 1990 had seen 746 men and women in training, a rise of 111 over 1989.

One of the most remarkable changes to have taken place in recent years is the ratio of active to retired clergy: it has almost reached 50:50. And alongside the 10,989 male and female clergy in stipendiary ministry are some 6,000 retired clergy with permission to officiate. Without the assistance of retired clergy there would be a manpower problem of gigantic proportions. But even these figures do not present a total picture of the active and part-time workforce. There are perhaps as many as 1,500 clergy working in hospitals, the armed forces and prisons, or as industrial, school or college chaplains. An absolutely accurate assessment of manpower is impossible to come by, for there are clergy who go missing altogether. The current *Crockford's Clerical Directory*, which lists the names and addresses of all Church of England clergy, nevertheless has the names of some 140 clergy, including a retired bishop, for whom no address is known.

At an organisational level, the Church of England's established links with the state proliferate through a network of boards and councils, committees and commissions, funds and societies, and of course through its connections with the Queen's household, awash as it is with clergy: the Clerk of the Closet, the Prelate of the Order of the British Empire, the Dean of the Chapels Royal, the Lord High Almoner. No diocesan bishop can 'take possession of the revenues of his see' (in reality, a monthly cheque from the Church

Commissioners) until he has done homage, normally at Buckingham Palace, where he is 'introduced into Her Majesty's presence' by the home secretary while the Clerk of the Closet to the Queen, currently the Bishop of Chelmsford, hovers in attendance with the rest of the Household-in-Waiting.[19] The Queen has thirty-six chaplains, who sport red cassocks, and their names are suggested to the Queen's private secretary by the Clerk of the Closet. Their duties are not too onerous, merely to preach in the Chapels Royal. The Chapels Royal? They comprise the chapel at St James's Palace, where on the Feast of the Epiphany offerings of gold, frankincense and myrrh are made, and the chapels at Hampton Court and the Tower of London. Then there are the Royal Peculiars, Westminster Abbey and the Queen's Free Chapel of St George within her Castle of Windsor. The Queen is Visitor to Westminster Abbey and, aided by the Duke of Edinburgh, she personally interviews and appoints the dean and canons of Windsor. Hidden away off the Embankment is the Queen's Chapel of the Savoy, another 'free' chapel – free of episcopal oversight – to which the Queen appoints her own chaplain; this she does in her fairy-tale role as Duke of Lancaster. Here use of the Book of Common Prayer is religiously preserved. Here, too, can be heard one of London's finest choirs.

The Church of England has a galaxy of organisations designed to impregnate national life with Christian philosophy. The National Society (Church of England) for Promoting Religious Education, patron, the Queen, address, Church House, is just one of them. There is an Action for Biblical Witness to Our Nation, very much against 'the sinfulness of fornication, adultery and homosexual practice'. There is an Actors' Church Union, 'to bring spiritual help to members of the profession who are in need.' Its president is Bishop John Yates, head of staff at Lambeth Palace. There is something called the Alcuin Club, founded in the last century to promote liturgical studies, and an Ancient Society of College Youths, which sounds a bit like a contradiction in terms but is ancient indeed; it came into existence in 1637, and still has an honorary secretary, who lives in Towcester. There is an Anglican Society for the Welfare of Animals, a fellowship dedicated specifically to praying for missionary work in the

Arctic, a Bible Reading Fellowship and an association of divorced and separated clergy wives. The Bishop of London may or may not have discovered that he is president of the Church Schoolmasters' and School Mistresses' Benevolent Institution, founded in 1857 'for the relief of financial distress among members of the Church of England in the teaching profession'. There is a Divine Healing Mission and an Ecclesiastical Law Society, a Family Life and Marriage Education Network and a Federation of Catholic Priests – by which they mean priests within the catholic tradition of the Church of England. There is a Victorian Guild of All Souls, who pray for the dying, the dead and the bereaved, and a Guild of the Holy Ghost the Comforter. No doubt much to the distress of the Action for Biblical Witness to Our Nation, also listed in the *Church of England Yearbook* is the Lesbian and Gay Christian Movement.

After 160 years the Lord's Day Observance Society is still in action. There is something called the Martyrs' Memorial and Church of England Trust, a Melanesian Mission, and a Movement for the Reform of Infant Baptism. The Missions to Seamen is one of the Church's most famous missionary societies, with centres in 100 ports. The Princess Royal is president. Not yet graced by royal patronage is an operation called Message, set up in 1969 by 'Miss N. Coggan', now the Hon. N. Coggan. She was the daughter of the archbishop of Canterbury, Lord Coggan, and what Message does is provide a service 'offered by local groups of churches through the medium of two-minute recorded telephone talks explaining the Good News of Jesus Christ as revealed in the Bible'. That is probably the Church's newest missionary endeavour; its oldest is also one of which few will have heard, the New England Company, founded in 1649. It operates from Saffron Walden. There is a Parochial Clergy Association, a Prison Service Chaplaincy, a Protestant Reformation Society, a Retired Clergy Association and a hospital for the clergy, St Luke's, in London. Universities and public schools run missions. There is a society to perpetuate the memory of King Charles the Martyr, better known to history as Charles I, instigator of the Civil War. Devotion to Our Lady is fostered 'throughout the Anglican Communion' by the Society of

Mary, and friendly relations with the Old Catholic Church are maintained by the Society of St Willibrord. At Benson in Oxfordshire can be tracked down the principal of Turners Court, founded in 1912 'to train deprived adolescent boys in a trade and to give them a social background to enable them to stand on their own feet in the world'. There is a Guild of Vergers; there is a 'resource centre' called the William Temple Foundation, 'engaged in thinking through the theological implications of aspects of urban and industrial experience', and there is a newspaper for bellringers called *The Ringing World*. These are merely examples of Church organisations, catering, as one may imagine, for a wide variety of needs, and staffed by clergy and laity of every political and liturgical hue. Add to all these the evangelising Boys' Brigade, 'upfront and unashamed in commending Jesus' according to its upstanding vice-president, the singer Cliff Richard, and the Mothers' Union, concerned since 1876 with 'all that strengthens and preserves marriage and Christian family life', and you have a rare mix of activity and opinion.

The Church of England may be a very parochial Church, with a theologically illiterate laity, one half of whose members are surprised to find that the other half go to confession and most of whose members could not tell you what a deacon is, but because it is an Established Church it operates with a spotlight permanently focused upon it. Hence its scandals, when they occur, become headlines, its opportunities for service in the community are there for the taking, and the interest it generates seems never ending. It also serves as a whipping boy for a multitude of discontents, and as a seemingly natural recipient of stupidity and hypocrisy. Complaining in the *Evening Standard* on 11 December 1992 about the 'bland twaddle' of the established bishops on the subject of the separation of the Prince and Princess of Wales, Stephen Glover wrote: 'We may not want to be told that we are wrong, but we still want to be told what is wrong and what is right, even if it does not make a blind bit of difference to the way we behave.' To minister under those circumstances, whether the Church is by law established or not, must sometimes seem like a rather thankless task.

THREE

The Making of a Bishop

THE Church of England is an episcopal Church; at the end of the day, for all the local allegiance parishioners may feel towards their parish, and however secure a parish priest may feel in his parish (known too as his living, or benefice), ultimate authority resides in the bishops. Only a bishop can ordain a deacon or priest, no priest or deacon can officiate without a bishop's licence, and every time a priest moves to a new parish he must be instituted into his living by the bishop. Of course no bishop can be consecrated except by other bishops, and all the bishops are vested with a specifically prophetic and teaching role. Although the Church of England has two provinces, Canterbury and York, both presided over by an archbishop (also known as a primate or metropolitan),[1] within his own diocese the diocesan bishop virtually reigns supreme. Seldom does an archbishop issue an order to a diocesan bishop (for fear it might not be carried out); he would make a request, for it is very debatable whether an archbishop has any real jurisdiction over the diocesan bishops in his province. He can only rule the province through and with his fellow bishops; he cannot overrule them. An archbishop, after all, is only a bishop who happens, for a time, to hold a specific office; there is no ordained ministry of archbishop, and no such thing in the Church of England as an emeritus archbishop. On resigning an archbishopric, the holder properly reverts to the style and dignity of a bishop.[2] So central are bishops to the mystique of Apostolic succession that there is a strongly held theory that no matter how reprehensibly he may behave, a bishop's orders are indelible, and that unlike a priest he cannot be unfrocked. It may be possible to remove a bishop from his see but he will always remain a bishop – even without the opportunity to officiate as one.

Just as the ordained ministry of the Church – deacon, priest and bishop – represents a hierarchy, so the organisational structure of the Church is based on a hierarchical pattern. At the base of the pyramid are any number of parishes, grouped for convenience into archdeaconries. London has half a dozen archdeacons, but most dioceses survive with two or three. The first known archdeacon in England was Wulfstan, appointed archdeacon of Canterbury in 803. At least every three years the archdeacon must carry out a visitation in his archdeaconry, inspecting the fabric and contents of churches, granting certificates for repairs and keeping a pastoral eye on the clergy on behalf of the bishop. He inducts new incumbents into their benefice and usually presents candidates to the bishop at an ordination service. In the southern province, for some reason the archdeacon of Canterbury enjoys the privilege of enthroning diocesan bishops.

Within the archdeaconries are a number of rural deaneries, groups of parishes whose clergy meet in a rural chapter under the rural dean to discuss and take action on matters of common concern. Rural deaneries also comprise laity, and together with the clergy they meet in the deanery synod. The prime task of the rural dean is to serve as a means of communication between the bishop and the clergy. The rural deaneries form individual dioceses under the jurisdiction of a diocesan bishop, and the dioceses in England are collected into two provinces, the dioceses chosen to serve as archbishoprics, Canterbury and York, remaining fixed. A small Anglican Church like that of Burundi, Rwanda and Zaire, with only ten bishops, may consist of only one province, and one of the bishops will be elected to serve as archbishop. A large Church like the Anglican Church of Australia has a number of provinces, each with an archbishop, one of whom is elected primate of Australia, but arrangements throughout the Anglican Communion vary a good deal. In the Episcopal Church in the USA there are nine provinces and no archbishops, just 'a presiding bishop and primate'.

The diocesan bishop may share his episcopal work with one or more suffragan bishops, depending on the size of the diocese, and by part-time, and very occasionally full-time, assistant bishops. Suffragan bishops have their own see, but it is not a diocesan see (the suffragan see of Dover, for example, is in the diocese of Canterbury), and although they do not exercise the full legal responsibilities of a diocesan bishop, today many are in almost total charge of an area of the diocese, and are often known as area bishops. (Oxford covers three counties and now has area bishops.) There are still those (although seldom the bishops themselves) who find this an unsatisfactory exercise of episcopal orders, and in a perfect world there would be much smaller dioceses and no suffragans, but the administrative and financial implications of creating new and smaller dioceses make such a move utterly impractical. A suffragan bishop carries out on behalf of the diocesan bishop particular episcopal functions like ordinations and confirmations, and many are now given specific areas of the diocese in which to supervise the pastoral care of the clergy. They do not automatically sit in the House of Bishops (six from Canterbury and three from York are elected as members), and suffragans are never eligible to sit in the House of Lords. An assistant bishop is a former diocesan or suffragan bishop living in retirement in the diocese, who has been invited by the diocesan to continue exercising his episcopate, mainly by carrying out confirmations. No bishop would be consecrated in the Church of England to be an assistant bishop; all Church of England bishops are consecrated to a specific see.[3]

Suffragan bishops are chosen by the diocesan bishop, whose commissaries they are.[4] (Archdeacons are also chosen by the diocesan bishop.) Under an act of 1534 the diocesan was required 'to name and elect two honest and discreet spiritual persons to the King requesting His Majesty to give one such of the said two persons as shall please His Majesty such title, name, style and dignity of bishop of one of the sees named in the Act'. Today two names still go forward, not directly to the sovereign but from the diocesan bishop to the prime minister, who invariably forwards the first name to the Queen – who equally invariably ticks it. The reason Downing Street never interferes in the choice of suffragans is that they do not qualify for a seat in Parliament; conversely, one argument for Downing Street continuing to have a serious say in the appointment of diocesan bishops is that they do stand in line for the House of Lords. Hence the role of the prime minister where suffragans are concerned is purely ceremonial. But a General Synod working party on Senior Church Appointments published a report in October 1992 recommending that, as far as suffragans were concerned, Downing Street should bow out and the names of not one but both potential bishops, in order of preference, should be sent to the Queen via the archbishop of the province.[5] Within hours of the report being published, both archbishops let it be known they had not been consulted and wanted no part in this novel constitutional procedure. There is within the British Constitution a general principle that the sovereign acts only upon the advice of her ministers; in any case, any actual involvement by the prime minister in the appointment of suffragans is a fiction, so there seems little point in exchanging one fiction for another.

When choosing a suffragan, there is at present no formal obligation on a diocesan bishop to consult anyone, but it can safely be assumed he always turns to his archbishop, if only as a matter of courtesy; the archbishop, after all, has to consecrate the new suffragan. Should a bishop propose to the prime minister – in effect, to the Queen – the name of someone wholly unacceptable to the archbishop, the archbishop could always decline to consecrate, but then presumably the Queen could order the archbishop to consecrate. What would happen should the archbishop refuse is perhaps best left to the imagination, but invocation of Richard II's Statute of Praemunire, under which Cardinal Wolsey was indicted in 1529, involving possible imprisonment and confiscation of goods, is believed to be a faint possibility.[6] Be that as it may, the working party took a dim view of the lack of any formal process of consultation, and suggested the setting up of an Appointing Group, consisting of the diocesan bishop as chairman, an archdeacon, a rural dean and five others. Their task would be to consult, approve a job description and search out three potential candidates; why three, when it was proposed that only two names should go forward to the relevant archbishop, remains a mystery. It took the working party five years to come up with this brainwave, and when the General Synod discussed it for the first time in 1993 it received a lukewarm reception.

Meanwhile, left to their own devices the diocesan bishops seem to be taking appropriate care. When the High Church Bishop of Chichester needed a new suffragan for Lewes to succeed an equally High bishop, Peter Ball, who had been preferred in 1992 to Gloucester, he chose an evangelical, the warden of Cranmer Hall Theological College in Durham. Ball's promotion coincided with the preferment of another suffragan, Nigel McCulloch of Taunton, to the diocesan bishopric of Wakefield. Archdeacons have often been seen as bishops in waiting, and the bishopric of Taunton was duly filled by the archdeacon of Ludlow, who seems admirably suited to a rural episcopacy; his hobbies include beekeeping and bricklaying.

Complaining about the present bench of bishops,[7] a member of the General Synod told me, 'The bishops are a nice bunch of men but they're not particularly holy or intellectually gifted. On the whole, the Church of England has ceased to attract high flyers, but the bishops reflect the quality of the clergy. They're not very bright or inspiring, but perhaps they never have been.' Never? One only has to recall some of Archbishop Fisher's contemporaries in the mid-twentieth century: Cyril Garbett of York, George Bell of Chichester, two major theologians, Kenneth Kirk of Oxford and A. J. Rawlinson of Derby, F. R. Barry of Southwell, Spencer Leeson of Peterborough and Leslie Hunter of Sheffield. Whatever former bishops may have lacked, it wasn't brains. Apart from the archbishops, only two diocesan bishops are household names today, and both for the wrong reasons, because both are in fact outstanding diocesans; the Bishop of Durham, David Jenkins, is a liberal theologian frequently reviled as some sort of Satanic fifth-columnist, and David Sheppard of Liverpool is best known for his prowess at cricket.

'I think the bishops are kindly, hard-working and conscientious,' another cleric told me, 'but very few are good preachers or scholarly.' Perhaps four could be accounted scholars: the Archbishop of York and the Bishops of Durham, Chichester and Ely. What the Church most notably lacks is eccentric bishops, but it sadly lacks eccentrics now in most departments of its life. An eighteenth-century rector of Cranley, James Fielding, was reputed to be a highwayman; Archbishop Ramsey's donnish comments and bizarre accidents were legendary; where resides the modern rector of Stiffkey? One of the deans made the point that now that diocesan bishops are chosen in effect by a committee, a more monochrome bench of bishops is almost bound to be thrown up. 'On the other hand,' he said, 'if you look around it is hard to say who of quality has been overlooked.' He made the point that dynamic leadership was lacking because 'they have to hold everybody's hand. Bishops were more radical in the past when the parish clergy were more secure than they are now. The clergy were quite happy to run their own show, and they didn't much bother about the bishops. Those ordained between the two world wars had enough money and enough people in the congregation and they were secure enough not to want the bishops on their tails. When I was ordained in 1951 the older clergy actually didn't like the bishop coming round. Today the clergy complain bitterly if he hasn't been round three times in a week. It used to leave the bishops much freer to be their own man. Now they've got to keep everyone happy.'

The Clergy Appointments Adviser, Canon Ian Hardaker, confirmed this crucial point. 'When I was ordained thirty years ago my rector would have thought that the less he saw of the bishop the better. Now I sense that most clergy get a bit worried if they don't have the opportunity of meeting their bishop as often as they might hope. The role of the priest is not so well defined as it used to be and the sturdy independence of the English parsonage has vanished. They are now more dependent on guidance and they see the bishop as the leading member of a team, whose constant support they expect to receive.'

Whereas until Geoffrey Fisher's time bishops were not infrequently recruited from the ranks of headmasters (Fisher had been appointed headmaster of Repton at twenty-eight, William Temple at twenty-nine; Archibald Tait and Frederick Temple had both been headmasters of Rugby, and Arthur Benson was the first headmaster of Wellington), a bishop today is more likely to have been principal of a theological college. Robert Runcie, George Carey, John Habgood of York and David Hope of London all were. And whereas, in the past, few suffragan bishops expected preferment to a diocese, today a period as a suffragan seems to have become a recognised training ground for greater things. University education for the bishops has changed too. In 1992 only 68 per cent had gained their first degree at Oxford or Cambridge. Eight had been to Durham, six to Leeds and five to London. Another marked difference is that of age. Few men are consecrated as young now as Gerald Ellison, forty when he began his episcopate at Willesden, progressing to Chester and eventually London, or John Robinson, forty too when he became bishop of Woolwich.[8] But neither do they hang on into their dotage. In 1892 the *Spectator* felt it was its duty to call upon the bishops of Chichester, 'close upon ninety', Bath and Wells, 'close on eighty-four' and Norwich, who was eighty, to contemplate retirement, and suggested that all bishops should step down at seventy-five. This they are now in fact obliged to do at seventy, and many retire between sixty-five and seventy, in contrast to Vernon Harcourt, who died in harness as archbishop of York in 1847 at the age of ninety-one.

When it comes to assessing the merits of former and current processes whereby the diocesan bishops are chosen, it has to be said it is almost inconceivable that some of the most outstanding Church leaders thrown up by a theologically indefensible system – Michael Ramsey or Mervyn Stockwood, for instance – would have survived the voting system regarded as such a virtue of the Crown Appointments Commission.[9] The only truly experimental appointment made by the Commission has been that of David Jenkins, in 1984. Before succeeding John Habgood as bishop of Durham he was professor of theology at Leeds University, and has been turned by the press into the best-known episcopal voice in the country, in other words, into a rogue elephant, which is a depressing thought if you go along with the Dean of Winchester's belief that 'David Jenkins is not a very radical theologian, and he speaks for a good many intelligent people. Anyone who has done A-level New Testament knows you don't actually need to believe in the revival of a corpse in order to believe in the Resurrection.' On the other hand, there are those who believe that theologians who think out loud should remain in universities. 'What people want to know,' a parish priest reminded me, 'is whether God exists, why their wife has cancer and what will happen when they die. Public arguments led by bishops about the Resurrection are no help at all.' The same parish priest complained bitterly after a confirmation service that his bishop had turned up in the church hall in a suit, not a purple cassock. 'The people wanted colour and glamour,' he moaned. 'The bishop just looked so ordinary.'

If not necessarily archetypical, the character and career of the youngest diocesan bishop, Nigel McCulloch, enthroned as bishop of Wakefield in 1992 at the age of fifty, after serving for six years as a suffragan, may be some indicator of the sort of man being entrusted with the spiritual guidance of the Church of England as it heads for the twenty-first century. He combines a gift for friendship with dedication to hard work, seeing, it is said, 'a face, and perhaps a pastoral opportunity, behind every piece of paper'. He shares with many of the younger bishops an almost compulsive desire to get round his diocese at the speed of lightning, and to try, as a bishop, to retain his love of parish work. When he was appointed to St Thomas's Church in Salisbury in 1979 there was a congregation of about eighty and the bishop of the diocese was contemplating closing the church; McCulloch revived the parish, and the congregation shot up to 300. He was nurtured on the controversial book *Honest to God*,[10] is flexible on such issues as homosexuality and the ordination of women and, perhaps most typically of all, bestrides the High and Low wings of the Church; no previous generation trained at Cuddesdon Theological College would have been happy to be called an 'evangelical catholic with an enquiring mind'. One of the problems for a man like McCulloch is the burden of expectation he carries into his episcopal office, for the sheer grind of paper and committee work, unless sensibly delegated, can wear away at early enthusiasm. No one really knows what it is like to be a diocesan bishop, and when you find out it is too late to turn back. It takes a man who would have been a success in almost any sphere to keep his head above the ecclesiastical quagmire.

McCulloch's predecessor at Wakefield, David Hope, now bishop of London, had the courage to admit on television to the boredom of much of his job, and one can be certain he was referring to the mountain of administration; pastorally he became a hit in London overnight. For someone like Hope, there may be the added dimension of loneliness by virtue of his being a bachelor, although marriage is no guarantee of company; one chaplain told me he had never known the bishop's wife to appear in his chapel, and he rather thought that first thing in the morning she went for a swim. There were in March 1993 six bachelor bishops (if you include the peripatetic Bishop of Gibraltar), of whom two were members of religious orders. While the lack of a wife has never been a positive bar to the episcopate, it must be said it has been a rarity, and one can only guess at the degree of queasy disquiet that keeps the number of bachelor bishops to an absolute minimum.[11] Loneliness, however, is to some extent endemic to the calling of a bishop. In his autobiography, another bachelor, the former bishop of Southwark, Mervyn Stockwood, has written, 'A bishop . . . is necessarily a lonely person. And it is not easy for a lonely man to carry such a burden for twenty years.'[12] Many bishops, even those who are married, rely heavily on the companionship, or at any rate the shared priestly presence, of their chaplain to alleviate some of the loneliness of the job. They can off-load some of the drudgery on to him and unwind with him at the end of the day, as often as not with a stiff whisky. One chaplain who objects to the compulsory retirement age for bishops remarked, 'Bishops don't have to be middle managers or bureaucrats. They should be the still centre of their diocese. You don't retire from being a father, you grow older and wiser. This idea of compulsory retirement is a fad of society that has rubbed off on to the Church. Bishops have chaplains and secretaries to do the organising for them.'

Unfortunately not all bishops are good at delegating, and one chaplain told me his bishop never consulted him over the planning of his diary. For most bishops, the day starts in their private chapel with silent prayer, matins and a celebration of the Eucharist. 'We all hope Saturday is going to be our day off,' a chaplain said, 'but if the Synod meets, bang goes Saturday. Some bishops want an unmarried chaplain, partly because he will not be too choosy about housing. But if a chaplain is to serve his bishop he must be available at all hours, just as the bishop needs to be free to meet his clergy's needs at almost a moment's notice. Even when the bishop gets back from the House of Lords at two o'clock in the morning he will be in chapel at seven. His priorities spring from his time in chapel. He always makes time for anyone who has any sort of problem, whether it's a priest or a churchwarden worried about his priest. He would make an appointment just like that.'

One of the most common pastoral problems confronting bishops at present is debt. Collections taken at confirmation services go into the bishop's discretionary fund, and from this source bishops are increasingly bailing out clergy who have run up credit card bills they cannot pay. Their wife may have lost her job, they may have been rash enough to place their children in private schools. Ironically, an ordinand is required to sign a declaration that he is not in debt before he is made deacon. Other causes of clergy debt are less mundane. 'Money for some clergy is a problem' a chaplain told me, 'because they espouse a life geared towards the good life. The bishop depends on rural deans to alert him if a clergyman has a debt problem, and we always try to deal with it as quickly as possible.' Holidays for sick clergy who cannot afford to go away are also a common drain on the bishop's private resources.

Because of their public persona, bishops are wide open to criticism. Some of it is a good deal sharper than it used to be, and appears in more unexpected places. When there was a suggestion, later abandoned, that the Mothers' Union might, for purely pragmatic reasons, support the legalising of brothels, the Bishop of Sodor and Man, Noël Jones, received a roasting in the *Church Times* from Paul Handley, briefly a former member of Dr Carey's staff. He said a letter written by the bishop to the *Daily Telegraph* – 'the most outrageous contribution to the debate' – had demonstrated why he was not bishop of somewhere bigger. What the bishop had written was, 'The policy of the Christian Church in faith and morals is not to be determined by small groups within it,' to which Mr Handley, in his weekly column, retorted, 'Bishop Jones clearly has no idea how the Christian Church comes to a mind on anything. That bit about "small groups" not determining policy is worth quoting back at him next time the

House of Bishops decides anything which the main body of the Church finds unacceptable.'

There is no training to be a bishop. Before being consecrated bishop of Durham in 1952, Michael Ramsey fell back upon reading Pope Gregory the Great's *Regula Pastoralis*. When, in years to come, he had Simon Phipps to stay at Lambeth Palace on the eve of his consecration as bishop of Horsham, he invited Phipps to the study after dinner. Not unnaturally, Phipps imagined the archbishop was going to pass on some sage advice. The minutes ticked by. Big Ben could be heard chiming across the Thames. Eventually Phipps suggested they should go to bed. 'The only advice he had given me about being a bishop,' Phipps can still recall, 'was to take every fifth Sunday off, and to leave a space in my diary every week for the crisis which was likely to emerge. I thought it was wonderfully characteristic of him to say two completely mundane things and to leave the rest to God.'[13]

Until 1977 – the year the Crown Appointments Commission was set up to give the Church a greater say in the choice of diocesan bishops – the prime minister, if he consulted the Church at all, did so only as a matter of courtesy, and then he usually only sounded out the views of the archbishops. Ultimately he exercised an exclusive right to submit the names of diocesan bishops to the sovereign, without consultation with anyone if he wished, or even to submit the names of people contrary to the expressed wishes of the archbishop concerned. As if this wasn't bad enough, since Victorian times the allegiance of prime ministers to the Church of England, while sometimes total, has sometimes been tenuous and even non-existent. At least three have been atheists. Many prime ministers, it is true, exercised Church patronage with a remarkable degree of conscientiousness, but rather than seek sensible advice from the Church, prime ministers like Palmerston, Lloyd George and Churchill, with no knowledge of or interest in ecclesiastical affairs, frequently consulted personal cronies, such influential outsiders as Lord Shaftesbury (in the case of Palmerston) or Brendan Bracken (in the case of Churchill).

Even when some intelligent attempt was being made by the archbishops' appointments secretary, in collusion, since 1966, with his opposite number at 10 Downing Street, to gather information on which to base a recommendation, the process was reminiscent of *Alice in Wonderland*. The appointments secretary would scurry, like the White Rabbit, from parsonage to deanery, taking tea and soundings, noting down black marks against the names of 'unsound' men, his ear keenly adjusted to the mispronounced vowel, his eye to any gaucheness unbecoming in a bishop's wife. The wonder is that under such a haphazard and theologically indefensible system some very remarkable bishops emerged, men of scholarship and learning, sometimes with a crusty temperament but often profoundly pastoral. They came, of course, almost entirely from the public schools, those most favoured being Eton, Winchester, Marlborough, Shrewsbury, Rugby, Harrow, Westminster, Charterhouse, Haileybury and King Edward's, Birmingham. Most also had a father in the ministry, and many were connected by birth or marriage to the peerage or the landed gentry.[14]

The Crown Appointments Commission is a semi-permanent body whose secretary, Hector McLean, is also appointments secretary to the archbishops. Along with the two archbishops and the prime minister's appointments secretary (a full-time post since 1947), he is an ex officio member of the Commission, but neither he nor the prime minister's appointments secretary has a vote.[15] Because the secretary of the Crown Appointments Commission, in his capacity as appointments secretary to the archbishops, has a hand in drawing to the attention of the bishops potential new suffragans, provosts, archdeacons and residentiary canons (he may even be asked to advise about deans), he is quite simply the most influential lay person in the Church of England, far more influential, in the long term, even than the secretary-general of the General Synod.

The other permanent members of the Commission are three elected by the House of Clergy of the General Synod and three elected by the House of Laity, and these half-dozen members, permanently subject to pressure groups, can be elected to serve for the duration of two synods; hence they could be in the business of choosing bishops for a decade. Each diocese has what is called a Vacancy-in-See Committee, convened at the start of each synodical cycle.[16] This comprises the suffragan bishops, the dean or provost and one archdeacon as well as elected clergy and laity, and if the bishopric falls vacant, four of its members are elected to the Crown Appointments Commission.

Dioceses are encouraged to make public the names of the Vacancy-in-See Committee so that they can be openly canvassed by interested people. With the two appointments secretaries present, the Committee draw up a Statement of Needs, describing what they see as the requirements of the diocese and the kind of bishop it would like. A few weeks later the two secretaries return to the diocese, and in the course of a day and a half they may meet between 100 and 150 people from the Church and the local community. They then draw up their own report for the Crown Appointments Commission, and it is this report, together with the Statement of Needs, that provides the raw material on which the Commission forms a view about the wishes of the diocese.

Nominations for a vacant bishopric may come to the Commission from anyone. One of the Commission secretary's jobs is to provide biographical information, much of which will be readily to hand, but in the case of a last-minute nomination of some obscure candidate some frantic rushing round in search of relevant facts may be necessary. Names are discussed in the Commission in alphabetical order, and there is no indication who has put them forward. The first question generally addressed is whether a candidate matches the description of need supplied by the diocese. The second question will be, What will he bring to the totality of the Church? I was told, 'If the answer to the second question is uncertain, it does not necessarily rule that person out, because it may be right for the Church at large for the diocese to have priority. There is a very considerable effort to get this balance right.' I was also told that Dr Carey's preferences tend to come down on the side of the diocese's requests, but this may simply be because he is himself at heart a diocesan bishop.

In order to boost the spirituality of the occasion (the Holy Ghost, after all, is meant to play some part in the selection of bishops), the Commission meets, whenever possible, in a religious or a retreat house. Between afternoon tea and

Evensong they will spend perhaps an hour and a half considering the Statement of Needs from the Vacancy-in-See Committee and the report drawn up by the two secretaries. After supper they take a look at the full list of candidates, which may number anything between a dozen and eighteen. These names will have been put to the secretaries in one of two categories, mandatory or discretionary. If a member of the Commission writes to say he wants a candidate to be regarded as mandatory, his name will be discussed. Alternatively, they may say they have heard that someone might be good but they know nothing about him and so they invite the secretaries to do some research, and in those circumstances the secretaries have discretion to put the name forward or withhold it. The bulk of the names are mandatory.

By bedtime the Commission aim to have arrived at a short list of not more than five and quite possibly only three, so that if eighteen names were submitted, clearly the majority entered the race with exceedingly long odds. Upon this short list the Commission sleeps. Next morning, after matins, Eucharist and breakfast, the first thing the archbishop in the chair will ask is whether anyone wishes to re-present any name discarded the night before.[17] The short list is then discussed in detail in order to reduce it to two names by voting, and when voting has been completed the chairman takes care to ask the diocesan representatives if they feel their case has had a fair hearing. A final two names are necessary because the Commission is obliged to send two names to the prime minister, and these names 'may be given in order of preference'. If the Commission does not avail itself of this right, as sometimes it does not, it is tantamount to saying the Commission cannot agree or make up its mind, and is asking the prime minister to make the decision. Even if the Commission does state a preference, however, there is no obligation upon the prime minister to submit their preferred name to the Queen, or indeed to submit either of the Commission's nominees; the prime minister can reject both names and ask the Commission to start again.

Each of the two names sent to the prime minister must have received eight out of twelve votes; then there is a final vote to decide on the order of preference. When it comes to expressing a preference, the Commission is taken to have done so if one candidate gets eight or more votes and the other four or less. If the leading candidate has only seven or six votes, then the prime minister is made aware of the votes for each candidate 'and he or she can see that no determining preference from the Church's point of view has been expressed'.

If the Commission discover the prime minister has sent the name of their second preference to the Queen it may be because, having written to their first preference to see if he is willing to allow his name to go forward, the prime minister discovers he has a reluctant bishop on his hands, but not many people decline a bishopric. It is more likely to be a case of political intervention. When terms of reference for the Crown Appointments Commission were being drawn up under James Callaghan, the prime minister's veto over the Church's nominees was retained as a kind of quid pro quo, and although the prime minister can send to the Queen only a name submitted by the Commission, he or she is at liberty to submit the Commission's second choice, or to call for new names ad infinitum. On at least two occasions during her premiership Margaret Thatcher declined to act as a rubber stamp. After Jim Thompson had been a very popular and successful area bishop of Stepney for nine years he was telephoned in 1987 by a member of the Commission (who had, of course, stepped well out of line) and told he was going to become bishop of Birmingham. He was, says my informant, 'flabbergasted', as was the Commission, to discover from the newspapers that Mrs Thatcher had spotted a wet – worse, a Labour sympathiser – a mile away and had advised the Queen to appoint their second choice, one of Thompson's fellow London suffragans, Mark Santer, for the past six years the area bishop of Kensington. (But this ploy rather backfired when it transpired that Santer was in favour of nuclear disarmament.) When the first vacancy arose after Mrs Thatcher's departure from 10 Downing Street in 1991, the Commission seized the opportunity to put Jim Thompson's name forward again, and John Major accepted it without a murmur. Thompson succeeded George Carey as bishop of Bath and Wells.

At the commencement of every meeting of the Crown

Appointments Commission everyone stands and recites in unison a declaration not to disclose anything that is said or transpires. Hector McLean told me, 'There has been no leak that I can identify with certainty. There may have been one or two occasions when someone appeared to be caught out by being asked a seemingly innocent question, but that is quite different to a deliberate leak. By the general standards of today I reckon that's not too bad.' It is common knowledge, however, that Jim Thompson's nomination for Birmingham was not the first occasion on which Mrs Thatcher had played a decisive constitutional role in the appointment of a bishop. In 1981, when the Commission was torn between John Habgood of Durham and Graham Leonard of Truro for the bishopric of London, the third most senior in the Church, Mrs Thatcher, not only a Methodist by upbringing but, in so far as she later adopted some sort of social allegiance to the Church of England, an evangelical by inclination, sent Leonard's name, although he was the Commission's second choice, to the Palace.[18] The fact that he was a leading Anglo-Catholic was neither here nor there; he was politically sound, and this was a decision she never regretted. By the mid–1980s, according to her biographer, the distinguished political journalist Hugo Young, 'she was in the habit of saying to anyone within earshot that the Bishop of London was the only man in the Church of England who made the kind of sense she was looking for'.[19]

Michael Ramsey, although he always wanted the Church to have a greater say in bishop-making, came in for a good deal of criticism for taking too little personal interest in Church appointments. Since 1977 it has not been possible for either of the archbishops to stand apart from diocesan appointments, for both are ex officio voting members of the Crown Appointments Commission. This is one of its advantages, for one of the most important tasks of any archbishop is to help build up a strong bench of bishops. And after all, the archbishops, who may serve on the Commission for fifteen years, do have to work closely, in the House of Bishops, with those whose names the Commission recommends. But even allowing for the virtues of continuity, what must be of very dubious merit is the fact that the six elected members from the General

Synod may serve not just for two consecutive terms of five years but, after a break of five years, may be elected to the Commission yet again. The balance of membership is weighted far too heavily in the direction of bureaucratically tainted interests and tittle-tattle.

How much influence is exercised by the Queen? She certainly takes a particular interest in the nomination to one bishopric, that of Norwich, for, although not officially in such a close relationship to her as the dean of Windsor, the bishop of Norwich is expected to keep a fatherly eye on Sandringham, and the Queen does not wish anyone in such close proximity who is not sympathetic.[20] Michael Ramsey always maintained that the reason Donald Coggan succeeded to Canterbury was that he got on so well with the royal family. Without exerting any sort of improper influence, it is perfectly easy to imagine, while the archbishop of Canterbury is staying the night at Windsor Castle, the Queen dropping into the conversation the name of someone she knows in connection with some vacant diocese – and just as easy to imagine the archbishop bringing that name forward, as he has every right to do, to the Crown Appointments Commission. There would be no guarantee that name would emerge as a nominee, but if it were known that he was the Queen's favoured candidate he might be hard to resist.

If the diocesan bishop is the linchpin of the Church, and the diocese is the most important structural entity, the cathedral is obviously the most visible symbol of that diocesan dimension. Every town with a cathedral automatically enjoys the status of a city, and implanted deep in the English subconscious is the cloistered atmosphere we all associate with a medieval cathedral close, the tea shops and the deanery, the eighteenth-century canons' houses, the open green, the tranquillity, and the sense that the old cathedrals exude of a timeless witness not just to the worship of God but to breathtaking craftsmanship and manual skills carried out by ordinary people. Close by will be the bishop's house or palace, but much in evidence, too, will be notices which read 'By Order of the Dean and Chapter', for in fact the cathedral belongs to the dean and chapter, not to the bishop; a cathedral is so called because it contains the bishop's cathedra, his chair, but whatever jurisdiction he may wield within the cathedral depends on the ancient statutes. In many cathedrals the dean cannot even give consent for the bishop to celebrate unless the chapter agrees, and the bishop spends far more time in his own private chapel than he does in the cathedral, where the statutes may permit him to preach only at Easter and Christmas.

The bishop generally ordains deacons in the cathedral, but his most important role is as visitor. Not all visitations go off smoothly. In 1991 the Bishop of Salisbury criticised the dean and chapter for their management, and reproached them for competing in the leisure industry. Six months after digesting 'some 31 closely typed pages of evidence, argument, ideas and philosophy', the chapter concluded that 'a less formal and legalistic approach might have better served the purpose which initially led the Dean and Chapter to request the visitation'.

The history of England's cathedrals is complex. Chichester, Exeter, Hereford, Lichfield, St Paul's, Salisbury, Wells and York are known as the Old Foundation; they were originally bishop's churches and have always played a central role in the life of their diocese. There are others – Canterbury, Carlisle, Durham, Ely, Norwich, Rochester, Winchester, Worcester – known as the New Foundation; all save Carlisle, which was Augustinian, were originally Benedictine monasteries, and hence were closed to the public, unless, like Canterbury, Durham and Winchester, they contained the shrine of a saint, in which case pilgrims arrived, often in considerable numbers and furnished with alms. Since 1840 cathedral deans have been appointed by the Crown; they often live in a house quite as large and lovely as the bishop's, and when the bishop comes to the cathedral for his enthronement the dean has the pleasure of slamming the door in his face.

Modern dioceses – Birmingham (1905), Blackburn (1926), Bradford (1919), Chelmsford (1914), Derby (1927), Newcastle (1882), Portsmouth (1927), St Edmundsbury and Ipswich (1914), Sheffield (1914), Southwark (1905), Wakefield (1888) – have a provost, not a dean. He is appointed by the bishop, not the Crown, because his cathedral has parish status. There are modern dioceses like Guildford (1927) and Liverpool (1880) with a new cathedral, but most newly created dioceses have taken over for their cathedral an already existing, large parish church. Southwark's cathedral predates the diocese by about 350 years. Just to confuse the issue, there are new dioceses – Guildford, Liverpool, Manchester (1847) and Truro (1877) – which have a dean, not a provost.[21]

To assist the dean in the running of the cathedral there are usually four residentiary canons, two of whom will be entirely engaged in cathedral duties. They live in the cathedral precincts and are 'in residence' a certain number of months each year, to conduct services, preach, hear confessions or counsel visitors. Two residentiary canons may have duties elsewhere. In the cathedrals of the Old Foundation, the offices of chancellor, treasurer and precentor have been retained, although a canon who happens to be precentor is no longer required to be able to sing. Originally the chancellor would have been a theologian, and the treasurer would have been in charge of endowments and fabric. The 'cathedral chapter' means the dean and residentiary canons, who form what is known as the administrative chapter; they are responsible for the spiritual life of the cathedral. They try to come to a consensus but occasionally the dean may have to exercise a casting vote. Usually he cannot be outvoted on any proposed change in the liturgy. The administrative chapter will probably meet twice a month, to discuss the state of the fabric, the services, their pastoral responsibility to visitors and their own staff arrangements. Even a small cathedral like Chichester may employ 85 people and depend on a further 1,000 volunteers. Most cathedrals run a gift shop and a restaurant. One of the best is at Ely.

Each cathedral also has a number of honorary canons, known in some of the cathedrals of the Old Foundation as prebendaries. They are chosen by the bishop as a mark of good conduct and long service, and together with the administrative chapter they form what is known as the greater chapter, which probably meets only once a year, and may enjoy the patronage of a number of livings.

Nowhere does financial expenditure and Christian witness receive a higher public profile than in the management and maintenance of the great medieval cathedrals, although it should be remembered that parish churches, of which there are 16,000 serving 13,000 parishes, also retain historical links and provide spiritual solace on an unimaginable scale. Bolton Abbey, St Mary the Virgin in Oxford and Bath Abbey all attract over 300,000 visitors a year, and in 1991 a total of some 12 million visitors were drawn to English parish churches before they started stomping through the cathedrals, as often as not causing tragic damage. Three and a half million people visit Westminster Abbey each year, among them souvenir hunters who think nothing of breaking fingers off the statue of Wordsworth, removing pieces of mosaic from the shrine of Edward the Confessor or damaging the crown of Henry V.

To be dean of a cathedral used to be the natural ambition of an academically gifted churchman, and in terms of prestige, a deanery was seen as an end in itself; very few deans (the Bishop of Chichester is a notable exception to the general rule) go on to be bishops, and today their stipend is on a par with that of a suffragan. A dean, after all, is already lord of all he surveys. Unfortunately, that is now, as often as not, a vast pile of stone and timber rotting and crumbling away before his eyes. Not only have deans, like bishops and archdeacons, discarded their gaiters, they are nowadays more likely to be entrepreneurs than scholars, for with their chapter of canons they have become custodians not only of what is left of the Church's ancient liturgy and glorious music but of medieval shrines, stained glass, carvings and intricate architecture which costs a great deal of money to maintain. Canterbury claims the cathedral costs £7,000 a day, and running a cathedral calls for great financial expertise. It also requires the kind of tact and grasp of public relations often lacking among the retired service chiefs increasingly being appointed to undertake administration. 'Sacking upsets tenor of Westminster Abbey' the *Guardian* announced in one of its famous punning headlines when reporting a row that had broken out at Westminster Abbey, where the 'chief administrative officer' is an admiral; after twenty-seven years a chorister had failed to get his contract renewed because, it was alleged, he sang flat. When St Paul's Cathedral woke up to the fact that they were £600,000 out of pocket, and imposed a wage freeze on their 110 full-time staff, one aggrieved employee complained, 'The brigadier talked about discipline. He told us, "I am a solidier." He's not. He is the registrar of a cathedral.' Someone else complained to the *Church Times*, 'We were talked to as if we were a bunch of squaddies.'

In the subsequent absence of both registrar and dean it was left to the Archdeacon of London to clarify the situation. 'It was more like a team talk before a football match,' he said. 'I think we must try to meet more often. Our annual staff party has been a way of building relationships, but we didn't have one last year because it couldn't be afforded.' Thus St Paul's meanders on its miraculous way, relying on Christmas parties to maintain staff morale. It was not aware of its financial plight until it dawned on someone to check how much the 2 million annual visitors were donating: 15p per person. Then they got into hot water when they imposed an entrance charge of £2.50. One Anglican priest, ordained in St Paul's, wrote to the press to say he had transferred his allegiance for purposes of prayer to Westminster Cathedral. He thought the practice of charging for entry to a place of worship 'borders on blasphemy'. Another brigadier is clerk to the chapter at Salisbury. He cooked up a scheme for distributing to cathedral visitors discount vouchers redeemable at the city's branch of McDonald's. 'This cathedral is a source of inspiration to hundreds of thousands of people,' the brigadier explained. 'If that means indulging in a little honest commercialism, so be it.'

Money is of course a real headache, and a dean can envisage spending the whole of his ministry weaving his way through a tangle of scaffolding. Work on restoring Worcester Cathedral, which began in 1989, is expected to last fifteen years. State aid amounting to £75,000 saved the roof; a total of £6 million is required. English Heritage are increasingly coming to the rescue; over two years they are making £690,000 available for Ely, and over three years £870,000 for Salisbury. Other recent grants made by English Heritage vary from £2,000 for Manchester to £337,000 for Lichfield.[22] Some cathedrals seem more adept than others at meeting their own repair bills; an appeal for £7 million for Winchester Cathedral produced an astonishing £6.5 million in two years. 'Bordering on the miraculous' was how the dean, Trevor Beeson, described an achievement unmatched by any other cathedral. Dean

Beeson's achievements have given him licence to examine in some detail the problems and failings of cathedrals and their staff.

Preaching at the University Church of St Mary the Virgin in Oxford on 5 May 1991, Trevor Beeson remarked that Lincoln's attempt to raise money by the exhibition in Australia of its copy of Magna Carta 'was not only a financial disaster but also exposed to public view a most unedifying personal conflict between the dean and canons which no one, not even the Bishop of Lincoln, is able to resolve.' Shades of Barchester! While on the subject of his fellow deans' shortcomings, Beeson reminded the congregation that 'the administrative arrangements at Exeter were, it seems, not sound enough to prevent the head verger from stealing at least £47,000 from the collection boxes'. Worse had befallen Salisbury. Having 'lost sight of £700,000 in the ailing British and Commonwealth Finance House' the cathedral was 'now doing battle not only with its city but also with the bishop's wife over a proposal to drive a new road through the Close'. What next? he asked.

Reflecting on his time as Dean of Lichfield, John Lang was to write in an article in the *Church Times*, 'The first few . . . years were without doubt the unhappiest of my whole working life.' Dr Lang put his finger on the crucial issue, the relationship between dean and residentiary canons; if that is not harmonious there will be disaster.

Those who complain in a mindless sort of way about the witness of the Church in the twentieth century need to throw their minds back to the age of pluralism that followed the Reformation, when bishops and deans seldom resided in their diocesan city, patronage was a matter of handing out livings to friends and relations, and with absentee deans and canons, cathedral worship slumped into a shambles. At the same time, there was an enormous increase in income from Church land, and those cathedral staff who did remain on duty grew fat on the proceeds. Although towards the end of the nineteenth century Walter Kerr and Edward Benson initiated reforms at Salisbury and Truro (where Benson was bishop), it was not until very recent times that two outstanding Church leaders, Frank Bennett, appointed dean of Chester in 1920, and H. C. N. Williams, provost of the new post-war cathedral at Coventry, demonstrated the possibility of using a cathedral as a major centre for worship and mission. One result, allied to the boom in the tourist industry, is that cathedrals have become symbols of pride and achievement, not mere shrines smelling of mothballs. Anyone who compares the sad and deserted atmosphere of many Gothic cathedrals in northern France must be grateful for the fund-raising gifts of the modern dean.

As Dean Beeson pointed out in his sermon, it is because of the 'astronomical sums of money' needed to keep the buildings in good repair, and to maintain their expanding life, that 'the old statutes, customs, traditions and people associated with cathedrals are being stretched to breaking point. The inherited organisation is often quite unsuitable for the tasks that have to be performed. The consequence, all too often, is inefficiency, frustration and stress, and what we read about cathedrals in the newspapers, and much else which mercifully doesn't reach the public eye, is often a symptom of this problem.' Because they are lumbered with medieval statutes, the old cathedrals are still governed by four or five people, the dean and chapter. Few chapter members have any serious managerial or financial skills, and even if they had, they are supposed to be clergy, not part-time businessmen. Trevor Beeson believes it is time to bring skilled lay people on to the governing bodies. Cathedrals in the past provided refuge for scholars, and many deans and canons produced seminal work from their home in the cathedral close. 'This vital asset,' says Beeson, 'has been largely lost, submerged under the busyness that requires deans and canons to be amateur financiers and shopkeepers.' He has suggested that cathedrals 'develop an effective partnership between clergy and laity, and, learning from the experience of universities and hospitals, not allow the cathedrals to fall into the hands of the accountants'.

But despite the unceasing financial grind, pay a visit to Trevor Beeson's deanery and who would not want to be a dean? At a time when one of Beeson's predecessors would rather live in Holborn than Winchester, Charles II took over the deanery, building, in 1673, the last great gallery in an English domestic house. It used to be the library; now it is the grandest study in the Church of England. The house has six bedrooms; the main bedroom takes 25 square yards of carpet. But it is the cathedral that attracts the visitors, half a million every year. 'We could do with more, really,' Beeson told me wistfully. 'They provide us with half our income. We suggest they give £2 a head, and about one in three does. It costs £600,000 a year to run the cathedral before we touch the fabric.' Apart from being a priest in charge of a magnificent house of prayer, Trevor Beeson is a considerable writer and broadcaster, yet he now spends 80 per cent of his time on administration and raising money. Why, I asked, did he quit a residentiary canonry at Westminster Abbey in 1987 to take on such a burden?

'You don't investigate the place before you are appointed. I just got a letter from Margaret Thatcher with the strict admonition that I must not go near the place or talk to anyone except the bishop. You're not allowed to case the joint. You can't even see the house. It's a great act of faith! My predecessor had been a contemplative. He had been here seventeen years, and had really done nothing except just keep it going. There was no educational programme, and I found enormous resistance to change from the chapter. It had enjoyed peace for decades! After I'd been here twelve months the treasurer told me we were £73,000 in the red. It came as a great surprise. Nobody had noticed. But can you wonder? The cathedral had been run by sixteenth-century statutes, which were geared just to keeping the place ticking over, and hopefully to prevent change.'

I asked if he thought it true that deans on the whole deserved the label liberal? 'I think traditionally they have always been. The bishops have been conservative and the deans have been scholars and a bit liberal. E. G. Selwyn of Winchester, for example, was an international scholar.[23] Now there are not the scholars about in the Church. The new idea is to have a dean as manager, not as scholar. If a scholar was dean he wouldn't want to run the show, and if he did, he would have no time for scholarship anyway. Again, in the old days all the deans automatically sat in Convocation. Today their collective influence is nil.'

Another reason for a dearth of scholars in the Church is the amalgamation of country parishes, where in the past the parish priest had time to think, read and write. Yet another is that a university career offers higher pay, longer holidays and better research facilities. 'All people are doing is keeping the show on the road,' said Beeson. It was an expression I heard more than once while researching this book.

Reverting to the archaic way a dean is appointed, Trevor Beeson thought the Crown should not today appoint anyone the bishop did not want, which was not the same thing as saying the bishop would necessarily get the man he did want. He recalled a former bluff and breezy bishop of Chester receiving the new dean with the encouraging words, 'Well, m'lad, you may 'ave bin the Crown's choice but I don't mind tellin' you, you're not mine.' Conversely, the first a dean of St Paul's knew that he had a new bishop was when he read of the appointment in the paper.

The deans meet in London four times a year. One of the things they can all take pride in is the standard of cathedral music, which has never been higher; at parish level, church music is generally held to be abysmal. Many cathedral organists are appointed very young and they too are of the highest calibre. 'What we are doing every day in cathedrals could be done on television or Radio Three just as it stands,' in Trevor Beeson's opinion. A cathedral like his, permitted a large choir, has a choir school in the precincts, for boys between seven and thirteen. Chichester too has a choir school, but their statutes only permit a choir of twelve boys and six men. A major problem for cathedral music is the pay available for a master of the choristers, and many need a second occupation to make ends meet. Career prospects are unsatisfactory, too. There are really only two prizes, St Paul's and Westminster Abbey.

In 1992 Peterborough – or rather, the Crown – took a risk in choosing as dean Michael Bunker, vicar of St James's, Muswell Hill, an extreme evangelical parish church in north London. It was a risk because cathedrals, to quote Trevor Beeson, are 'community churches. You can't muck about with them. There is too much history tied up and they are too big.' No one has suggested that the new Dean of Peterborough, said by his former parishioners to be 'terribly sensitive to the way people feel', is planning to introduce conservative evangelical worship or charismatic services into what is undoubtedly a High Church cathedral, but he might be in serious trouble if he did, just as a catholic dean who started reserving on the high altar and using the Latin rite would deservedly come a cropper. But whether he likes it or not he will certainly have to wear vestments.

One reason people retire to a cathedral city is to be assured of a choice of matins or a sung Eucharist, 'and a lot of people who attend cathedral services are on the frontiers of faith and don't want commitment to parish life. You can come here,' says Beeson, 'and no one will get hold of you and ask you to take the collection or help to run some parish organisation.' What visitors may find, as they do at Wells, is a welcome to receive communion even if they are not an Anglican, or an invitation to become a Friend of the Cathedral, at an annual subscription of anything between £2 and £10. Friends help to raise funds: £500,000 in recent years for Canterbury, who plan to spend another £850,000 in 1993 replacing the eighteenth-century Portland stone floor in the nave; £100,000 to restore the organ at York. But the numbers of committed supporters is said to be on the decline. After a recruiting drive in 1991, one cathedral managed to enroll just five new Friends.

Those who over the years were responsible for the redrawing of diocesan boundaries often took little notice of the geographical position of the cathedral. Their role as a centre of the diocese may not be easy to carry out if they are now situated at one end of it, as Chichester notoriously is. The town of Rye, at the far eastern end of the Chichester diocese, is no further from Guildford than it is from Chichester, and is actually closer to Canterbury, Rochester, St Paul's and Southwark, not to mention two cathedrals in France, in Calais and Boulogne.

A simple example of how a cathedral can serve a non-parochial purpose may be found in Southwark Cathedral, where at the west end a beautifully designed plaque has been inserted into the floor as a memorial to those who died nearby on the Thames in a boating accident in 1989. Southwark not only has a chapel dedicated to John Harvard, founder of the American university, who was born in the parish and baptised in the church,[24] but also a chapel set aside for prayer 'for all who live or die under the shadow of HIV or AIDS'. As recently as 1928 the dean of Gloucester was dim enough to imagine that structural damage might be caused if a recording was made in his cathedral, and not even reassurance from Elgar could convince him to the contrary, but ever since 1724 the Three Choirs Festival, involving Gloucester, Hereford and Worcester, has flourished, and Winchester, Salisbury and Chichester have a music festival too. Encouragement of all the arts has again become a major duty undertaken by cathedrals, as it was in the Middle Ages; John Piper's window and Elizabeth Frink's lectern at Coventry are examples of inspired patronage.

In the summer of 1992 a commission, chaired by Lady Howe, wife of the Conservative politician Lord Howe, was set up by the archbishops 'to examine the future role in Church and nation of the cathedrals of the Church of England and to make recommendations as to how best that role could be fulfilled, including proposals for their government and support'. It was not expected to report for two years, and one can safely assume two or three more years will then pass before any recommendations are accepted and put into practice, but almost certainly the commission will suggest a radical rewriting of the statutes, to allow a far wider representation of laity and experts to take part in the governing of cathedrals. They may well also recommend replacement of the freehold, at present enjoyed by deans and canons, with fixed contracts.

They should also look closely at the lazy way in which bishops often make appointments when searching for residentiary canons. 'The only reason he became a canon is that he made such a dog's dinner of the parish church,' I was told of one appointment in the Midlands. Referring to deans and a few canons – St Paul's Cathedral are Crown appointments – Trevor Beeson said in Oxford in 1992, 'The Crown appears to take a great deal of care over its selections, but the same cannot be said of all the bishops, at least, not over appointment to canonries. The temptations facing a bishop in this area of his work are considerable. What is to be done with a clergyman who has laboured hard and long in a series of parishes, who has served faithfully on a number of diocesan boards and synods, who is too old or too tired to be given another major parochial appointment, yet is deserving of some recognition or preferment? A cathedral stall may be a convenient answer to that question.

'Or how is a bishop to solve the problem of a misplaced clergyman – a priest of some gifts who was appointed to a post of significance in the diocese but for one reason or another it hasn't worked out satisfactorily? Again, a cathedral stall provides an answer. Or a diocesan official – a director of ordination candidates or of social responsibility – needs to be found a base and a house, so why not appoint him to that vacant canonry? The question of whether or not such men have anything to contribute to the mission of the cathedral or are capable of working in a team is rarely asked. Other considerations are often regarded as more important.'

How, asked the dean, are bishops to be protected against such temptations, and cathedrals preserved from their consequences? He suggested that consultation, in the case of canonries, between 'those making the appointment and those who will live with its consequences' should be made mandatory, and that the dean and chapter should be given a power of veto. 'It is,' he said, 'intolerable that those entrusted with the leadership of a cathedral's life should not have a decisive voice over the choice of those who will share that leadership with them.' At present, a canon appointed at the age of forty-five may enter into a freehold allowing him to hang on to his stall for a quarter of a century. A ten-year leasehold would, Trevor Beeson thought, enable deans and canons to move on to new work 'with satisfaction and dignity'.

The working party on Senior Church Appointments believes the process of selection of deans and provosts will become increasingly important as the role of the cathedrals continues to expand, through educational and artistic programmes as well as by catering for the spiritual needs of tourists and pilgrims. Hence they want formal consultation by means of the setting up of an Appointing Group consisting of ten people, to provide two names in the case of a dean, three in the case of a provost. They think the bishops should continue to appoint provosts, and that nominations for deaneries should go to the sovereign from the appropriate archbishop, not, as at present, via the prime minister. Some of this makes sense, but not all of it. They seem to think the filling of a provost's post too important to be left to the bishop to fish around on his own but that the bishop should continue to appoint; why he has to be burdened with three names, and the archbishop – always assuming the archbishops do ever take over from the prime minister – with two names is far from clear. Why two names have to be produced at all when, as in the case of suffragan bishops, the first preference is automatically to be sent to Buckingham Palace is an even bigger mystery. Leaks from an Appointing Group of ten are inevitable, so there would be disappointed would-be deans. There would also be a bill to be met for the cost of servicing the Appointing Groups. The sum of £70,000 per annum has been suggested. The greatest danger inherent in this mania for giving everyone a say, roping in outsiders and generally appointing by committee, is that names which survive that kind of scrutiny tend to be safe names, the ones that offend fewest members of the committee. And with major organisational and financial problems on its hands, the Church can less and less afford to depend upon safe appointments.

FOUR

Money Matters

KENNETH Leech, who for six years was race relations field officer at the Board of Social Responsibility, found the building where he worked a place 'in which vast numbers of people carry on their work in separate compartments without any overall theological and political strategy'.[1] Astonishingly enough, he was writing about Church House, an unlovely bureaucratic pile adjacent to Westminster Abbey with a chilling chapel few, if any, committees ever use for a Eucharist. Its secular atmosphere does indeed seem far removed from any worship or Christian witness it is supposedly supporting through a seamless flow of wisdom, decisions and paperwork. With entrances in Dean's Yard and Great Smith Street, it is a rabbit warren round which no one ever seems able to find their way; the lifts, when they work, are always full of bishops anxiously enquiring if they are on the right floor. Through open office doors can sometimes be glimpsed tables sparsely laid for private lunchtime meetings. When the General Synod is in session, meetings seem to be taking place in conspiratorial huddles round every corner, some to speculate on vacant appointments, others to try and fix a vote.

At the apex of this bureaucracy is the General Synod Office, presided over by the secretary-general. There are committees and advisory committees; boards of Ministry and of Education; and a Board for Social Responsibility with advisory boards to the Board. There is a Committee for Communications and a Council for Christian Unity; a Commission that cares about Cathedral Statutes and a Diocesan Commission charged with the onerous task of wondering if more suffragan bishops are needed. There is a Hospital Chaplaincies Council and a Legal Advisory Commission. There is also a Legal Aid Commission, a Liturgical Commission and, in the basement, one of the best Italian restaurants in town.

When, in 1970, the General Synod (and the whole edifice of synodical government) took over from the old Church Assembly, radicals believed that Church government would become more democratic and less self-centred. But because dioceses and deaneries were encouraged to participate in synodical government, delay was built into the system from the start. It was also thought necessary for measures to be debated thoroughly before being sent to Parliament for ratification, to try to prevent any loss of confidence in the Church's competence to legislate, and this too has led to complaints that changes in pastoral organisation or the revision of services all take too long to implement. Like the Church Assembly, which existed from 1919 to 1970, the General Synod consists of three houses, Bishops, Clergy and Laity, and if any concept of democracy now exists it is in the attempt to provide consensus, contained in provisions whereby no house can be overridden by a majority of the other houses.

With the advent of the ordination of women to the diaconate there has been a minor shift of emphasis within the House of Clergy, which currently contains 25 women deacons. In total numbers, the Synod is smaller by about 200 than the unwieldy Assembly (the diocese of London, for example, sent 16 laity to the Church Assembly; now it only returns seven to the General Synod), but the Synod has been packed with ex officio members. Fifteen deans or provosts and no fewer than 43 archdeacons are entitled to a seat. Diocesan bishops constituting the House of Bishops have always effectively sat in the Church Assembly or General Synod in an ex officio capacity, but now they have been joined by nine elected suffragans. Then there are clerical representatives from universities, and in the House of Laity such splendid creatures as deans of the Arches, vicar-generals and Church Estate commissioners.

The archbishops of Canterbury and York are joint presidents of the General Synod, but a panel of chairmen, lay and clerical, appointed by the archbishops, take it in turns to preside over the majority of debates. This is one major improvement over Church Assembly arrangements, when the archbishop of Canterbury, if he was present, always took the chair – in the case of Fisher, like a headmaster; in the case of Ramsey, like an absent-minded professor. But the archbishop of Canterbury remains influential when it comes to deciding what is debated; business for inclusion on the agenda may be submitted by boards and councils, working parties, diocesan synods or private members, but no item will make its way on to the agenda unless it is agreed by the standing committee – whose chairman is the archbishop of Canterbury. In June 1992 the standing committee reported, 'Behind much of the criticism of the length of Synod meetings lies a feeling that some things get on to the agenda which ought not to be there. There has in the past been a feeling that Boards and Councils have generated reports that Synod did not want and should not have spent time debating.' A long-standing desire to see the number of Synod meetings reduced from three a year to two (partly on grounds of cost) has at last been achieved, and this can be done only by curtailing the number of items earmarked for debate.

Items placed on the agenda as private members' motions indicate both the Synod's wide range of interests and attitudes, and its propensity for wasting time. Recently a layman from Sheffield wanted the legal limit for therapeutic abortions reduced to eighteen weeks. Another, from Chichester, wished to express concern 'at the mounting level of personal debt'. A lay woman from Norwich wanted ordination candidates trained to face 'tensions between their vocation and marriage and family life', and a suffragan bishop was anxious for the standing committee to bring forward proposals for the lifting of direct state control over the appointment of diocesan bishops, and the authorisation by Parliament of Synod legislation; in other words, he wanted disestablishment. A dean wished to have the promotion of 'sex tourism with children' banned and an archdeacon wanted the Synod to recognise the need 'for a stronger and clearer ethical investment policy on the handling of Church assets'. Someone else thought the Synod should spend time debating 'the overabundant provision of food' at Synod meetings (a suggestion tailor-made to cheer up any journalist), and it was even proposed that valuable time should be consumed by discussing the abolition of all clerical titles other than Reverend. (Archbishops are the Most Reverend, bishops the Right Reverend, deans and provosts the Very Reverend and archdeacons the Venerable.)

Obviously crucial to the general tone of the Synod and the outcome of its business is the kind of clergy and laity elected every five years. Inevitably they will be people anxious to steer the Church in a particular direction, and most will be steeped in an unmistakable ecclesiastical aura; they will enjoy gossip, paperwork and political in-fighting. The laity will also be white, middle-class and middle-aged, either self-employed or retired, people able and willing to give up several weeks a year to meetings in London and York. The House of Laity is not as upper-crust as it used to be; in 1992 there were only two peeresses, a baronet, one knight, a judge and one Privy Councillor. But although members of the House of Laity may also have a toe in their parochial church council or their deanery or diocesan synod, and may therefore claim to be in touch with the grass roots, by no stretch of the imagination can they pretend to be socially or ethnically representative of the Church of England.

When the Synod sits in the debating chamber, long-lens cameras, a radio booth and television lights suggest that in some respects the Church has come to terms with the twentieth century. (Archbishop Ramsey refused to allow television cameras into the 1968 Lambeth Conference.) Church House press officers now stalk the landings with mobile telephones, and so media-conscious has the Church become that at the 1992 debate on the ordination of women more seats were reserved for the press than the public. When the press look down at the assembled Synod members, they see not one young face, and very few black. Members talk about 'personhood' and discuss such riveting topics as the Draft Incumbents (Vacation of Benefices) (Amendment) Measure (GS 954B). No wonder they feel the need to crack a joke occasionally, always greeted on cue with hearty laughter. Every time they pass up and down the staircase they get assessed by portraits of past luminaries, with names like Sir Philip Wilbraham Baker Wilbraham, Bart. On sale to raise money for St Luke's Hospital for the Clergy are truly awful mugs priced at 'only' £3. The ties at £5 look better value. But the impression that predominates is of a sea of paper. Members clasp papers to their knees. There are trays encircling every room full of papers, for reports flow from the boards and councils of the Synod like a tidal wave.

But the most serious criticism of the General Synod has to do with its desire to maintain the status quo, an inevitable outcome of its non-representative nature, especially that of the House of Laity. For within the Synod is focused that tribal element that has characterised the Church for centuries; white male dominance, a clear contradiction of the principle of inclusiveness preached by Christ. Those in favour of the ordination of women to the priesthood believe that instead of Synod debates on the subject being enlightened by reasonable theological insights they were tarnished by arguments that bore witness to a subconscious understanding of woman as a second-class form of *Homo Sapiens*. On two other important issues, the Church's responsibility towards blacks and homosexuals, the Synod has in recent years shown at best a lack of resolve to shed the exclusivity that makes the Church appear a club for 'normal' people, at worst a moral cowardice that must have frightened off all but the most devout.

In 1989 the Committee for Black Anglican Concerns asked the Synod to ensure that arrangements were made for the election of at least two dozen members belonging to minority ethnic groups. It was instructive to see the way in which most members of the Synod were perfectly happy to accept the notion that forty-three archdeacons could be considered a distinct group whose presence was deemed essential in the Synod while pleading that to make special provision for black people would constitute some sort of inverted racism. As Peter Selby says in his book *BeLonging: Challenge to a Tribal Church*,[2] what makes race such a difficult phenomenon to deal with in the life of the Church is the ease with which it can be denied. There may have been practical arguments against doing what the committee requested, but these would have paled into insignificance in comparison to the overriding reason for voting in favour, the absolute necessity to send from the Synod a clear signal to the parishes and the country that members of minority ethnic communities are welcome, have a contribution to make to Church government and should be positively encouraged to step forward. But the Synod, lacking initiative, insight and imagination, let a golden opportunity slip by. It often seems that what is most important to the Synod is observance of its standing orders and the delivery of effusive speeches of thanks for the gracious manner in which Sister Sophistication of the Convent of the Lost Sheep has chaired the debate.

Because the General Synod constitutes a national forum, with press, radio and television present, it is often tempted to be seen to be concerned with all sorts of issues it knows nothing about. There is a dearth of informed opinion in the Synod on a host of matters that come up for discussion. Perhaps just two members possess expert knowledge of energy conservation, but that will not prevent scores of others rising to their feet to say something that will neither be reported nor make any difference to government policy. They tend to forget they are debating only yards from the House of Commons, where, even if debates are childishly rowdy, a good many people *are* well briefed.

'We spend an awful long time on legislation, chasing hares all over the place,' a member of the House of Clergy told me. 'I think the Synod is far too large. How can you have a good discussion with 550 people? Only twelve or fourteen people will ever get called during a debate. The vast majority of members just have to sit there. I find it all so boring.' 'Synodical government has loomed too large in the Church's life,' one of the deans told me, 'because it has wanted to do too much and it has not been able to attract the best sort of people to do it. It's become a full-time job.' Paul Welsby has put it even more bluntly: 'At its inauguration in 1970, many churchmen hailed synodical government as a panacea for the many ills that beset the Church and, like their predecessors after the establishment of the Church Assembly in 1919, were doomed to disillusionment and frustration.'[3] It was extraordinary, the initial rush of enthusiasm and support; in 1970, 2,500 candidates stood for 500 seats. Why do they want to stand? Surveying those elected five years on, of whom not one was a representative of skilled or unskilled manual workers, Professor Kathleen Jones concluded there were few members who could provide 'more than a personal anecdote' in debates on, say, 'the immigrant population of Britain' or 'the poor and the rootless'.[4]

But nothing very much ever changes, and it seems that each generation of Church Assembly or Synod members has to learn from first-hand experience just what they are letting themselves in for or, in the case of the ex officio bishops, what is entailed by compulsion. When Cosmo Lang retired as archbishop of Canterbury in 1942 he noted in his diary,

> So I bade farewell to Convocation and the Church Assembly. I must frankly confess that this was not to me a very grievous loss. Convocation had always been a trouble and a trial, especially the proceedings of the Lower House. And although in a measure I always enjoyed the duties of Chairman of the Church Assembly, it was often wearisome to be tied to the Chair during long debates in which the most frequent speakers were often the least able or useful; and it was difficult to suffer the inevitable bores gladly.

As central to Church affairs as the General Synod are the Synod's geographical neighbours, the Church Commissioners. They are traditionally credited with being awash with money, and their alleged connections with prostitution in Paddington and gold mines in South Africa have also for a long time been the stuff of popular journalism. Correctly they are called the Church Commissioners for England, and in their composition Church and State go hand in hand. All the diocesan bishops are members. So are the Lord Chancellor, the Lord President of the Council, the Chancellor of the Exchequer, the Home Secretary, the Speaker of the House of Commons, the Lord Chief Justice . . . the entire cast of Gilbert and Sullivan. The four members who matter, however, are the secretary and the Three Church Estates Commissioners; the First Estates Commissioner is appointed by the Crown, the Third by the archbishop of Canterbury, and the Second is always an MP, who answers for the Commissioners in the House of Commons and presents to Parliament measures passed by the General Synod. He is appointed by the Queen on the advice of the prime minister; the current Second Commissioner is the Rt Hon Michael Alison.

In a nutshell, the Church Commissioners manage the assets of the Church, some, like farmland, often historic; others, like commercial property, not so ancient. They also hold a stock exchange portfolio. From their income they pay, among much else, the entire stipend of diocesan, suffragan and full-time assistant bishops, together with their official expenses, which include the upkeep of the bishops' houses and the wages of their staff. Differentials in pay at the bottom of the ecclesiastical ladder are very small; as in so many professions, they widen out considerably nearer the top. Along with deans and provosts, suffragan bishops receive £19,410, and most diocesan bishops £23,160. (All stipends quoted were fixed in 1992.) Bishops also get a car, a chauffeur (diocesans only) and a gardener. Winchester is paid £26,160, Durham £31,380 and London £35,560. With the possible exception of London, who is a metropolitan in all but name, it is hard to see any justification for differentials for other bishops, who are senior only for historic reasons; they carry no extra responsibilities. Indeed, it could be argued there is no case in a Christian organisation, which supplies housing and pensions for all, for a bishop to be paid more than a curate. However, the archbishop of York is in receipt of £38,150 and the archbishop of Canterbury £43,550, about the same as he would earn as dean of a university faculty.

Except for the dioceses of Oxford and Sodor and Man, the Church Commissioners also provide the stipend of every dean and provost and of two residentiary canons at each cathedral, and they make a grant towards the stipends of archdeacons. The cost of all these salaries and expenses comes to about £2.5 million a year. The Commissioners also provide about half the money required for clergy stipends, and almost all the money needed for pensions; in fact, about a quarter of the Commissioners' income now goes to paying pensions, a proportion of income, starting at about £7,000 per annum per clergyman, which will almost certainly continue to rise.

Notwithstanding the fact that at the close of the nineteenth century there were discovered to be 1,500 retired clergy subsisting on less than £67 a year, many of them lodged in workhouses, for centuries the Church of England's parish clergy and congregations have been accustomed to relative wealth. That is to say, in the case of the clergy, only a few struggled on a pittance and many lived a life of luxury, for either they were presented by a kindly patron to a well-endowed benefice or they were younger sons of the aristocracy, with nothing better to do than take holy orders and build an enormous country rectory. As for the bishops, many were comfortably off too, their sees having amassed wealth since the Middle Ages. But the newly created Victorian sees were not well endowed. In 1876 Edward Benson was dubious about exchanging the chancellorship of Lincoln Cathedral for the bishopric of Truro as he doubted whether he could maintain his large family on £3,000 per annum. Congregations reluctantly dipped into their pockets when the collection plate came round, on some vague assumption that they were giving to charity, which sometimes they were, and when the vicar left it was automatically assumed that another would be provided, much as free milk was later to be delivered by the welfare state.

Church revenues have long since been pooled and ironed out, and no one today would be mad enough to get ordained in order to live a carefree and riotous life. The national average stipend for a parish priest in 1992 was about £12,800. Taking into account the value of a noncontributory pension scheme and a free house, in real terms this stipend was reckoned to be worth about £20,000. But the laity still have no clear idea how the Church is financed. They contribute to something called a quota, collected each year by the diocese, but what the money is spent on they have no idea, and it seldom occurs to them to enquire how the clergy are paid. When money impinges on their consciousness it is generally related to a gaping hole in the roof, and maintenance costs can now bear down at local level like the proverbial ton of bricks. An appeal for £80,000 to repair the spire, tower and sanctus bell at All Saints', Malden, may be met, because Essex is a wealthy county and All Saints' is a tenth-century church. With the American Ambassador as patron of a £250,000 appeal for repairs to the London church where T. S. Eliot worshipped – St Stephen's, Gloucester Road, now an American tourist attraction – this parish is in little danger of extinction. But the largest church to go up after the Reformation, an 1853 Gothic revival in Bloomsbury, the

University Church of Christ the King in Gordon Square, was closed down in 1992; it was costing £1,400 a week to run, and the congregation – students and local hotel residents, mainly – was contributing just £75 a week.

Even in a more usual residential area, personal contributions to the Church are pathetic. They can on average be as low as £2.50 a week, and seldom in any diocese rise above £3. This is largely because congregations have never developed a realistic attitude to finance, and this in turn is because they have not had to pay directly out of their own pocket for the services provided by the Church, especially for the presence in their midst of a parish priest. Until now, 45 per cent of the cost of clergy stipends has been given to the dioceses by the Church Commissioners. But the Commissioners need to find an extra £5 million a year just to pay clergy and widows' pensions, and their contribution towards stipends is to be cut by 30 per cent. For not only have the Commissioners' expenses gone up, their income, as a result of the recession and somewhat imprudent investment in the property market, has fallen.[5] Instead of rising to this challenge and telling parishes quite bluntly to cough up more money – lots more of it – the dioceses are busy freezing parochial posts. It cannot be easy for congregations to grasp the seriousness of their situation so long as the First Church Estates Commissioner urges members to give another 30p a week.[6] The Archbishop of Canterbury had the matter in more realistic perspective when he said, 'Ask for a little and you will get a little. Put before people the picture of a Church pleading for small change to enable it to struggle along, and you will get small change.' But Dr Carey himself is struggling against a General Synod whose members are prepared to argue against giving 5 per cent of net pay to the Church.

The archbishop's own diocese is fairly typical. In 1992 it had a budget of £4 million, of which £3.2 million was earmarked for stipends and the maintenance of clergy houses. Some £900,000 was due from the Church Commissioners. But Canterbury diocese has been told that over the next three years this grant from the Commissioners will be cut by £90,000 per annum, so that by 1996 the Church Commissioners will only be contributing £630,000, less than 20 per cent of the total cost of maintaining the clergy, assuming that sum will have risen, with inflation, to £3.6 million. There will only be one place from which the balance can be made up; from the quotas paid to the diocese by the parishes. When preparing their budget for 1992, the Ely Diocesan Board of Finance concluded that with the usual stipend and salary increases, parish quotas would need to rise by 40 per cent, but they kept the rise down to 20 per cent by the simple expedient of cutting stipends and deferring repairs to buildings – a short-sighted policy if ever there was one.

There are two problems about fund-raising from parochial sources. The first is that parishes see all giving as charitable giving, and once it is driven home to them that the running costs of their parish priest amount to about £19,000 a year, and that before long, if they do not make a substantial contribution to those costs, they will have no parish priest, they are liable to withdraw genuine charitable giving upon which others depend. It costs £2,200 a day to run St Luke's Hospital for the Clergy, and at present 500 parishes send £100 a year or more; the United Society for the Propagation of the Gospel and the Church Missionary Society, both heavily reliant on parishes for support, were to reduce their spending in 1993 by £1 million. Many 'worthy causes' will go to the wall unless parishes steel themselves to maintaining clergy stipends as well as supporting charities. The other problem is psychological. There is plenty of money around to be scooped up (Christian Aid increased its 1991–92 income by £9 million to £42.1 million), but Church people see financing the Church on a day-to-day basis as alien to Anglican concepts of genteel behaviour. Getting parishioners to covenant, which provides tax advantages, is a headache in itself; rather than sit down and write out a cheque or a standing order the woman-in-the-pew finds it far more fun to stand for hours over a simmering pot, making marmalade for the jumble sale. This she sees as 'doing something for the Church'. It makes her feel she has taken trouble. Organising a church bazaar does take a lot of time and effort, but it is seldom cost-effective. The problem is compounded when a request for extra funds is seen as an appeal to bail out the Church Commissioners, upon whose expert investment policies the Church has relied so heavily in the past. To most people they are a nebulous institution, part of that mysterious world that for some inexplicable reason is still thought to owe the Church a living.

'More committee'd than committed' is how one wag in the General Synod has described the Church of England. The Church also, unfortunately, gives the impression of having money to burn. In 1991 the Bishop of Oxford went to the High Court to have the Church Commissioners' investment policies scrutinised (he is himself a Church Commissioner); the Commissioners were vindicated, and a bill for £100,000 had to be paid. A year later a parish priest in the diocese of Chichester was accused of adultery, and after two consistory court trials and two appeals he was deprived of his living and the Church picked up bills to the tune of £300,000. Nevertheless bishops hurried home from the July 1992 General Synod to see what enthusiasm they could muster for 'sacrificial giving'. The Bishop of Norwich told his diocese he wanted £7 a week from parishioners, not the £2.70 they were then contributing, and that unless they did give more generously parishes would just have to wait for incumbencies to be filled. Chelmsford and Lincoln were already planning cuts in their stipendiary ministry, and earlier in the year the Durham diocesan synod had decided to suspend all vacant livings and to replace freeholds with five-year contracts – all in the name of financial prudence. As a Durham priest pointed out, 'A failure to make appointments from outside the diocese in the foreseeable future will quickly result in the formation of sterile closed shops. A spiritual and forward lead from bishops and diocesan senior staff is now required. Meanwhile, a steady stream of able young men and women who are ready to give properly is moving out of the established Church into the "community churches" where on the one hand they see freedom from diocesan bureaucracy and on the other, theological liberalism.' At a nondenominational service held at a conference centre in Brighton during the summer of 1992, led by a charismatic American evangelist, £17,000 was collected from the congregation.

Of course the problems many parishes face just to stave off physical disaster are enormous. When a pinnacle from the 300-year-old spire of St Michael and All Angels at Kington St

Michael in Wiltshire came crashing through the roof of the nave during a service in 1990, the parish was faced with a repair bill for £133,000. St George's at Cam in Gloucestershire, built in 1340, needs £150,000 to renew the roof and rehang the bells. It is going to take £92,000 to repair the eighteenth-century organ of St Peter and St Mary Magdalene in Barnstaple, Devon. Norfolk is particularly rich in medieval churches; one of them, St Peter and St Paul at Carbrooke, needs £60,000 to install a heating system and repair the chancel roof. It has cost £280,000 just to clean and restore the west front of Bath Abbey; the Friends of the Abbey need to raise a total of £2.5 million to clean the church throughout. St Lawrence parish at Alton in Hampshire are appealing for £300,000; St Peter and St Paul at Charing in Kent, the only English parish to have had a saint (St Richard) as vicar, need £125,000. An Edwin Lutyens church, St Jude-on-the-Hill in Hampstead Garden Suburb, has a 'Father' Willis organ in need of renovations costing £80,000. The parish of the Victorian Gothic Christ Church and St Paul's, Forest Hill, are praying for a staggering £500,000, while the rector of one of London's largest parish churches, the late eighteenth-century St-John-at-Hackney, hopes for £200,000 – to provide facilities for the homeless and mentally ill. The custodians of a much earlier eighteenth-century church, built by Hawksmoor, St Alphege's in Greenwich, where Thomas Tallis is buried, say that rewiring, relighting, redecorating and repairs to the organ will cost £350,000. And so it goes on. And it is not just ancient buildings that are in trouble; Edward Maufe's St Thomas the Apostle at Hanwell, built in 1933, needs £130,000 'to remove asbestos from the internal walls'. Only half a century older, St Saviour and St James in Pimlico needs £357,000 for repairs to the roof, plasterwork and the flooring.

Quite apart from local bills for maintenance and repair, how has the Church's overall financial crisis come about? One of the Church Commissioners told me, 'The Commissioners have been hit quite severely by the recession because a very large part of their assets have been held in farms, which have not been productive for a long time. And if you are into farms it is very difficult to get out of them. On top of that the Commissioners have gone heavily into property, which served them well in the 1980s, but property has turned very sour on them. They borrowed substantial sums to engage in property development, and rising interest rates have put up the cost of their borrowings. And the collapse of the property market has made it difficult for them to let property.'

It would be fair to say the Church Commissioners have made good judgements as well as bad. They invested in the MetroCentre in Gateshead, Tyneside, which has been a success, and, although strongly pressed to invest in the ill-fated Docklands Scheme in London, fortunately did not do so. But they came unstuck over the poll tax, committing themselves in 1989 to meeting the cost of the clergy's community-charge bills, which ended up as a much larger sum than anyone had expected. 'No one said at the time this was imprudent,' another Commissioner reminded me, 'but in the light of hindsight it was a larger commitment than we should have taken on. Many of us did not have a totally clear picture of what the financial position was.

'Eighteen months ago [i.e. at the start of 1991] it became apparent that not only had a gap opened up between the sustainable income of the Commissioners and their level of expenditure but, projecting forwards for a number of years, that gap was not going to close. You can stand it for two or three years, but with income not catching up with expenditure, something had to be done, or capital would have been eaten into. That was what led to the Church Commissioners deciding they had got to cut back on the support they give to dioceses for stipends, and over the next five years that support will be reduced from about £60 million to about £35 million. This loss of £25 million in grants spread over five years, ending in 1995, is the loss that is hitting the dioceses, and dioceses have been used to increases each year, not cuts. The cuts are not going to be evenly distributed. They are heaviest in dioceses thought best able to afford them. But the sums are quite substantial. Last year Chichester, for example, lost just under £100,000. This year it will be £200,000 and, over the next two years, £250,000 each year. These cuts will have to be made up through the parish quota. There is no other source of income.'

Management of the Church Commissioners' assets is left to

a small and select Assets Committee, with the First Church Estates Commissioner sitting as chairman, the Bishop of Peterborough appointed to keep an eye on the ethical aspects involved and a handful of experts in property and investment, chosen by the archbishop of Canterbury. They are responsible for £2.5 billion of assets, and in their hands they hold not just the stipend of the archbishop of Canterbury and the upkeep of Lambeth Palace but the future pensions of all the clergy. The unaccountability of this committee, the infrequency of its meetings and the lack of expert advice readily available to it causes grave concern in certain quarters. A member of one of the other committees told me, 'I think there are large questions that need to be asked. Management of the assets is very much shut off from the rest of the Commissioners' business. The Assets Committee have complete control. They don't even report to the Board of Governors. The Board is not given an opportunity to discuss how the assets are performing, and all they receive is an annual statement of how much money is available to be allocated.

'What really worries me is that the Assets Committee don't even meet once a month – and as a Church Commissioner myself I only discovered that by digging about. And when they do meet they do so for just two hours. There is, on the Committee, only one expert in each field, and I believe the expert is simply listened to and never tackled. Now, that is a very slender base for the effective supervision of £2.5 billion. When I compare the Church Commissioners with the sort of resources employed by big City investors – well, it makes you think! Twenty-five investment analysts is not out of the way elsewhere. I believe it is high time serious thought was given to handing over a good deal of investment to investment houses in the City. You could keep the Assets Committee, to whom outsiders would report. That would provide a far more professional operation.

'With a huge asset base of this size I find it difficult to persuade myself that the effort put into the management of it is adequate to get the best results. There also needs to be a greater accountability and a greater degree of openness. I strongly believe the Assets Committee should be accountable to the General Synod. There is no objective external measurement of its performance. They have pushed the assets a lot harder than they should have done to extract income from them. The system is half a century old. The staff ought to be spotting things in the first place, but I don't think they're all that well equipped to do it, and the Committee can't spot things fast enough if they only meet once a month.'

Another of my financial informants, by no means wholly critical of the Church Commissioners, said, 'I am amazed at the meekness with which the Church has taken this turn-around in the Commissioners' fortunes. I think the Commissioners have got a reasonably good story to tell about how it happened, but it is causing major difficulties in many of the dioceses. But they seem to think it's like cholera – an act of God. People are reacting without asking whether it need have happened in the first place. Personally, I think there is a danger of the Commissioners losing the confidence of the Church, but I also think that judgement on them should be suspended. If the economy picks up and the Church Commissioners don't manage to recoup their losses, and mistakes are still being made, dangers loom ahead of us. There is, I think, a degree of complaisance in the organisation which has been fostered by the absence of any significant questioning from the Church, and this I find dangerous.

'What I also notice is how little money Church people give in wealthy dioceses and how much more they give in poor areas. In Chichester it is as low as £2.50 a week, in Southwark it is almost £5 a week. If in a diocese with 50,000 members they all gave an extra £1 a week, that would produce £2.5 million a year. That would solve all their problems. It isn't sacrificial giving we're talking about. The Church doesn't know what sacrificial giving is.'

FIVE

Training for the Next Century

'WE are a lively, growing evangelical Church in renewal. I am looking for a colleague ready to take initiatives in ministry and particular responsibility for evangelism and outreach.' So read an advertisement in the *Church Times*, inserted by a team rector in the Oxford diocese. In the same issue there was a job going in the diocese of Truro; the diocesan secretary was looking for an incumbent 'in this rural and seaside parish of under 3,000 (rising considerably in the summer) who will actively and gently lead forward a community which includes people involved in farming, tourist industry, small industry, as well as retired and professional people, and will also further extend the church's ministry to holiday makers. Central Churchmanship. New house.'

There was no mention in either advertisement about an ability to weed churchyards, ring bells, keep accounts as well as one's temper, organise flower rotas and parish fêtes, sweep up confetti, get on well with the young, the middle-aged and the elderly, express, when appropriate, both joy and condolence, preach intelligently, drive a car or ride a bicycle, use a typewriter and edit a magazine. Both advertisements also assumed that applicants would know their way through the Bible backwards, would be competent to celebrate holy communion without spilling the consecrated wine (and would know what to do if they did), could put on vestments the right way round, conduct a funeral, baptise a baby, pray with the dying, would have some theological competence and know how to address a letter to an archdeacon. All this, and a great deal more, was quite simply taken for granted.

It always has been. Until quite recent times there was no formal screening for a clergyman at all, and only a minimum of training; a university degree, perhaps, and some knowledge of the Scriptures was deemed sufficient, and diocesan bishops were free to ordain whom they pleased. In theory they still are, but they almost always ordain now on the advice of heads of theological colleges, the college students, or ordinands as they are generally called, having been recommended by bishops' selection conferences run by the Advisory Board of Ministry, a board with offices in Church House and answerable to the General Synod.[1] The ancestry of the Board goes back to 1912, but its influence is much more recent; in 1928 a future archbishop of Canterbury, Michael Ramsey, was considered fit for ordination at twenty-three without passing through any selection procedure and after spending less than twelve months at a theological college – in his case, Cuddesdon. Today there is, by comparison, a veritable obstacle course to be negotiated by the would-be cleric, who needs, first of all, to believe he has experienced that hardest of all human experiences to define, a vocation.

This is generally deemed to be rather more than the equivalent of a schoolboy desire to drive a train, and is often manifested by a kind of permanent nagging, a feeling that however agreeable it would be to remain a server or indeed to drive a locomotive, what God actually wants is that you should be a priest. But many people are genuinely unable to disentangle a specific vocation to the priesthood from a commitment to Christianity, and one of the purposes of a structured selection procedure is to help men and women sort out whether it is the ordained ministry to which they are being called. A recognition and evaluation of vocation is in fact the hardest part of the obstacle course, both for the potential priest and for those in charge of his selection (for 'his' read also 'her', for, since women were accepted into the diaconate, selection conferences are of course testing the vocations of both men and women).

In 1983 the Advisory Council for the Church's Ministry, predecessor of the Advisory Board of Ministry, said that after wide consultation they had found it extremely difficult to reach a consensus on the subject of vocation, 'either on its definition or on the way to recognise it clearly. All are agreed that there is real meaning in the term vocation but we must conclude that it arises in different ways and takes many forms.'[2]

Legally a man or woman can be ordained deacon at twenty-three and priest at twenty-four, and in the past, the majority of clergy were. But, as Canon Hugh Marshall, chief secretary to the Advisory Board of Ministry, pointed out to me, 'The age profile has changed radically. Many more middle-aged men are being ordained.' A non-stipendiary minister usually has a secular job and, although he or she may serve in a parish or chaplaincy, receives no salary (i.e. stipend) from the Church. Training for the non-stipendiary ministry does not start before the age of thirty.

There are no statistics relating to initial enquiries; obviously there are people who discuss the possibility of ordination with their parish priest in a vague sort of way, and take the matter no further. But a potentially serious candidate, armed with leaflets entitled *Does God Need You?* and *Ministry in the Church: Is It for You?*, will be referred to their diocesan director of ordinands, and, as Canon Marshall explained, 'There is some sorting-out at this initial stage, if that's not too strong a phrase.' The director of ordinands makes a recommendation to the bishop, who may or may not interview the candidate himself before sponsoring him for a bishops' selection conference, of which there are some fifty a year, each one attended by up to sixteen candidates. In 1990, 359 male deacons (77 of them non-stipendiary) were ordained, and 121 women deacons (of whom 42 were non-stipendiary), so that somewhere along the line (generally at the selection conference stage) between a quarter and a fifth of seriously intentioned candidates do not make it to, and through, theological college.

Canon Marshall said that research has not shown why fewer men than in the past are coming forward for ordination under the age of thirty, but there are many people who believe they are being positively discouraged, on the grounds that direct entry to theological college via school and university does not offer ordinands a sufficient taste of secular life, and that they should knock around a bit and gain experience of other occupations; there are even people – like Nicolas Stacey, who many years ago left the parochial ministry to work for a charity and the social services – who are in favour of men and women coming in and out of parochial ministry during the course of their careers, having two strings to their bow, in effect.[3] But if the Church continues ordaining a majority of new clergy in their mid-thirties, it is hard to see from what pool of experienced priests they will in future be able to choose a wide cross-section of bishops.

A bishops' selection conference lasts three days, and five selectors, appointed by the bishops, work with a selection secretary, who also acts as a sixth selector; those selectors chosen by the bishops are a mixture of clergy and laity, men and women, and care is taken to ensure they have no connection with any of the candidates. The conference makes a recommendation on each candidate to the sponsoring bishop, and Canon Marshall said, 'The vast majority of times, the bishop will accept the recommendation. From our point of view, if bishops were frequently rejecting recommendations it would say something about the selection process. Equally, if they were just rubber-stamping it would suggest the bishops were not taking the responsibility for decisions themselves.' The age range of candidates at a conference may be between twenty-three and sixty, and many candidates will be married, but ordination at twenty-three or twenty-four is becoming increasingly rare, with the majority of candidates having had some experience of life other than school and university.

One of the selectors told me, 'The conferences have quite a feel about them of a retreat, because the whole thing is conducted in the context of prayerful worship, of waiting on God – although we don't actually put a stopwatch on how long people are on their knees.' Each candidate has four interviews: with the chairman, the selection secretary and two other selectors. One looks at educational abilities and the quality of their mind – whether the person can benefit from training; others try to assess pastoral ability and spirituality. A selector who wished to remain anonymous told me, 'It's not good enough for a candidate to say, "I feel I've been called by God to be ordained." You want to see in what context they have expressed their faith; through leadership in their local church, for instance. How much can they really show that their faith is part of their life? It's a fair question to ask of anyone – Why are you offering yourself now and not twenty years ago? Equally, you could ask a young man why he wasn't planning to be an architect. Doesn't God need Christian architects? Candidates come with references so we do not meet them cold. In particular we look at the way they relate to each other during the conference. And we need to remember we are only making a recommendation about training. After two or three years they may not be considered suitable for ordination by their college.'

Something that has changed radically is the head-on manner in which a selection board will tackle a candidate's sexuality. A lay selector from Truro said, 'Twenty years ago we didn't talk about it. Now we do. If a person is gay a decision to ordain is the bishop's. Being homosexual is not a canonical bar to ordination, but presumably bishops refuse to ordain if they think a gay man may not be discreet. If the bishop was not already aware that someone was gay and the selectors felt that this was a major issue they would want to draw the attention of the bishop to it. I think one has to say that different bishops will come to different conclusions. I have to be careful about making ex cathedra statements about this because it is an area that is extremely delicate.'

Some intensive work was carried out a decade ago to establish a set of criteria, still used by selectors today, for choosing candidates for training to the ordained ministry. 'The call to Christian commitment as a lay person must not be confused with the call to the professional ministries,' selectors are warned. 'Does the sense of call arise primarily from a neurotic need?' Precisely how the selectors are meant to know this is not made clear, but they are told, 'It is particularly important to judge the ways in which the call has already influenced the life and work of the candidate. Has it strengthened devotional life? Has it already shown itself in pastoral awareness? Has it persisted long enough to ensure that it will last?'

Specifically on the question of faith, we learn, 'It is not enough for candidates simply to reiterate their faith in Jesus

Christ as "Lord" and "Saviour", as many do. They must go on to say what they mean, coherently, in relation to their own experience, using language currently in everyday life.' The candidates' faith, selectors are told, 'needs to be put to the test and substantiated over a period of time, in order to make sure that, as one whom we consulted put it, "the fire in the belly is not a flash in the pan". We therefore felt considerable concern about "new Christians" [presumably they meant "born-again" Christians] coming to a conference.'

It may seem surprising how many conservative evangelicals, whose entire faith sometimes seems to be grounded on a certitude denied to others, are accepted for training when those preparing criteria for selection are sensible enough to write:

> God is greater than our hearts and minds or he would not be God. Certainty is therefore not to be had. A degree of agnosticism is an important positive element in the faith of a Christian. It is a God-given tool, provoking exploration leading to a greater understanding, even if sometimes we have to proceed by a *via negativa* . . . a glib and watertight faith that acknowledges no doubt becomes a tool rather of the devil than of God, for it can do harm both to the gospel we proclaim and to the person proclaiming it.

A fascinating variety of reasons for rejecting candidates emerge from these criteria. For example, 'Too many candidates at selection conferences appear to be waiting for some magic to be performed later at their theological training or by ordination or licensing. Such an attitude should certainly raise doubts about the strength of their vocation, motivation and faith.' An explanation, too, for why some clergy go off the rails transpires. 'Personality and character', the selectors are reminded, 'have always been important; but with the enormous pressures under which those in the various professional ministries of the Church have to live and work now and in the foreseeable future, we cannot stress sufficiently the importance of their maturity and stability of personality and integrity of character. They are, however, notoriously difficult to assess.'

On the subject of what at the time of the Reformation would have been known as wit, the selectors are told:

> It is important to distinguish between those who have little or no intellectual ability and those who have ability but, for lack of opportunity, have neither had their intellectual ability fully tested nor acquired any formal educational qualifications. With all the uncertainties of the future, the Church is going to need for its professional ministry people of an increasingly high calibre. They must be capable of doing theology in the strict sense of thinking about God. For this they will require some capacity for dealing with abstract concepts, clarity of mind and powers of analysis and criticism, and the imagination that gives them the ability to transcend the limitations of their own experience.

Some rather quaint advice is offered on the vexed question of class. The compilers of the criteria confess that

> the selection procedures and criteria have been felt at times to favour those who are middle-class and articulate. We believe that this is not fundamentally true but that sometimes considerable effort is required to ensure that the system does not create its own prejudices and allow them to operate half-hidden. If, as is so often claimed, the Church of England is predominantly middle-class, it is not surprising that a high proportion of candidates for ministry are middle-class.[4]

This is a circular argument, surely; one could make the equally obvious assertion that the Church of England is middle-class because it is largely among public schoolboys and university undergraduates that any attempt to foster vocations is made, and that the resulting middle-class clergy attract middle-class congregations. There are of course large numbers of working-class parishes, but few parish priests in any area make a serious effort to spot potential ordinands among their congregation. Like so much else in the Church of England, vocations to the priesthood are largely left to chance, and inevitably, in a middle-class-oriented society, those from less privileged backgrounds assume they will not be required in positions of leadership, and so do not apply. The lack of working-class clergy, like the lack of black clergy, has as much to do with the state of the nation as with the nature of the Church.

A desire to preach from six feet above contradiction, to wear fancy dress, possess the power to absolve from sin, to live in a male-dominated atmosphere and obtain a freehold for life have all traditionally been motives, if only subconscious ones, that for many clergy have made the idea of ordination an attractive one. Selectors today remain warned to be on their guard 'where the candidate's motivation appears to be neurotic. Any indication that a candidate is running away from something into ministry, or is seeking to find in ministry a way of solving a dependency problem, should alert selectors.'

With such exacting standards aimed at, it seems a miracle that anyone passes muster at all. There must also be a temptation, which to its credit the Church seems to have resisted, to drop educational and personal standards in order to swell its manpower in times of deployment and recruitment difficulties. But, as Canon Marshall explained, 'The Church doesn't say we need to fill *x* number of places. It may or may not matter that we are filling every post. I would want to ask, what is God saying to us in this situation?'

I suggested that he might be saying, 'Close down the Church.'

'Yes, he might. On the other hand, we are committed to offering a ministry to the whole country. What has clearly been said to the Church over the past fifteen years is that the ministry of the Church is not just the full-time ordained. Just as in the last century the clergy tended to be the educated, so the role is changing and the role of the congregation is changing. To someone who uses a fall in ordinands as a criterion of failure I would say that is not the only criterion. If we take an analogy – although I'm not sure if it works – we are reducing our armed forces. Does that mean to say we are less well defended? Or have needs changed? Whereas twenty or thirty years ago there were 15,000 full-time clergy, and now there are 10,000, thirty years ago there were fewer people involved locally in the ministry of the Church. But how you evaluate the lower numbers of clergy with the rise in lay participation I agree isn't easy.'

Discontent about the ordination training they received is often heard from middle-aged clergy, a discontent that has taken some of them outside the structures of the Church altogether. Christopher Brown, who now works as director of the NSPCC, claims to have spent his final year as an ordinand stuck in the country studying meditation and medieval canon law. 'That,' he has said, 'was the preparation the Church gave me for working in south London. Still after thirty years I deeply resent that waste of a year in my life.'[5] The colleges were very slow to take on board twentieth-century insights into sexuality and psychology, and until recently many students left college ill-prepared for pastoral work. (Some would say the pendulum has swung too far and today they are ill-prepared theologically.) In 1968 there were still twenty-five theological colleges, but the drop in the numbers of ordinands during the 1960s meant that by 1968 some 20 per cent of residential accommodation was empty, and closures and amalgamations followed; Ripon Hall merged with Cuddesdon, Salisbury with Wells, and in Cambridge Ridley Hall and Westcott House joined forces with a Methodist foundation.

Today there are fourteen colleges (of which five specifically cater for catholic ordinands and six for evangelicals) and fourteen part-time courses. A candidate is free to choose which college he or she will attend, and churchmanship, the courses on offer and geographical suitability will all come in for consideration. Candidates with a strong catholic disposition will probably aim to go to the College of the Resurrection at Mirfield, Chichester, or St Stephen's House in Oxford. Two other colleges with a slightly broader catholic tradition are Lincoln and Westcott House in Cambridge. Evangelical candidates have never been in any doubt where to head for: Oak Hill in north London, Wycliffe Hall in Oxford, Cranmer Hall in Durham, St John's College in Nottingham, Trinity College in Bristol or Ridley Hall in Cambridge. Ripon College at Cuddesdon and Salisbury and Wells in Salisbury are now more mixed from a churchmanship point of view than the other colleges, and The Queen's College at Birmingham is interdenominational. There are also theological colleges in Edinburgh and at Llandaff where clergy destined for the Church of England sometimes train. The colleges are independent foundations, but the courses they offer are validated by the Advisory Board of Ministry on behalf of the bishops.[6]

Between them the colleges have a surplus of at least 200 ordination training places, and they are said to be losing about £300,000 a year. So once again the axe has been threatened. If recommendations made in a report which was due to be considered in detail by the House of Bishops in July 1993 are accepted, the training of ordinands will cease from July 1994 at Mirfield, Oak Hill and Salisbury, with the numbers of part-time courses being reduced to eight. If the theological college at Mirfield does close, the number of strictly Anglo-Catholic colleges will be reduced to two. The report, *A Way Ahead*,[7] which came in for instant and widespread criticism, is based on the work of two committees, the steering group for theological courses and the advisory group on full-time theological training, both chaired by the Bishop of Lincoln.

What the Bishop of Lincoln's report to the House of Bishops envisaged in the immediate future was 760 students in training in just eleven colleges. If there was an upturn in the numbers of ordinands, they reckon the surviving colleges could accommodate another 100. What effect a further closure of colleges would have on morale remains to be seen. Ceaseless retrenchment is unlikely to encourage additional applicants for selection conferences. What is almost certain is that many admirable clergy ordained in the days when a bishop alone determined the suitability of a candidate for ordination would be rejected by a selection conference today – if they ever got there in the first place; some were both working-class and semi-literate. In his pamphlet *The Anglo-Catholic Social Conscience* Kenneth Leech pays tribute to a remarkable eccentric, Joe Williamson, who conducted a spectacular ministry in Stepney, particularly among prostitutes. Father Leech asks:

> Will priests of the Williamson type ever appear again in the Church of England? Can the contemporary establishment hold people like this? I often wonder if Joe would have got through a present day ACCM [Advisory Council for the Church's Ministry, forerunner of the Advisory Board of Ministry], or would have passed GOE [the General Ordination Examination]. I doubt it. So we need to ask: does our present system encourage a more

> stereotyped, conformist and monochrome type of cleric: liberal in theology and politics, who is often termed the SLD at the Parish Eucharist?[8]

Patrick Morris (not his real name) is thirty-two, married with three children under the age of six. He has his own thriving business – or he had; he has decided to sell his business, and his home, and to go for two years to a theological college to study for the priesthood. His wife and children are going with him. There is no guarantee that after two years at college he will be ordained.

Patrick had a conventional religious background, with no sudden conversion on the road to Damascus. 'I rather wish I had had one,' he says. 'I first began to consider the possibility of ordination five years ago. I think I was seeking for something more than just Sunday services. I couldn't read when I was a child but I was in the choir.' He left his comprehensive school at sixteen, went to work for his father and later opened up in business on his own. His third child was born after he had begun to explore the possibility of ordination.

The first thing he did was consult his parish priest. 'He gave me certain tasks to do, like reading and following a rule of life, a guided prayer life really. I was given a breviary. About a year later I went to see the diocesan director of ordinands, who pointed out that I hadn't got many academic qualifications, so he sent me on an eighteen-month part-time theological course, and suggested I should have a spiritual director. I chose a retired Anglo-Catholic priest in a neighbouring parish. At the end of the course I went back to the director, and I also saw one of the bishop's examining chaplains. That was a two-hour interview, and at the end of it he told me he was going to recommend to the director that he recommend to the bishop that he should sponsor me as an ordination candidate. I never actually saw the bishop.

'I was given a questionnaire to fill in and I had to get medical certificates and provide the names of five referees, including my parish priest, another priest who knew me and someone outside the Church.

'The selection conference was held at a diocesan retreat centre. You hear how terrible it's going to be. When I left the house I was fine but I must admit on the train I thought I was going to be really ill. Knowing my luck, I was the first to arrive. I suppose I was nervous not knowing what I was in for. There were testing moments during those three days, but the selectors, two of whom were women, were very nice. It turned out not to be a grilling session, and they explained we were not competing against one another, which was just as well. There was an undergraduate from Oxford, an airline pilot, a teacher in civil engineering, a university lecturer and me with my GSE Woodwork Grade 1.

'I thought that when I went to a selection conference I would be one of the oldest there. In fact, there were a couple of chaps of about twenty, but I was still one of the youngest. There were sixteen of us, all men as it happened, and we were split into two groups. Two selectors were with us all the time, and they had all our papers and background. The other two had only the briefest information. We had four interviews, and a pastoral situation to deal with, a delicate situation between two families. We also worked as a group, which was intended, I suppose, to test our qualities of leadership.

'I thought it was all absolutely fair, and at the end you were given a chance to say if with hindsight you wanted to alter anything you'd said. It was a relief when the three days were over because it was very tiring and draining. An important part of the conference was the time we spent together in prayer. There was a very strong love of God in everyone there. You would not have been there without that. I think out of sixteen I was the only catholic.'

Patrick only had to wait ten days for a letter from the director of ordinands to say he had been selected for training. He then had something like nine months in which to break the news to his parents (who were nonplussed), to sell up his business, dispose of his house, arrange with the college for accommodation and with the diocese for a grant. If all goes well, and his bishop is recommended by the college to ordain him deacon some time in 1994, he will start life again, aged thirty-four, as an assistant curate with about £10,000 a year on which to feed and clothe a wife and three children.

Wycliffe Hall in Oxford claims to be the most popular

theological college. The staff say it is. The students agree. Wycliffe, after all, is full and has a waiting list. 'We have been full for several years now,' the acting principal, David Wenham, told me. 'Last year we stopped interviewing very early on. We would like to take more students, although providing accommodation for married students – 50 per cent are married – presents a problem.' That may well be a problem peculiar to any theological college situated in a university town, where flats are at a premium. Wycliffe also acknowledges that any theological college immediately adjacent to a university (St Stephen's House and Ripon in Oxford, Ridley Hall and Wescott House in Cambridge) will probably be high on a student's preferential list. But much of Wycliffe's current popularity stems from its traditional evangelical teaching, for, although no statistics exist, it is widely acknowledged that more evangelicals than catholics are offering themselves for ordination.

'At a pinch,' says Dr Wenham, 'we could take ninety students. At present we have eighty, of whom sixty-seven are Anglican ordinands. The remainder are research or exchange students. The average age is about twenty-nine. One man is fifty. Before seeking ordination they have worked as pilots, solicitors, doctors and schoolteachers. Some have been fruitfully involved in lay ministry, as churchwardens and so on, and now feel that the most important thing in life is to bring people into relationship with God.'

'Into relationship with God' is instantly recognisable evangelical language, and Wycliffe, although ironically inhabiting Victorian buildings once part of a Puseyite convent, was founded in 1877 to counteract the catholic influence of the Oxford Movement. A portrait of John Wycliffe, the fourteenth-century 'scholar and heretic', according to *Collier's Encyclopedia,* adorns the chapel's otherwise plain windows; Wycliffe was master of Balliol, and his unorthodox ideas gave rise to the preaching of a sect known as the Lollards. Specifically, the Hall was established to teach a commitment to 'the full gospel of redemption through the atoning and victorious resurrection of Jesus Christ' and 'the need for personal faith in Jesus Christ as Saviour and Lord'. It affirms 'the essentials of evangelical Anglican belief' but denies that it is identified with any particular 'brand' of evangelicalism.

It is true that during training Wycliffe students go on exchange visits to Mirfield, where they experience the smell of incense, but it would be disingenuous to imagine Wycliffe to be in any other business than that of producing mainstream evangelical clergy, men and women whose areas of doubt are easily removed by reference to an appropriate biblical passage, and whose belief in God is rooted not so much in an intellectual acceptance of the probability of divine creation as in an absolute certainty that they are personally in touch with the living Jesus.

And to that end, students would claim that Wycliffe Hall is the most popular college not just because it is full but because they consider they receive at Wycliffe as good a training as they could get anywhere. One has to assume they mean at any other evangelical college. One student told me that he knew of an evangelical college principal elsewhere who had said he would welcome a drop in the number of ordinands, a remark he regarded almost as heresy. One very much gets the impression at Wycliffe that they do not need to be 'identified with any particular brand' of evangelicalism, for brands become somewhat irrelevant when immovable principles guide your curriculum. 'We lay great stress on teaching that Scripture is inspired by God,' a member of the staff told me. 'The Bible, after all, was inspired by God, so as far as both salvation and revelation are concerned, the Bible is uniquely authoritative. We do of course recognise that it is a human book as well as divine, and when we come to interpret the Scriptures we need to draw on resources both of reason and tradition. But,' he added, 'Scripture has an authority and a trustworthiness that sets it above reason and tradition. Ultimately it commands our obedience.'

He conceded that Scripture could be abused, that it could be used merely to confirm a view already held, and that hermeneutics should be taken very seriously. A surreptitious peep at my dictionary later told me that hermeneutics were 'the principles and methodology of biblical interpretation'. Biblical teaching and preaching, he added, were evangelical priorities because they were an expression of obedience to Christ.

So, it might be argued, was the celebration of holy communion and the granting of absolution, not to mention the ordaining of priests, but for evangelicals the Bible seems to take precedence over the sacraments. One student told me there were only two 'pukka sacraments', baptism and holy communion, for these were the only two 'ordained by Christ'. He complained that bishops spent far too much of their time confirming people, a statement which may bring a wry smile to the face of bishops who only wish they had more confirmation candidates on whom to waste their time. He explained that marriage, for example, was not a sacrament, merely a covenant. It is no time at all, when talking to evangelical theological students, before one feels oneself being sucked into semantics. The Bible lies in front of them on a coffee table, waiting to be pounced upon to prove a point. They are extremely friendly but wary, as if they expect you to try to trip them up. But all insecurity vanishes as soon as the Bible is introduced into the conversation along with evangelical-speak; should James, twenty-four and already slightly bald, have to face a family whose teenage son or daughter had committed suicide, he prayed he would be able 'to come alongside and bring Christ into their situation'. I formed a mental image of a barge coming alongside a jetty, and perhaps I was meant to. For Duncan, twenty-nine, the expression 'Glorify God and enjoy him for ever' was clearly part of everyday parlance. His hearty handshake had earlier warned me I was in the company of good old-fashioned muscular Christianity; I half expected to be invited to spend the weekend under canvas.

A catholic student may loll on his bed to talk to you, and his hand will simply hold yours in an affectionate greeting. Evangelical students tend to stay in their chairs, with their legs crossed. You cannot imagine them giving a bereaved parent a hug. This is not from want of opportunity to see how the other half live. Duncan did the rounds of the churches in Cambridge while an undergraduate, but decided the Anglo-Catholics were 'too fussed about who was to be crucifer. At solemn Eucharist they got very excited about the choreography. Dare I say it, they seemed to be dilettante, but the people in the Christian Union struck me as normal.' He served at communion in his college chapel, attended Little St Mary's, Higher than which in Cambridge you cannot get, and ended up at the Round Church, the apotheosis of evangelicalism. Here he found Jesus.

There was no such search for certitude for James. He sang in his parish choir and knew at the age of nine that he was not just a Christian but an evangelical Christian; it was the age at which he started praying to someone he says he could identify as a father, and now he is destined for a surburban team ministry with a population of 30,000, the mother church having become famous in recent years for its 'out-and-out evangelical outreach'. Both James and Duncan looked at various parishes before deciding where to go; Duncan in fact looked at four parishes, turned down two and was turned down by one. It seems the vicar wanted a curate 100 per cent keen on youth work, about which Duncan was only lukewarm. 'I was too honest,' he says. He is amusing and quick-witted, in contrast to James, who seems more nervous about showing his feelings, but both are extremely pleasant. They are also very positive. 'I take the Thirty-Nine Articles very seriously,' says James. 'Very seriously indeed.'

Both young men are delighted with the new Archbishop of Canterbury. James, it seems, experienced Dr Carey's pastoral care of his clergy in Bath and Wells, and was very impressed by 'his enormous commitment to mission'. He also liked the way Dr Carey would telephone clergy wives out of the blue. 'I'm very excited, and feel positive about Dr Carey's appointment,' he says.

Something Duncan feels very positive about is Walsingham, in Norfolk, whose tinselly shrine is a great draw for Anglo-Catholics. He was once 'on a bit of a day out, to be honest. We had a pub lunch, it wasn't really a pilgrimage.' This presumably was at the time he was sampling the Church of England's varied wares, and he decided that 'places like Walsingham give the wrong indication – as if you can locate faith externally'.

It is amusing to catch students imitating modes of speech they have picked up from tutors, or maybe from hearing clergy on television. 'What I think I would want to say' is a favourite episcopal opening gambit these days. 'What I think I would want to say,' Duncan says several times, 'is that I don't claim a monopoly of the truth, but I do claim it for the Bible. I began to get stirrings when I studied the Reformation. Could I really be saved through the grace of God rather than my own efforts?' He admits that catholic liturgy is very beautiful, but he comes down on two fundamental truths. 'Liberal theology I find entirely unconvincing. It has a very damaging effect.' And then he adds, 'Evangelicalism is authentic Christianity.' So that is that.

Although there are students at Wycliffe from Sri Lanka, Kenya, Nepal, Germany and Canada, there seems to be a continuing emphasis upon training a ministry that will still expect to find in this country a ready-made parochialism; the Mothers' Union, jam-making, Boy Scouts, outings, jumble sales. 'Coffee gatherings' as well as Bible studies feature on the programme for the wives of ordinands, as if to get them used to opening endless tins of Nescafé. Meanwhile, their husbands learn how to preach. 'An ordained minister in the Church of England [staff at Wycliffe eschew the word priest whenever possible, and Duncan involved himself in a definition of presbyter vis-à-vis priest] is a representative of the established Church,' I was reminded, 'and as such they have a status in society. They are expected to speak publicly for the Church, so we place great emphasis on the importance of communication. Exegetical skills must be matched by communication skills, whether skills in preaching, apologetics or counselling.' They rightly place great emphasis too on prayer, most of it corporate. Perhaps it is from their corporate prayer that they draw their inner strength, for few of the trappings or props of religious belief are in evidence; there is a spartan self-abasement about the place. It is not that the students' rooms are uncomfortable; far from it. Many are spacious and well furnished. They just seem to be without colour, and a certain earnestness pervades the atmosphere; you would not wish to stray too far from the straight and narrow, or else a students' meeting might be convened to save you. Any mention of sex is focused straight away on marriage, and the defence of same. Much concern is expressed at Wycliffe about the breakdown of clergy marriages, and the staff feel that not enough attention is paid in society at large to the support of marriage as an institution. Here again they are almost certainly right, but one goes away wondering how well equipped an evangelical ordinand will be to counsel anyone with a sexual problem that goes beyond fancying the girl next door. Not everyone depends on the Bible for comfort and support as much as they do.

Wycliffe believes the Church needs a ministry that is 'theocentric, with worship at its heart' and 'theomorphic, with Christ as its model'. I was told, 'The minister must be one who is familiar with the gospel, and capable of proclaiming and explaining that gospel in a society which can no longer be assumed to have prior knowledge of, or familiarity with, the Christian proclamation. Because of the secularisation of national education and the proliferation of "religious studies" courses at universities, it can no longer be assumed that students possess an extensive knowledge of the Bible, of Christian history or the main elements of the Christian tradition.'

For students under thirty, who have not yet had an opportunity to study theology at a tertiary level, Wycliffe offers a three-year certificate in theology, containing a dozen papers that provide 'a rigorous grounding in the basic core elements identified as appropriate to the needs of those preparing for Christian ministry'. A study of the Pentateuch and ecclesiology does not sound like a load of fun, but to the keen young evangelical heading for the stony ground of Islington or Muswell Hill it is, I am led to believe, meat and drink.

Clergy at an evangelical college will probably wear a collar and tie; at a catholic college they may be decked out in a velvet jacket, stock and dog collar. A monk may drift across the lawn. The Sacrament will be reserved in the chapel. The atmosphere seems more relaxed despite their falling-off of ordinands, for somehow they seem to see the possibility of fun in ordination. Candidates have bottles of wine in their rooms.

Since 1839 the Theological College at Chichester has been in the mainstream of catholic training, yet in almost every respect it presents a fresh and lively aspect. In 1987 it moved into new buildings, lacking intimacy compared to the old, in the opinion of some, but on first inspection, once you can locate the front door, seeming to offer a very pleasing modern campus. In 1991 a new principal, Canon Peter Atkinson, was appointed at the age of thirty-nine, and in order to help inaugurate an entirely new curriculum, in 1992, after being a priest only two years and aged only thirty, Dr Christopher Knights was appointed tutor in Old Testament studies. Even more surprising, perhaps, for a catholic college closely identified with a traditionally rather High Church diocese, whose Anglo-Catholic bishop strongly opposes the unilateral ordination of women to the priesthood, in 1992 Chichester appointed a woman deacon as vice-principal; she has special responsibility for teaching doctrine. Previously doctrine tutor to the University of Kent's diploma course in theology and a member of the British Council, Christine Hall's formidable qualifications including fluent Romanian.

Although many theological college principals become bishops, and the Church has not yet got around to advertising vacant sees, the job of principal to a theological college, along with other academic posts, is nowadays advertised. Canon Atkinson is on a ten-year contract, from which he could ask to be released sooner (should he suddenly be offered a bishopric, presumably!). However, he did tell me, 'I miss parish life like mad,' so he may just as easily leave after five or six years to renew his links with the Boy Scouts or the Mothers' Union. Meanwhile he has forty-seven students to think about. 'Not all are ordinands. We have two women in training to be deacons, and four students who are not in residence, so we have forty-three in college. Three of the men are non-ordination candidates, here to read a certificate or degree course on their own initiative, and they are paying their own way. A third of our students are married and they live out, but we give them a study bedroom where they can work in peace.' Fifty-five full fees, he said, would finance the college 'in a very satisfactory way'. To make up the shortfall they depend on letting the college for conferences during vacations.

Canon Atkinson said he had been 'impressed and surprised' by the demand of overseas students to read theology in this country and he was planning to build up a bursary fund to enable the college to offer more places to foreign students who might not have the financial backing to come to Chichester. Already they had two students from the Bahamas, two from Egypt and a priest from Kenya. Having trained in England, these students would return home – 'the only basis on which their bishop would encourage them to come here'. Canon Atkinson feels strongly on the subject of vocations to the traditional priesthood. 'There is,' he said, 'no substitute for a strong stipendiary parochial ministry of priests and deacons. The Church of England is not doing enough to encourage vocations of black people in this country – but then, I don't believe the Church of England is doing enough to encourage vocations among white people. Historically this has not been the responsibility of theological colleges, but my feeling is that colleges could be a bit more active. And parish clergy are rarely the ones who initiate the sense of vocation in members of their congregation. I think they should. Everyone leaves it to someone else.'

The age of students at Chichester in 1992, not one of whom had come from a clerical family, ranged from twenty-five to sixty. The average age was around thirty, and most had therefore had some experience of a secular occupation. Canon Atkinson did not give the impression of being wholeheartedly in favour of this trend. 'There has been a strong policy,' he said, 'of encouraging young candidates to go off for a number of years and "gain experience", but Archbishop Runcie helped to adjust the balance by reminding the Church that it needed young clergy who would have a long haul in the ministry as well as the older man.'

The pastoral care of students at Chichester seems to have a high priority and to have been worked out in an interesting way. The principal provides an annual report on each student, describing his or her progress in their spiritual growth as well as their academic studies, and to compile these reports he relies on information supplied by the tutors. The students know that anything they say to their tutor may be relayed to the principal, and eventually to their bishop, so they are allowed to see the principal's report, sign it to confirm they have read it and can even forward their own version of events if they wish. On the full-time staff is also a chaplain, to whom the students can talk in total confidence, and nothing said to him is passed on to anyone.

With the decline of extreme Anglo-Catholicism the students at Chichester are today more 'catholic' than Anglo-Catholic, but Canon Atkinson maintained the catholic tradition 'is visibly represented in a number of ways. We have a daily Mass, and we take the daily offices very seriously. Students attend morning and evening prayer every day and compline once a week. What we expect of them is that they work out a rule which they stick to. Our rule of worship in fact more or less reflects the canonical obligation on deacons and priests.' In the chapel at Chichester there is no mistaking the college's origins in the Oxford Movement. The Sacrament is reserved in a tabernacle and votive candles are lit before a statue of the Virgin Mary. Canon Atkinson described their mode of worship as 'simple, but recognisably catholic. We have a concelebrated Eucharist. I think our catholic tradition is there in the particular emphasis we give to spiritual direction, to the importance of such things as retreats and the use of silence and so on. These things are not exclusive to the catholic tradition but are characteristic of it. We are not in any sense Anglo-Catholic or doctrinaire. We aim to teach good self-critical theology in such a way that candidates will come to whatever conclusions they do on contentious theological matters with a degree of theology behind their conclusions.'

Was Canon Atkinson concerned about the apparent ascendancy of the evangelical wing of the Church of England? 'I think the advance of evangelicalism matters in the sense that I would be very sorry indeed to see the Church of England swing wholly in an evangelical direction. The catholic wing has some very important things to say. I wouldn't want to see fewer evangelicals coming forward for ordination but I would love to see a revival of confidence and nerve within the more catholic end of the spectrum.'

Did he sense a lack of intellectual credibility among evangelicals? 'I think there is a danger of uncritical and untheological fundamentalism within the evangelical upsurge. I would not categorise the evangelical predominance as purely fundamentalist, that would be a gross distortion, and the evangelical colleges are certainly places where good theology is being done, but I think there is a mood, within the evangelical and charismatic resurgence, of anti-intellectualism. Yes, I do see a growth of fundamentalism within the Church of England, that is, within the evangelical resurgence, and that is disturbing. I'm not worried about charismatic services within catholic worship because I think that where it flourishes within a strongly liturgical and sacramental form of life the balance is ready-made.'

What about the intellectual calibre of ordinands, about which much sniping goes on among older clergy? Canon Atkinson said he did not think the Church needed a clergy entirely composed of doctors of philosophy, but he agreed that with some marked exceptions the intellectual leadership of the Church was not brilliant. He mentioned as an outstanding exception Rowan Williams, who at forty-one had just resigned as Lady Margaret professor of divinity at Oxford to become Bishop of Monmouth. I pointed out that as Monmouth was in Wales, Williams had been lost to the Church of England. Yes, said Atkinson, but he might come back one day. As far as his own students were concerned, he re-emphasised that 'Chichester has always stood for strong commitment to the parochial ministry, and that is my aim and the aim of the college – to produce good deacons and priests. But my ambition for all our students is that when they leave here they don't just switch off their studies. Having said that, it is not necessary that they should all be intellectuals.'

On the vexed issue of a student's sexual orientation, over which a veil of almost complete lack of interest was at one time drawn by college principals, and into which they are now being encouraged by certain evangelical fundamentalists to pry with indecent determination, Canon Atkinson was as frank and interesting as on every other topic. 'I don't interrogate students about their sexual orientation or practice. That is a matter of policy, and I believe that to be the right thing to do. And orientation, of course, is not a matter any bishop would regard as a bar to ordination. I don't single out the difficulties of being a gay deacon or priest particularly, although we do certainly talk about the personal domestic issues of parish life, of being a person who needs their own space and privacy, and who needs their own relationships, family life or household. I think we air most of those sorts of issues in the course on pastoral studies.

'In the present climate, since the bishops have issued their recent statement,[9] if a gay student came to ask my advice I think we would look at the statement together, talk it through, and come to what conclusion we could as to whether there was any reason for him to talk to his bishop in the way he had come to talk to me. I think it would be different in the present situation if he came to tell me that he was living with a partner in an actively homophile relationship.' This is at present specifically proscribed for the clergy but not the laity. 'I think in the light of the bishops' statement any bishop would feel entitled to say that I had failed to inform him of a material situation about one of his candidates.'

'So,' I suggested, 'he might not come to talk to you at all?'

'He might well not.'

Which was not very satisfactory?

'It is unsatisfactory because for ministerial formation to take place, an open and honest relationship between staff and students is necessary. If there are areas of personal life which we are all discouraged from talking about, but which nevertheless may affect the person's suitability for ordination, something of a conspiracy of silence descends over one aspect of a student's preparation for ministry. That is bad for the student concerned, and can only serve to entrench the feeling – already too strong among the Anglican clergy – that bishops are there to be kept at arm's length, outwitted, avoided or generally "managed". That attitude has already done too much damage in the Church. So at present we are all caught – ordinands, college staff and bishops – with an unresolved difficulty about what and how much we should say to each other.'

And what about the possibility that Canon Atkinson and his colleagues are training ordinands for whom no post will be available because of a shortage of money? 'I think the way out of it is straightforward: for the laity and clergy to give money on a generous and sacrificial level. Then the Church would be able to pay for stipendiary clergy. But I think there is a loss of nerve about. How can a diocese that has decided not to ordain any deacons encourage vocations to the ministry with any credibility or conviction? I think it's a recipe for disaster. The Church needs to offer its lay people a vision of a Church worth paying for, and that comes in part through having a strong ministry. Too many parishioners have seen their parishes amalgamated, and there has been a great loss of confidence. It is the recapture of vision and enthusiasm that would make all the difference.'

It seems amazing that on leaving his post as vice-principal of Chichester in 1992, Bill Croft, who joined the staff in 1983, could write, 'When I first arrived at the College there was no such thing as a thought-out rationale for the training programme as a whole.'[10] By the academic year 1990–91 an entirely new curriculum was in place, and one of the mysteries to an outsider is how the students, who have recently included candidates from the Church in Wales, an Indian Orthodox priest, two subdeacons from Turkey, a Roman Catholic seminarian from Bavaria and a Lutheran student from Sweden, cope with college years consisting of only about thirty-two weeks when course units include apologetics, ascetical theology, biblical studies, Church history, doctrine, liturgy and worship, moral theology and study of the Old and New Testaments. Many students complained to me of the long vacations, made more pointless for some by lack of finance.

But cope they do, gaining as they go along, it seems, a quite extraordinary inner calm, although sometimes, not surprisingly and quite rightly, admitting to uncertainty. A rather serious student, due to be ordained deacon in eight weeks' time, told me he was extremely nervous at the prospect. He already had a curacy lined up, and was due to live alone, at the far end of a working-class town parish, in a house that badly needed decorating. 'The parish have been very good to me,' he said. 'I offered to do some painting myself and they sent me a cheque for £200.' This raised gasps of admiration from a circle of his friends, gathered to talk to me in his room. They all agreed that this had been a generous gesture. What, I asked, did they dread most about the range of tasks that lay ahead? 'Church!' one blurted out. Everyone roared with laughter. It was a very ecclesiastical joke – and rather a High Church joke at that; one cannot imagine such mock profanity on the lips of an evangelical. They were all, in fact, in a quiet and unaffected way deeply committed to the Church. Clearly they loved it and each other. There was a joker in the pack, the college lad, who was not only immensely outgoing and friendly but both funny and witty. His attempts at lunch to carve up a cheese-cake, most of which ended upside down on the table, endeared him to us all. 'What I really worry about,' he told me, 'is the way people will look up to me when I'm ordained.'

Had the ordination of women been a burning topic of conversation during their time at college? A former teacher, married with two small children (he had abandoned his family to sit next to me at lunch), said it was such a sensitive issue, over which people's feelings could so easily be hurt, that he believed everyone had done well to keep their thoughts to themselves. He had, too, a horror tale to tell, from personal experience, of a parish that had exploded after ructions between the parish priest and the congregation, some of whom, apparently, had tried to dictate policy over baptism. 'I never want to go through anything like that again in my life,' he said, not with passion but deep feeling.

A young woman training to be a deacon, with no strong desire to be priested, had given up an administrative job in the Church bureaucracy. The young man in whose room we met had been an engineer. They all spoke highly of their bishops. The woman had been impressed by the courtesy with which the former bishop of London, Graham Leonard, a leading opponent of the ordination of women to the priesthood, had received her. The joker was extremely impressed by *his* bishop because he had written to him in his own hand – 'The only diocesan bishop who does write to ordinands in his own hand,' he claimed. Not so, the former teacher corrected him. His bishop did so too, and he told us how he had spent much of his episcopacy taking food to the door of his house to feed the poor. Not one word of backbiting or disgruntlement disfigured their conversation, and I felt that a parish which acquired any of them would be fortunate and privileged. 'The Church is in crisis,' volunteered the joker, who had a slightly more fundamentalist use of language than the others, 'and we are all called to renew it.' This sounded a bit like jargon, and he agreed there was a sense in which the Church had always been in crisis. 'It is being judged by God all the time, I suppose.' He agreed that since the Church had never been perfect, that, too, must always have been the case. Why, I wondered, did these unpretentious, delightful and intelligent young people want so much to live on £10,000 a year and to carry on the battles of generations? And would the Church be worthy of them?

'There is still a feeling that proper training for the ministry is done in colleges, and we have got to live with that. But it might be right for a bank manager to go on supporting his family while in training.' Thus Canon Martin Baddeley, principal of the Southwark Ordination Course, explains the ethos of the part-time course he runs, at present attended by thirty men and twenty women. They come from the dioceses of London, Rochester, Chelmsford and Guildford as well as Southwark. Seven are Methodists and three are members of the United Reformed Church. 'They all train together and we try to talk about the provisional nature of the Church. Hopefully God is drawing us on to something else. Thirty years ago who would have envisaged the possibility of Anglicans and Methodists even training together? It is unlikely that fifteen years ago anyone would have believed that a Roman Catholic would have lectured here on ethics.'

The Southwark Ordination Course, a pioneer in non-residential training for the ministry, is housed in a particularly ugly church near Blackfriars Bridge. Only about a quarter of those attending are destined for a stipendiary ministry, and while they are training they all remain in full-time employment. The rest will go into non-stipendiary ministry – 'a horrid term,' in the opinion of Canon Baddeley, 'because it describes something with a negative. They will be attached to a parish but not paid by the Church. The term "minister in secular employment" is coming to be preferred. It is more positive.'

For many people, course training means less upheaval for their family. Most are professionals, although a few have no qualifications at all. 'Our great hope is that they will do much of their learning from each other. I want to train people who are prepared to think about their faith, so that they can explain it confidently, carefully and thoughtfully to people outside.

'A great deal of ordination training is trying to encourage the right kind of self-confidence. Some people are not used to speaking in public even in small groups. We have had a weekend on storytelling. For that we had a professional storyteller who came, and the woman had an amazing gift for encouraging people who do not normally dare open their mouths. We sat round in a circle and in turn made up a story. It was an exercise in trying to overcome self-consciousness.'

Those who sat around making up stories included a cashier, a marketing consultant, a number of housewives, a computer programmer, a teacher, several social workers, a taxi driver, a nurse, a company secretary, a university lecturer, an engineer, a civil servant, a financial consultant and a solicitor. 'It's very rare,' says Canon Baddeley, 'that we get anyone under thirty because that's currently the age at which the Church of England seems to think that people mature. If they are being trained for non-stipendiary ministry, the Church feels that they should be established in their secular work and that they should have had time to think things out.'

The Southwark course lasts three years and consists of evening classes, residential weekends and summer schools. In their third year the students do what is called a theological audit of their job; they have to describe their secular work, and then, reflecting on the three years of theological study they have done, describe how theology challenges or supports them in their daily job. Out of an intake of twenty, two or three can be expected to drop out, and perhaps the same number will ultimately be failed, so that the overall drop-out rate would appear to be higher than from among theological college students.

Before becoming Bishop of Bradford in 1992, David Smith (previously suffragan bishop of Maidstone) was the archbishop of Canterbury's link with non-stipendiary ministers. He has always had a special interest in the future shape of the parish ministry, and while he is optimistic about the future in general, he has serious reservations about the way that lay ministry has been developing outside the context of any coherent plans for the parish as a whole. He even believes the role of the deacon needs sorting out. As far as non-stipendiaries are concerned, he told me, 'A non-stipendiary minister is trying to work out the Christian gospel in a secular context. I do not see his ministry during the week as pastoral, but as prophetic. What he is actually doing is talking about what it means to handle the materials he uses in his work, how his particular work fits in with the idea of God the Creator.'

If the non-stipendiary minister is on a theological quest, and is not particularly engaged pastorally, why does he need to be a priest at all? 'This is something they have been wrestling with for some time. The fact that they are known at work to be a priest gives them – I hesitate to use the word – credibility. But they are very much, to use the jargon, people who work on the frontier.'

'Appalling' is how the bishop regards the title 'non-stipendiary minister'. He said, 'It introduces money into the formula. I don't see it at all as a way of providing the Church with free clergy on Sunday. I see it as an extension of ordained ministry among people whose time will be largely spent earning their living. If you had a priest who was a teacher in a school, I would look to that person to help the parish to be much more supportive of people in the field of education. Whether a parish feels a closer rapport with a priest who goes out to work depends entirely on the individual minister. They form a link with the outside world in the way that perhaps a stipendiary parish priest cannot. As a crude model, I see an analogy between the evangelical parish which used to send a missionary to Africa: the non-stipendiary minister is today being sent into the world by the parish, only closer to home.'

For the scheme to work it depends on incumbents being prepared to sponsor a member of their congregation who wishes to be trained as a non-stipendiary minister, and the choice to become non-stipendiary has to be made at the start of training. 'If a parish priest says he is not prepared to have a non-stipendiary, then it is extraordinarily difficult for that person to be sponsored and trained. I wouldn't say that resistance was widespread, but I have come across it. There are also difficulties in placing a non-stipendiary minister in a parish if he moves because he changes his job. Then there are some who face redundancy. Once a non-stipendiary minister gets the taste for being a clergyman he may move into the stipendiary ministry. In Canterbury we had a first-class rector who had been a non-stipendiary apple farmer.'

The Bishop of Bradford told me he had a lot of sympathy with the idea of clergy acquiring two skills and moving in and out of parochial ministry, but he thought it was very difficult in practical terms. 'Most clergy could not afford to live in the parish in which they minister if they had to find a house on their stipend. I would prefer to see further development of ministers in secular employment. But I think the role of the stipendiary clergy needs to be clarified a great deal. We have inherited an honourable thing, the Jack-of-all-trades parish priest, but now, with fewer ordinands, this is no longer tenable. When you have six churches in a united benefice, the actual expression of the persona of the parish priest is less satisfactory. He needs to be able to delegate a great deal more to lay people, and to non-stipendiaries. And he must be prepared to let them have power and take some real decisions. I cannot for the life of me see why a parish priest should be involved in producing the parish magazine. We have to look again at what a priest is ordained to do. I do not see that the president of the Eucharist has to be the leader of every act of worship. In some country parishes it is quite impossible for there to be a Eucharist in every church every Sunday except at the expense of multiple heart attacks among the clergy, and various non-Eucharistic acts of worship are being devised and led by lay people with guidance from the parish priest. That, I think, is the vicar's task – to train other people. And he must let them get on with it. His own role must be more and more clearly defined.

'With the advent of local management in the field of education, this has produced an enormous amount of paperwork and bureaucracy for schools. Where they are Church of England schools, or by tradition the vicar is chairman of the school governors, paperwork can take up a huge amount of his time. One parish priest told me there was no one else to do it so he spent three days a week acting as chairman of the governors. I sympathise, but I think it is wholly unacceptable. We only have x number of clergy. We have to look after their wellbeing, physically, spiritually and mentally, and therefore we have to look at their role and what they do.

'Over the next decade I foresee a smaller number of stipendiary clergy, with a clearer role and in good heart. I see an increasing number of non-stipendiaries and lay ministers, and I think we need to get these roles sorted out. I don't want to put the Holy Spirit in a straitjacket but I do think getting a bit of order into the place is not a bad idea. In the parish I see the laity having a much greater role, clearly distinct from that of the parish priest. Generally speaking, I do think that over the next ten or fifteen years the question of role is going to be absolutely crucial, because if everybody is expected to be able to do everything you will have low morale. If you are going to talk in crude terms about professional clergy, I want them to be even more professional than they are at present. I expect the parish still to be a very crucial element in the Church of England, very crucial indeed. But I expect to see the Church relating to the wider community even more fully than it does at the moment.'

The bishop said he could well envisage some deacons remaining in deacon's orders. 'It may be that deacons will all be non-stipendiary. I am clear there is a difference between a priest and a deacon but we have to make up our minds whether the deacon is redundant. My own view is that the case for redundancy is far from proved.'

I told the bishop that many opponents of the ordination of women to the priesthood seemed to fear that it would be a step towards the laity celebrating holy communion. 'I see the possibility of lay celebration as a serious anxiety on their part,' he said. 'Certainly I do. But my own view is that the Church of England is a long way away from lay celebration. I personally would be among those who needed to be convinced. What worries me far more is that when I was ordained, almost all my year were under thirty and single. There are going to be increasingly fewer leaders to choose from with a lifetime's experience of ordination if we go on ordaining older men.'

Having got through theological college or a part-time course and been ordained, students need to find incumbents prepared to take them on as curates. Someone in need of a curate may approach college principals to see who is available. Alan Burton (not his real name) thought he was all set up when, on the eve of his ordination, he found that the vicar whose parish he was about to join was having an affair with someone else's wife, and the bishop quickly pulled him out.

What I particularly wanted to know was how well Alan felt his theological college had prepared him for the real world of a priest.

'I feel a lot of people expect too much of theological colleges. For example, one of our students said we needed to be taught how to cope with crises in the parish, and the principal used to say, "Well, to be quite honest, you'll only learn that when you're in the parish, working closely with your incumbent. What we are here to do is teach you about the Bible, theology and Christian ethics so that you can apply your spiritual formation in practice." '

What about practice as opposed to theory? Had he, for example, been taught how to hear confession?

'No.'

Shouldn't he have been?

'No. Because, for a start, we cannot hear confession as a deacon, and also the bishops' guideline is that we don't hear confessions until our third year of ministry anyway.'

Was he taught at college how to celebrate?

'No. Well, we did have a couple of sessions on what to do at the altar as a deacon. On the practical side it is largely on-the-job training. At college it was largely theoretical. The only exception was with regard to funerals. A funeral would be the first public service you would take, often within the first few days of being a deacon. But usually deacons are not permitted to take marriages, and in some dioceses they do not even baptise.

'My vicar has taught me an awful lot. But the problem is that curates tend to become clones of their first incumbent.

'What I learned at college was the liturgy, ethics, the Old and New Testaments, skills concerned with articulating the faith, preaching – the intellectual side rather than the practical or pastoral. Most of the ethical questions we were concerned with were things like a just war and the rights and wrongs of abortion. You learn to put this to practical use in the parish on your feet. The training was enough for us to be able to make a start.'

I asked how the college he went to prepared him to accept other people's expectations of him as a priest, but somehow the answer rather missed the point of the question.

'The most important part of our life in college – and we were told this from day one – was developing a life of prayer. We were encouraged to live a holy life in preparation for being set apart. There was a great emphasis on spiritual formation. The principal said that at the end of the day it didn't matter how good our grades were, what mattered was whether we were men and women of prayer. Unless he was sure that we were, he would not recommend us for ordination. We were all expected to have a spiritual director. With my spiritual director I would discuss anything and everything. In fact, I still do. It's essential to have a confidant other than your own incumbent. Marvellous though my vicar is, there have been times when I've felt like packing my bags and going. It's because you are working so closely with someone. It's quite similar to a relationship a married couple might have. There are bound to be tensions.

'Many assistant curates these days are middle-aged, and these tensions are often caused by this fad for late ordination. The old relationship used to be a father-and-son relationship in many respects. Now it has got to be seen as a managerial relationship.'

He said he believed in providence and he thought it providential that he had landed up in his present parish. Was he glad he was in it?

'Yes. Despite the ups and downs, which are usually trivial. We don't have clashes of personality, it's more a clash when the administration goes wrong. I can envisage the trivia of administration undermining my calling, to be perfectly honest. There are some days when instead of spreading the Christian faith we spend our time appeasing people, sorting out flower rotas and just keeping the show on the road. I can imagine, when I have my own parish, setting aside two or three hours a day simply for administration, and it's not attractive.

'At college we had a course on pastoral psychology, given by a clinical psychologist who was also a priest. It was very good. It gave me various counselling tools I could use. We had a course on counselling as well.

'Officially we were told that we could be sent down for a variety of misdemeanours, one of which the principal called "gross sexual misconduct", but he didn't actually elaborate! In fact, something as personal as your own sexuality tends to be dealt with by your spiritual director. It simply would not be appropriate for a student to go to the principal and say, "I think I may be gay." As a student one is constantly aware that one's whole life is being monitored. You need a spiritual director who is bold enough to say, "And what about your sexuality?" We were having dinner once. I had seen him for sacramental confession, and he did say, "How do you cope with being a single man, a single man who is, you know, straight, in a virtually all-male environment, in which you know quite a number are gay, knowing that the opportunities of meeting women are pretty slim?" These were questions that cropped up and one would talk through. They are questions which continue to occur to me now. It was well known that a large number of the students at my college were gay, and it was just accepted. There was no real problem about that. As for how they resolved their sexuality, it was exactly the same problem as confronts a single straight man. To be quite honest, I could go to various clubs and pick up loads of women and have a rare old time and completely make a mockery of my priestly orders as a heterosexual, as much as a gay priest could. I accept, however, that if I met a woman I wanted to marry, my marriage would be blessed, and if a gay priest met a man he wanted to live with, his union would be condemned. And I suppose, as a fairly liberal-minded sort of person, I feel that that's not on. We *were* taught situational ethics, after all.

'It is not for me to tell a person what they should do. Counselling comes down to where you stand theologically, and how you understand the Church and the Christian revelation. And if you are going to understand the Church and the Bible and the Christian revelation as being a set of do's and don'ts, then I'm afraid I have to say I don't believe in that. If you see Christian revelation as a way of enabling people to live life to the fullest, and through living life to the fullest attain a relationship with God, and through that life they can actually become adult, that opens up a whole area of creative choices in the ethical problems which confront people.

'It's only because I've been to a theological college that I feel like this. Unless I had been able to pursue largely academic questions I wouldn't have that foundation to build on. College makes one do some very serious thinking.'

I asked the Archbishop of Canterbury, himself a former principal of a theological college, Trinity, Bristol, and a former lecturer at two others, Oak Hill and St John's, Nottingham, if he was satisfied that the colleges were training in the right way for the twenty-first century, producing students able to cope with the basic theological questions ordinary people ask – about the meaning of life, death and suffering?

'Yes, I am,' he replied without hesitation. He then expanded. 'I think our colleges are much better now than they used to be. In the late fifties we were quite amateurish. We are much more professional now, with a much better balance between ministerial and intellectual training. Where I would say we still need to make progress is in pastoral training. It's not adequate. If I had my way, and if we had more money, I'd make a two-year course three years and a three-year course four. We could then construct a very substantial sandwich course. I'd like there to be chunks of time when a person, under an experienced incumbent, is tested in preaching, teaching and communication. I don't actually think the average person wants clergy to come with ready-packed answers to the problems of evil and so on. What they want is clergy who care, who love and who visit. I want to release the clergy from behind their desks and their computers to get out with people, into the pubs and clubs, and to visit more than they're doing now.

'This can only start with encouragement from the bishops. Two years ago I spoke to a young clergyman who said to me he never visited, and I told him he'd lost credibility in preaching. Because if you don't know how people live, then really your teaching will be unrelated to their lives. I hope he took my advice.'

SIX

Head-Hunting for Patrons

THE scene was a small, not overcrowded church hall in the centre of a prosperous residential town, a town with its own theological society. The guest speaker was one of the suffragan bishops from their diocese. About forty people, mainly laity, had assembled on a Tuesday evening to hear him speak on 'The Idea of the Parish' – not, as the bishop was the first to admit, a subject which seemed, on the face of it, to overflow with theological content. He was introduced by the mayor, resplendent in her chain of office, which made the occasion more formal than it need have been. She was, by chance, a member of the diocesan synod, and twice addressed the suffragan as 'My Lord Bishop'.

'My Lord Bishop' was obviously a very modern bishop, clad not in purple but in a black stock, which perfectly matched his black beard and closely cropped black hair. He did not wear a pectoral cross, but he did wear steel-rimmed glasses, and this gave him a slightly sinister look. On the other hand, his mild manners could have been mistaken for those of a popular schoolmaster, which he once had been. Consecrated at the age of forty-five, like so many bishops today he had also been principal of a theological college.

'The structure of the Church *is* a branch of theology;' he told his polite, middle-aged, middle-class audience, adding, 'And the Church *does* need reforming.' It was important, he said, to recognise that our present parochial structure was designed for a basically rural society. People needed saving from the idolatry of the parish. The original parish had not been a fixed geographical area, but a 'camp site' presided over by the local bishop. 'Hang about,' he enjoined his audience at one point, but hang about as they might, they were subjected to a 45-minute talk which amounted to the kind of history lesson – about tithing, the Dark Ages and private patronage – one might have delivered to a class of reasonably intelligent sixteen-year-olds.

And then, 'Where do we go from here?' the bishop suddenly asked. But if he knew he was not saying. Just at the point where I thought he was going to produce a blueprint for the future he suggested that everyone should have coffee, after which he would be happy to take questions; these, he very much hoped, would be in the form of statements, for he was anxious to be told himself how the Church should proceed. Having been consecrated so young, he will, it is almost certain, one day be offered a diocese. He came across as a perfectly amiable noodle.

The word 'parish' derives from the Greek *paroikia*, meaning a sojourn, for those who belonged to a local community of Christians believed they were merely temporary residents on earth, their true home being in heaven. It was not until the fourth century that the parish became a firmly located geographical area as a subdivision of the bishop's diocese. One of the most baffling aspects of the Church of England's parochial system has always been the relationship between the diocesan bishop and the patrons of the livings in his diocese – and how a clergyman is actually appointed to a living. Today about a third of all livings are in the gift of the bishop; the remaining two-thirds have patrons who may be the fellow of an Oxford college, or the next-door vicar, the lord of the manor, some colonel absent in India, a dotty old spinster more interested in cats and begonias than whether the new vicar is married, even an atheist or a Roman Catholic.

These are the descendants or inheritors of those who built parish churches in the Middle Ages at their own expense and decided they would like to retain some say in the appointment of a parson. 'Patronage is entirely illogical,' the clergy appointments adviser, Canon Ian Hardaker, told me. 'Yet we would not find it easy to devise a system of appointments that would serve us better. I think it leads to quite a healthy variety of different people within each diocese.' In 1991 Canon Hardaker interviewed 508 priests or deacons, including 22 from overseas, seeking a parochial position. Anyone who wants his help fills in a questionnaire, and twice a month he publishes a list of current vacancies, those he has been asked by patrons to advertise. Patrons in turn are circulated with information about people seeking a job. Canon Hardaker said, 'I am assisting bishops and patrons in head-hunting.' Not every priest who asks for his details to be circulated can be helped in this way. Canon Hardaker explained, 'I have to ask the question, If the truth is told about this man or woman, is there any reasonable prospect of their obtaining a post – and should they? I don't want to be used by someone who ought not to be in stipendiary ministry.'

Canon Hardaker's head-hunting is organised in an office behind Church House, from which he sallies forth to attend bishops' staff meetings and post-ordination conferences. Until the recent reduction in posts, clergy were crossing diocesan boundaries in increasing numbers, many in order to move nearer to aged parents or to further their wife's career. But it is only since 1977 that they, together with clergy from overseas and many school and service chaplains, have had help through the clergy appointments adviser in getting matched up to an appropriate parish, where the stated preferences of the parochial church council remain tediously stereotyped: 'the youngish clergyman who has cut his teeth on his first incumbency, with an interesting wife and well-behaved, beautiful children'. Sometimes, said Canon Hardaker, the archdeacon plays a crucial role in advising the parish about the sort of person they really need. He finds country parishes more flexible than those in towns, as they may well need to be; the days when a clergyman nearing retirement could take it easy in a cosy hamlet and preside over the harvest festival have gone. 'Those that are most difficult to fill are the really remotely rural, where the workload may be considerable. In the wolds of Lincolnshire a priest may now have a dozen parishes, each with its own churchwardens, buildings in need of repair and a great variety of services. And these are areas where social services, like buses, the post office, shops and schools, are all being withdrawn. He won't be able to afford two cars so his wife may well be stuck at home all day, with no prospect of finding a job anyway. And the nearest fellow clergyman may be 20 miles away.' For a country parson today, services on a Sunday at 9 a.m., 10 a.m. and 11 a.m. in three different churches, and Evensong in a fourth at 6.30 p.m., is commonplace.

It seems hardly surprising, therefore, that as far as the clergy are concerned, their stated preference seems to be for 'a country-town parish, where there is one church, physically in the centre of the town, and a recognisable community. It fits very comfortably with the Anglican ideal. There is a tendency for the clergy to find that kind of ministry particularly attractive.'

Other parishes in which Canon Hardaker finds it difficult to interest his clients are large, often vandalised housing estates. 'It is difficult for people to work where their church and house are constantly under threat from vandals, and it isn't easy in these parishes to develop a lay ministry. On rather desolate housing estates the priest finds himself trying desperately to meet the ordinary human needs of people, and often finds himself quite overwhelmed by the demands.'

In 1942, Noel Bales was inducted as vicar of Marshland St James in Norfolk. And there he remained until his retirement in 1992, at the age of eighty-four. Nowadays, the average length of time a priest remains in one parish is six and a half years. 'Some parishes need a quick short job doing,' Canon Hardaker explained. 'Some people are good at creating new things quickly and then they need to move on. Others work more slowly and need to stay a long time.' When a parish does fall vacant, the parochial church council draws up a statement of need and elects two representatives from the congregation to act on the parish's behalf. There is only 'moral pressure' placed on the patron to advertise the post, and some patrons agree to advertise but tell the parish they will have to pay. Hence by no means every vacancy gets advertised. If the patron is not an Anglican, he has to get someone else to act for him. The patron is responsible for producing a shortlist of applicants, and it is the patron who has the final say. Ultimately, however, it is the bishop who grants a licence to officiate, so if the patron and the bishop end up in deadlock, the process of finding an incumbent starts all over again. The 1986 Patronage (Benefices) Measure was intended to give more involvement to the parishes in the choice of an incumbent, whose stipend, increasingly, they are going to have to finance, but the degree of parochial involvement still remains minimal. Unbelievably, a parish cannot even submit names for consideration.

'Rough and ready but proven over the years' is how the Archbishop of Canterbury described to me the Church's methods of deployment. 'The bishops' problems are not so much concerned with those who want to move as with the clergy we can't move, the ones who don't want to move – like a man in Bath and Wells who has been there since the 1940s. It really is sometimes a difficulty when you see a parish going down the drain and you can't do anything about it. Because lay people are now much more critical, I think actually it's going to be more difficult for some clergy in the days ahead to get a job. There's going to be a small number of priests who are unemployable. That will worry us because of the pastoral implications. But I do hope the Church of England will still find a place for even the most awkward and difficult of customers. Part of the genius of the Church of England is that we've had our fair share of eccentrics.

'Legally and historically the freehold developed to protect clergymen from difficult bishops, and to protect evangelical clergy from the hardness and harshness of the rest of the Church of England. But I hope those days are past. The difficulty with the freehold now is that it makes it very difficult for a bishop to deploy people properly. At an institution the bishop says, 'Receive this cure, which is both yours and mine,' but the reality is that the moment you institute a clergyman it becomes *his* cure, and not yours. So I believe it's terribly important to reform the freehold, and in the next couple of years a measure will go through the General Synod which I hope will lead to greater accountability of the clergy to their bishop, so that the bishop can deploy his clergy in a responsible manner.

'Proper evaluation is essential. In the diocese of Canterbury we have an annual review. We look at the clergy's reading, retreats, sabbaticals, family life, what financial help they might need and so on. Personal and strategic development is for the sake of the Church as well as the individual clergyman, because ministry is not about *my* satisfaction, it's about building up the Kingdom of God.'

'Central in tradition and warm in heart' is how one patron described his parish in the diocese of Lincoln when in July 1992 he asked Canon Hardaker to circulate its details. 'Churchmanship is Evangelical/Charismatic/Renewal,' said another, in Birmingham, whose attendance was said to be ninety in the morning and thirty in the evening. They were seeking a vicar 'who is an evangelical man, born again and renewed in the Holy Spirit and who is able to give sound Bible-based teaching'. Accommodation available for this prospective paragon was a vicarage 'with five bedrooms, two reception, study and spacious and secluded garden.'

The patrons of Chapel Chorlton, Maer and Whitmore were seeking 'an imaginative, intelligent and pastoral priest of a moderate catholic tradition to serve this lively United Benefice'. An 'enterprising congregation' drawn from a population of 2,000 'in 40 square miles of beautiful, surprisingly isolated country' were 'eager to grow as Christians and to make more consistent contact with younger parishioners.' Another parish wished their new team vicar 'to be willing to work ecumenically, particularly in developing relations with the local Methodist church'. The Hatfield team ministry were offering an assistant priest 'a very pleasant Tudor cottage in the churchyard' and 'expenses paid in full'.

Reorganisation of parochial life is nothing new; it underwent an upheaval in the nineteenth century, when the Industrial Revolution rendered medieval structures out of date. But change which people like Canon Hardaker, ordained thirty years ago, have had to absorb are momentous. Group and team ministries came into existence in the 1980s. Churches have been declared redundant and turned into flats, parishes have been amalgamated, team vicars stripped of their freeholds and Anglican churches opened for use by other denominations. Not only have parts of the liturgy been modernised beyond recognition, nomenclature has changed quite dramatically. Clergy in catholic parishes, once known as Father Smith, are now almost universally called Father John, and most bishops too have reverted to an earlier mode of address: Bishop David, Bishop Eric. Like the new custom of standing for the Prayer of Consecration and to receive Communion, it has an air of the Orthodox Church about it.

For the next ten years parishes are expected, whether Orthodox by instinct or not, to grapple with something peculiarly Anglican, that is to say, something ill-defined and ill thought out. Thanks to the evangelising success of the Church Missionary Society in Uganda, Kenya and Nigeria, there are now a great many black African evangelical bishops, who got together at the 1988 Lambeth Conference to call for a Decade of Evangelism. There was not much debate for no details were available, and those who felt uneasy about inaugurating something so vague concurred because not to have done so might have been misconstrued. Officially launched in January 1991, the Decade of Evangelism met in England with a predictably mixed reception, warm in some quarters, distinctly lukewarm in others. I asked Mrs Marion Mort, one of the organisers of the Decade, what its purpose was.

'We are looking at all those opportunities which are offered both to the congregation as a community, and also to individual Christians, to make Christ known. Now I don't mean by that that you rush up to everyone you come across to ask them whether they're saved. I can't think of anything more off-putting. But you know how traditionally reserved we are as English people. Therefore people don't speak easily of what is in their hearts. The fact that you admit to saying your prayers, reading the Bible and going to church gives someone you're talking to permission to ask questions. So they may say, "You don't believe all that crap, do you?" '

'Lest too rosy a picture be given of the first year of the Decade it must be said that many parishes remain virtually unmoved . . . And voices doubtful about and critical of the whole concept are not lacking.' This is official, for it is a comment from the 1992 *Church of England Year Book*. But by the spring of that year it was claimed by the Church of England's Board of Mission that 'thousands of English parishes are rising to the Lambeth challenge "to make Christ known to the people of his world" '. One might have supposed the Church had been doing this for nearly 2,000 years, but there has been a change of tactic. In Walsall 'a Christians in Sport service attracted more than 500 people to hear two well-known Christian footballers'.

In the diocese of St Albans prizes were offered for the parish church putting on the best display of the Christian faith to the casual visitor; 'unchurched children' on a council housing estate in Birmingham were 'being turned into members of Explorers'. 'These encouraging stories,' said the Bishop of Wakefield, 'confound the prophets of doom and show that the Church of England is on the move.'

Despite the fact that the Church of England has a total of 4,903 church schools – mostly primary – comprising about a fifth of schools in England, it is the 'unchurched children' who particularly worry Mrs Mort. 'We have fallen into the trap,' she said, 'of assuming that because we are a country with an Established Church there is, throughout the population, a knowledge of Christianity. This is not true. Young people in their late teens and early twenties do not know about Christianity because they are the children of parents who do not know. It becomes clearer and clearer that the people who have the job of teaching religious education are not themselves knowledgeable about the Christian faith.'

It becomes clearer and clearer too that the Christian faith is simply not being taught. The 1988 Education Reform Act stipulated that religious education should be compulsory but made no provision for it to be included in the national curriculum. David Pascall, chairman of the National Curriculum Council, reckons that half a century after the 1944 Education Act made religious education a statutory requirement, two-thirds of primary school children receive 'little or no observable' teaching in the subject. He has said that even when children are given religious education between the ages of eleven and thirteen, 'it is only too often for a mere half an hour a week. By my calculations, that means that an alarming number of children could be receiving something like fifty hours of religious education in their whole school life.'

Oddly enough, research in the 1980s showed that schools fully run by local authorities often paid more attention to religious education than Church schools.[1] But the day has passed when many Church of England schools are able to retain any credible say in religious education. At Slough and Eton Church of England School, 98 per cent of the children are Asian, and alongside a reluctance to include religious education in the national curriculum goes a demand, in a multi-faith society, for faiths other than Christianity to be taught. Many teachers, the majority of whom have no faith of their own, no doubt regard the teaching of one religion per week enough of a bore. An indication of the drift to secularisation may be gauged by the fact that thirty years ago, no shop other than a bakery would have opened on Good Friday; today every shop opens and no one knows what Good Friday is. Yet Mrs Mort remained optimistic. 'By the year 2001 [the year when the Decade of Evangelism ends] I would hope that stories from the Gospel will once again be common currency in our land. One of the symptoms of decline in Christian belief and knowledge of the Gospel is the fact that people don't know the stories.'

But ten years is surely too long a period over which to try to sustain the momentum for a Church initiative devoid of targets other than those of the most generalised nature. My guess is that, like the simplistic Call to the Nation trumpeted in 1975 by two evangelical archbishops, Donald Coggan and Stuart Blanch, the Decade of Evangelism will simply fizzle out, in England, at any rate. This will be no bad thing if the Church spends more of its time and resources dealing with problems that stare it in the face at parish level, problems it can actually do something about. One of these is the contentious issue of race, contentious to a large extent because it is so easily denied; but it can safely be said to exist in the Church of England, for if it did not the Church of England would uniquely be the only predominantly white, middle-class society in the world from which racism, subconscious though much of it undoubtedly is, had been eradicated. 'Racism is writ deep in the whole understanding of life of people in this country,' in the opinion of the Bishop of Croydon, Wilfred Wood, who was ordained in Barbados in 1959, by chance in the year of the Notting Hill race riots, and is now the Church of England's token black bishop – although, without undue immodesty, he would say that his colour had nothing to do with his invitation to become a suffragan bishop. 'Slavery and colonialisation have distorted proper relationships and have created a sense of the superiority of white people and the inferiority of black people. I don't need to be convinced about this because I was given an entirely English education in the colonies. No one had bothered to write the history of the Caribbean, and so my own attitude to foreigners were England attitudes: the bullnecked German, the lazy Spaniard. As for Africans, I thought they lived in trees. Yet I had met none of these people.'

Before being consecrated in 1985, the Bishop of Croydon had served, for eight years, as the bishop of London's officer in race relations, and part of his task now is to foster vocations among black men and women, bearing in mind that the majority of black clergy at present serving in the Church of England (they number fewer than 100) were not even born in this country. For four years he was chairman of the Committee on Black Anglican Concerns (a subcommittee of the standing committee of the General Synod), and in 1991 the committee produced a report called *Seeds of Hope*. This revealed that in precisely one diocese there was a commission for race relations, with three full-time staff, and that in a quarter of dioceses there was no provision at all for dealing with racial matters. Twenty-three dioceses – virtually 50 per cent of them – employed no one in either a full or part-time capacity to address 'racial justice issues'.

In 1980, when Mervyn Stockwood resigned the see of Southwark, Wilfred Wood served as a member of the Crown Appointments Commission charged with recommending Stockwood's successor, and was very impressed when a lay member of the Commission said he thought they ought to consider bishops from overseas. Wood imagined he meant black bishops, and only realised later that the layman had in mind someone white, British born and bred like the Bishop of Portsmouth, who used to be bishop of Johannesburg. In 1990 the Chelmsford diocese adopted an equal-opportunities policy, but when *Seeds of Hope* was debated in the General Synod in November 1991 it was reported that Sheffield, for example, although it has a small black and Asian community, had no black member on the diocesan synod, no black clergy and just one black churchwarden in the entire diocese. The

Archdeacon of Sheffield suggested that senior diocesan staff should submit themselves to 'racism-awareness training'.

A priest formerly in the Oxford diocese, Martin Flatman,[2] recalled that as a curate in Reading he had asked a West Indian who had attended church regularly in the West Indies why he never went to church in England. 'Well,' he said, 'the first Sunday I was in this country I put on my best clothes as I had always done back home and I went to the local church. Everyone looked at me and shifted in their seats and looked uncomfortable, and when I walked out the vicar took me on one side and said that he would rather I didn't come again as I was upsetting his congregation.'

The Bishop of Liverpool, David Sheppard, told the Synod that very few black people went regularly to any church after the age of ten or eleven, and that youngsters needed to see role models of adults taking leading places in the life of the Church. Ten days before the Synod debate, when the team rector of Hackney Marsh, Stanton Durant, who had been educated in Barbados, was installed in Liverpool Cathedral as Archdeacon of Liverpool, two-thirds of the congregation had been black, supporters of the new archdeacon from east and west London. Their presence, said the bishop, had been 'an eye-opener to Christians in Liverpool'. But while in no way disparaging the loyalty of the archdeacon's friends, it is not difficult to pack a cathedral for a special event, as the crowds who flock to attend some special memorial service attest. In 1992 a service organised in Liverpool Cathedral to celebrate the diamond jubilee of the Women's Day of Prayer in Britain was expected to attract a congregation of 800; 2,000 turned up. To get in to the enthronement of a bishop you need a ticket.

In 1992 a report commissioned by the social responsibility committee in the diocese of Sheffield found that about 200 black people, said to be 1.6 per cent of the total worshipping community, attended an Anglican parish church in Sheffield on an average Sunday morning. 'The Church of England still has a long hill to climb if it is to be taken seriously by black people in our society,' it noted. It found that fifty-four churches in the diocese had black members, and only ten black people served on their parochial church council. What must also be a source of discouragement to Christians from minority ethnic groups is the stark fact that after thirty years of employing black clergy, the Church of England has produced only one black bishop and one black archdeacon. At the same time it has imported into jobs as diocesan bishops a large number from overseas – all white. And of course there is little chance of fostering vocations among black people living here if they have been made to feel unwelcome and have deserted the Established Church for some black independent church, as very many have. In his presidential address to the Southwark diocesan synod in July 1992, the Bishop of Kingston, Peter Selby, asked, 'Can we accept that long after we have ceased even to remember what the debate about the ordination of women was about . . . we shall still be ordaining hardly any of our black members?' He said many black people had long ago decided that the Church of England could never be a real spiritual home for them.[3]

The Bishop of Croydon told me, 'I have always taken the view that if you have a church which remains stubbornly white in an area where large numbers of black people are living, either the clergyman is racist himself or he is weak in dealing with racism. A church can be transformed overnight when a clergyman arrives who is just a good Christian. I remember one clergyman whose congregation complained that he was spending too much time at the door talking to black people instead of the white people who contributed to the organ fund, and he said, "Well, I've got to do it because none of you will." There is racism in the Church of England because the Church of England reflects life in England, and because English Anglicans see Christianity as the religious expression of national life and consciousness. The English think they can claim to be Christian but that they are at liberty to dislike Pakistanis.'

The bishop agreed that racism as practised by Christians is extremely subtle. 'The concept of physical violence and irrational hatred would be a very naive view of racism. Racism is the situation where the dominating and most important thing about a person is his ethnic origin. People say they are against race relations legislation because you can't legislate to make people good, but since I am in favour of strong race relations legislation I have to point out that there is a difference between prejudice and racial discrimination. Legislation is very helpful because it helps to condition people to act correctly.'

The bishop remembered one woman who was so outraged when he was appointed to a living in Catford in 1974 that she tore up her Christian Stewardship donations envelope, saying, 'If you want to give the Church to black people they can have it.' 'I wish,' said the bishop, 'there were more people like her, frankly, because she was outspoken and that was how she felt. What we have to work for is the day when the colour of a priest is irrelevant, where a congregation may be 99 per cent black and the clergyman is white, and vice versa. The mainline churches in Africa and the Caribbean are very conservative, so that Anglican liturgy is no problem to black people. The reason they have gone over to the independent black churches is that they have not been made to feel welcome and comfortable in the mainline churches in this country.'

The Church of England at its best can be experienced by visiting a parish like St Botolph's in the City of London, a few yards from Aldgate Underground station. Here, in a handsome eighteenth-century church that stood, originally, beside the old gate (Ald Gate) of London's city wall, millionaires worship alongside the homeless and the mentally ill, for many of the church's patrons are rich merchant bankers, who contribute some £75,000 a year towards the maintenance of a counselling service and day centre for those who gravitate to the parish in search of food, accommodation and companionship. The government provides another £75,000, leaving the rector, until 1992 Malcolm Johnson, to raise £150,000. Some 200 parishes and about fifty schools chip in with cash, tinned food, voluntary helpers and prayers.

St Botolph's, Aldgate, began its specialised ministry to down-and-outs when George Appleton, later archbishop of Perth and then archbishop in Jerusalem, was rector; he ran a soup kitchen for people who were getting drunk on methylated spirits. Now anything between 200 and 300 single homeless people daily make their way to St Botolph's, from as far afield as Tower Hamlets, Bermondsey and Hackney.

(St Botolph himself was a seventeenth-century Suffolk man who built a Benedictine abbey near Aldeburgh and befriended travellers.) Father Johnson arrived on the scene in 1974, and modestly recalled, 'All I had to do really was build up the staff'. By 1992 staff working as a team in both the church and the crypt numbered nineteen; they included three priests, a woman deacon, a lay Franciscan, social workers and secretaries. The parish runs four hostels. It was once disparagingly described by one of Fr Johnson's clerical colleagues in the General Synod as a sideshow.

Fr Johnson: 'Two workers are on duty all day dealing with casual callers. Three times a week we run a day centre, attended by about thirty people we know very well and can work with. The idea is to get them into discussion groups, get them to understand what their benefits are, get them somewhere to live, get them on their feet again. Three evenings a week there is an all-comers centre, when as many as 300 homeless people may arrive for a meal.

'Our resettlement team beg, borrow and steal flats from local authorities and housing associations. But many homeless just cannot cope. There is a riot in the crypt almost every day, because so many of the homeless are mentally ill.

'I only have to show myself in the crypt and everyone wants to talk about their faith. There's no worry about talking about God. It just sort of happens. Some of the social workers on the team are Christians, some are not. There is no hidden agenda. It's just a friendly place where people can learn about themselves and perhaps a bit about God at the same time.'

In 1991 Fr Johnson was determined to prove that the City fathers were not just supporting those who drifted into the Square Mile from other parts of London, and on census day he conducted his own count of the homeless in the City itself. He found ninety people sleeping rough. He has compelled the Department of Health to provide a surgery, so that people now have a doctor on tap, but he believes that in general 'voluntary organisations are letting statutory authorities off the hook. I spend all my time bullying them.'

Many of those who come to the crypt at St Botolph's, once the home of the dead, now of the homeless, do so for simple friendship and for a free meal. There is controversy among the staff as to whether dinner should be free, for many could pay something out of their unemployment benefits, but Fr Johnson believes it should be free for everyone or that all should pay, and clearly some cannot. 'For every nine of the homeless who have learned to budget, there will be one who is completely dotty, completely mad, who doesn't draw benefits, doesn't know how to cope, who's filthy dirty. Who am I to turn him away?'

One of the clergy divides his time between counselling and explaining to others about homelessness. 'We ought to go on and on about it and about what the Church can do about it. We ought to go on and on about certain things until people think we are boring, pushing various government departments into doing things like providing direct-access hostels. We should go on and on about the need to build more council houses. The trouble is, no one wants to hear, and I think it's very difficult for the Church to say anything because no one actually reports it. A recent debate in the General Synod on housing wasn't reported in the national press. So I get a bit fed up now and again.

'That's why Ken Leech [M. E. Reckit urban fellow] is on the staff. He's a very useful theologian who does his theology at ground level and then publishes something, and people do actually read what he says. Nobody seems to read what I say! Actually, I'm not surprised.' And he roared with laughter.

Fr Johnson saw St Botolph's as being run on an American pattern, as a parish that goes out and raises money in the commercial world in order to do whatever it wants, no matter what the diocese may want it to do. His father was a businessman, which may account for his fund-raising gifts, rare among the clergy. He said, 'There ought to be a little think-tank in every diocese, of people who know how to get money from charitable trusts, people who know about buildings. The diocese of Chelmsford are good at doing this. Far more planning is required to utilise existing buildings for new purposes.'

When in 1992 the BBC *Everyman* television series made a programme about the new Bishop of London, David Hope, they singled out the Bishop's visit to St Botolph's, partly, one suspects, because its woman deacon was prepared to go on television and accuse large chunks of London's male clergy of cottaging instead of campaigning for women priests; partly, one suspects, because it also rejoices in a young bellringer who was anxious to tell the bishop that he was gay and then to go on camera and tell the viewers that the bishop had told him that was no great deal and he was not to be ashamed of the fact. Easy though it was to smile, the fact is that few if any former bishops of London would have elicited such a confidence, nor have appeared so unruffled. In the wake of the bishop's visit, St Botolph's were searching for yet another full-time staff member, specifically to conduct a ministry to people with AIDS.

'This,' Malcolm Johnson explained, 'has come out of our ministry to gay men, and that came about because I'm gay. It's as simple as that.' The story of St Botolph's dual role, its ministry to homosexuals since 1974 run in tandem with its ministry to the homeless, has a rich vein of farce but also reveals the establishment at its most incompetent and insensitive.

It may come as a surprise to those of an older generation who recall the civilised but perhaps rather less than flamboyant Robert Stopford, bishop of London from 1961 to 1973, to learn that it was he who was instrumental in designating a parish for a priest who wished to work with the gay community in London. 'What I told Bishop Stopford I wanted to do was work very quietly to help people put their Christianity and their sexuality together,' said Fr Johnson. 'He was very interested in this. He said, "This seems to be a neglected area, let's see if we can get you a base." He found one place but that fell through, and then he resigned, leaving a note for his successor, Gerald Ellison (bishop of London from 1973 to 1981), saying, "Malcolm wants a City church." He thought a City church would be a nice quiet place from which to do this. So Gerald appointed me here, without knowing why! And *this* is absolutely hysterical. He didn't interview me, and we got to within two weeks of the induction when John Hestor, the rector of Soho [later canon precentor at Chichester Cathedral], who also thought it would be a good thing if someone worked with the gay community, went to see him, and just as John was leaving he said to the bishop, "I'm so glad you've put Malcolm Johnson into St Botolph's because now he can get on with his work." There was a *long* pause, and Gerald said, "*What* work?" John Hestor's reaction was, "Oh, God, I've let the cat out of the bag!"

'Anyway, Gerald didn't say anything. He inducted me, and when he came to lunch two months later he sat me down in my dining room and said, "Now, tell me all about it." ' At this point in his reminiscences Fr Johnson again went off into fits of laughter. 'So I said to him, "I'm gay myself, this is the sort of work I want to do, I think there's a great need. A lot of people who are gay are very religious. Let's see if I can do something." To which Gerald didn't make any comment at all. I don't think he really understood, because when the Lesbian and Gay Christian Movement started here in 1975 he was *not* very pleased.'

However, led by an ordinand of Robert Runcie's – whom Lord Runcie, when bishop of St Albans, declined to ordain priest, and who to this day remains that rare modern anomaly in the Church of England, a perpetual deacon – the movement rented accommodation at St Botolph's. Then came a watershed in the Church's ambivalent attitude towards homosexuals, a disastrous and very unpleasant debate in the General Synod in 1987, discussed in detail in Chapter 11. Fr Johnson recalled, 'I put down an amendment asking the Synod to affirm committed homosexual relationships and got forty-six votes – mainly from married women. Most of the gay men weren't there, of course. They were terrified. Anyway, after that the chancellor of the diocese [the late George Newsom] discovered that the Lesbian and Gay Christian Movement were in the tower, so although they had been there twelve years he decided I ought to apply for a faculty to have them.' (A faculty is a licence or permit granted by a diocesan chancellor or an archdeacon for any alteration to churches or churchyards, most commonly when permission is required to erect or remove something like an altar or a tablet.)

But the Chancellor had no intention of granting a faculty, merely of enabling fellow barristers to make money. Fr Johnson went on, 'I actually didn't want to apply for a faculty. What I said to the new bishop, Graham Leonard [bishop of London from 1981 to 1991], was "Give me a year and I will make sure they move, because the premises are not very beautiful anyway. I will make sure they go to a decent place, without any court case or legal tussle. Just trust me enough and I will make sure they move within a year." But he wouldn't do that. So I was whisked into court. It was absolutely unbearable. The old boy had a field day. I think he was about seventy-five by that time. His best throwaway remark was, "The Rector must throw himself upon the mercy of this court." Can you imagine that? I reminded him it was a Christian consistory court and that got up his nose, of course. In the end I had to withdraw because the costs were already twenty thousand quid. It was absolutely iniquitous.

'Having forced me to apply for a faculty I did not want and they were not going to grant, the diocese then forced me to get an eviction order, and I just had no alternative. A date was set for the eviction, but fortunately the Lesbian and Gay Christian Movement decided to leave the day before it was due to be served. So we had a big service and out they marched. It was very hurtful indeed. I don't think the gay Christian movement has forgiven the Church yet. A lot of damage was done. Enormous damage.'

Reverting to his parish's latest initiative, Malcolm Johnson explained, 'I want someone who will actually visit people with AIDS, in their homes and in hospital, and talk about God. I don't find any difficulty myself whenever I go to see AIDS patients, as I often do. There's no problem at all talking about God, about faith, death and about the way you live. I've never had difficulty discussing these deep issues with people who have maybe only three years to live, but I now want someone to do that work for me.[4] I just haven't got time.

'I have been to several conferences attended by people with AIDS, and I have always come away heartened. It's staggering, really.'

In conclusion, Fr Johnson told me, 'I'm just doing what any parish priest ought to be doing, looking to see what the needs are and trying to meet them. And of course on Sunday, even though we are in the City, I have a congregation. Sixty yesterday. It could be more but they're a very lively bunch. They have no hesitation saying what they think and they enjoy discussion groups. We work entirely as a team and on a consensus basis. The old idea that Father knows best has gone from here.

'The parish is an amazing mixture of people, and they are very loving towards me. Which after eighteen years is rather incredible. And just as well, as I see no prospect of moving. I've been too open about being gay.'[5]

SEVEN

The Lambeth Way

QUEEN Victoria believed that central churchmanship was 'the only true, enlightened, Christian and intellectual view of religion which exists'. She would have a shock today if she went in search of a traditional central church service, for one of the most noticeable changes that have occurred in the last few years has been the blurring of demarcation lines between forms of churchmanship, leaving central church, as a clearly identifiable form of worship, almost entirely a thing of the past. In fairly simplistic terms, what seems to have happened is that evangelicals – those on the Low or Protestant wing of the Church of England, who place great emphasis on the Scriptures – have jettisoned much of their recognisably Anglican liturgy in favour of experimental forms of worship, embracing in some instances charismatic fundamentalism with little intellectual backbone or spiritual content, while old-fashioned Anglo-Catholics – those on the extreme High or catholic wing of the Church of England, who place great emphasis on the sacraments – have toned down their extreme dependence on the outward trappings of catholicism, and have blended in more with the High Church party, those who used to be somewhere between central church and Anglo-Catholic.

Different forms of churchmanship within the Church of England are more easily recognised than described. Obvious pointers are the name given to holy communion, the time of day it is celebrated, the frequency of celebration on a Sunday, the vestments worn and the elaborateness or otherwise of the liturgy. Evangelicals may call Sunday the Lord's Day and holy communion the Lord's Supper; they will probably celebrate only once on Sunday and hardly ever during the week; they only wear a surplice, and nowadays there are evangelical clergy who even celebrate in a suit and tie. The church will be sparsely furnished, with perhaps just a cross on the altar; no candles, no statues, no ritual and not much fun. Because evangelicals believe that each individual has a kind of direct access to God, with no need of a priest to act as intermediary, evangelicals do not hear private confession, reserving the sacrament of absolution for the congregation en masse after they have recited the General Confession. No evangelical would ever make the sign of the cross; catholics frequently do so. Many evangelical clergy do not even regard themselves as priests, preferring the designation 'presbyter', originally a member of the governing body of an early Christian church, and sometimes known as an elder. All evangelicals, unless they have a doctorate or happen to be a canon or a prebendary, are addressed as Mister, Mrs or Miss. They very much reflect the ethos of the Anglican Church in the eighteenth century.

Many parishes easily identified as central church in the past, by their adherence to sung matins as their main midday service on Sunday, were encouraged by the Parish and People Movement,[1] inaugurated in 1949 to reinstate holy communion (which they may then have called the Eucharist) as the focus of worship, a task undertaken on behalf of the High and Anglo-Catholic sections of the Church of England in late Victorian times by the Oxford Movement, which originated under the influence of three Oxford divines, John Keble, Henry Newman and Edward Pusey. But even until only about a decade ago the typical Anglican central parish church remained unmistakable. The notice board would have advertised a 'family communion', probably at 10.30 a.m., a service which would have contained hymns and a sermon. Communion would have been celebrated in vestments but without incense. The Blessed Sacrament (the consecrated host) would have been (and often still is) reserved in a side altar – not on the high altar, as it would be in an Anglo-Catholic church. Confessions would have been heard 'by appointment' and the clergy would often have been called Father, but some parishioners might have addressed them as Mister. It was no nonsense Prayer Book Anglicanism, and even where sung matins as the main service had been replaced by a celebration of the Eucharist, matins would probably have been said in a side chapel before the eight o'clock said communion.

The differences between what was called High Church and the quite obvious Anglo-Catholics were never entirely clear-cut; they were really only differences of refinement. All catholic clergy (and laity, of course) see the role of the priest as that of a mediator between God and His Church; all catholic clergy hear private confession, and rather than try, as evangelicals do, to search out passages of Scripture to prove conclusively some doctrinal point or other, they believe in receiving the grace of God through the sacraments. A catholic church will be readily identifiable from its notice board; sung Eucharist on Sunday morning will indicate High, sung Mass or High Mass will indicate out-and-out Anglo-Catholicism. Marian worship may be evident by the presence of a statue of the Virgin Mary; votive candles may be lit; there will be that evocative smell of last Sunday's incense hanging in the air. There will be at least one celebration of holy communion in the early morning every day of the week, and on major saints' days there will be a High Mass. All the male clergy are called Father; women clergy are beginning to be addressed as Mother. On Sunday the Eucharist will be sung, in exceptional circumstances (at St Bartholomew's in Brighton, for instance) to a setting by Mozart or Haydn. Elaborate and beautiful vestments are worn; on parish business the clergy almost invariably wear a cassock; and a definite sign that the parish is Anglo-Catholic would be an announcement of vespers or benediction on Sunday evening.

However, there are middle-aged clergy trained in the High or catholic tradition of Mirfield or Cuddesdon who lament the death of Anglo-Catholicism almost in its entirety, and Kenneth Leech has described Anglo-Catholicism as continuing to exist 'as a kind of marginal movement which is increasingly cut off from all the creative currents in the Christian world'.[2] But pockets of very potent resistance can still be found, churches so bedecked with candles and statues of the Virgin Mary that a notice in the porch tactfully directs Roman Catholics to their own nearest place of worship. And when Anglo-Catholicism still comes alive it is not merely liturgical but incarnational, as thousands who, in 1992, mourned the death at fifty-six of Canon David Diamond, rector of St Paul's, Deptford, will attest. When he was inducted in 1969 the place was deserted; by the time he died there were seven clergy involved in a parish that had become cemented to the community. On one occasion he sent 12,000 parishioners to Margate in a single outing. Princess Margaret, who veers to the High wing anyway, and even the Queen were swept up in the general enthusiasm. Fireworks and bands became an integral part of the Festival Mass. But the term 'catholic' now seems to be used to embrace all those who would at one time have been labelled central, High Church or Anglo-Catholic, and as far as ecclesiastical politics are concerned, Anglo-Catholics are generally seen as being in retreat.

Unless you live in a large town with a tradition of civic worship, with a parish church which ever since it was built has been too big, and once a year plays host to the mayor and his mace, to find what used to be a central church service can involve a lot of traipsing about. And even in a safe town parish of this sort, one that caters for parishioners who do not want to be troubled by theological conundrums, matins will almost certainly have vanished, and has to be sought out – almost exclusively – in cathedrals, where it can often still be found in conjunction with a sung Eucharist. At Blackburn, for instance, you will find choral matins at 9.15 a.m. and choral Eucharist at 11 a.m.; at Exeter, sung Eucharist at 9.45 a.m. and matins at 11.15 a.m. But Lichfield have dispensed with matins altogether; so have Worcester. Southwell have a parish communion (very 'Parish and People', this) at 9.30 a.m. and matins at 11 a.m.; Christ Church, Oxford, provide matins at 10 a.m. and a sung Eucharist at 11.15 a.m. Only in London does your choice of service in a parish church remain as wide as it ever was. If you want extreme evangelicalism, go to St James's, Muswell Hill, where a 'family service' is on offer at 10.30 a.m. and 'evening praise' at 6.30 p.m. On the other hand, St John the Baptist, Holland Road, will provide you, at 10 a.m., with the Latin Mass, followed at 11 a.m. by a solemn Mass, and in the evening, at six, you can enjoy vespers and then benediction.

Strictly speaking, use at holy communion of the Roman

Catholic rite, as opposed to the Book of Common Prayer or the 1980 Alternative Service Book, is illegal, but in essence the Roman rite differs very little from the Series A communion service (Series B is more traditional), and a blind eye is turned to use of the Roman Catholic Mass. Many Anglican clergy use the Roman Catholic book for their private devotions anyway. Those who use it publicly do so because they think it better written than the Anglican liturgy, and they like to offer prayer in the manner adopted by the vast majority of Christendom.

One reason it is so difficult to find a central church now is that those who have not moved to a pronounced catholic position have become evangelical. 'Praise the Lord with us this Sunday,' a church which offers 'Sunday Morning Worship (and Communion)' at 10.30 enjoins the passerby. This was a church specifically suggested to me as central, which clearly it no longer is. Evensong is no longer Evensong but Evening Prayer, and texts from Isaiah adorn the notice board: 'The Word of our God Stands Forever' and, rather more intimidatingly, 'Seek the Lord While He May be Found'. In the next-door parish, its church only yards away, the nature of the services advertised for 11 a.m. and 6.30 p.m. is left entirely blank. 'Why don't you come to one and discover what goes on for yourself?' the vicar, a dapper little man with a pale-blue stock, suggested. Asked how he would describe the churchmanship within, he hesitated, and again suggested the best way to find out was to come to a service. 'Sometimes I don't wear any robes at all,' he said, and eventually agreed his parish was of an evangelical persuasion.

On the porch was a typed notice headed 'The Wages of Sin is Death'. It went on to ask, 'Do you know what this means? It means because you go your own way, do your own thing and to hell with everyone else . . . it means that *you* will go to hell.'

'By evangelical I mean we are Christ-centred and spirit-filled and we do what the Lord tells us,' the vicar explained. 'For the past five weeks we've had an evangelical outreach.' That apparently involved a massive distribution of literature to shops and houses. 'We are a praying community, that's why people are attracted to us. On Sunday we are studying the

Book of Revelation so there's some homework for you.' He looked at his watch. 'I've just come from one meeting,' he said, 'and I have another in half an hour so I really must go now.' So saying, he shook hands and departed.

The most important shift in the kaleidoscopic make-up of the Church of England has been the astonishing rise in the numbers and influence of evangelicals. Because of the lack of evangelical parishes into which to absorb the rising tide of evangelical ordinands, some have infiltrated what used to be central church parishes, where catholic clergy maintain they are preaching and practising evangelical churchmanship, the evangelicals saying, on the contrary, they are broadening their own horizons. The most influential evangelical layman has probably been the academic lawyer Sir Norman Anderson, who in 1970 came to prominence as chairman of the House of Laity of the General Synod, an achievement which reflected not only his own distinguished contribution to the widening of evangelical perceptions but the position of pre-eminence by then achieved by a once very demoralised wing of the Church of England. The most influential clergyman is by general consent John Stott, from 1950 to 1977 rector of All Souls, Langham Place, London, and now rector emeritus. His church, next door to the BBC, became a sort of mecca for evangelicals, largely because Dr Stott is not only sympathetic and profoundly knowledgeable but also (and this has in the past been regrettably rare for an evangelical) an intellectual.

'When I was ordained in 1945' Dr Stott recalled, 'evangelical Anglicans were a despised and rejected minority – tolerated but despised, mainly, I think, because we had very little scholarship. The leaders of the evangelical movement were good pastors, they cared for their people and were very faithful in the local church but they took little or no part in the wider life of the Church. Because they had a siege mentality they seldom even stood for election to the convocations.'

With hindsight, one can see that the American preacher Billy Graham's postwar 'Crusades' in London – the first, and probably the most influential, was held in Harringay in 1954 – produced a degree of lasting commitment among those of an evangelical persuasion to whom his message of personal salvation appealed, and quite a large number of those converts will have been potential ordinands.[3] But a specific change in the fortunes of the evangelicals can pretty accurately be dated from 1967, when the first National Evangelical Anglican Congress was held at Keele University. Dr Stott said, 'The evangelical party had been guilty of a double withdrawal, withdrawal from the visible Church into the parish, and from the secular world into our own pietistic circles. I think we repented at Keele of both these withdrawals, and the decision to take our place both in the Church and in the world was a very significant decision. It has led more than anything else to what has happened since, especially to our most gifted evangelicals getting into synodical government and so on.'

Although the present archbishop of Canterbury is an evangelical, and every evangelical theological college is full, the evangelical party remains under-represented on the bench of bishops in relation to the party's numerical strength in the country. The Church historian Paul Welsby regards the evangelicals as 'more powerful, articulate and intelligent' than they have been for many years. After Keele, he writes, evangelicals 'began to see the Holy Communion as "the main service of the People of God" and determined to work towards "the practice of a weekly celebration . . . as the central corporate service of the Church" '.[4] No words could demonstrate more clearly the gulf which then lay between evangelicals and catholics. For 130 years or more, many catholics have been in the habit of celebrating, or at least attending, holy communion on a daily basis, never mind weekly. But it was this move towards accepting the centrality of communion, and a decision, in common with other Anglicans, to use the new Series A and B services, that helped as much as anything to break down old misunderstandings, even old hostilities, between High and Low, and to help, in conjunction with the gradual loss of heart among Anglo-Catholics, in the construction of a more uniformly central-catholic brand of parish worship. Even bishops like Robert Runcie (archbishop of Canterbury 1980–91), who a generation earlier might have been happy to be regarded as Anglo-Catholics, as Michael Ramsey was, now preferred to be known as liberal catholics, thus helping to stress the collegiality of the bench. Because of the catholic breadth of worship throughout each diocese, it is virtually impossible for an evangelical, if he becomes a bishop, to remain closely identified with evangelicalism. Most adopt at least a central stance.

In addition to repentance for past mistakes on their own part, Dr Stott sees 'Anglo-Catholic retreat' as one of the reasons for evangelical advance. 'It is obvious that the Tractarian Movement was dominant in the Church of England for just over a century, and was dominant in a very rigid form, which has usually been put in terms of no salvation without sacraments, no sacraments without priests, and no priests without bishops in the apostolic succession. I would have said that that catholic rigidity is almost nonexistent today, and that the catholic Anglican leaders that I know are really searching for a new self-identity and definition which is much broader. So I think their retreat did create a vacuum into which to some degree evangelicals then stepped.'

The reason behind Anglo-Catholic 'retreat' was to a large extent that, as one Anglo-Catholic put it to me, 'we had been too successful'. They had fought for a century for the centrality of the Eucharist and for liturgical revision, both of which had been achieved, and at the same time they had looked to Rome as the unchanging rock upon which Peter had been commissioned to build the one Church. But when the Second Vatican Council, meeting from 1962 to 1965, chiselled away at that rock, encouraging the saying of Mass in the vernacular, dropping rules about fasting, permitting Mass to be celebrated in the evening (previously unheard of, now commonplace), Anglo-Catholics found the grass cut from under their feet; it seemed that they had become old-fashioned, with no longer any distinctive programme of their own. This was the vacuum the evangelicals moved to fill. It has to be said, too, that the Anglo-Catholics were sadly deficient in leadership at episcopal level. Although Eric Kemp of Chichester and John Moorman of Ripon were intellectually outstanding, neither ever made an impact on the country. Cyril Easthaugh of Peterborough, a morally courageous and exceptionally kind man, lost all intellectual credibility by the ineptitude of his speeches against Anglican-Methodist reunion. And Graham Leonard of Truro, later of London, managed to antagonise many of his fellow Anglo-Catholic clergy by the treatment he permitted to be meted out to women deacons in his diocese.

What distinctively remains of the Anglo-Catholic movement can easily be traced from the notice board in the churchyard of an inner-city late-Victorian building, with houses all around falling to the demolition hammers in order that a new roundabout may be built: 'Parish Mass 10 a.m.' 'On a holy day of obligation, something like Corpus Christi, we'll get through five Masses between us,' explains the vicar, who has been ordained twenty years. It is his day off but the telephone rings constantly, and in the middle of lunch someone arrives an hour early to take him to scatter some ashes, so he hastily dons a cassock. The vicarage is large and lofty, has seven bedrooms, and seems an embarrassing contrast to the squalor outside.

'A suburban parish might have a High Mass in the evening on a saint's day and they can be pretty well certain that everyone who wanted to get to Mass that day could do so. Here, that would just be ridiculous, because many people don't get back from work until eight o'clock at night. So the usual pattern is 7 a.m., 8 a.m., 12.15 midday, 6.30 p.m. and 8 p.m. That roughly caters for everybody. The parish is working-class and lower-middle, largely black, with large numbers of shift workers employed by the local health authority and British Rail. And there are vast numbers of nurses. On Sunday we have just over 100 adults at the ten o'clock Mass.

'What can you say about a parish like this? It's certainly not dead in the sense that people come to church. You don't get nominal churchgoers at Easter and Christmas in the way that you do further out in the suburbs, you only get your regulars, including about thirty children. There were twenty-eight in Sunday school last week. There are usually a few babies as well. The only people we're short of are teenagers, between twelve and eighteen, and I would have thought that was fairly common. It is the opt-out period. But we find that they come back. It doesn't worry me at all. You get foolish bishops who come along and say, "Oh dear, you don't seem to have any teenagers, it's a big problem for the Church," but I didn't go to church when I was that age and now I'm a priest.

'We use the Roman rite for all our services. We are, I

suppose, what you'd call Anglo-Catholic. No, I don't think we are at all eccentric as a parish. Our Sunday congregation live in the parish and they come because it's their parish church.'

Not only does the Church of England glory in a diversity of liturgical practice, but ambiguity about belief is one of its hallmarks, some would say *the* hallmark, belief in the literal truths of the virgin birth and the Resurrection proving no problem to some, incomprehensible to others. When two of his clergy went on television at Easter 1992 to discount the physical resurrection of Christ, their bishop was doing his best to pour oil on troubled waters when he summed up to perfection the sort of Anglican liberalism that so infuriates conservatives. 'The Church of England,' he said, 'allows very wide scope for its clergy both to teach the faith of the Church in traditional ways and to engage in the exploration of new ways of proclamation.'[5] This was too much for John Gummer, who, until he resigned his seat on 1 December 1992 in protest at the ordination of women to the priesthood, represented the diocese of St Edmundsbury and Ipswich in the General Synod. He mounted a Suffolk pulpit to denounce the BBC for 'promoting half-baked heresies'. He called the clerics 'misfits' and demanded to know how the Church of England could 'feed God's sheep if it allows these hireling shepherds to poison their food', a nice rustic turn of phrase coming from a minister of agriculture. The patronising analogy between parishioners and livestock is one that people of all persuasions resolutely decline to abandon.

It is no longer possible to sample some of the Church of England's Sunday wares without being reminded of 'The Lambeth Walk':

> Ev'ything free and easy,
> Do as you darn well pleasey . . .[6]

Built in 1938, surrounded by suburban housing of the same period and equipped with lavatories, a crèche, an office, a kitchen and a large, rather utilitarian, lounge, Holy Trinity seemed more like a conference hall than a place of worship. In the lounge, the ladies of the Women's Royal Voluntary

Services were preparing for a get-together, 'to thank those who took meals-on-wheels round last year'. The cold flan and sausages on sticks looked unappetising. The church itself was plain and whitewashed, with a salmon-pink curtain draped behind an altar adorned with a single cross. Over the gallery was pinned up, in red cut-out lettering, 'He Who Believes Has Everlasting Life'. There were twin pulpits, rows of chairs instead of pews, and large quantities of books for sale.

The spring 1992 programme of events can have meant little to the uninitiated: 'Barnabas – Mr Encouragement', 'James – Mr Camel Knees,' 'Apollos – Mr Speaker' and 'Andrew – Mr Livelink'. Other events included a Week of Prayer, a Gift Day for the Church, an Evangelical Alliance Weekend, a Men's Breakfast, a Women's Breakfast and a Lent Bible School.

For Sunday Morning Worship at eleven you do not want to be late or you may end up in the gallery. There will already have been an identical service at 9.30 a.m., attracting perhaps 150 people. But at eleven, it's a full house. From the ceiling is suspended a screen, like the kind they have at the pantomime, on which the words of the hymns are flashed up. This has the effect of making the congregation sing looking upwards. When they first arrive there is a message on the screen which reads:

> Holy is the Lord God Almighty
> Holy, holy, is the Lord;
> Holy is the Lord God Almighty!
> Who was, and is, and is to come!
> Holy, holy is the Lord!
>
> Jesus, Jesus, Jesus is the Lord;
> Jesus is the Lord God Almighty!
> Jesus, Jesus, Jesus is the Lord;
> Jesus is the Lord God Almighty!
> Who was, and is, and is to come!
> Jesus, Jesus, Jesus is the Lord.

An elderly choir, male and female, assemble in the sanctuary, the men in cassocks and surplices, the women in blue gowns. There is a pianist and a small string band, amplified. 'Let's be quiet before the Lord,' the 'associate minister', not even listed in *Crockford's*, tells the congregation, but instead of keeping quiet he immediately launches into a prayer. He is wearing a smart suit, shirt and tie. Then there is the first of seven hymns, 'Soon and very soon we are going to see the King', sung to a swinging, catchy rhythm. One lady holds up her right hand; a few half-hearted claps soon peter out. The singing isn't fervent, exactly, but more lusty than in many churches.

There is the first of two readings from Zachariah, an Old Testament prophet whose prophecies the parish has been studying in some detail over the past few weeks. It is read from the pulpit by a lay woman, and most of the congregation follow the passage in their own Bibles. A layman welcomes the young members of the congregation by way of a conjuring trick of sorts, having first of all said, 'Nice to see you, boys and girls – to see you, nice.' His white handkerchief represents a cloud, up into which God went, and down from which he has promised to come again. It is all faintly ridiculous. 'Lots of people don't believe Jesus is going to come again in a cloud,' the layman tells the children. 'Are you ready for when he comes?' The emphasis of the whole service, in the hymns and the sermon, is upon the Second Coming.

The second hymn, 'This earth belongs to God, the World, its wealth, and all its people', is sung to the tune of 'See, the conqu'ring hero comes!' but not in an arrangement that Handel would have recognised. There is a second reading from Zachariah, and then a 25-minute sermon, an exposition, in fact, on the readings for the day, preached by the vicar, a pleasant-looking man in his early forties who trained at Oak Hill Theological College and is therefore the real McCoy, a genuine modern Low Church Anglican. He too is in a smart suit, collar and tie. He could be mistaken for a friendly solicitor.

'We've been working our way through this man Zachariah,' he reminds the congregation, who again have their Bibles open on their knees. He talks quickly but adroitly, and despite slipping into atrocious clichés he treats the congregation like intelligent people. 'Fasten your safety belts, we are going to move on at a fair old speed', 'Isn't it true, when the chips are down, we turn to God?' and 'The whole show is going to be altered' are expressions that come as naturally to him as his need to present a literal interpretation of the Bible. 'The geography of the world will be rearranged at the Second Coming,' he assures us. It all sounds rather frightening. But a promise is a promise, and this parish believes that every promise ever made, whether nice or nasty, will be kept. 'When you kick the bucket you say goodbye to everything in life.' Well, no one would argue about that. He tells the joke about the admiral signalling to a lighthouse to shift over, and concludes, 'This immovable day [the Day of Judgement] will be the climax to history.'

The congregation take all this quite calmly, but they may have heard it before. There are many old and seemingly single men and women, quite a lot of teenagers, some of the boys with an arm round their girlfriend. There are also a good many young children, and the crèche is crowded. One hundred and twenty children attend Sunday school every week. There is a general confession but no absolution, and a spoken Te Deum and lots more hymns, all about the Lord who is risen from the dead. One goes:

> Make way, make way, make way, make way,
> For the King of kings, for the King of kings,
> Make way, make way, make way, make way,
> And let his kingdom in.

It is as though there is a need for repeated reassurance. The atmosphere, like the surrounding houses, is suburban and lower-middle-class; one could be at Butlin's. No one seems uplifted, and my overriding impression of the service is of its dullness and utter respectability.

A young 'warden' earlier brushed past me in the nave with a mug of coffee in his hand, and when I tell him I am writing a book about the Church of England he laughs, as though I have strayed into an alien building. Then he corrects himself. 'We *are* very Anglican,' he assures me. 'We celebrate the Eucharist at 9.30 a.m. and 11 a.m. on the fourth Sunday of the month and every Sunday at 8.30 a.m., using a modern version of 1662.' They also have something called a 'church plant' in a local school, they baptise children out of doors, they run a 'marriage-matters seminar', their news sheet carries advertisements for the Salvation Army, and notices of births which conclude, 'Praise the Lord!!!'

The warden is modest about any suggestion that his church is successful. 'One is always struggling.' But he agrees there are many other parishes who would be envious of their numbers. 'I would put it down to the preaching of the word.' A cynic might also put it down to the fact that this part of the world is liberally strewn with catholic churches, who share out among them the local catholic community, whereas his set-up is the only one of its kind for miles around, a magnet for fundamentalist evangelicals from many parishes other than his own.

At St Stephen's, the civic and parish church of a large, once fashionable, town, the bells peal out from a tower that has featured in many eighteenth-century prints. In the days of strict central churchmanship there would probably have been a sung matins at 11 a.m.; now the main service is a sung Eucharist at 10 a.m. The church is run in tandem with the even older and original parish church, and the vicar and his assistant curate dash between the two. According to the notice board at St Stephen's, you can be given a 'clergy interview' between 9 a.m. and 10 a.m. on Saturdays.

At the entrance, a churchwarden counts in the congregation. They number about eighty-five, strung out among the pews of a high, wide nave, so that the church looks emptier than it is. There is one small boy and his teenage brother but a dearth of young families. In the front sit two elderly ladies, both with a blue rinse. Guides have been optimistically printed in French and German, and the celebrant mimes part of the Eucharist in deaf-and-dumb sign language.

There is a processional hymn, and the celebrant, who is alone and preaches too, is preceded by a cross, two women carrying candles, a choir of eleven small boys and six old men and a young verger wearing a gown and carrying a wand. Wands and maces play a prominent part; for some reason, two great brass maces are later unhooked from the pews and carried to the altar together with the offertory and bread and wine.

The celebrant wears a chasuble but there is no incense. The Sacrament is reserved in a side altar, and confessions are heard. The clergy are called Father, and among the intercessions, led by an elderly doctor, are prayers for Father Richard, who has fractured his leg in five places while skiing.

An old man in a raincoat reads the lesson, and the Gospel is read from the centre of the nave. For thirteen minutes the curate preaches on 'Christ the Friend of Sinners', stumbling slightly over his well-prepared notes whenever he raises his eyes.

The pillars are draped with plain green banners but the most diverting ornamentation is the organist's beard, as bushy as Edward Lear's. There is a makeshift military chapel with some tattered regimental banners laid up, and three votive candles, 10p each, burning before a small statue in a niche. During the sermon the verger, having taken off his gown, sits at the west door writing up a ledger.

There was an atmosphere of acute embarrassment at the Peace, which consisted of a minimum of stiff British handshakes.[7] Indeed, the whole service was very polite, correct and English. 'Thank you very much,' said the sidesman as I placed a pound on the open salver. But exuberance there was none, and no town councillor, paying an official visit, would have felt out of place. Unlike many of their Higher counterparts these days, the congregation knelt for the consecration and to receive communion. Many genuflected as they left their pews. It was a form of catholic worship with 'safety first' writ large upon it.

After the ablutions a group from the congregation sang a Taizé chant,[8] but the whole service then ground to an anticlimax when the curate read out banns of marriage and other mundane notices; there were two seats available at £2.50 for the 35-Plus Group's outing to see *The Boy Friend*. And that was that. It was all over in one hour four minutes, and one could not help feeling that there had been a slight slip-up and this particular show had overrun by four minutes. An invitation to take part in the ubiquitous coffee session afterwards was easy to resist. The congregation were not unfriendly, just remote, undemanding and self-contained. Their service had been essentially 'C of E', a cosy get-together for people who do not want to get too close together. 'Dear Lord, make my family whole' one of the intercessions on the notice board read. Perhaps if they threw themselves into their worship a bit more it might do the trick.

On the back of the order of service was printed the following legalistic jargon:

> The material in this service, which falls within the alternatives permitted in The Order for Holy Communion Rite A of the Alternative Service Book 1980, is reproduced by permission of the Central Board of Finance of the Church of England. The incumbent and the parochial church council have agreed to use this service, in accordance with Canon B3 of the Canons of the Church of England. Copies of the full text are available for the inspection of the congregation.

So, the Board of Finance owns the copyright in the liturgy of the Church of England. No wonder it doesn't always take off.

St Ignatius is a sky-high church, overlooking smart Regency housing and in need of £400,000 to keep the rain from coming through the roof. The interior is an impressive setting for a sung Mass, and on a Sunday at least 100 gather close together in the centre of the nave; I am told that five years ago, before the present incumbent came, there might have been fifteen. Numerous people say good morning as I arrive, and two nuns settle down beside me, only to have to get up again to have a chat with someone. It often seems to be part of the Anglican ritual to grab the chance of doing a spot of business before a service begins.

There are many old ladies, some extremely infirm; there are also a lot of small children, who scamper around unchecked, but apart from a boy of sixteen who leads the procession, swinging the incense, there seem to be no adolescents.

There is plenty to hold one's attention before the service begins: a large spotlit crucifix on the south wall; a veiled statue of Our Lady before which burn half a dozen votive candles; another colossal statue, of St Michael, sword raised aloft. An altar has been placed halfway up the flight of steps leading to the high altar, on which the Sacrament is reserved, and it is at the lower altar that Mass is celebrated, with great dignity, facing the people. But first the parish priest comes out to say good morning to the congregation. 'Good morning,' they reply in unison. He thanks them for supplying bric-a-brac to help raise funds for a young priest in another diocese he is supporting, in connection with which he cracks a joke: 'Do shove anything you like through my letterbox – so long as it's cash or a cheque.' He announces a 'cockney St Valentine's – a party with chips' – and asks the congregation to remember someone in hospital with septicaemia. He then wishes Audrey and Mavis a happy birthday, and singles out Nicholas, a little boy of four, who seems overcome with embarrassment. 'He will have been pleased later,' I was assured.

In comes the procession, incense, cross, two candles and four priests, one of them limping heavily and holding the lectionary aloft in one hand. Only the celebrant, on this occasion the vicar, is fully vested in alb and chasuble; the three concelebrants, all retired and part-time helpers, wear only alb and stole because the church does not possess four matching chasubles. There are six male singers and servers, but exceptional participation in the liturgy by the congregation renders a choir superfluous.

The first lesson, from Isaiah, was read by a tall, very good-looking young man (although afterwards people kept saying to me, 'He's not as young as he looks'), who turned out to be the churchwarden and gay. I had assumed that a boy parked on his lap by his mother when she went up to receive communion was his son. 'Oh no,' he said, laughing, 'I just love children.' The second lesson was read by an equally young and attractive member of the laity, the mother of three young children and wife of an ordinand. Both she and the churchwarden wore a pullover and jeans.

During the thirteen-minute sermon (this seems to be the statutory length of time in catholic churches), preached by one of the retired Anglo-Catholic clergy living in the parish, a sermon supposedly about the Apostles which degenerated into complete waffle about the Queen and the efficiency of her staff and household, two little brothers played hide-and-seek behind a side altar. After their father had received communion and the boys a blessing, all three lit candles before the statue of St Michael and knelt in silent prayer. There was in fact a lot of private worship going on during the Mass. The Peace was exchanged on a massive scale, everyone turning to their neighbour and to those in other pews to hold hands or embrace, and the concelebrating clergy came among the congregation too, kissing the women but daring only to shake hands with the men. One day perhaps the Church of England will be in full communion with the Eastern Orthodox Church and then we shall all get a kiss. In true Orthodox style, however, the congregation stood for the prayer of consecration, and at least half of them stood to receive communion.

I got a free cup of tea afterwards because I was a visitor, but I was told with a wag of the finger that I should have to pay next time. Opinion seemed divided among those I talked to as to whether the vicar, dead set against the ordination of women, encouraged open discussion within the parish or merely used the parochial church council as a rubber stamp for his own decisions. I was told he feared he was no good at his job and was so nervous before celebrating Mass that he could scarcely speak, yet he conducted the seventy-minute service in a calm tone of voice and with faultless precision.

One of the nuns kept peering over my notebook to try to see what I was writing down. She belonged to a community with only four members living in their local house, and they divided their nursing and pastoral skills between this parish and one other. Someone else explained there were two members of the diocesan synod in the parish, who could be relied upon to see that people's views were passed from the diocesan to the General Synod. She said she was against the ordination of women because it was such a divisive issue, and that such issues only diverted people from worship.

As for worship itself, the following day, in order to celebrate the feast day of St Scholastica, there would be a Mass at 8 a.m. and another at 6.15 p.m., and indeed, there would be two celebrations every day throughout the week, Friday's being to commemorate St Cyril and St Methodius. On Saturday two sittings for breakfast would be served, at nine and 11.30 a.m., and it was at these breakfasts, I was told, that new members of the congregation were often recruited. There are no conventional church organisations in this parish, but four dozen laity have formed themselves into four prayer groups, and they share in visiting the sick and the housebound. 'It's strange,' one of the members of a prayer group told me, 'the vicar doesn't think that anyone loves him, which is very sad, yet he's very good at getting us to love one another.'

There was, for sure, an unforced atmosphere of mutual good will, and a feeling that the congregation did constitute a community. Their parish was in a town large enough for anyone who did not care for the style of worship to go elsewhere, and although inevitably some had drifted away because they felt ill at ease with a vicar who was not easy to talk to, many more had found a sense of identity and a spiritual home that felt genuinely warm (the draught in church was another matter), particularly where their attitude towards young children and gays was concerned, in both instances untypical of England and its Established Church. As the procession had filed out at the end of Mass, a little boy stood by a pillar with his hands in his pockets to watch them pass, which seemed as natural as the constant bowing of the two nuns at the name of Jesus.

In *Friends in High Places*[9] Jeremy Paxman has written of people who detest going to church on Sunday 'finding no familiar hymns, being invited to shout "Alleluia", shake hands with total strangers and stumble through services which seem to have been rewritten every three months'. The Dean of Winchester concedes that 'the amount of variety has become a very messy business. If I was starting again I would take the 1928 Service and develop that. What we are short of is people with imagination to put on services. What has been happening with liturgical revision is rather technical. Liturgists are very rarely the people who know how to stage liturgy. It is musicians and artists who know how to present.'

Where the liturgy has gone into free fall is at the extreme evangelical end of the spectrum, and particularly among evangelical charismatics. The charismatic movement is, however, extremely elusive, the word 'charismatic' itself being in the loosest possible use, with charismatic Anglicans attaching themselves to things called, for example, Kingdom Faith Ministries. The point has been reached where an Anglican priest can write (to the author), 'The services we have are not very

Anglican at all and are very free in the Spirit.' He was also good enough to 'pray for God's richest blessing and anointing to be upon your writing project'.

The word 'charismatic' used to have a perfectly clear meaning; it meant a person like President Kennedy or Pope John. Such people were said to have charisma, 'the special magnetic appeal, charm or power of an individual that inspires popular loyalty and enthusiasm'. But according to Longman's dictionary, charisma does also mean 'an extraordinary power (of healing) divinely given to a Christian', and the Church's ministry of healing is now virtually synonymous with charismatic worship, much of it inspired by evangelical fundamentalism. As long ago as 1915 the Guild of St Raphael was instituted, especially to reinstate the laying-on of hands and the sacrament of Holy Unction, and the Churches' Council of Healing was established by William Temple in 1944. It was in 1952 that the Convocation of Canterbury commended to the Church the modern revival of spiritual healing, which for centuries had been neglected, but sensible safeguards laid down for spiritual healing by an archbishops' commission in 1958 were disregarded by a minority of maverick clergymen who began to practise exorcism, without supervision, often without good reason and sometimes with catastrophic effects.

It still remains a dodgy extension of parochial ministry, with too many lay people with too little to do believing they are called to healing and counselling, just as in the secular world people with no training or aptitude cheerfully label themselves – and are accepted as – social workers. I was told by the Bishop of Bradford, 'People in many parishes seem to be called to the ministry of healing and nothing else. What I want is some clarity about which forms of lay ministry ought to have official authorisation. When lay people, particularly those involved in the charismatic movement, say they feel called to share in the ministry of healing, counselling or the laying-on of hands, I think there are great opportunities and great snares. The snares are that you get somebody involved with more zeal than discretion.'

A parish priest who takes healing and exorcism responsibly is Canon Dominic Walker. 'People,' he told me, 'will come to a healing service with a host of problems. I would always want to stress that healing takes place within a relationship with God. But sometimes an agnostic is healed. The first time I laid on a healing service was at the Elephant and Castle. A man arrived on crutches, hobbled down the aisle very slowly and received anointing and the laying-on of hands. Then he put his crutches under his arm, walked out of the church and was never seen again. Afterwards the cockneys at the Elephant and Castle said to me, "That was a good 'un, Father. Where did you 'ire 'im from?" They were quite sure I'd employed an out-of-work actor, and I have to admit, on reflection, it may have been someone pulling my leg.

'I think we have got to get away from the idea that healing is a matter of magic. It has to be seen in a much wider context of healing within the broken world in which we live. I see healing as one of the signs of the Kingdom of God. The demand given to the disciples was to heal the sick, cast out demons and proclaim the Kingdom of God.'

As far as exorcism is concerned, Canon Walker said, 'We avoid the word "exorcism" now and call it the ministry of deliverance.' But each diocese now has an exorcist appointed by the bishop, someone with medical or psychological knowledge. Canon Walker said the need for exorcism is very rare, and that when it is administered it is done after taking psychiatric advice and in the context of prayer and proper aftercare. He himself is a diocesan exorcist, and described a case in which he was involved:

'I once saw someone in a psychiatric clinic. The doctors asked me to go round because they had tried medication without any effect, and the woman was getting worse rather than better. During the exorcism she spoke in different voices, the voices of three different men, claiming to be three different spirits. She threw herself to the ground and started going into a snakelike position. Her language was enough to make a docker blush, and I commanded in the name of Christ that the three spirits should leave. At the end of it she collapsed, and then regained consciousness. It poses the question, what happened? Some of the doctors were a bit worried that something might have come out of her and into them. My own feeling is they were just deep, unhealed wounds in her subconscious mind which needed to be brought to the surface and released.

'At the end of it you feel absolutely exhausted. You really do feel you have been in a battle. It was not all that long, about twenty minutes, but it felt like hours. When I got home I was ashen and someone said, "What's wrong? You'd better have a stiff whisky." The woman enjoyed a miraculous recovery and went home a few days later.

'Most of the people we get have seen ghosts, and these are psychological projections. Two-thirds of poltergeists are young people who are cut off from their feelings because they have denied them. Often they come from a home where there is a very strict moral atmosphere, and they may be trying to live two lifestyles, one, restricted, at home, and one more free, at school. Most of the people who come for help are in fact from outside the Church, after they have tried everything else.

'At a service of healing, whether you anoint as well as lay your hands on people depends on whether you have any oil on you at the time. Oil used to be seen as a sign of healing. It was poured into wounds. Once a year a supply of oil is consecrated and blessed by the bishop and distributed among the clergy.'

A service for the consecration of oil was held at a large parish church in one diocese on the Tuesday of Easter Week in 1992. Laity and a few nuns packed the side aisles, and before the diocesan clergy appeared in procession, one of their number rehearsed the congregation, waving his arms wildly and exhorting them not to drag the Gloria.

As clergy from all over the diocese arrived, there was a scurry to the vestry of birettas, leather and duffel coats. In the congregation were earnest young theological students with earrings, altar boys, and an evangelical clergyman who never wears vestments and refused to dress up even for this occasion. As the procession entered, many of the clergy smiled a greeting to their friends. One was pushed in a wheelchair. Two were black. Patriarchal grey beards waved, smartly clipped ginger ones remained static. Some of the clergy wore cowls, some university hoods, and many wore fancy stoles. A prebendary sported red buttons. There were those who walked with their fingertips touching, and one actually appeared to be in a trance. At the rear came five assistant bishops, one in a borrowed white mitre, then the suffragan, and then the diocesan bishop. To renew their commitment to the diaconate, the deacons filed to the front of the altar steps. After the bishop's sermon the other clergy renewed their commitment to the priesthood.

The three oils were blessed: oil for the sick, as enjoined by St James; the oil of baptism, its symbolism being 'that of an athlete or soldier using oil to make his limbs supple and strong for his contest'; and the oil of chrism. While the last of the oils was being blessed, all the clergy stretched out their right hand, and this they did again at the consecration, after which one cleric received communion with a camera slung round his neck. Taizé chants were chanted, the bishop intoned the final blessing, and the clergy must have been tempted to leave at a gallop when side drums started beating up the last hymn. As the bishop moved down the nave, a child began to scream, but most of the congregation dutifully genuflected.

Since about 1978 Anglo-Catholics have been aboard the charismatic bandwagon. According to their 1992 *News*, 'Charismatic renewal is the movement within all the churches emphasising the power of the Holy Spirit at work in the life of every Christian.' A member of the National Committee of Anglo-Catholic Charismatics is Father James Naters, superior general of the Society of St John the Evangelist, the first religious community for men founded in England since the Reformation – in Oxford, in 1866. I went to the community's London house, in Westminster, to talk to Fr Naters about the charismatic movement.

'It is really a movement of openness to the Holy Spirit, to go where the Holy Spirit leads,' he explained. 'The Anglo-Catholic Charismatic Convention was formed by a group who had been praying together in the East End, who thought the catholic wing of the Church was not listening to what charismatics might be saying. The Anglo-Catholic side is very definitely church-based and sacramental. There is a free spirit, but the liturgy is retained. It gives the Eucharist a much freer atmosphere. There is opportunity for free prayer, and people from the congregation can contribute. And there is a great deal of praise and singing of choruses. After the Eucharist there is a time when people can come up for healing, with the laying-on of hands, and anointing if necessary. That usually goes on for quite a long time. One reason I think the charismatic movement is seen at its best in the Roman Catholic Church, where it originally sprang up in American Catholic universities, is that, there again, it is church and sacramentally based. But at its best I would also say the evangelical Church of England charismatic movement is very good.

'One of the things about charismatic renewal is that it does change people's lives. They do have a deepened sense of commitment. And I think one of the things charismatic renewal is doing is hastening the cause of unity.'

Fr Naters explained that healing was often given to people with depression, 'but people sometimes come up for physical healing, and you sometimes see physical healing happening'.

I suggested we were now in the realm of miracles.

'Yes, I believe that miracles do happen. I do indeed. Have I seen one happen? Yes. I was once asked to speak in the Midlands, where the parish priest used to have a monthly healing service, and during the Eucharist we invited anyone to come up who wanted to ask for prayers for healing, with the laying-on of hands, and in some cases anointing, and I remember one old lady coming up with terribly, terribly swollen legs. She had to be helped by people on either side, and she was walking with great difficulty and was obviously in great pain. So I laid hands on her and prayed for healing. The next time I met her she came up to me and said, "Look, I'm all right. I can walk without help. I don't need my stick. Praise the Lord!" '[10]

A service of healing can be a low-key event, and to the jaundiced eye, a somewhat chaotic one. On the windswept outskirts of an industrial town in the Midlands, in an area of massive deprivation and squalor, of high-rise flats and abandoned gardens, the vicar runs an equally down-at-heel church, with minimal local support and in need of £6,000 for basic repairs. There is a day centre attached, intended mainly for people with mental problems. Here, at midday, perhaps a dozen receive soup and sandwiches and, if they want it, 'counselling' from the churchwarden, whose husband turns out to be a major surprise, a Jewish convert who is also a lay reader. He wears a cloth cap, which he never removes.

Once a week there is a healing service in the day centre, a filthy place, frankly, and one wonders what inverted pretensions rule out the Lady Chapel, where the Sacrament is reserved and where some sacramental atmosphere might perhaps be worked up. Instead, dressed in a cardigan and homespun stole, the vicar seats himself at a coffee table and opens up his travelling box of tricks, from which he extracts a cross, two candles, a paten and a chalice. The churchwarden and a bearded man in blue jeans, who takes little oral part in the service, strum on guitars. The reader reclines on a sofa. Normally, the vicar explains, there might be a dozen present, and they all seem embarrassed by the small turnout, which includes a man called Bill, clearly a former mental patient, and a lady who brews the tea. But at least they haven't rented a congregation for my benefit.

The churchwarden announces a hymn; the refrain is 'His name is wonderful'. Bill follows the words with a magnifying glass. 'Jehovah, is that another name for God?' he asks when the hymn is over. 'It's *the* name for God,' the churchwarden volunteers. The next hymn is about 'Blessed Jesus, my redeemer'. 'I've just cracked this code' is Bill's next contribution to a liturgy that seems as shapeless as the vicar's cardigan. 'That's great,' he is told. We move on to the general confession, and the lay reader, garrulous at the best of times, is invited to comment on the Gospel reading. This he does at length.

Then comes the charismatic note. 'We should worship God with our whole body,' the vicar explains. 'And we shouldn't be afraid of our emotions coming into worship. If the priest holds up his hands at the altar, why shouldn't the congregation hold up theirs?' The tea lady raises her hands a little. 'Sometimes,' says the vicar, 'when I go deeply into prayer I groan.'

'Who created God?' Bill suddenly demands to know, loud and clear. I am beginning to think he is the most intelligent person present. A kind of ecclesiastical schizophrenia has gripped this parish, which may account for the poor attendance at Mass and the general air of mess and muddle and decay; they are trying to be evangelical Anglo-Catholics, with some very un-catholic biblical exhortations, and banners proclaiming Jesus, strung up everywhere. In the church, tambourines lie in a heap in case at a charismatic service held once a month the congregation feel inclined to liven up the proceedings.

Once again Bill comes to the rescue. 'I had a dream the other night,' he says, 'in which I was told I must say the creed every day.'

'Why don't you?' snaps the reader.

'I haven't got a copy.'

'*I'll* get you one.'

For the next hymn the tea lady decides to stand up. Then the vicar calls for intercessions, and after a blissful moment of silence the reader asks for guidance for all those who are confused. He had me in mind, I imagine. There is another hymn, and I begin to feel the whole event is a kind of self-indulgence; while celebrating, the vicar remains seated, and in the middle of the prayer of consecration the churchwarden dashes out of the room, only returning to fiddle about in her bag. I have never attended any occasion less reverential.

Everyone receives communion, standing, the reader still with his cap on. After the ablutions the vicar, his shirt hanging out of his trousers, also decides to stand – for yet one more hymn, at the end of which he asks, 'Would anyone like the laying-on of hands today?' This is what I have come to witness. But there are no takers. The vicar gives a blessing, and just as I think it is all over, the churchwarden introduces yet *another* hymn.

'Made plenty of notes, have you?' asked the vicar afterwards. 'Well, I hope it's been enlightening.' Indeed, it had. This had been a catholic and supposedly charismatic celebration of the Eucharist at its most bizarre and depressing. Outside, the unchurched parishioners continued on their own disorientated way.

I had been told that St Matthew's held charismatic services, so I telephoned to check if this was so. After several futile encounters with an answerphone I eventually contacted the vicar's wife, who demanded to know if I was a born-again Christian. Clearly disconcerted to discover that I was not, she then took it upon herself to cross-examine me about which church I attended. Eventually I elicited the information that although some services were more 'open' than others, almost anything could happen at any time. It had been a great pity, she said, that I had not been there last Sunday, when people in the front pews were seized by the spirit almost immediately; she and her husband were just off on holiday, so why didn't I come round on their return, when she would be preaching? Did I realise the last four vicars had all had a nervous breakdown? It was clear she was anxious to be interviewed and appear in the book, so why didn't I stay to lunch as well? To my relief, she later telephoned to say they had two people in terrible trouble who were now coming to lunch, and as they needed to talk would I mind postponing my visit? I said, not at all. 'Bless you,' she said. I still attended the service, however.

Inside the door a churchwarden and the vicar were shaking hands with everyone. Discounting the family of a baby boy due to be baptised, there were not more than fifty-five or sixty in the congregation, and until half a dozen children trooped in, accompanied by some straggling adults, half an hour late, there was not a single child or teenager. For all the desperate attempts I discovered the vicar's wife was making to dismantle any liturgy ever invented, almost all the parishioners had stubbornly remained on the wrong side of elderly.

The building was bare and cheerless, without a candlestick or a cross. Coffee and fellowship would be on offer after the service, the vicar announced. He wore a suit and a clerical collar and seemed quite nice and rational, in contrast to his wife, who exhibited all the hallmarks of an hysteric. On Wednesday, he said, there was to be the Ladies' Bible Study, and next Sunday, at 12.30 p.m., there would be a church family picnic. We were to pray for good weather; on the other hand, 'We do praise God for the rain, too, don't we.' The Mission for the Month was the Bible Society. He then handed us over to a layman, who was going to lead the service.

'I greet you all in the name of the Lord,' he said. 'The theme of the service will be Spending Time with God.' First we were to bow our heads and be very quiet, and ask God to cleanse us so that we could come into the Lord's presence with clean hands.

There was no need of a choir for, led by a nicely strumming musical ensemble, the congregation sang three hymns on the trot in a pleasantly swingy manner. There was some spasmodic hand-clapping, and a few hands were stretched out in the approved charismatic manner. But so far it seemed more like a breezy sing-along than a service. The father and both godfathers of the baby wore a shirt and tie but no jacket and the vicar baptised without bothering to don even a surplice. He then returned to his seat in the congregation (presumably there were other times when he earned his stipend), and from then on we were in the somewhat bizarre hands of his wife, whose performance during a 35-minute 'teaching talk', as she called it (not the sermon I had been promised), would have been hilariously funny had it not been so embarrassing; poorly prepared, badly delivered and devoid of all theological, intellectual and even emotional content.

'Right, we're going to talk about Time,' she said. 'Time is a very precious commodity, isn't it, mothers. How do you spend your time? How do you spend a typical day, I wonder?' She then mimed brushing her teeth, washing her face, eating her breakfast, rushing to work and falling asleep. When she got to some vague analogy about a day without Jesus being like a cake without any raising agent, an elderly man and woman walked out.

The burden of the 'talk', delivered in a breathless fluster, was to recommend that despite the rush of life we all make time to have a quiet time with God. 'A quiet time is a private audition with the King of Kings,' she proclaimed. I think she meant 'audience'. She spoke of 'maximum quality time', and reckoned twenty minutes a day was the very least amount of time one should devote to being quiet with God. Those, like monks and nuns, who do this sort of thing professionally would probably reckon it was about eight hours. She then rushed around putting on tapes, usually in the wrong place; dancing ('I'm not a dancer,' she confessed, 'but I dance for the Lord'); lying flat on her face; and, despite the theme of being quiet, generally making as much noise as she knew how. There was a good deal of talk about the devil and his demons, intent on causing distractions, and about the power of darkness. However, we were assured there were twice as many angels as demons, so that was all right. References to Biblical texts came tripping off her tongue: 2 Timothy, 2: 15; Mark 11, 24. There was also a good deal of 'Now, where have I got to?' Or, 'Something's missing, never mind.' 'What have we here, folks?' she asked her audience, who remained as placid as suet puddings. 'A Bible! This Bible is God's blueprint. It is utterly and totally trustworthy.' The Bible had been heavily scored in different-coloured crayons, and the congregation were invited to come up afterwards and inspect the underlinings.

Props included a tambourine, a briefcase and a map, which the lay leader tried to pin to the pulpit. No one could possibly have read it. 'Pin the word of God up on your kitchen sink,' she advised. When we were in heaven we would be worshipping and praying all the time so why not start now? She rattled her tambourine. 'Don't you clap your hands at a football match? How much more worthy is the Lord to be clapped!' And so it went on. As though she was determined to try out the entire charismatic repertoire, she wandered around at one point singing complete gibberish, but nothing she did seemed to catch on. Clearly the Holy Spirit, like the vicar, was having a day off. No one in the congregation, try to whip them up as she might, would oblige by speaking in tongues; no one began to dance in the aisle. On the contrary, four old biddies at the back of the church were having a cheerful chinwag, and a little boy began to pass the time by playing skittles with a collection of old batteries.

'You need to walk around while you pray,' the vicar's wife was prattling on. 'It's hard work but it keeps you awake. Be systematic. I have a system, but I haven't time to tell you about it now.' We were, however, vouchsafed the information that if we did spend time with God, who was our best friend, 'he would whisper secrets in our ear'. The most revealing moment came when, at one flustered juncture, she called out, 'What's the word I want, Jim?'

'Sacrament,' her husband replied.

For the final hymn the congregation were invited to hold hands. About a dozen did so. If any member of the congregation wanted prayer afterwards, there were prayer groups they could talk to. In the interests of modernity and in a desperate attempt to revive an ailing parish, out of the window had gone some old-fashioned but structured and intelligible evangelical Morning Prayer. In had come self-satisfaction ('I have never heard that passage so well read'; 'Thank you, Jean, for that time of quiet') and ultimately a patronising and boring mockery of a once virile Anglican tradition.

When I met the Archbishop of Canterbury at Lambeth Palace, I took the opportunity to ask him whether, like John Stott, he saw the charismatic movement as a fourth strand to Anglican churchmanship or whether he thought it had rather gone up a cul-de-sac?

'It's difficult to know,' he said. 'I'm not in touch with it these days. What it contributed to church life generally was popular music. Everyone felt they could make a contribution. But it's been divisive because it seemed to open up a chasm between the switched-on Christian and the average run-of-the-mill Anglican, between the first-class and the second-class, between the saint and the straggler. That's very unfortunate indeed. In my own church in Durham[11] I tried to bring in positive features of the charismatic alongside the positive features of Anglicanism generally. I made the church more sacramental but I drew upon good charismatic music. I'm all for the eclectic approach. Whatever God brings in, let's use. Let's not be too sniffy about it. We mustn't live in the past, but we mustn't abandon the past.'

EIGHT

Bars and Bombs

IMAGES, particularly those projected by cartoonists and satirists, even by novelists, tend to linger long after the reality has changed, sometimes beyond recognition. The image of the clergy remains, for many, that of the incompetent high-pitched curate, the bumbling, slightly sanctimonious parish priest and the rotund bishop, laced up in gaiters and living it up in a palace. Bishops have not worn gaiters for at least thirty years, a fact ignored even by as sharp-eyed an observer of the social scene as Alan Bennett, who has the bishop coming to lunch in gaiters in one of his brilliant *Talking Heads* monologues, written in 1988. Only a quarter of the diocesan bishops live in anything that could remotely be designated a castle or a palace, and then only in a small part of the building. The rest will have been converted into diocesan offices. And many parish priests have no curate at all. If he lives in the country, the parson will not, like his eighteenth-century predecessor, be riding to hounds but in a second-hand car, from village to village, distributing what one theological college principal has described as Communion on Wheels.

His suburban or industrial counterpart may also have a clutch of churches to care for, helped by a team ministry. And of course there are clergy working full-time in a multitude of non-parochial situations, some already well-defined, like school, hospital or prison chaplaincies, some in the rarefied atmosphere of cathedrals, some among those who are dying of AIDS. If a clergyman does not fancy working in a parish but feels called to be an administrator, there is no shortage of openings within the Church's bureaucracy. You can be secretary to the Committee for Ministry Among Deaf People, chaplain to Derbyshire College of Higher Education or Wolverhampton University, assistant secretary for industrial and economic affairs to the Board for Social Responsibility, or run the Communications Unit for the Committee for Communications. You can be a broadcasting officer, or secretary of the Hospital Chaplaincies Council. Out in the sticks you may fancy the job of pastoral assistant to the Bishop of Bath and Wells, or officer for evangelism in Norwich. You could be canon librarian at Rochester Cathedral or parish development officer in Wakefield. You could apply to be warden of Lincoln Diocesan Conference and Retreat House, or by ingratiating yourself with the Supreme Governor of the Church of England hope to be appointed a canon of Windsor. If you want to escape from the rat race completely, and feel a vocation to the religious life, apply to the abbot of the Community of Our Lady and St John or the minister general of the Society of St Francis. Become chaplain at Eton or work for the Missions to Seamen. The field for extra-parochial employment is almost limitless. There is even a chaplain to the Eurotunnel.

Of course, there is nothing to prevent a Church of England clergyman from working overseas, and although the Victorian urge to convert the natives has rather subsided, missionaries attached, for instance, to the United Society for the Propagation of the Gospel can still be found in Africa, the West Indies, South America, India, Pakistan and East Asia. Commitment to social justice nowadays takes priority over Bible-bashing, and great emphasis is laid on training indigenous leaders – to the extent that the society, with an annual budget of £5 million, employs only about 110 staff in forty countries. The Church Missionary Society, founded in 1799 to 'proclaim the Gospel in all lands', still provides missionaries for twenty-eight African and Asian countries, but the missionaries take up their work only at the invitation of the local Church. Many missionaries are lay people, often married, and sometimes accompanied in their missionary work by their children, for a vocation to missionary work has often gripped a whole family, whereas vocation to parish work is much more likely to be felt only by the priest himself, even if he has a family.

To be bishop of Gibraltar in Europe (was there ever a more ridiculous designation, especially as the bishop's writ runs to

North Africa?) you certainly need to be fond of travel – of flying, at any rate. Church of England chaplaincies in north and central Europe used to come under the jurisdiction of one of the suffragan bishops in the London diocese, and those in southern Europe and around the Mediterranean were in the care of the bishop of Gibraltar. But in 1980 a new diocese of Gibraltar in Europe was created and added to the Province of Canterbury, so that not only does the bishop, with diocesan offices in London, have to hop from Malaga to Majorca, from Athens to Rome, he has to find time to attend residential meetings of the House of Bishops and sit through debates in the General Synod before flying off again to Luxembourg, Paris, Finland . . . It is just as well the present bishop is a bachelor. As well as a cathedral in Gibraltar there are pro-cathedrals in Brussels and Malta (of which the bishop is also dean); there are eight archdeacons and perhaps 130 chaplaincies of one sort or another. Some, like Las Palmas, sound enticing, but the life of a Church of England chaplain overseas, struggling to maintain an Anglican presence in an alien climate, can be an isolated and lonely one; some might even say, rather pointless.

In Tangier, for example, a chaplaincy with a rather chequered history (one chaplain within recent memory was driven to suicide), there is a church which, out of season, may attract a congregation of twelve for the 11 a.m. communion service, four of them visitors. There is a Muslim caretaker, who, if you happen to mention you know the bishop, will kiss you on both cheeks and say, 'Thank you, thank you,' and there are plenty of reminders of the old country: a chancel, for example, built in memory of Sir John Hay Drummond Hay, 'GCMG, KCB, Grand Cross of the Dannebrog, For 40 Years British Resident at the Court of Morocco', and a plaque on the wall to commemorate a squadron leader shot after escaping. 'Good Hunting, Tim,' it reads. There is a pew reserved for the churchwarden, and the scanty congregation sit as far apart from one another as possible. There is of course no choir, no Scout troop, no Mothers' Union. I asked the chaplain, John Featherstone, what the pastoral opportunities in a situation like this were.

'Very few. Sometimes I'm visited by Bible-bashing types

who seem to think I should be converting Muslims, which even if I wanted to I don't think is possible. I was here once before and I left because I didn't think I had enough to do. There are no baptisms or weddings, just the occasional funeral, but now I'm resigned to the fact. I fill my day largely by reading. And there are people I visit, because there are people here who are very lonely. A lot of the expatriates in Tangier have lived their lives entirely for pleasure, and as they get older and can't gad about they get more and more lonely.

'We don't have a PCC, we have what's called a church committee, which consists of me, the treasurer, the churchwarden and a secretary. There are only twenty-six on the electoral roll. They squabble among each other, and grumble because the local red wine goes sour, or the church is cold. It's a bit like living among seventy-year-old adolescents, frankly.'

Mr Featherstone sees more of the local Spanish archbishop than he does of any Anglican priest. The nearest chaplain lives in Casablanca, some 300 miles away. 'I was supposed to be going over last Easter to Gibraltar to see the suffragan bishop,[1] but he said he was so busy he could only give me twenty minutes – and it's not worth taking an aeroplane and going over to Gib for a twenty-minute conversation with a suffragan bishop.'

The church in Tangier, St Andrew's, is self-supporting as a result of legacies, for the town was once home to some fabulously wealthy people. But most are now dead, and they are not being replaced. 'One wonders how much longer the bishop will keep a chaplaincy like this going,' says Mr Featherstone. 'I definitely feel it is worthwhile keeping Christian worship alive here as long as possible, but for a congregation we depend a lot on tourists, and the Gulf crisis in 1991 killed tourism for quite a long time. Our congregations fluctuate enormously. We could have thirty, we could have ten. We advertise services in all the main hotels, but I suspect the Muslim staff don't like it. And I sometimes wonder how happy the couriers are, because they like to get a commission on excursions on a Sunday morning, and *they* don't want tourists trooping off to church.'

How does someone like Mr Featherstone end up in a place like Tangier? 'I'd been teaching for twenty years in England,

and when I retired I was still quite energetic but I didn't know anyone in the establishment; I didn't know any of the bishops. So I must have written to the Bishop of Gibraltar, who offered me Zagreb, which meant learning Serbo-Croat, so I came here, in 1987.

'Then I spent a year and a half in a parish in England, where things didn't work out very well, so I came back to Tangier. I don't speak Arabic but I get by with French.' He says the bishop is thinking of combining Tangier with Gibraltar. 'And how will the expatriates react to that?'

'Very badly, I should think. But you have to admit it, the number of serious Christians here is very, very small.'

The day I called at a busy general hospital in the Sheffield diocese there was one Muslim patient, there were eight Jewish, fifteen Roman Catholic, twenty Free Church and 250 registered as Church of England, so it is small wonder that almost every full-time hospital chaplain in England is an Anglican. There are some 370, but the chaplain I had gone to see, an evangelical who had been in the job ten years, spends only two days a week on the wards because he is also district chaplain to the local health authority, and among his duties is organising part-time chaplains and visiting day hospitals, residential hospitals and the mentally ill. To that extent his job is ecumenical, and he was fulsome in his praise of the part-time Catholic and Free Church chaplains who visit his own hospital.

He had formed a desire to work in hospitals while still at theological college, but his background includes twelve years in Southeast Asia with the Church Missionary Society, a spell of teaching, three years in an industrial parish in Durham and another brief period in charge of four country parishes in the West Country. He had also trained as a physiotherapist, and had no plans to return to parish work.

'I was at a conference of hospital chaplains the other day, and it was good to be with clergy who were happy and content and fulfilled in what they do. Lots of parish clergy aren't.' Many of the day-to-day concerns of the parochial clergy are a far cry from a job that requires a bleeper in your pocket. At any moment the chaplain could be summoned to someone dying, and obviously death is at the core of his ministry.

'I deal with death and bereavement every day, and I meet people all the time who actually want to die. I'm going to see a lady in a moment, in one of the residential homes, who has no contact with her local church but sees herself as a Christian, and she is very angry with God because he won't let her die. She's had strokes, she's incapacitated, she's depressed and she's actually dying of cancer, and what she wants is to die immediately.

'I think one of the important parts of my job is to let people express this kind of feeling, and not to feel there is anything wrong in saying it. I think about my own death quite a lot. I think death is fascinating. Actually, we have a joke at home. When we go out to dinner parties my wife says, "Don't talk about death." ' I suggested that perhaps her reason was that they wouldn't be asked again, and he roared with laughter.

On admission to the hospital every patient is given a leaflet about the chaplaincy and they can ask to see a chaplain if they wish. Otherwise, it is rather hit and miss. Some 40,000 patients pass through every year, and the chaplain finds that on some wards he is tipped off whom to see, on others the medical team, while friendly, fail to see his role as any part of their own healing process.

Nevertheless he regards his pastoral opportunities as enormous. 'I am here for whatever people want me for. With some it will be to cheer them up for a few minutes, for others to administer the Sacrament, or to explore areas of anxiety, about whether they are going to die, or about the limitations they will have to face after their operation or their stroke. It's a very direct contact with people with particular needs, and a relationship of trust has to develop pretty rapidly. It is an enormous privilege to be alongside people at this particular critical moment, but there may be sixty new patients in a ward in a week, so the chance of meeting everybody is nil.'

He had hardly ever worn a clerical collar in thirty years, and he would take the Sacrament to the dying in a suit, but he said the majority of hospital chaplains do wear a dog collar. He also nearly always declines to take a funeral, thinking it far better to refer the bereaved to their parish clergy. What he does do is spend a lot of time with the staff. 'This week I saw a therapist who works with old people, and she wanted to talk to me because she has to go home and nurse her elderly parents; her father is very aggressive with her, and she realised she was getting very tired and aggressive with her own patients here. There was someone else this morning who had been in trouble with the police, and someone who is working out his homosexual orientation. Actually, what sparked him coming to see me was that his partner had died.

'We are understaffed and overworked, and with the change to trust status people are worried about their jobs. The high ideals with which people entered the health service are clashing with the need to budget. Many people feel a tremendous conflict in dealing with this. I have to make sure the authority is interested in purchasing a chaplaincy service. Personally I don't mind all this, because it makes me look at what I am providing. It makes you think very hard about what you're doing.'

He said he loved his work and could not ask for more, had discovered great tolerance among the mentally ill, would never again wish to be employed by the Church, but admitted to depression, particularly when tired. His remedy is rather simple. He has a long sleep. He was also grateful that he received regular supervision. His job had also confirmed an attitude he inherited from his mother, a great sympathy for people who choose how and when to die.

'I feel we have a right to make that choice. Every week I hear someone say, "Why won't God let me go?" It is not so much a question of a fear of pain, because most pain can be relieved now, it is a matter of the quality of life. More and more old people have thought this through and are very aware and intelligent about it. They are very concerned about loss of independence. In medical circles, the whole question of euthanasia is rising rapidly to the top of the agenda. My wife and I have both made wills saying in the event of a car crash we are not to be kept alive like cabbages. But at present it's very much easier said than done.'

The local prison, built in mid-Victorian times to look like a castellated adornment to the town, has delicious views of the countryside from the chapel. There is not much else to recommend it. 'You're ten minutes late,' a warder informed me when I asked for the chaplain, and I was told to wait in the waiting room, a room so depressing I was only too glad to step through electronically operated doors into the heart of the prison itself. In order to talk to the chaplain, a retired primary school headmaster who had been ordained only two or three years, I had to sit in the chapel, for his own office was being used by someone else for counselling. There was a holy-water stoop attached to the door, but otherwise it was obviously interdenominational. A Roman Catholic Mass is celebrated twice a week by a part-time Catholic chaplain, and once a month the main Sunday service is taken by a Methodist minister.

'I'm Anglo-Catholic myself,' the chaplain explained as he showed me his vestments. 'Smells and bells! You name it and I'll do it! I can't show you the plate, that's locked up – for obvious reasons.'

Apart from a year as a deacon he had had no parochial experience, and was attracted to the work of a full-time prison chaplain because of the relationships he could form with the inmates. 'It's like a big boys' school, really. I like to think I'm useful, sometimes being with people in great times of grief, when they've had a bereavement on the outside, and generally trying to help people when they get depressed and fed up. And of course we have a normal liturgy, the same as any other church.'

In theory the prison holds 500 inmates, but with one wing temporarily out of commission there were about 410. 'Last week we did very well, we had forty-five to the main service. It's usually a steady thirty, because these days we are competing with visits on a Sunday morning. In the old days, when there were no Sunday morning visits, it was easy to get a full chapel. It seats about ninety. I would think about three-quarters of those who come to chapel are committed Christians.'

He was due the next week to conduct a service of blessing for a prisoner who had contracted a civil marriage. 'What I do find takes a lot of time is hearing confessions. The quote goes, "I want to make it right with God." And that's a very touching part of one's work.' He once heard a confession to murder.

'The lifers left in December. When you have lifers and other long-term people it adds dramatic stability to an institution. Many of the chaps here are only on remand or are awaiting transfer to another prison. They may only be here six months. There's a waiting list for Wormwood Scrubs.

'But even so the pastoral opportunities are absolutely immense. One could become residential and do the job twenty-four hours a day and still not meet the need. But obviously one has to cope with one's own sanity. I play squash, and I've got an allotment. I work here five days a week, and while I'm here I give my absolute all. And when I leave, I throw the keys in, and that has to be that.'

The chaplain arrives about eight in the morning, and collects a computer sheet of the names of everyone admitted overnight – usually between eight and a dozen. There were once thirty-one new admissions, and he managed to see all thirty-one in one morning. 'I went home exhausted!' After new prisoners have been received, the chaplain is the first person to visit them in their cell. He gives them a brochure, explains how to apply to attend the chapel, and says, 'If ever you feel very lonely or fed up, put in an application and one of our team will come and see you.' He said the first reaction might be blasé or very pleased to see him. 'It varies a lot.'

But most of his pastoral work is accomplished by walking the blocks, simply by being a constant presence within the prison. He cannot visit a cell between noon and 1.30 p.m., or again between about 4 p.m. and 6 p.m., for at these hours there are only two warders on duty on each block and all the prisoners are 'banged up'. He is known variously, to prisoners and warders alike, as David, Father David, Vic, Rev or Gov. Wherever he moves, he does so through a haze of cigarette smoke. The trusty in charge of cleaning smokes in the chapel. Everyone smokes in the hospital wing. They all smoke in the classrooms, and the duty governor was leaning cheerily against the door of his office, pipe in mouth. A Mormon asked the chaplain if a book he had requested had arrived. Then we were buttonholed by a chap whose grandmother was to be buried at noon that day; was there a prayer he could say? The chaplain told him to come to the chapel at 11.45 a.m.

Everywhere the chaplain goes he asks the officers if everything is all right. 'I always try to sense whether there is any trouble brewing, whether the lads are getting restless. You almost develop a sixth sense. You begin to see different groupings emerging. I had a glass of water thrown over me once – clean water. It could have been the other! A chap was being transferred to another prison and I just wanted to wish him well, but something went wrong, and he chucked a glass of water at the governor. I was standing behind the governor, who ducked. I didn't.

'Every day throughout the year it is the chaplain's duty to walk the wings, to be accessible and to visit the punishment block and the hospital. I'm also available to the officers. Some make use of me, some don't.'

The previous evening, a prisoner had tried to hang himself from the window of his cell. 'His cellmate was somewhat traumatised by the whole affair, so I spent a good deal of time yesterday talking to him. He had been instrumental in saving his cellmate's life. The chap who attempted suicide is okay now and regrets what he did.'[2]

Prison chaplains are appointed by the Home Office and licensed by the local bishop. In 1992 the first three Anglican women deacons were appointed to full-time posts as prison chaplains. An induction course is about all the training they get for the job. What qualifications did a priest or deacon need to be a prison chaplain? 'You need to be fairly unflappable, good in terms of relationships with people, and have an ability to cope with several things going on at the same time. I think a lot of these things could also apply to a primary head teacher.'

The prison chaplain I met walks the echoing corridors of his claustrophobic parish in an atmosphere of constant clanging and shouting and alternating heartiness and despair. It is all a long way removed from the ecclesiastical politics of Church House or the parish fête. Or indeed the romanticised version of prison life as depicted on television in *Porridge.* One of his most distressing tasks is to break to a prisoner the news of someone's death, and every report of a death outside has to be checked by the chaplain, for there are people who will inform the prison that someone has died just to inflict additional suffering.

'It's despicable, but I have had to cope with three hoaxes. If you're unlucky, checking out a death can be a two-hour job. It's always my task to go and break the news to a prisoner. Sometimes when they see me coming they say, "Oh, no!" '

I had taken up nearly an hour and a half of the chaplain's time, and shortly the prisoners were to have lunch and then get locked in their cells. It is a pretty frantic schedule. There was someone waiting in the chapel to pray for his grandmother; that night there might be another attempted suicide; there was a young man due for release in two days' time, pushing a trolley of curry into a lift.

'Is it all right?' the chaplain asked.

'No!'

As I left, the chaplain said, 'You haven't asked if I enjoy the work. The answer is, by and large, yes, very much. The bit I don't like is breaking the news of a bereavement. Reading the Eucharist is fine if you've got people who are committed to what they're doing, but if you've got a couple of lads who have just gone up there to chat, I find that a bit distracting.'

Finally he said, 'A prison chaplain mustn't mind being made a fool of. I believe everything – and I believe nothing!'

'Many thanks for your letter and I'm glad that you were pleased with the result. I have thought over what you said and have decided that my name should not be used. One is tempted to see one's name in lights but I feel that I am only one of many and that there are many more service chaplains who could tell their tale and explain their ministries in a far more eloquent and constructive way.

'In many ways the life of a service chaplain is no different to that of his civilian counterpart. It is my belief that the crux of all ministry ultimately is that of suffering . . .'

So let us call the army chaplain who flew several hundred miles to give me lunch at the Guards Barracks in London Arthur King. After spending eight years in two parishes of his own – 'I'm a country person by nature,' he told me, 'and I used to see myself as a kind of ecclesiastical James Herriot' – he decided 'there wasn't really enough to get my teeth into', felt a call to adventure, and persuaded his wife to agree to a three-year trial period as an army chaplain.

'I knew nothing about the army,' Arthur King recalled. 'The very idea of marching for miles and miles appalled me.' But march he did, because initially he served with an infantry battalion, after training for a month at Sandhurst (all chaplains are obliged, largely for administrative reasons, to accept commissioned rank) and for two weeks at the Royal Army Chaplains' Department Centre at Bagshot, 'to learn the difference between a corporal and a sergeant'. Although he went on parade to learn drill, he did not handle a weapon, except to learn how to make one safe, for no chaplain goes into battle armed. The joke is that he learns to run instead. This, however, chaplains seldom do. Many have been decorated for gallantry.

'Colonel' King said, 'I've never found having a commissioned rank a problem. It's no more a barrier with a soldier than a clerical collar is in a parish. The chaplain is given rank not for himself but for the benefit of the people he works with. If I went to the commanding officer as a civilian clergyman he might not have much sympathy, but if he sees me as part of his team, it actually gives more power to my elbow.' However, no chaplain makes day-to-day use of his rank; all are referred to as Padre.

Officially the army no longer enforces compulsory attendance at church, but unofficially things are not so straightforward. 'I remember the first service I took in the field. We were on exercise in Jamaica. I'd been told to expect twenty, and 200 turned up. It was obvious the whole company had been told to turn out so I went to see the sergeant major afterwards. "Look at it this way, Padre," he said. "There are a lot of people who would not have been there out of choice and a lot who would have liked to have been there, but it takes courage for a soldier to step out and say, 'I'm going to a church service.' So if I tell them all to be there I take the blame." '

Despite constant anxiety experienced by his family, and very nearly losing his life twice, Arthur King had so far survived sixteen years as a chaplain. How did he keep in balance his vocation as a priest and the military ethos in which he had to operate?

'By prayer. If a chaplain hasn't got that then he might as well pack his bags and go home. I've had eight postings and

I've had a wonderful time, but there have been times too when my faith has been taken to the edge. I've done more than one trip to Northern Ireland, and most of the tours I did were fairly quiet. But the last time I was there, in 1986, I was in a location where they brought in a bomb. Which killed two of the guys who were with me. I was about 100 yards from where the bomb went off. It was a big bomb, about 1,000 lb. It was quite devastating. It was a bad tour, actually. We lost three people. Two other guys were wounded. I was hurt as well. That did have an effect on me. I was there when they died. There were lots of things, actually. I don't know if you're going to put this in the book. Are you? If so, I'll modify it a bit.

'I think when you see that kind of thing for the first time, it's not like somebody dying in bed, it's not like going to visit someone who's dying in hospital. It's not even like being at the scene of a car accident, horrendous though that may be. Because you are aware afterwards that your own life has been very much at risk. It made me realise that somewhere out there was someone equally intent on killing me. When you see the reality of hatred in a broken body it does have an effect on you. It took me two years to get over it.

'War itself, and that kind of incident, is set apart from normal human experience. I can now understand, for instance, why veterans have reunions. It's a place where even forty years on they can talk and spew out some of their experiences from a great depth, because spoken about in other people's company it doesn't mean anything. I find that very true now of people who have come back from the Gulf. It was also true of people from the Falklands and Vietnam, but not of the soldier returning in 1945 because he was coming back to a community that knew what it was to be bombed, who had actually seen death and destruction on their own doorsteps. Today, soldiers return to a society which knows very little about service life and nothing at all about personal involvement in war.

'I often wondered why I had to go through the experience in Northern Ireland, and part of the crucifying experience for me was that I had a senior chaplain who couldn't understand it at all. I visited the families of the wounded and saw the families of the two who had been killed, and took the ashes of one of them back with me to Ireland. On the Sunday morning, when I'd stopped running around, I returned to barracks and asked if I could celebrate. It was rather like getting on a bike again after you've fallen off. The senior chaplain was there and I asked if I could talk to him about the whole thing, and it was quite obvious by his reaction that he just didn't want to know. For me, that was a devastating blow, because it brought it very sharply home to me, who cares for the carers?'

On manoeuvres in Germany in 1980 King had already broken his back. He had to tell his wife that he had been injured and very nearly killed in Northern Ireland. By the time the Gulf War broke out in January 1991, he was senior chaplain to the 7th Armoured Brigade. 'I knew what we were going to face when we went to the Gulf, or I had an idea, because of the incident in Northern Ireland. My greatest fear was for those who were going to face death for the first time. For myself, I didn't actually expect to come back, to be honest with you. But Ireland had strengthened my faith, and I had the tremendous conviction in the Gulf that no matter what the depth of despair, God is always with you.'

He was the first army chaplain to arrive in the Gulf and he remained there six months. During that time his elder son was so anxious he failed his A levels. At our interview in the summer of 1992, King remembered, 'I've actually lived under worse conditions, but not for so long. The heat at the beginning was quite horrendous. But there was a lovely atmosphere throughout the brigade headquarters, and the brigadier had some rare gifts of leadership. They had been good to work with in peacetime but they were a thousand times better in war. Every day we had services. I took a Remembrance Day service with about 3,000 present. In a shed. And I would wander round and talk to the men, perhaps two or three together, and I would say, "As I'm here, how about joining in a prayer together?" And in that couple of minutes you had a chance to enter into something very special. The interesting thing was that many of them would ask you, not is there a "service" but is there communion? The altar might be a table, or some boxes on the back of a vehicle, anything you could find to put your communion kit on. We didn't have a lot of wine so I used to tincture the bread rather than give them the chalice, to make the wine last. It was very moving, because you would look the soldier straight in the eye as you gave him communion, and he looked you straight in the eye, and you knew what he was thinking, and he knew exactly what you were thinking as well: this may be the last time.

'I remember one incident when we lost a young driver in the convoy I was with, and at eight o'clock that morning I conducted a service. The RC chaplain gave an address, and he preached from the raising of Lazarus. The text was, "Let him go free." And you had 200 guys in front of you, some of them quite hard men, who were deeply moved. But one thing I found was that when soldiers are operational they haven't time to grieve, and you do the grieving process for them. It's a kind of vicarious suffering, if you like.

'I'm sure there are many soldiers who fought in the Gulf whose sense of spirituality has changed, because you can understand why Jesus and the prophets went into the desert to find God. There is nothing else there.'

Arthur King said he was not a pacifist, but neither did he believe in a just war. 'That may seem strange. I think there can be a situation in which war becomes the lesser of two evils, but I don't know if you could ever call that a just war, because there are no good wars, and there never have been. Anybody who has been in a war would say that. But I believe that at the end of the day force is sometimes your only resort, especially when you are dealing with someone like Saddam Hussein. It did go through people's minds, why were we out in the Gulf? But when we had finished what we had to do I think we knew why we had been there. There were reasons beyond just that of oil. Having spoken to so many Iraqis, and seen how evil that regime was, my only regret – and it is a very great regret – is that we stopped when we did. It's an unresolved war.

'But of course, I'm not called upon to kill. It's my job to be with those who are. After coming back, I have an intense feeling of wanting to see things grow. I've taken a greater interest in gardening, for instance. It was a joy to plant bulbs and to see all this life coming up. Which must have a lot to do with the fact that last year I placed a lot of people in the ground, and I wasn't even sure who they were.'

I had some difficulty getting into Open Door, a day centre run in Brighton for people diagnosed HIV positive, all of whom in theory know – although some may not have accepted – that they have a mortal illness from which they will die while still quite young. I had some difficulty because Marcus Riggs was run off his feet and all too frequently importuned by visitors, many of whom, like representatives from parishes anxious to learn how they can help, had a more urgent call on his time than authors. However, at the second shove the door did open, and I struck lucky. It was, Father Riggs told me, a fairly quiet day.

Nevertheless the small sitting room on the ground floor was crowded. So was the office, where clerical garb hung on the wall, and so was the dining room in the basement, where lunch was being served. This, I was told, was the most important room in the house, 'where an awful lot of support is received round the kitchen table'. We grabbed mugs of tea and went upstairs. In the hall, Fr Riggs was stopped by a young man with a tale to tell about his friend who had met with an accident. He had fallen out of a window. Another young man in flower-embroidered trousers swayed beside him. 'It will have been a drugs-related accident, I imagine,' Fr Riggs explained. 'The chap who was telling me about it has been off heroin for ten days and is doing quite well. But the one in the flowery trousers is so off his head he doesn't know which way up he is.'

We were now on the first floor, in the residents' small sitting room, where a women helper was feeding a baby. Fr Riggs sat in the window, framed by two enormous house plants, into the pots of which, for the next hour and forty minutes, he continually flicked his cigarette ash.

Fr Riggs, who is known to everyone in Brighton, Christian or not, as Father Marcus, was thirty-six at the time of my visit.[3] With his close-cropped beard and wearing a leather jacket and grey open-necked shirt, he might have presented an image of the archetypal trendy vicar. On the contrary, he was unsentimental, down-to-earth, and very clear about what he is trying to do. He is trying to relate the gospel to life as far away as possible from the parochial system. In his own words, he is not 'some desperately radical way-out sort of person, just a fairly average priest being who I am and getting on with it'.

Open Door is run as an integral part of the diocese of Chichester. The diocese purchased the house, in a narrow residential street a few yards from the sea, and pay the minister's stipend. Yet he is free to celebrate in the diocese wherever he is asked. 'I'm a dab hand at clergy holidays,' said Fr Riggs. 'The main difference between being here and in a parish is that I don't have to organise lots of services, which I'm quite relieved about. And at Open Door you meet an even more diverse range of people than you do in a parish, from business directors to people who sleep under the pier. And you get much more honest people.'

There are two bedrooms, for people who may need a brief holiday. There is a shower room on the ground floor for those in a wheelchair. There are facilities for acupuncture and massage. But essentially the house is a community where a simple lunch is served every weekday to perhaps thirty callers, where the front door is open between 10 a.m. and 5 p.m., where those with AIDS are encouraged to help and support one another and to strike a positive attitude towards what is left of their lives, blighted as so many of those lives have been in the first instance by drink and drugs.

'Early on,' said Fr Riggs, 'we seemed to attract people who were fairly chaotic. We've a lot of people who have had drink and drugs problems for years. You cannot undertake every task, and we tend to concentrate on those whom other people find difficult. The reason a lot of people dependent on drugs feel comfortable here is that their history is usually one of conflict with authority, and there is no authority here. I refuse to be in charge. Nobody is. Or God is! We don't have staff roles. There's no structure at all. This gives people space in which to identify their problems, which may concern housing, money, loneliness, and find ways of tackling them. We tell people this is a community and they are expected to look after each other. For example, if nobody cooks the lunch there is no lunch.'

It is so often because they are on drink or drugs, not necessarily because they are homosexual, that many of the callers at Open Door have AIDS. 'People into self-destruct often have an incredibly negative self-image. They are almost cruel to themselves. And if you are off your head with drugs and have sex with someone, condoms aren't an issue. But the most important single factor in the spread of HIV is probably alcohol. People are well aware when they are stone-cold sober that you just don't screw without a condom, but when people are drunk, they think, what does it matter? Having unprotected sex is absolute madness but there's madness going on everywhere.'

Married couples come to Open Door, and Fr Riggs believes that AIDS presents much worse problems for heterosexuals than for homosexuals.[4] 'Gay men are more used to being open about sex. Talking about sex with a heterosexual partner remains one of society's great taboos. Where AIDS is concerned, the problem for heterosexuals is babies, because you can't have babies if you use a condom. And many of the younger ones want babies. We have one baby whose father is positive and the mother contracted AIDS because she wanted a baby. There's another guy who comes here whose wife doesn't know he is HIV positive and he's having to tell her he's off sex for the moment, because he can't suddenly say, Shall we use a condom?

'There are two rent boys who come here and virtually all their customers are married men. Most of the female prostitutes in Brighton have AIDS. There are probably thousands of people out there with HIV. It's quite frightening, really. What we can do about it I don't know. America is five years ahead of us, and in New York the biggest killer of women between twenty and thirty is AIDS.'

The youngest caller at Open House to have become infected – 'although he wasn't sure if he'd been infected by being screwed or by sharing needles' – was a boy of fourteen. 'He had real problems getting here because he was supposed to be at school and every time he came here he had to tell his parents he was in detention.

'We have a church youth group from Burgess Hill coming on Sunday night, and we've found more and more that the best people to carry out education on AIDS are the people with HIV. What the group don't know is that when they get here their leader is going to be whisked off to the pub by me, and the youngsters are going to talk to a couple of lads with HIV who are only two years older than themselves.'

Marcus Riggs depended for back-up on three or four clergy he visited quite often, but he said his main support came from the staff. 'It is bliss working with lay people. I never want to work in a clergy team again as long as I live. But if I did work in a parish with someone older I'd insist on working with a woman. The idea of working with another priest just does my head in.

'By working at Open Door I've learned an awful lot about how I should go about being a parish priest if I was offered a living. I no longer use theological terms or concepts. I've stopped being a clergyman. I'm a priest. But in so many parishes the vicar-is-in-charge mentality remains rife, and it has to do with the insecurity of a lot of clergy, who actually need to be in charge. The clergy need to look hard at the way they relate to people, and the last place people who come here are likely to look for spiritual help is the institutional Church. Their experiences of parish churches is that they are incomprehensible, because much of what goes on in parishes bears no relation to people's experience of real living. The Church is often about why you are not the person the Church wants you to be, not about who you actually are. For midnight Mass at Christmas, four of our callers came with me to a parish church. When I celebrated Mass in the house at Easter, thirty-nine attended, because they knew that the worship going on here would relate to them as human beings.'

One advantage of Fr Riggs's roving commission was that it enabled him to encourage local parishes to adopt responsive attitudes towards those with HIV. 'I always preach on the gospel of the day,' he said, 'but I usually manage to work something into my sermon about AIDS.' Those parishes he found most sympathetic were in villages and on council estates; those least responsive, with one or two exceptions, were conservative evangelical parishes and extreme Anglo-Catholic ones. 'The problem is clergy who are not honest about sex. There is a major problem with gay clergy anyway, because the vast majority either live life in compartments or just can't cope with who they are. I see clergy who have got a drink problem, and they have all been gay and unable to cope with it. They are lonely, and very often have to say things they don't believe to be true. It must be soul destroying, really.'

You might think he would have found his own work soul destroying. In four years he had buried more than forty young people with AIDS. On the contrary. 'It's a great luxury being a priest here. I should think 5 per cent of the callers go to Mass, but all are searching spiritually, and I don't have to do those awful funerals for people you didn't know, when the widow tells you everyone loved him and he was a wonderful person and he'll be missed, and that's all you've got to go on. It's far easier to bury people you know, and after a funeral we all have a great knees-up. But it is true that with gays the family often fails to give support to the surviving partner. I went to visit a guy whose boyfriend had died just before Christmas, and his sister was there. They were very close except that the one thing they had never talked about was sexuality. The two men had lived together for nineteen years and you knew perfectly well the sister knew they were a gay couple but it had never been talked about. I told him, of course she knows, why don't you tell her and get it over and done with.'

Fr Riggs exhibited impatience with all forms of humbug, an impatience far more commonly encountered among clergy who have found fulfilment in non-parochial ministry than among parish priests who still feel they need to glance over their shoulder at their congregation all the time. He said, 'I've learned that trying to live out the gospel is only going to work if you are prepared to be open and honest with each other and share what's really going on. And I've learned that never again am *I* going to play role games. I'm not going to play vicar games any more. This life isn't a trial run. I've come to terms with being mortal earlier than a lot of people because I've buried so many people younger than myself.'

He was equally impatient with attendance statistics. 'I don't think the Church is in retreat at all. The Church is numbers-orientated, and I don't care if the numbers go down, quite frankly, because I don't believe in the numbers game. If you find effective ways of communicating, the numbers go up.' And he cited a nearby church where ten years earlier there had been a congregation of twenty, now there was one of 150. 'At a church where I've been doing an interregnum, numbers have gone up from sixty to ninety and all I've done is preach and say Mass.

'One of the major handicaps to a parish becoming a real community is often the parish priest, because you can become a real community only if you are open and honest with one another, and priests are often the worst at it. I have no qualms about frightening people off. If people leave because they can't cope with you proclaiming the truth as you perceive it, that's their problem. What concerns me is that when I snuff it I am able to look God in the eye and say, "Well, I did the best I could with the resources you gave me." And who I am is all I have to offer.

'The Archbishop of Canterbury seems to think if we are all fundamentalist and pushy we'll get there. I don't believe that at all. I don't think the Kingdom of God is about being pushy. If the Church is in crisis it is because there are an enormous number of people who worship in our churches who experience little connection between what they believe and what they've been challenged to do, which is to proclaim the Kingdom of God. After every sermon I listen to I ask, "So what?" And after 99.999 per cent of the sermons I hear, there is no "So what?" So nothing! "That was very nice, wasn't it." But if there's no "So what?" the gospel hasn't been heard.'

NINE

The Religious in Retreat

IT still comes as a surprise to many people to realise that within the Church of England are monasteries and convents. Monasteries in particular seem to be associated only with the past – swept away by Henry VIII. The great monastic tradition predates even the existence of parishes. In many areas, abbeys and monasteries formed the nucleus of religious life, and those who live and work as monks and nuns, whether ordained or not, are collectively known as religious. The first monastery in Britain was founded at Galloway in 397 by St Ninian, 200 years before England had an archbishop of Canterbury. At the Council of Whitby, held in 664, St Hilda strongly advocated maintaining the 'Celtic' form of Church administration, whereby the monasteries acted as the focus for administration, but she and her adherents were overruled, and the 'Roman' form of administration, based upon the diocese, was adopted. By the accession of Henry VIII there were sixteen dioceses, and after destroying the monasteries he created another six. (By no means all the pre-Reformation dioceses coincide with the forty-three dioceses in England today.)

During the Middle Ages, many of the monasteries had become renowned as centres of learning. The Benedictine abbey at Durham was built as a shrine for St Cuthbert, and buried with him at Durham is a monk of Jarrow, the Venerable Bede, author of the *Ecclesiastical History of the British People* and generally regarded as the greatest scholar of the eighth century. Bede recalled that from the age of seven he had passed all his life meditating on the Scriptures. 'Amid observance of monastic rule and daily chant of liturgy in the church,' he wrote, 'I have always loved to learn, to teach and to write.' Of Matthew Paris, a thirteenth-century monk and historian of St Albans, it was said that his 'copious chronicles' provided 'a mass of information about contemporary Europe and the Near East which is not to be found elsewhere'. Until 1220, almost every book illustration was produced in a monastery.

Henry VIII took a scythe to the monasteries partly because the general corruption within the Church had seeped into the religious life, partly because many were within the episcopal jurisdiction of bishops on the continent, and Henry wished to sever all ties with Rome. Cardinal Wolsey suppressed no fewer than twenty-two monasteries in order to begin work on building Christ Church in Oxford,[1] and for three centuries following the Reformation no monk or nun was to be seen in England. But it was almost inevitable that the nineteenth-century revival of interest in Catholic ritual, together with a rediscovery of the primacy of the sacraments, should have led to a revival of interest in the religious life. A sisterhood of Anglican nuns, the Society of the Holy Cross, was established in London in 1845, ironically in the very year that one of the three founders of the Oxford Movement, Henry Newman, was received into the Roman Catholic Church. Twenty years later the first monastic institution to be recognised appeared on the scene, under the direction of the vicar of Cowley, in Oxford, the Rev R. M. Benson; its members are often referred to as the Cowley Fathers. By this time one of the best-known communities for women, St Mary the Virgin, had also been founded, at Wantage in Oxfordshire in 1849. There are now forty-five communities for women and ten for men, consisting of some 860 women and 250 men. In essence, they all adhere to the original principles of St Benedict, who died in 543: monks and nuns live, work and pray as a community, usually for a good deal of the time in silence, but the practical ways in which they may fulfil their vocations vary a good deal.

The Community of the Resurrection at Mirfield in Yorkshire, founded in 1892 by Charles Gore, runs, among other things, a theological college (although there are recommendations for its closure). The Society of St Francis (the Franciscans were reintroduced into England in 1922) run a school for maladjusted boys. Like Mirfield, the Society of the Sacred Mission, founded one year later than Mirfield, has produced bishops from among their brethren, and carry out work in Japan, Australia and South Africa. The Bishop of Truro, Michael Ball, and his twin, Bishop Peter Ball, were founders of the Community of the Glorious Ascension. The sisters of the Community of the Epiphany in Truro, founded in 1883, help with parish work and in old people's homes. The Community of St Andrew at Westbourne Park in London, founded in 1861, engages in education and has among its sisters deacons and deaconesses. In 1987 the sisters of a Benedictine community, the Salutation of Blessed Mary the Virgin at Burford in Oxfordshire, decided that monks and nuns would share a contemplative life. Almost all religious communities conduct retreats or provide accommodation for private retreats; some farm, many distribute food to the poor, and at Mirfield, in particular, theologians of distinction have found the inspiration to write. In all these ways the modern religious communities reflect the inspirations of the earliest founders.[2]

Perhaps the greatest variation between monasteries lies in their buildings and architecture. You might easily walk past the front door of the Monastery of Christ the Saviour thinking you were not within a hundred miles of a religious community, in this case the Community of the Servants of the Will of God, founded at Crawley Down in West Sussex in 1953. In 1985 they set up their second monastery, in Hove, in a dull Edwardian terraced house, the only house now, apart from the spacious vicarage opposite, to be occupied by one family. This is an area of bedsitters, of students and down-and-outs. The monastery itself has lace curtains in the windows, and dustbins in the front garden.

Instructions for arrival, given over the telephone by the Prior, were extremely exact; ten minutes to noon. The first ring on the doorbell went unanswered. Was I early or late? Life here, as in all religious communities, is precisely regulated. I had been told that at noon there would be a service in the chapel (sext, as it happens), then there would be lunch, and as I had been invited on a major saint's day we should be allowed to talk. After lunch, said the Prior, we would wash up, then go back into the chapel; then we could have a chat. It all sounded rather forbidding. As it turned out, it was also an extremely cold day, and I had felt obliged to wear a suit. The brothers, however, were dressed in blue denim tunics they had run up themselves, and blue jeans, and they were well wrapped up in several pullovers – a wise precaution, for not a single radiator had been turned on and the house was freezing cold. I was seated in the chapel by the Prior, and as others came in they scarcely looked at me. One old boy had a frightful cough (they were all suffering, more or less, from coughs and sneezes), and he kept being given reproachful glances by a fellow brother. There is no way here for the uninitiated to differentiate between those who are ordained and those who are lay members; no one wears a dog collar. The chapel was bare, so I stared at the flock wallpaper, for apart from a couple of icons there was nothing to gladden the eye. Indeed, I found the whole house profoundly depressing.

A nice German lady eventually sat beside me. She and a younger woman from Birmingham were living with the community as what they call Seekers, trying to discover if they had a vocation to join the community, and if these two Seekers do apply to join, the community will have to decide whether to extend its membership to women. The German lady shared her plainchant book with me, for half the pages in mine were missing.

Before lunch I was quietly introduced to the small community. One visitor turned out to be the superior, who normally resides at the Monastery of the Holy Trinity at Crawley Down; another was a young man with his hair tied in a bun who had spent some time as a Seeker, had decided the monastic life was not for him, was now out of work and was being given a free lunch. The food was all laid out before we sat down (they seldom eat meat, more for economic reasons than from any principle, but someone had given them a turkey so this had been casseroled), and we stood for such a lengthy grace I feared the food would get cold. Before sitting down we all raised our glasses in a toast. I failed to catch to whom the toast had been proposed; it sounded like 'happy saint's day' but I may have misheard, and the drink turned out to be a mildly potent brew, some sort of home-made wine, for which the German lady had been responsible.

The turkey was excellent, as were the potatoes and cabbage. Then they tucked into Christmas cake, sent from New Zealand by relatives of one of the brothers. Surely, I suggested, it must have cost a fortune to post? Yes, but had these kind relatives sent a postal order, and a cake had been purchased locally, it would not have been the same. Conversation was general and animated; normally someone reads a book.

The Superior explained that they had expanded into Hove at the suggestion of the bishop in order to work alongside the local parish priest. The Community of the Servants of the Will of God is now forty years old, but compared to the ancient monastic orders, it is a novice. 'How do you found a new community?' I asked. 'Could I found one?'

'Not unless you were called by God to do it,' the Superior explained.

It is quite pointless talking to religious about the religious life unless you are prepared to suspend your own disbelief, for they use a language that makes sense only if you speak it too. Their lives are what one might call 'God-centred'. Almost every statement of importance is prefaced with or by the assumption that one's task is to discover God's will, and that basically God is in charge of events and knows what He is doing. These attitudes do not, however, come across in any dogmatic way; they come as naturally to members of the community as someone else saying, 'On Monday I shall go to the office because I have my living to earn.'

'We don't choose this life,' I was told. 'God chooses us to live it.' So what of free will? 'You could reject God's call, of course. The basic test as to whether you are drawn to this life is one of self-sacrifice. You have to go through a dying to self.' What great sacrifice had the Prior, a former secular parish priest, been compelled to make? He paused to consider, and decided it was giving up going for long walks.

Their belief in prayer is absolute. 'I was wondering who to invite to lunch today,' the Prior told me, 'and then your letter turned up.' The day in Hove is rooted in prayer, and begins liturgically with vespers in the parish church at 6.30 p.m. followed by a celebration of the Eucharist. The community then return to the monastery, just nine doors up the road, to go into Greater Silence until 9.30 the next morning. In the evening in their own chapel they say the 'Jesus Prayer', and they are up at 4.30 and back in the chapel to sing matins at 5 a.m. For an hour they pray alone in their cell, and at seven return to the chapel for lauds. 'How many hours a day do you actually spend in prayer?' I asked. The Prior caught himself beginning to tot them up, and then said, 'In effect, Michael, it's twenty-four.' I suggested they must sleep at some stage. Ah, but even when asleep one is still a part of the community's life of prayer. 'How many hours a day are you writing? Even when you are not writing you are thinking about your work, aren't you?'

Above our heads a banging and crashing broke out. 'That's Brother Patrick making the bread,' the Prior explained. 'At Crawley Down we have a small farm and a few cows, but basically we are dependent on what people give us. We don't own anything personally. We have a clothes store, and people give us socks and things like that. No, we don't have any pocket money.' They never take a holiday either, but they do go into a kind of busman's retreat or 'rest period' at Crawley Down, and if an elderly relative is unwell they may be permitted to pay a visit, but usually only for a day. No wonder it takes seven years to become professed for life; no one would want to make a mistake.

The community would say that the primary aim of their life was to deepen, through prayer, their dependence upon God so that 'the whole of life becomes a continuous act of praise and intercession'. And they would go on to say that their aim was 'not merely to celebrate the Eucharist, but to live a eucharistic life, in other words, to allow the basic movement of the Eucharist – Christ's gathering and uniting of all things in himself, by the Spirit, to the Glory of God the Father – to be the basic movement of our own lives'. And if this means nothing to an outsider, so be it.

At 9.30 a.m. the brothers meet in a room leading to the chapel (it was here that the Prior and I talked, and he did turn on an antique gas fire, or I should not have survived), and this is when tasks for the day are allocated. And it is at 9.30 a.m. that they enter into Lesser Silence, which means they can speak when strictly necessary. 'On Thursdays we have supper a little earlier than usual, about 5.20 p.m., and that is a talking meal.' Corporately or alone in their cells they are at conscious prayer for at least three hours a day, and talk for nothing like so long. 'God works with and through people who pray,' said the Prior. 'He makes himself known to us, humanly speaking, through the Spirit.'

Was there anything the Prior would sooner be doing than living the contemplative life of a monk? 'No,' was the instant answer. And then, very gently, he added, 'Don't misunderstand me, Michael. It just isn't a real question.'

The parish priest of St Patrick's, John Sharpe, arrived two years before the community, to find the church 'only just hanging on by its fingertips'. He wonders, in fact, whether the Church in his area, an area he described as 'profoundly unstable', had ever taken root at all. He felt a mission to build up a decaying parish, and knew what sort of tasks lay ahead. The bishop, Eric Kemp, had a plan to resurrect the area by introducing the ancient model: religious community, theological students and parish combined. So an outpost of students from Chichester Theological College took up residence in the rambling vicarage. 'It worked to an extent, but the parish was just so run down. I don't think the bishop understood just how hard one had to work to do anything at all. The students all had their own academic work to do, and after two years they left. Just as they left, the monks arrived.

'We have adopted many of their patterns of worship, which has been very helpful. They've given us a sort of stability, I suppose, in an area that is *very* unstable. They have helped us to develop the prayer life in the parish, which I think is of paramount importance. But they don't actually integrate deeply with us. I feel that we are one community, but I doubt whether they do.

'What has occurred is a remarkable revival of worship, largely among people who had never been to church before. In 1983 there might have been fifteen at the Sunday parish Mass. On a Sunday there are now at least 100, and during the week, when the community come to the church for Mass in the evening, a congregation of thirty is a regular occurrence, some of them people who have drifted in from the night shelter.'

I decided to put some of these claims to the test, and wandered into the church at 6.45 on a Wednesday evening. An assortment of tramps, alcoholics and the mentally ill were all jumbled up with parishioners in pews ranged round a free-standing altar in the nave, and vespers was under way, the plainchant being led by a young estate agent. Father Sharpe, in alb, sat in the centre; I recognised two monks from the monastery, one of whom smiled as I entered. Another was in alb and stole, ready to assist at the Mass. At the back of the church a boy of about fifteen, wearing jeans, gaily swung a censer. He had a bit of a cold (caught from a monk? I wondered), and blew his nose from time to time.

Some of those who were going to stay in the night shelter sat at the back, against the wall, and after vespers, when Fr Sharpe moved into a corner to put on his chasuble, he rustled them up into the body of the congregation. Behind me an old tramp sat huddled in a blanket, and there was a good deal of bronchial wheezing. No description of the liturgy could by itself convey the unselfconscious devotion of the service. Extempore prayers, for handicapped children in particular, were offered by a lay woman; a new young worker from the night shelter (he would be preparing breakfast in the morning) read the lesson. The boy server seemed immensely efficient, only breaking down in giggles after the consecration, for which everyone gathered in a strange intimacy round the altar, within feet of the celebrant.

A home-baked roll was consecrated; the paten and chalice were modern earthenware. Yet there was nothing folksy about the occasion. At the Peace I was embraced by two religious, and everyone moved round to kiss or shake hands. I commented afterwards to a friend, a priest who had gone along with me, on the youthfulness of many of the congregation. 'They go because they love God,' he told me. Everyone, including many of the down-and-outs who were almost certainly not confirmed, received communion. It was a gentle, moving experience, which seemed by the nature of those present – unwashed, wearing mittens, unpatronised and essentially unimpressed and at home – to offer a glimpse of what worship may have been like in the Middle Ages; a rediscovery within the English Church of a marriage of reverence, impressive ritual and sensible simplicity. All this had been brought about by placing a tiny religious community in the street.

There are no parish organisations. Fr Sharpe told me, 'Our main function is worship. We sing morning and evening prayer and Mass every day. Yet more people come to see me here than they have ever done anywhere else. I hear more confessions than ever before, and in a pastoral sense I'm much more of a priest here than I've ever been before. And really we are dealing largely with pagan people, so our general attitude is to welcome people into the community without fussing too much about baptism and confirmation. If initially we fuss about the sacraments, then people will just be frightened away. Once they've joined us and feel at home and have got used to the Christian way, that's the time to broach the question of baptism and confirmation.

'I've always been dissatisfied with Sunday evening worship, so at 5 p.m. on Sunday we have simple Taizé chants, the lighting of the evening lamp, then a laying-on of hands – a very simple affair. There is an exchange of the Peace, then a short sermon which people discuss afterwards. We have tea, and then go back into church for a very simple form of benediction.'

What seems to have happened is that the spirituality emanating from St. Patrick's sparks a response in people whose lives are often tragically disoriented. 'Many people here have no family backgrounds. A lot of people in this parish are in very, very difficult circumstances; financially, spiritually, morally, everything you can think of. I'm not altogether sure at present who lives next door. It's all tiny rooms, and people sometimes come here simply to get lost.'

The night shelter was opened in the winter of 1985, and in the first six years it provided 30,000 beds: a thin mattress on a stone floor, blankets, security, warmth, a supper at 9.30 and breakfast in the morning. 'We take anyone who comes, whatever their state. Originally everyone had a terrible drink-related problem. Then we saw increasing numbers of mentally ill, because of the closure of mental hospitals. And now there are a tremendous number of people using us who have just fallen on hard times.' On 27 May 1993 one such, Andy Corrigan, was stabbed to death in the church.

How did Fr Sharpe feel the bishop rated the success of the experiment? 'I don't know, to be honest. Once a year I go and see him and tell him what I'm doing, whether he likes it or not. But personally I feel we have claimed the church back for God. It's prayed in. We have put down some roots. The neighbourhood know we are here. But it remains a very shifting population. Just as it looks as though someone is settled and things are working out, they up and move on. If I get into a muddle there are a number of routes I can take out of it. For lots of people, it seems, there is no way out of the muddle. It just gets worse and worse as they get older and older.'

At this point in the conversation the doorbell rang, and Fr Sharpe let in a young man. He sat in the dining room, gently rocking on a chair. While Fr Sharpe was sorting out some literature for me, the young man saw me standing in the hall, about to depart. Rigidly he held out his hand, and when I shook hands he held on to me. He might have been thirty, it was hard to tell; several teeth were missing, he reeked of alcohol, his face was blotchy and he was clearly undernourished. Some incoherent tale about his children emerged among the tears. Drink was ruining his life, he told me, still holding my hand. I told him Fr Sharpe was free to see him now, and left him with the only person he had thought to turn to at five o'clock in the evening. Any idea that people no longer call upon the clergy when they are in distress is ludicrous.

When the Community of St Peter, a nursing order of nuns in Woking, Surrey, was left a legacy, it asked the bishop of Guildford what it should do with it. Build a retreat house, he said, and so a purpose-built retreat house was opened in the grounds of the convent in 1968. To some extent it serves as a diocesan retreat house, providing accommodation for ordination retreats and ordination selection conferences, but the warden, Barbara Ingamells, who is employed by the Community, is more or less free to organise her own programme, and a varied affair it is too. There are retreats for gardeners, for those interested in sacred dance, for parishes, for people who want a silent retreat conducted by a favourite priest, for those who have never been on retreat before, for people who just want to get away on their own for a day or a weekend.

Mrs Ingamells's husband, licensed by the bishop but also employed by the Community of St Peter, is chaplain. Two of the sisters work in the house, one as sacristan, the other in charge of domestic arrangements. With twenty-nine bedrooms in almost constant use and the needs of different styles of retreat to be catered for, it seems amazing that the house is so quiet and orderly. I arrived on the second day of a silent retreat being conducted for two dozen people who had come from Wales, London or the south coast. Most had seen an advertisement in *Vision*, the journal of the National Retreat Association.[3] All but two were women, and all but a handful were old. One lady was nearly blind and had brought her guide dog. They were paying £76 each for four nights, which included the conductor's fee. The cost of a visit run by the staff is £19 a day.

We tiptoed into the library, past retreatants wandering around in the hall, gazing at the bookstall. I soon came to the conclusion that silence might prove a greater hardship for the warden than her visitors, she was so fluent and light-hearted, the kind of person almost anyone might feel tempted to unburden themselves to in a very short time indeed. She thought her retreat house was fairly typical.

'We have a broad selection of people who come to us,' she explained. 'Although we are Anglican-based we have people from all denominations, and retreat work is spreading terrifically through the Free Churches. One of our biggest retreats is for Methodist ministers, because they have no retreat houses of their own.

'On the Anglican front, what we are finding is that people are coming much more as individuals. They still come on organised retreats, but often they ring and say, "I'm just dying to get away for a few days, can I come?" And provided we have a spare room, yes, we'll take them. We provide almost whatever they want. If they just want to come and be alone and quiet and go out for walks and do their own thing, that's fine. If they want an individually guided retreat in which somebody will talk to them each day and guide them through their retreat we'll do that, because my husband and I are both trained. If they want to come to whatever's going on in the house and join in, they can.

'Next weekend, for example, we have a parish in Reading bringing twenty-two people. My husband and I have been asked to lead that retreat. At the same time I have a young person who is thinking of going into the ministry coming to stay. She comes to see me on a regular basis to talk about her situation. I've also got two other people coming on Saturday just for the day. They will join in the Eucharist and a meditation, otherwise they're going to do their own thing. And at the same time there's somebody who rang up and said she just wants to get away completely, she doesn't want to do anything set, she just wants to be on her own. So I shall have all these different things happening at the same time. What we try not to do is put a talking organisation alongside a silent retreat, because that destroys the peace and silence of the house.'

Silence: there are those who cannot wait to be embraced by it, others who are naturally apprehensive. 'A lot of them come with anxiety and trepidation the first time, but I think they find it much easier than they expected. We did have two people who couldn't stand it and left after the first day. But usually they don't find it half as difficult as they think they will. You don't go around ignoring everybody. You smile at people. You open doors for people. You get to know people tremendously well in silence. You really do. It's one of the strange things. The meals are taken in silence, but you're passing things to each other. Silence is a means to an end, not an end in itself, the end being that the person who comes on retreat is totally free to communicate with God, to think their own thoughts, just to be themselves.

'Having a meal in silence isn't such a strain as you would think. About a fortnight ago my husband was serving crême caramel and he dropped one down somebody's neck. Everybody got the giggles. Things are much funnier in silence. The other day we had a cheesecake with a very hard base, and everybody was stubbing their spoons, and one table got the giggles, which set everyone else off. But it doesn't matter. The Lord has a sense of humour, so why worry?

'We play music during meals and it does cut out the noise of knives and forks. Usually quiet classical things. You have to assess your group. This lot we have now would want classical music, definitely. For one group I played what I thought was some beautiful panpipe music but at the end of the retreat one lady complained she couldn't eat her breakfast with "that horrible squeaking noise".'

The day I was there, a Mozart chamber work was followed by the Unfinished Symphony. It is difficult to know where to look when eating in silence, because you cannot stare at the person opposite, and the tension on my table was certainly eased when one of the nuns, who, like the warden, was seldom far from laughing, mimed politely to know if I would like more gravy or vegetables. We had roast chicken, cabbage and boiled potatoes, rhubarb and custard (was I back at school, I wondered? But fortunately I like rhubarb), and fruit and cheese. Skirts and woolly cardigans seemed to be the order of the day. A few faces were permanently pursed, others gave one a friendly smile.

I plucked up courage to approach the conductor, an austere and elderly Anglo-Catholic priest who rather alarmingly demanded to know if I was a Christian, one of only two people in the course of my research who did. I suggested that in order to go on a retreat such as his – during the week and at a cost of £76 excluding fares – you needed to be retired and well-off. He saw nothing wrong with this, just as he dismissed the idea that going on retreat was the same thing as going on holiday. Indeed, he claimed to be a severe retreat conductor, and described a retreat as hard work. Nor was he fussed by people – fans, really – who tended to follow him around. 'For this conductor we are always chock-a-block full, with a waiting list,' I had been told. Who was he, the cleric wanted to know, to turn away regular retreatants? He only regretted the necessity for him to take so many retreats a year – about fifteen – because of the lack of good retreat conductors. It was, he said, a gift, and if you had it you should use it.

The pattern for each day of this retreat was identical: Eucharist at 8 a.m., an address at ten, a meditation in the chapel at 12.30, lunch at one, tea at four, an address at five, supper at 6.45 and another address in chapel at 8 p.m. followed by compline. Those who come on a retreat for beginners are allowed to talk on Saturday afternoon, 'so that they can relax a bit if they are not used to silence. We provide a Taizé evening for them, with the chapel alight with candles, and people sitting on the floor, all very atmospheric.' Mrs Ingamells is treasurer of the Anglo-Catholic Charismatic Committee, hence her interest in liturgical experiment.

Who else comes to St Columba's House in Woking, not necessarily on retreat but for a conference? Groups from the General Synod, the hospice movement, the Church Army, the Bible Society, the United Society for the Propagation of the Gospel. With chairs instead of pews, the chapel is very versatile. 'People can do what they like with the chapel,' I was told. It is a large and airy but reverent building, with the Sacrament reserved and other tinges of Anglo-Catholicism, as one would expect in a retreat house attached to a convent.

There is no formal training for running a retreat house. You just pick it up, but both Barbara Ingamells and her husband attended a three-year part-time course on counselling and spiritual direction run in London by the National Retreat Association. According to Mrs Ingamells, there is a very fine line between counselling and spiritual direction. 'Some people come here to sort out a particular problem in their lives, and if they wish we will talk and pray with them. Other people may come for an actual spiritual direction session. They usually come at regular intervals, to talk specifically about their spiritual lives. We are both available to lead one-to-one retreats, which is the up and coming thing now. An eight-day retreat is the norm.'

The words of Jesus as recorded in Chapter 6 of the Gospel according to St Mark, 'Come with me by yourselves to some place apart where you can rest quietly', seem to be being heeded by more and more laity of all persuasions. When the retreat and conference centre at Glastonbury (described in an estate agent's brochure at the turn of the century as 'a gentleman's residence with interesting ruins in the grounds') was opened in 1931, 450 people made their retreat there; today the annual figure is 2,000. There are about thirty diocesan retreat houses providing some 1,000 beds, and a dozen religious houses that conduct retreats, providing another 250 beds.

Abbey House in Glastonbury was in silent retreat for 144 days in 1991. Martin Oliver, the warden at Glastonbury, made the interesting point that 'with a larger number in society living singly and experiencing silence for long stretches in lonely lives, it is good to offer a retreat in which they may share their faith and their interest with others in "safe" surroundings. They very quickly become a temporary community and there is much mutual problem confiding and support.'

Amanda, who did not go on her first retreat until she was in her forties, was now so hooked she was training to lead retreats herself. Her first retreat had been organised by her parish, and she still recalled that for her 'it was wonderful. It opened up something within me. It put me on a completely new path. I found a need within myself and I am now seeing that need in other people. That first retreat was a silent one and it was my first experience of silence, and for me it was, well, just wonderful.

'Going on retreat with your parish helps people to grow closer together. How does it work? I don't know, to be honest. I think it is where God takes over and we have to step back. It's very difficult to talk about retreats, because they are such a personal thing. Everybody takes away something special for themselves, and after the retreat the benefits are still working within you. My husband would tell you it has changed me completely. I'm a much more peaceful person. I don't rush around any more, and it's made me much more tolerant. Much, much more tolerant. And more understanding, I hope. I am less judgemental than I used to be. Ask my two sons! These sound very pious words, but I believe that by going on retreat I have handed my life over to God.'

While the need for retreat houses seems to be ever on the increase, many of those who run retreats, nuns and monks in the religious communities, are in serious decline. The first priority of the first post-Reformation English monastic order, the Society of St John the Evangelist, was to conduct retreats for the clergy, and this task, at St Edward's House in

Westminster, it still performs. But the Society's Oxford house has been reduced to four members, and in London there remains only a dwindling nucleus of a religious community hit, like many others, by a dearth in vocations. Most of the brothers (all but one are ordained) are in their seventies.

'What we would like,' the Father Superior, told me, 'is one or two men coming to us at the age of thirty or forty, but there would still be a great age gap. There was an influx of members to the religious life after the war, and at one time we had seven or eight novices, not all of whom stayed. With us the novitiate lasts two years, during which time people are making up their minds whether this is really the life for them, and the community is deciding whether they seem to be suitable. But I would say there has been a general falling-off in numbers since the late 1950s, certainly the 1960s.'

This he attributed to a reluctance by people in many walks of life to commit themselves; as comparable examples he cited marriage and the drop in vocations to the priesthood. But then he recalled that the Franciscans, based in Birmingham, still attract quite a number of new people. 'Although,' he added, 'while quite a lot come, quite a lot go!' St John the Evangelist – the Cowley Fathers – last recruited a novice two years ago, but he transferred to an autonomous American congregation of the Society in Massachusetts, where there are at present eighteen brethren, two in their eighties but most a good deal younger than the inhabitants of St Edward's House.

It was in 1904 that St Edward's House was built for the Society, a brief walk away from Westminster Abbey. From its charming roof garden, mainly tended by the Father Superior, there is a splendid view of the Houses of Parliament. Off the library is a small Lady Chapel, where the Sacrament is reserved and holy oil kept in permanent readiness, for here a good deal of spiritual and physical healing takes place. But the monks and their guests gather for the daily offices in a larger, panelled chapel with an imposing canopy over the altar and a statue of the Virgin Mary. It is uncluttered, indeed unadorned, but relaxing; life at St Edward's House is generally conducted in a fairly relaxed atmosphere. Few rise before 6 a.m., matins is said at seven, the Eucharist is celebrated at 7.30 and breakfast is eaten in silence; but everyone chatters after terce at 8.45 a.m.

The monks are back in chapel for sext at 12.45 p.m., and lunch is a very informal affair, with no general grace and everyone helping themselves to excellent soup and wholemeal bread, cold meats and salads, fruit and cheese. The refectory has acquired two fifteenth-century carved panels, and the other treasure in the house is a seventeenth-century icon from the Cathedral of St Petersburg, which hangs in the sitting room.

To round off the day the community say Evensong at 6.30, listen to music at supper and go into silence after compline, at 9.30 p.m. Hearing confessions (there is always a confessor on duty between noon and 12.20 p.m., 4.00 and 4.30 p.m. and 6.00 and 6.30 p.m.) and offering spiritual advice and guidance, fills part of any day. As the Father Superior explained, 'So many people who want to come and talk say, "My vicar hasn't got time." Many parish priests are so busy doing this and that, they haven't got time to really sit down and talk to people at length. But some have come to know us through a retreat and then ask if they can come on a more regular basis. It may sound rather funny to come to a monk with marriage problems but people do.'

So how do monks like Father James Naters, the Father Superior, keep abreast of the problems of the modern world? 'Through television, through newspapers, through meeting people.' He has even learned to use the word 'outreach'. 'Our one lay brother has been very much involved in working with the homeless, and with youngsters at Centrepoint, and with the mentally ill. He's also been asked to speak at seminars on problems like AIDS. We are very glad he has got this outreach. None of the rest of us have quite that same outreach. But there's another member of the Society who's recently discovered he is slightly dyslectic and he is now hoping to teach youngsters with dyslectic problems.' Another ordained brother has a regular counselling time with dropouts at St Martin-in-the-Fields.

St Edward's House can accommodate up to nine guests, and those retreats conducted by its own members are silent. Many people use the house for a one-day meeting. Yet it seems that while religious communities like the Society of St John the Evangelist continue to fulfil a need for people on the outside, they have not rekindled desire among a new generation to join them on the inside. There is of course far more to being a monk than disdaining worldly goods and pleasures; there is the positive commitment to a life of daily prayer and contemplation, the routine of worship, the virtually unvarying company. The original rule of life drawn up by Father Benson for the Cowley Fathers, drawn both from Benedictine and Dominican traditions, has been modified and is no more rigorous than the rule of life observed by many of the largest and best known of the Church of England's male communities, like the Community of the Resurrection. Yet they too are suffering from a shortage of vocations. The Mirfield Fathers left South Africa in 1970, and now they have decided to abandon their connections with the twelfth-century Royal Foundation of St Katherine in Stepney, withdrawing no fewer than five priests and a lay brother from 'the maintenance of regular praise and prayer' in buildings dedicated to providing accommodation for conferences, retreats and clubs. Unless new vocations to the religious life do materialise, the sense of serenity that greets one on the doorstep of a monastery like St Edward's House, a serenity that is the by-product of a lifetime of concentrated worship, will become a vanishing memory.

When Doris – who now signs herself Doris of the Cross – said she wanted to join a nursing order of nuns, her stepmother told her, 'I can't understand you, you'll have to do what you're told, you know. And don't come here in those long gowns picking up all the microbes off the streets.' Sister Doris, now Mother Superior of the Community of the Servants of the Cross, has been trailing her 'long gown' along the streets, hospital wards and lately the corridors of the Convent of the Holy Rood at Lindfield in Sussex for half a century (she was professed in 1943). Had she any regrets about the life she chose when still so young?

'None at all. I didn't want to get married, I just wanted to give my life to nursing. I was a bit miserable when we came here to Lindfield, because there was no nursing, and I thought, what *am* I going to do? But when we came here it was luxury.

We had lino on the floors. And a bit of mat by the bed. And hot and cold water in our rooms. We even had a hot-water bottle and an eiderdown.'

At seventy-five the Mother Superior was one of the youngest of the sisters. She darted from her room into the hall when I arrived, whisked me back into her room, sat me down by the window and began at once to recount the history of her order. There were just a dozen sisters left, eight of them over eighty. The nursing they used to do has been taken over by the National Health Service, there are virtually no new vocations in sight, and hers appears to be one of numerous Anglican orders of nursing sisters threatened with extinction.

They were founded in Fulham, in 1882, moved to Worthing after eleven years, 'where we nursed what you call geriatrics these days', and finally settled, in 1967, on an estate near Haywards Heath, rather worldly on the exterior but spoiled by ugly extensions. The Mother Superior explained, 'We are dedicated to the Holy Cross and to works of reparation – making good for our own sins and for the sins of the whole world. It's been a hard life, but I don't want to give up easily.

'But the nursing became too heavy. We used to have sixty patients and no outside staff. We built an extension when we came here because we had twenty sisters then. We didn't know what work we should have to do, because obviously we could no longer do nursing. Then we were offered retreat work.'

As well as serving as a diocesan retreat house, the community lays on facilities in its hall for clergy meetings, golden weddings, quiet days for groups. They follow the rule of St Augustine, but in deference to the advancing age of the sisters there is a certain relaxation. 'Some naughty nuns still get up at four o'clock,' the Mother Superior told me. 'That's not necessary, but I can't get them to stop. I get up at 5.20 a.m. Actually it was 4.20 this morning, but that was a mistake. Have I done a penance? No, it was an accident! I didn't do it on purpose!

'Our sisters are long-lived because they are active. I think it's when people retire that they go senile. I've proved that. If you give an old lady something to do she's quite happy doing it. If they haven't got anything to do they become rather naughty. They go round during silence in the afternoon talking to the gardeners.'

The Mother Superior had more serious criticism to make of her sisters, alas. 'They get so niggardly with each other when they haven't got anything to occupy themselves. They get very, very scratchy. The chaplain has had to speak to them once or twice to sort them out.'

But with inevitable tensions building up as the community tries to adjust to old age and to the loss of its original purpose, the overriding vocation remains intact. 'The purpose of the religious life is to serve Our Lord unbiased. We are not committed to anything else. We commit ourselves entirely to this sort of life. I would feel at sea if I was free.'

I asked what the general consensus was in the house on the question of the ordination of women. The response, 'No!', came with the velocity of a bullet from a gun. 'I think a woman's work is in a house, in a family.'

Foolishly, I suggested that hers was not.

'It is, you know. Very much so. It's my job to look after the other sisters.'

They have a half-day off once a month and a full day once a year. 'They can go shopping on their day off as long as they don't buy anything very expensive. If they want to go and see a relation or a friend they can. We don't touch our pensions, it all goes to the bursar, so if they want money they come and ask.'

The Mother Superior, in her sitting room lined with books, with a clock that had long since ceased to tick, and flowering bulbs on the windowsill, could well have been a kindly headmistress. In the kitchen she introduced me to Sister Monica, 'the odd-jobber', wearing an apron. She plays the organ for the local church (an additional small source of income for the community) and spends much pleasurable time feeding wild cats.

Books were stacked rather haphazardly throughout the house, and there was an atmosphere not so much of the cloister as, well, a run-down girls' boarding school. New recruits used to bring with them whatever capital they possessed. 'I didn't have any to bring,' the Mother Superior confessed, rather wistfully.

This is hardly surprising. She was one of seven children, and only ten when her mother died. She recalled her childhood in New Zealand without enthusiasm. 'My stepmother and I didn't get on well together. We could suffer each other for a while but if she ever said anything about one of my brothers or sisters, then we came to grief.'

A diminutive nun bubbling with amusement called Sister Margaret saved up her annual day off to go on an air flight, her first ever. She had met an air hostess while browsing in Woolworth's, and the air hostess arranged for the trip to Genoa. 'I wasn't frightened. Oh, not a bit. I had a most *wonderful* time. It was fun, it was wholesome.' The crew all signed a card for her, inscribed 'To a Jet Setting Nun'.

Sister Margaret toddled off to make tea, which she wheeled in to the Mother Superior's room on a trolley. 'I won't have any, dear,' said the Mother Superior, eyeing two cups and plates. My visit had been arranged for Ash Wednesday, so I asked if she had given up afternoon tea for Lent.

'Lent doesn't begin until Sunday,' I was informed.

'I thought Lent began on Ash Wednesday.'

'Well, they tell me it doesn't! But come to think of it, we certainly didn't have meat for dinner. We had soup and dumplings. Quite often we have dumplings, don't we, sister? Sometimes it's stew and dumplings. Sometimes it's mince with a dumpling.

'If a novice came I'd let her see how we live, how we tick over. We put out an appeal on the local radio last year, for helpers for our sale, and one of the people who replied is coming to see if she wants to be a novice. There is another coming who's a deacon. I think they are both over fifty. If they were younger there would be too big an age gap. This is giving me hope.'

A parish from Enfield, or part of it, lie sprawled on the lawn in the sunshine. The setting is a beautiful Jacobean stone house in the Cotswold town of Burford, 20 miles west of Oxford, a house with a detached chapel built in 1662 to commemorate both the Restoration and the new Book of Common Prayer. They have gone on retreat for a day to the Priory of Our Lady, the Church's first experiment in a mixed community.

There are separate telephone numbers for the brothers and sisters, but unless the community soon attracts more women novices, their number may become a spare line. The community was only saved from extinction by Archbishop Runcie, who had used the house for consecration retreats; in 1987, following a dreadful spate of deaths among the nuns, he suggested men should be admitted. Brother Robert and Brother Thomas were the first to arrive. They have since been joined by Tom, who is twenty-nine and used to work in banking, and eventually by three others, so that now the community consists of six monks, three of whom are ordained, and three nuns, one of whom, Mary, the last female novice to enter the community, is the Mother Prioress. The Benedictine titles Dame and Dom (originally mistress and master) have been dropped, and strictly speaking even Brother and Sister are taboo; they are all known only by their Christian names.

Robert was on duty and opened the front door. 'I'm on the typewriter at the moment,' he said. 'Come in and look at the books. Mother will join us for tea at half past four.' I was gratified to find some of my own books on sale in the hall, where retreatants who did not care for sunbathing sat in a silence as stony as the walls, and did not even look at me. Robert reappeared, having presumably got off the typewriter, and bowed me into the refectory.

'Benedict,' he explained, 'was quite specific, you must never call anyone by their Christian name, you should always call them Brother. But the Church reflects changes in British society, and we are following the spirit of Benedict but not the letter. He was writing at the time of the collapse of the Roman Empire, and there were two problems confronting the Church; the emancipation of slaves and an enormous number of soldiers looking for jobs. And what he was seeking in monasticism, which was originally a lay movement anyway, was an absolute equality. When, before the Second Vatican Council, people were known as Brother or Father, depending whether they were ordained, the lay brother was regarded as a dogsbody. That's all gone. Myself, I answer to everything, as long as it isn't rude.'

Robert is in fact a priest, a former chaplain to Trinity College, Cambridge. He had considered the religious life while training at Westcott House. Although he looks quite young, he said, 'My pilgrimage has been a very long one. You could write a book about it. How do you test a vocation? I don't know, really. I suppose I'm testing it because I'm living it. We take it in stages. We take simple vows for three years; solemn vows mean a commitment for life. I'm in my fourth year. The belief that we take vows of poverty, chastity and obedience is a popular misconception. They were invented by St Francis of Assisi. The traditional monastic vows are stability, conversion of life and obedience. Stability means you will make this place your home and the people in it your family until the day you die. Conversion of life means your whole life will be given over to Christ, which certainly includes a commitment to celibacy. Conversion has to occur day by day, week by week. It is not a flash on the road to Damascus. It affects everything – your attitude to people, and to the way you live your life. A monk no longer even has his own body at his disposal.'

The house was a monastery in the distant past, but when its numbers slumped to two monks it became one of the first casualties of the dissolution of the small houses. The female Benedictine community bought the property in 1949, and at that time Mass was said in Latin, plainchant was the order of the day, and I would not have been admitted even to the refectory. Only a doctor or a priest could get past a leather door that marked the bounds of enclosure. Had I managed to penetrate the chapel I should have had to sit at the back and wait for communion to be brought to me. Much has changed, but I doubt whether this would have worried the essentially laissez-faire James I, who stayed in the house on his progress from Scotland to London in 1603, still less his grandson Charles II, who made use of the place for the horse racing at Burford, lodging Nell Gwynn at the Bull Hotel.

The day starts at six with private prayer and meditation. At 7 a.m. the community are in the chapel for lauds, which lasts about forty-five minutes. After breakfast they carry out domestic chores. 'One week you may find yourself responsible for guests, the next the laundry, or preparing vegetables.' At 9.15 they are back in chapel for terce, 'and then we have a daily conference just to go through the diary so that everybody knows what's happening. Then, unless you are the cook, we have a morning work period given over to study – a study of the Scriptures and the rule of St Benedict. Benedict had a balance of study, manual work and prayer. His rule directs you to the Scriptures and the Scriptures point you to Christ.' At noon they celebrate the Eucharist. 'We moved it from early morning to the centre of the day because we have a number of people who come as day guests. Lunch is silent. There's a reading. At 2 p.m. we have nones.'

The community owns 12 acres of land, which includes a graveyard and a Christmas tree plantation, 'which is one way we earn our keep'. They also run a dried-flower business and a printing press, and Brother Stewart mounts icons. In addition, they have accommodation for five guests. 'Having resident guests is actually quite hard work. People often want to natter, and sometimes they have quite serious problems they want to talk about. Because we have such limited accommodation we don't like people staying more than one week. They have to fall in with the routine of the house, although there's no three-line whip to go to chapel. But this isn't a hotel – although, if Robert Runcie hadn't rescued it, it might easily be one by now – and we are very cagey about people who want a cheap weekend in the Cotswolds, because we make no formal charge. We leave an envelope in the bedrooms and invite people to make a contribution. We suggest sixteen quid a day. The local pub charges £32 for bed and breakfast. Sixteen pounds literally covers our costs. Having worked in a bank, Thomas does the sums and makes sure we get it right.

'We need to go deeper into our monastic life,' said Robert. 'Our guests are virtually living on top of us. You meet them in the corridors. You meet them going into the loo.' So the community are appealing for a quarter of a million pounds to refurbish a guest house. They remain an enclosed order in the sense that they do not go out to parishes or conduct missions overseas, 'but the grill has gone. The purpose of our community is to give glory to God after the manner of St Benedict, by the offering of our lives. We are living out our baptismal vows in a particular way, which many people think is cranky. Certainly the idea of stability in a very mobile world seems crackers. People are used to sort of zapping round all over the place. But you are stable here because you can't run away from yourself or run away from God, and a lot of people do run away into hyperactivity.' He was just explaining that they did not have booze at Burford – 'well, we do have a drink on Christmas Day, but it would be very hard to become an alcoholic in a religious community'[4] – when he suddenly jumped up and chased a couple out of the garden. The young man, after all, was wearing only a pair of shorts. Apparently he said to Robert, 'What religion are you?'

'Christian, I said.'

Back on the subject of his vocation, Brother Robert said, 'It's very easy to be romantic about the monastic life. It is not like that. The romanticism wears off in twenty-four hours. It can be very boring. It's very monotonous. It's very samey. You need a lot of stamina and perseverance to keep going.'

So why did he continue?

'Because I want to do it. Why does one do anything? I'm here because I want to be here. I believe in God. And I believe that God loves me. And being me, being Robert, is about being a monk. It's about singleness, I think, probably. Being a single person. But I am also someone who needs to live in a community. It gives a shape to your life.'

Was he single because he was a monk, or a monk because he was single?

'That's a good question. I actively chose not to marry or to have any other lifestyle, cohabiting with anybody. That was me. I knew that any sort of marriage was not for me before I became a monk. I do recognise myself profoundly at a basic sort of level as a sort of single person. If I wasn't here I would be living by myself. That is me. But everybody has their own story to tell and their own pilgrimage. I'm not sure you can generalise just from me. But for me, there was also the call to community, to be in fellowship with others. That must have something to do with loneliness, embracing one's interior loneliness and exploring what's going on inside. And of course it's all muddled up with God, the God who loves me – though sometimes I doubt whether he does. And with having the confidence to love oneself.'

How, as a monk, did Robert express his love for other

people, especially, perhaps, the other members of the community?

'Whose feet do you wash? This is the great monastic question. Whose feet do you wash? If you are a Christian, love must be a characteristic of life. The monastic life can be lived with great selfishness – doing your own thing, not doing anything for society. But actually, charity is the hallmark of Christian life. In a monastic community it is expressed in the love of the brethren, but those who are married have chosen their partners. I didn't choose to live with the rest of this community, any more than they choose to live with me. God has chosen the odd bods to live with me and vice versa. And that in itself is an amazing experience, because I wouldn't have chosen to live with the people I'm living with. You can't escape from them. They sit next to you at the dinner table. They sit next to you in chapel. You can't escape them. They are in the next room down the corridor from you. So if you cannot love the brother or sister whom you have seen, you cannot love God whom you have not seen. So you begin with the people you are given to live with.

'In the stranger you meet Christ. Therefore our service to the world and the Church is to a whole galaxy of people, including an organ grinder in Oxford High Street, who never leaves us any money because he's broke, but we listen to all his woes; a single woman from Birmingham, living with her elderly parents, who's unemployed; two married ladies from Wales; the director of a big national charity; a married couple from Potters Bar, one of whom's a wood carver; a hospital chaplain from the Midlands; a solicitor from London; a young comedian on BBC2; a student doing a PhD.

'We have a number of women applying to join our community, which is very exciting. There were six sisters when I came here and since then three have died. We honestly thought the whole notion of a double community was going to die out. But it looks as if, please God, that's not going to happen.'

One of the least typical yet most flourishing of the religious orders is the Oratory of the Good Shepherd, dedicated to prayer, discipline and pastoral concern, one of whose founders, in 1913, was Eric Milner-White. He had just been appointed chaplain to King's College Choir School, Cambridge, where in 1914 he briefly taught the future archbishop of Canterbury, Michael Ramsey. For twenty-three years he served as dean of King's and later was dean of York. In fact, the first members of the order were all Cambridge dons, and today those who join take a vow pledging them to study. They also take a vow of celibacy, and they depend perhaps far more than other religious on self-discipline, for they live and work, in the United Kingdom, the USA, Australia and South Africa, not in a religious house but mainly as parish priests. Some are academics. Six are bishops.

The Superior of the English Province, Canon Dominic Walker, believes the secret of the Oratory's success is that 'it's a form of the religious life which is appropriate to the twenty-first century'. They have fifty professed priests and brothers, with ten newly professed members to their credit. It seemed odd that after eighty years they were only now in the process of applying to the Advisory Council on Relgious Communities for official recognition in England.[5] (They are already recognised officially as a religious community in America and South Africa.) Fortunately for them, a member of the council happens to be the Bishop of Portsmouth – who is also a member of the Oratory.

The brethren meet once a month in small groups – in chapters, in fact, with a prior in charge – and once a year as a Province, when they hold a General Chapter and go into retreat. As they live largely in the secular world they do not take a vow of poverty but they are required every month to account for their expenditure. One of their most distinguished members was Canon Eric Mascall, from 1962 to 1973 professor of historical theology at King's College, London, who died in 1993. The late Alec Vidler, editor of *Theology* from 1939 to 1964 and a canon of Windsor, was a member for sixty years.

Canon Walker rises at 5.30 a.m. each day so that he can spend an hour in prayer before making a brisk seven-minute walk to his parish church to celebrate Mass, and he will probably say three or four offices during the day. 'But,' he told me, 'one or two of the old brethren say all the little hours. We have one dear old father who is now blind, and if you go to see him he is always saying an office. He'll have a cup of coffee and say another office! He knows them all by heart.'

The Church of England has never been short of places of pilgrimage. Lindisfarne, the site of Becket's murder in Canterbury Cathedral, and the tombs of St Cuthbert and the Venerable Bede at Durham come readily to mind. But the Shrine of Our Lady of Walsingham is a phenomenon, a mecca for so many people now that if you want to go on an organised pilgrimage with your parish, and be sure, during what they call the season, of an altar at which to hear Mass (and there are fifteen chapels), you need to book a year in advance. The 'season', their really busy time, runs from Holy Week through to November, when anything up to 500 groups of pilgrims descend upon what still remains a remarkably small and unspoilt village, only a few miles from the north Norfolk coast and inaccessible by British Rail.

A quarter of a million people, so it is estimated, visit Walsingham every year; some, of course, are frankly sight-seers, but the constant stream of young and old, fit and lame, laity and religious who enter the shrine in silence, to hear Mass, attend benediction, make their confession or drink from the holy well is a sure sign that something is astir which cannot be attributed to the tourist industry. There is a hospice with a refectory and 250 beds where 50,000 pilgrims stay for a weekend every year. There is constant lively activity, with parties arriving and leaving simultaneously, one party ascending from the well, the children happily splashing water off their hands, while another party close by is saying the Hail Mary. 'An awful lot of religion goes on here,' the assistant administrator, Peter Walters, told me, and I could well believe him.

Even on a visit early in Lent, when numbers were such that no fewer than three parties who had failed to book could still be accommodated, thanks to the ministrations of a nun from the Society of St Margaret who rushed round preparing altars at a moment's notice, it seemed incredible that so much activity could be organised by just two resident priests. They are assisted by retired clergy, but partly because of the concentrated pressure of work, and partly because of the inevitably rarefied atmosphere, Father Walters also told me, 'I get away on holiday to get my hands dirty whenever I can.' His form of holiday activity involves visiting children in Colombia who are at risk of ill-treatment and death – even being set alight with petrol – at the hands of the authorities.

It was in 1061 that the lady of the manor of Walsingham, one Richeldis de Faverches, claimed she had had a vision of the Virgin Mary. So she built a replica of the Holy Family's house at Nazareth, and throughout the Middle Ages Walsingham was a place of pilgrimage. But in 1538 Richeldis's shrine fell victim to Henry VIII, and it was not until a young Anglo-Catholic priest, Alfred Hope Patten, was inducted as vicar of St Mary's, Walsingham, in 1921 that the cult of the Virgin Mary was revived in the village. Within a year he had his parishioners saying the rosary before a statue of Our Lady and the Child, and in 1931 he acquired land on which to build a Marian shrine, now known as the Holy House. The present church, built to encase both shrine and well, was erected in 1938, but as late as the 1950s Sir Ninan Comper was at work on the reredos in the Holy House.

Close by the memorial to Father Patten is a box for intercessions, always crammed full, and every evening at six o'clock, at the shrine, prayers are offered for the sick, the dying and the dead. In the vestry, Fr Walters showed me the intercession book, pages of names of people waiting to be prayed for. Routine services also include a Mass in the shrine at 7.30 every morning and another at 11.30 a.m. in a chapel in the grounds. On weekdays, at 2.30 p.m., there is a sprinkling at the well, when pilgrims take a sip, sometimes a considerable gulp (reducing one little boy to helpless hiccups), from a ladle containing holy water. The priest then makes the sign of the cross on their foreheads, and pours water over their hands. A plea appeared in the *Walsingham Review* at Easter 1992 for pilgrims to take only 'small bottles of holy water and not to bring large containers' as Norfolk was in its fourth consecutive year of 'less than average rainfall'. This 'had involved the Shrine in considerable expense in deepening the Holy Well'. The well was originally only 10 feet deep, and engineers had to be called in to sink a shaft another 20 feet.

The most esoteric events take place on Saturdays, when in the evening there is a candlelit procession in the grounds with the figure of Our Lady borne aloft, and on Sundays, when in the afternoon the Sacrament is carried in procession, pilgrims kneeling as it passes, as everyone would automatically have done before the Reformation. But whereas not so many years ago Walsingham was structured entirely for the benefit of extreme Anglo-Catholics, today, I was told, 'anything goes, from the Roman Mass to the Book of Common Prayer'. Indeed, it is impossible to believe that so many pilgrims, from St John's, Sevenoaks, and Holy Trinity, Winchmore Hill, from Luckley Oakfield School and St Michael's College, Llandaff, from St Mark's, Stockton Green, and St James's, Darlington, are all served by clergy in birettas. Many of the people who visit are from inner-city parishes, many more than in the past are black, and many are from the north. There is an annual pilgrimage for politicians (John Gummer is a Guardian of the Shrine), and ecumenical groups and university students walk to Walsingham carrying wooden crosses.

The attraction of Walsingham, especially among the young, is such that thought is being given to the provision of camping and recreational facilities (there is nothing for young people to do in the evening but go to the pub), and to the building of dormitories. One reason for the arrival of ever increasing numbers of children is that pilgrimage is now on the GSE religious curriculum. The pressure on space in the summer is so great that some feel the church is now too small. There are visitors who register shock at the plethora of altars and candles, statues and votive lamps, and yet it is not the interior decor that shocks – if anything does – but the sheer numbers of very ordinary-looking pilgrims. They are not making any of the extravagant gestures one might find on the continent. No one crawls up to the shrine on their knees or crosses themselves twenty-eight times in front of every icon. Yet somehow, because such ordinary parishioners are here in such numbers, it seems so very un-English.

On Spring Bank Holiday Monday in May there is a national pilgrimage, which can turn into something of a scrummage, for the numbers are swollen by extreme evangelicals who turn up with banners and protests. Six pilgrims were present in

1931. The police estimated there were 8,000 in 1992. The 'Waltzing Ham Show' these spoilsports call it, and there is generally a good deal of mockery mingled with the day's festive atmosphere. It is the Marian dimension to the national pilgrimage rather than the concept of pilgrimage itself that draws the Protestant fire. 'But in fact,' Fr Walters himself protested, 'we are Jesus-centred, and not at all bizarre.'

There is also a good deal of ecumenical activity at Walsingham, and not solely because some of the Roman Catholic clergy wandering around the place were once Anglicans; there is a chapel within the shrine church set aside for use by the Orthodox, and in the event of a shortage of beds elsewhere, Roman Catholic pilgrims sometimes stay at the Anglican hospice. Methodists are increasingly coming to Walsingham, and Anglicans and Roman Catholics in the village share evening prayer on great feast days. Few leave Walsingham quite as they found it, reminded, perhaps, of T. S. Eliot's injunction in a poem about another holy place, Little Gidding:

> You are not here to verify,
> Instruct yourself, or inform curiosity
> Or carry report. You are here to kneel
> Where prayer has been valid.

Three Dutch ladies queue up to thank Fr Walters for his 'homily'. Two teenagers sit on a bench drinking Coca-Cola, and Fr Walters politely pretends to remember meeting them on a previous visit. They are scarcely fifteen. A young man cannot wait to thank him for all the arrangements; he is looking immensely relieved and rather pleased with himself, having just led his first parish pilgrimage without mishap.

It was on his own first visit to Walsingham, as a boy, that Fr Walters was moved to make his first confession. Some years later a letter inviting him to be assistant administrator arrived out of the blue. He thinks four years in the job is long enough for anyone, but when I met him he was not looking beyond November 1992. 'I've told my bishop that if women are ordained I shall go over to Rome,' he said. No doubt some of his evangelical Anglican brethren thought he already had.

TEN

Dr Who?

WHEN it comes to Church affairs in this country, the focus of attention is the Primate of All England. This is a relatively new development. Archbishops of Canterbury did not necessarily attract the spotlight in the past, and other bishops often exerted more influence. For centuries, bishops of Durham were both civil and military rulers of the northeast, and it was not until 1836, on the death of the last prince-bishop of Durham, William van Mildert, that the regal authority of the palatine diocese finally reverted to the Crown. And in Victorian times the bishopric of London was considered a far more arduous posting than the archbishopric of Canterbury.

But with a levelling-out of influence among diocesan bishops there has coincided not just a national but an international rise of interest in the office of the archbishop of Canterbury. Since Geoffrey Fisher's time this has partly been due to the archbishop's involvement in the World Council of Churches, the Anglican Communion and the Ecumenical Movement; since Michael Ramsey's it has been increased by the perception of the archbishop as a liberal leader upon whom those in distress feel free to call for help. Ramsey broadened the office immensely, travelling widely both on ecumenical and Anglican Communion affairs and involving himself in social and humanitarian issues, like the welfare of Commonwealth immigrants. This liberal stance was to a large extent followed by Robert Runcie. The press in any case find it convenient simply to equate the Church of England with the archbishop of Canterbury.

Randall Davidson's stint at Canterbury, from 1903 to 1928,

virtually ran in tandem with the first quarter of the twentieth century; this was a stretch in office which no one would attempt to emulate today. Such are the physical and intellectual demands now made on any archbishop of Canterbury that fifteen years in office must be reckoned the absolute maximum; bearing in mind that he must retire at seventy and is unlikely to be appointed until he is in his early fifties, he has little chance of staying in office longer than fifteen years anyway. But there are those who see no reason why the term should exceed a decade. His workload has become truly formidable. He retains ultimate responsibility for his own diocese, with its 265 parishes and a diocesan synod which meets twice a year and over which he presides. He is a president of the General Synod, chairman of the House of Bishops, a chairman of the Crown Appointments Commission, a president of the Central Board of Finance and chairman of the Church Commissioners. The archbishop is also chairman of the standing committee of the General Synod and serves as a member of its legislative committee. He is president of the Lambeth Conference and of the Anglican Consultative Council, and chairs meetings of the Anglican primates. He is expected to retain close ecumenical links with Church leaders throughout the world as well as within the British Isles, he attends the House of Lords and endless official dinners, consecrates new bishops appointed to the southern province, ordains and confirms, is expected to prepare better sermons than anyone else, to undertake patronage on an enormous scale, address conferences, perhaps write books, and produce some instant comment on almost any social or moral issue of the day.

When assessing the current state of the Church of England, and in particular the level of leadership it has received from its modern archbishops, it is necessary to bear in mind that the Church this century has suffered two grievous deaths. The first, in 1944, was that of William Temple, a socialist and philosophical theologian, after only two years as archbishop of Canterbury. As bishop of Manchester and then as archbishop of York he had become a legend in his lifetime, and he is remembered today especially for his leadership of the Life and Liberty Movement and for calling, as early as 1917, for freedom for the Church from the 'intolerable hindrance' of parliamentary control. His personal goodness and sincerity moved and impressed all who knew him. 'Prodigal in his gifts, lavish in his generosity, wide in his interests, abundant in his energy, holy in his dedication' is how a former dean of Westminster, Edward Carpenter, has described William Temple.[1] Paul Welsby writes that he 'possessed exceptional intellectual power and prophetic insight [and] was able to hold in synthesis theology, philosophy, politics and economics'.[2] All this was combined with genuine humility and a great gift for friendship, and Temple's life's work on behalf of the Church and the nation was expected to come to fruition in postwar Britain. But that was not to be. 'Temple's death,' said the provost of The Queen's College, Oxford, 'seemed to shake the Western world as if one of its pillars had been removed.'[3]

The bishop who by all the laws of common sense and natural justice should have succeeded Temple was George Bell of Chichester. Churchill, however, roused himself from the state of torpor into which he usually slumped when faced with ecclesiastical matters (he often delegated the task of sounding out potential bishops to Brendan Bracken, the minister of information, much as Palmerston, equally ignorant about Church affairs, had depended for advice on Lord Shaftesbury), and decided that under no circumstances would he recommend to the king that a man who was opposed to the indiscriminate bombing of German civilian targets should go to Canterbury.[4] The job went instead to a man with as good a brain as Temple's (Geoffrey Fisher was a Triple First) but with a mind working on a far smaller scale, obsessed as it was with the details of canon law revision. Fisher had many half-hidden qualities as a pastor, but his impetuosity, intellectual arrogance and lack of vision seriously impaired the sixteen years he spent at Lambeth. During the 1940s and 1950s there had been grave concern about recruitment to the ministry (the current lack of vocations is nothing new), and the dean of St Paul's, W. R. Matthews, believed that the bishops and clergy 'worked hard on canon law when the future of the Church became day by day more precarious'. Dr Matthews went so far as to compare the bishops' time-consuming engagement in canon law revision to 'a man who occupied himself in rearranging the furniture when the house was on fire'.

In 1961 Fisher was succeeded by his former Repton pupil Michael Ramsey. During Ramsey's time as archbishop of Canterbury, the Church suffered its second untimely catastrophe, the death in 1972 of his namesake Ian Ramsey, a creative and congenial genius whose speciality was the study of natural law in ethics. Formerly Nolloth professor of the philosophy of religion at Oxford, Ian Ramsey had been bishop of Durham since 1966, a man, again according to Paul Welsby, 'of immense moral and intellectual stature who had a unique appeal and became the most influential figure on the episcopal bench'.[5] In many ways he seemed to be the reincarnation of Temple, and there was open talk that he would succeed Michael Ramsey at Canterbury. He would have brought to the job great integrity, but on his death from a heart attack, induced by overwork, a chasm yawned. Eventually, in 1974, it was filled by the evangelical archbishop of York, Donald Coggan, for there seemed to be no one else of sufficient seniority or proven ability in place. Unfortunately, during Dr Coggan's six years as caretaker at Canterbury he was partnered at York by another evangelical, the delightful but less than dynamic Stuart Blanch, and they could not be said to have formed a strong or even a complementary team. More and more it can be seen that with the premature deaths of William Temple and Ian Ramsey the Church of England was robbed within the space of a quarter of a century of two potentially great archbishops of Canterbury, and it has never really recovered from their loss.

Much of the adverse publicity that befell the Church of England in Ramsey's and Runcie's time did so because on occasions both archbishops stood out against government policy; much, however, resulted because the Church of England seems so peculiarly adept at scoring own goals. If, as happened in 1970, a bishop, having taken an early and gift-laden farewell of his diocese, hotfoots it to Tenerife in the company of a 'club hostess' by the name of Miss Lovejoy, it is hardly fair to blame the *News of the World* for following him.[6] Two major scandals that sullied and saddened the Runcie years, detracting from many of those years' achievements, were indicative of the amateurish way in which the Church still handles almost anything more complicated than campanology. It is, after all, quite an achievement for an archbishop to lose control over a member of his staff to the extent that he ends up incarcerated by terrorists, but this is what happened in the case of Dr Runcie's secretary for Anglican Affairs, Mr Terry Waite.

It is always difficult to write objectively about someone whose newsworthy conduct has turned him into a sort of folk hero, but in *Archbishop* Jonathan Mantle makes a veiled attempt.[7] The Archbishop, says Mantle, was always pleasantly surprised to see Waite, but was 'too busy to know, as a rule, more than vague details of Waite's movements'. Terry Waite was a member of the Archbishop's household which makes even more astonishing Mantle's assertion that after Waite had been advised by the Foreign Office, the British ambassador and by the archbishop himself not to return to Lebanon, 'none of them had any physical or legal authority actually to prevent him from doing so'. Of course neither the Foreign Office nor the ambassador had authority over Waite, but an archbishop scarcely requires legal authority to give implicit instructions to a member of his household, and the normal consequence of disobeying instructions is to face the sack. Instead, having been allowed to swan around the world without supervision as some sort of maverick crypto-diplomat, Waite rushed in where an angel with a grain of prudence would have heeded professional advice, and his almost inevitable capture, on a mission that has been described by Geoffrey Wheatcroft as 'a kind of deranged post-Imperial delusion of grandeur',[8] left Runcie paralysed with worry for half his archiepiscopacy.

However foolhardy Terry Waite's conduct may have been, no one would have wished upon him the hardship he endured, and at least the suffering he brought on his own head was in part a consequence of altruism. While Waite languished, liturgical and ethical discontents were swirling over the Church of England, and many of these were to coalesce in the other disaster that came to haunt Lambeth Palace while Dr Runcie was living there, a disaster which also epitomised two of the clergy's besetting sins, undirected ambition and, at times of real crisis, a pastoral insensitivity towards individual people that tends to make a mockery of their generalised pontificating about love and charity. Only naivety on an unimaginable scale would have permitted publication of the anonymous Preface to the 1987/88 edition of *Crockford's Clerical Directory*, which led to the suicide of the author, Gareth Bennett, a suicide for which no one to this day has acknowledged a shred of culpability.

Dr Bennett was a fellow and chaplain of New College, Oxford (where from 1959 to 1979 he was dean of divinity), an eighteenth-century Church historian, an Anglo-Catholic, a frequent speaker in the General Synod and a member of its standing and policy subcommittees. On the face of it, he might appear to have been on the very inside of the establishment, but in fact he had become an outsider, the sort of useful, talented person the charmed inner circle of the establishment always considers expendable if there is any danger of their rocking the boat, and especially if there is any danger of their speaking the truth. With the drift towards liberal theology, Bennett had become an outsider partly because, like so many others, he had become profoundly disillusioned with what he saw as a creeping erosion of the Church's catholic ethos.

'A symbolic moment in the history of Anglicanism in the late twentieth century' is how William Oddie, a former librarian at Pusey House, now a Roman Catholic layman, has described the death of Gareth Bennett in a book in which he argues that Bennett was driven to suicide by a Church he had loved.[9] Dr Bennett's views were well known, many shared them and he had not exactly been commissioned to contribute a Foreword to *Hints on Flower Arranging in the Vicarage*. *Crockford's* Prefaces had a robust tradition for plain and often controversial speaking; that was their purpose. The two men who commissioned Bennett were James Shelley, then secretary of the Church Commissioners, and the secretary-general of the General Synod, Derek Pattinson, since retired, knighted and ordained. They gave him carte blanche to write what he wanted without fear of editorial interference, and they chose him precisely because they knew the kind of topics on which he was longing to blow off steam. Dr Bennett produced a 13,000-word article which it was left to Mr Pattinson to put into production. According to the Archbishop of York, Dr Habgood, Mr Pattinson only 'scanned it hurriedly'.

This was a little unfortunate. Even though freedom of expression may have been offered to an author, on occasions it is an editor's duty at least to draw his attention to the likely consequences of publication. But, because of the childish cloak of anonymity always accorded to the writer of the Preface, Bennett and Pattinson relaxed their guard, and both were unprepared for the backlash in store. Previous anonymous Prefaces had notably failed to spare the blushes of archbishops Fisher and Coggan, and much of the hypocritical nature of the subsequent closing of establishment ranks took the form of defending Runcie by attacking Bennett – on the spurious grounds that Bennett had sheltered behind anonymity in order to criticise the Archbishop of Canterbury. In any event, Runcie's failings, such as they were, could be read as a symptom rather than a cause of the Church's ills.

Taking a broad view of the current state of affairs, Dr Bennett castigated the Anglican Communion for its refusal to face up to questions of authority, and the General Synod for failing to devise any coherent policy for the Church of England. He accused the theological colleges of training 'a whole generation of priests with a minimal knowledge of classical Anglican divinity or its methods', and he regretted the 'virtual disuse of the prayer books based on the English Book of Common Prayer'. Dr Habgood he dismissed as 'the leading theological relativist among the bishops'. (He may have had a point. Commenting on television in December 1992 on the separation of the Prince and Princess of Wales, Dr Habgood said, 'Separation, in a curious way, affirms the sacredness of marriage.') Dr Bennett also poured scorn upon the way Dr Coggan had 'indifferently led' the 1978 Lambeth Conference. Pressure to ordain women to the priesthood, the advance of liberal theology, a discarding of rigid attitudes to abortion, divorce and homosexuality all excited his quivering quill.

Most of this was ignored, however. Through no fault of his own, Dr Runcie was at the time particularly vulnerable to press scrutiny, and it was the 'attack' on Runcie that was to prove fatal. Bennett suggested that the archbishop tended to take the line of least resistance, did not know what he was doing, had a clear preference 'for men of liberal disposition with a moderately catholic style which is not taken to the point of having firm principles', and exerted undue influence in the appointment of bishops. 'He has,' Dr Bennett wrote, 'the advantage of the intellectual pragmatist: the desire to put off all questions until someone else makes a decision.'

The Church establishment was seized by paranoia, and later blamed its actions on 'considerable media pressure'. It is true that the *Daily Mail* offered Dr Bennett £5,000 for a confession, the *Sun* suddenly discovered it had got a religious-affairs correspondent on its staff, and overnight Dr Bennett found himself in demand for questioning on practically every news and current affairs programme, but the Church was responsible for publishing this dynamite, and the press could only have been encouraged in their hunt for the culprit by comments like the Bishop of Peterborough's ('a sour piece of anonymous malice') and the Bishop of St Alban's ('cowardly and disgraceful'). Dr Habgood, by instinct an authoritarian who does not care at the best of times for the Church to come under attack, was said to be on the warpath, with every intention of discovering and revealing the identity of the author. This he has firmly denied, but in his essay on the subject in *Confessions of a Conservative Liberal* he tells us he decided to deny the truth of Dr Bennett's allegations against Dr Runcie for fear 'the Preface's verdict was accepted and its accuracy [remain] unquestioned'.[10] Hence he issued a statement referring to 'a sourness and vindictiveness about the anonymous attack on the Archbishop of Canterbury' and expressing a hope that the public would treat 'this abuse of privilege with the contempt it deserves'. He said, 'The entirely negative tone of his whole Preface is one of its most depressing features. I think the Church would be wise to regard it as an outburst from a disappointed cleric who manages to pinpoint some of the real problems which face the Church of England and the Anglican Communion, but has nothing constructive to offer about the way ahead.'

Dr Habgood seems to have been sure the author was male and a cleric, and Dr Runcie 'strongly suspected the author was Gary'.[11] Having discussed the matter with Dr Runcie before issuing his statement, Habgood must surely have known who Runcie thought had written the Preface, a conclusion supported by internal evidence fairly easily deduced from the Preface itself. Indeed, anyone at the centre of ecclesiastical politics could have produced a very short list of likely authors, and, of course, many did. Instead of restricting himself to a defence of Dr Runcie, Dr Habgood used his statement to lash out at a man with very few clothes on his back. The point was most effectively and eloquently made by the Bishop of Peterborough, who informed *The Times*, 'Already the vultures are circling around this man.'

But it is not sufficient to suggest that Dr Bennett ended his life simply because he thought he was about to be exposed as someone who had piled criticism upon the head of a personal friend for whose resignation the press was already baying, or because at fifty-eight he realised his hopes of preferment had vanished. The establishment knew that he was the author, and he knew they knew. He also therefore knew precisely what they thought of him. How was he ever to sit around the same table with them again? The Church was his whole life, and these men were not just business friends, acquaintances or colleagues; they constituted a surrogate family. He killed himself because his entire world had caved in and there was nowhere for him to hide. The Church had made sure of that. Once Dr Bennett had gassed himself, Dr Habgood changed his tune and described him as 'a good and gifted man' and 'a gentle critical scholar'.

Until now, Dr Runcie's part in this unsavoury drama has not, it seems, been accurately reported. For example, it has often been alleged that he tried to telephone Bennett, and that hearing the archbishop's voice, Bennett silently replaced the receiver.[12] 'The telephone call to Bennett is an invention,' Lord Runcie told me. 'I believe that in his diary a telephone rang but it was not me. I do not recollect thinking about ringing him up.' According to Jonathan Mantle's biography, after returning to Lambeth Palace from consecrating the man destined to succeed him, George Carey (he had been appointed bishop of Bath and Wells), Dr Runcie sat up 'most of the night . . . with the newspapers and his Head of Staff, Bishop Gordon, trying to pin down the identity of the author'.

But Lord Runcie maintains that this is also quite untrue. 'Some of Jonathan Mantle is remarkably good popular writing,' he concedes. 'It is undoubtedly the most readable of those unsolicited biographies. But frankly, his account [of the Bennett affair] is full of fantasy.'[13]

Dr Runcie became certain the author *was* Gareth Bennett at a Eucharist at Pusey House in Oxford. 'Afterwards,' Lord Runcie told me, 'Gary came up and was particularly effusive in appreciation of my sermon.' But he coupled this with a 'very shifty sort of apology' for his inability to attend a forthcoming meeting of the General Synod's policy sub-committee – a meeting at which discussion was bound to focus on the authorship of the Preface. And publication of *Crockford's* was due between that Sunday Eucharist and the policy sub-committee meeting. Dr Runcie had seen an advance copy of the Preface and had been 'mulling over the authorship' although, he said, 'I confess that I wondered quite why my press office and General Synod characters were jumping up and down so much.' But Dr Bennett's behaviour at Pusey House cleared his mind. 'When I got into the car outside Pusey after lunch, I turned to my chaplain and said, "Now I know Gary Bennett wrote that Preface." '

As well as scandal and criticism, the modern archbishop of Canterbury is vulnerable to a grossly overloaded work schedule. One of the causes is the archbishop's ever increasing involvement with the Anglican Communion (a term first coined in 1885), a loose-knit alliance of independent Churches and provinces, all, theoretically, in communion with the Church of England and with each other, but whose communion, since the advent of unilateral ordination of women to the priesthood, is now somewhat quaintly referred to as 'impaired'. There are probably 70 million Anglicans worldwide, living in more than 450 dioceses in 164 countries, and the number of provinces has grown to 29. Since 1867 their bishops have met roughly every ten years, and always in England, at an assembly called the Lambeth Conference, over which the archbishop of Canterbury, as *primus inter pares*, presides. The initiative for the first Lambeth Conference came from the Anglican Church of Canada, anxious to resolve a dispute about the interpretation and authority of the Scriptures then raging between the archbishop of Cape Town and one of his diocesans, the mildly eccentric Bishop Colenso of Natal. Colenso permitted African converts to remain polygamously married; the archbishop, Robert Gray, tried to depose him; Colenso resisted and schism ensued. On that first occasion seventy-six bishops gathered for four days in the chapel at Lambeth Palace. Today the numbers attending, together with assorted consultants and wives, is around 700, and meetings sometimes last a month. At the 1878 conference 100 bishops discussed 'modern forms of infidelity'. Still in hot pursuit of sin, a decade later 145 bishops had transferred to the library at Lambeth to discuss intemperance, purity and divorce, although they did take a look too at socialism and the care of immigrants. By 1897 the Lambeth Conference was warmly commending the concept of deaconesses, and a thoroughly contemporary flavour gripped proceedings in 1908, with 242 bishops now making the journey to London; on the agenda were the ministry of healing, possible revision of the prayer book and the supply and training of the clergy.

Sex reared its ugly head again in 1920, when the Conference rejected outright the use of contraception; by 1958 they were all for it – within marriage, of course. In 1958 most of the bishops also came out in favour of nuclear disarmament. By 1968, with 462 diocesan bishops booked in, the Conference had to leave Lambeth Palace, where nevertheless a garden party was held, and move into the dreary environment of Church House. Paperwork took over, committees proliferated, and the ordination of women to the priesthood was discussed. Ten years later Dr Coggan shifted the venue to the University of Kent in Canterbury, where some of the American bishops found their accommodation rather spartan, and some of the African bishops discovered their president to be out of touch with the way cricket is played in the colonies. With his agenda running hopelessly behind schedule, Dr Coggan said to one guest, 'We are a quarter of an hour late for lunch, bishop. I wonder if you could come to the point.' 'I am an African,' said the bishop, 'and it takes me a long time to come to the point!'

The most striking factor about the Anglican Communion is

the relocation over the past century of its ethnic power base. Even as recently as 1968 it seemed that white North American bishops dominated the proceedings; today not only are the majority of Anglicans African and black, but by initiating, for instance, the Decade of Evangelism in 1988 the black African bishops have assumed an important, possibly an overriding, international influence. The Archbishop of Cape Town, Desmond Tutu, is far and away the best-known archbishop in the world, and while the Church of England agonises over gay clergy the Church in Africa is fighting for human freedom, for life itself. Africa's bishops get imprisoned; the worst an English bishop suffers is a flat tyre on the way to a public school confirmation. On the wall of the converted garage of a small suburban house in Basingstoke hangs, in a frame, a pillowcase. In the pillowcase are four bullet holes. The bullets were intended for the retired bishop in Iran, Hassan Dehqani-Tafti. One went through the hand of his wife as she threw herself across him to save his life. Later, their charming and brilliant twenty-four-year-old son Bahram was murdered.

Bishop Dehqani-Tafti was president bishop of the Episcopal Church in Jerusalem and the Middle East, and the front-line activities of persecuted primates like Dehqani-Tafti and Tutu call into question the archbishop of Canterbury's continuing supremacy as president of the Lambeth Conference and even as host. In 1988 a Canadian bishop spoke in French; Africans and others celebrate a non-English liturgy; the Church of England, with its increasingly ill-disciplined forms of worship and widespread abandonment of sacred music, is no longer seen as the norm. And the archbishops of Canterbury and York are the only primates appointed through government channels, which means they may be perceived by Anglicans overseas as being in thrall to some political master.

Although presiding over the Lambeth Conference often brings out the best in English archbishops – it did so in Ramsey and Runcie – there seems little reason to an outsider why the presidency should not circulate among the primates; in 1988 the chair was successfully taken at different sessions by various primates. Dr Carey was firmly stamped on by his fellow primates when he suggested the next Lambeth Conference should be held in the year 2000; it will in fact take place on schedule in 1998, and already there is talk of holding it in either Canada or Kenya. If this does transpire it would be natural for the Canadian primate or the archbishop of the Province of Kenya to play host and preside.

But one problem about the Anglican Communion (and it is a problem that particularly affects the archbishop of Canterbury's workload) is a reluctance on the part of overseas Churches to let the archbishop of Canterbury relinquish his place of honour. American bishops still love an excuse to visit England, and many Africans have an urge to see the archbishop in a papal role. As a member of the Archbishop's staff put it to me, 'their tribal traditions fit in beautifully with episcopacy and hierarchy. It would,' he said, 'be very difficult to imagine anyone else fulfilling the Archbishop's functions in relation to the Anglican Communion. There is no wish within the Communion for the presidency to rotate. The Archbishop of Canterbury is the senior bishop by creation. They would all find it unacceptable to ignore the roots of the Anglican Communion, and you must remember that many need to make contact with their roots because they are extremely isolated.'

Dr Carey has been packing as many as seven overseas visits a year into his itinerary, and, although not all are lengthy, the planning and preparation take time. Even before his enthronement, he went to Ireland for a meeting of the Anglican primates.[14] In August 1991 he spent two weeks in Papua New Guinea, and in January 1992 four days in Jordan and Israel, taking part in the Orthodox Christmas in the Church of the Holy Nativity in Bethlehem. He was at the Standing Committee of the Anglican Consultative Council in the USA for a week in April, visited the Falkland Islands – a parish outside any diocese, of which, in effect, the Archbishop is vicar – and in May paid a visit to North Carolina. In May, too, he went to Rome, where he paid an informal visit to the Pope. In August he led a pilgrimage to Bec in Normandy. Between a visit to Prague for the Conference of European Churches and a thirteen-day visit in September to the Episcopal Church of the United States, he had just one day at home in which to turn round. Then he was in Istanbul in October, hobnobbing (as Michael Ramsey would have said) with the Ecumenical

Patriarch. In December he was in Sri Lanka, an area under his metropolitan jurisdiction, to consecrate a new bishop. It is no wonder that someone who wrote to the archbishop's chaplain in July to request an interview was told there was small chance of one for about four months 'simply because his diary between now and the beginning of October is such that he is hardly at Lambeth'. He was off again in January 1993 to South Africa and in April to inaugurate the new province of Korea.

A quarter of a century ago the role of the bishop was under light-hearted discussion among a group of radicals, and one priest said, 'If I was archbishop of Canterbury I would tell them all to stop doing whatever it is they are doing and stay at home for a year and think.' Such sentiments are still occasionally voiced, as the role of the diocesan bishop spirals out of orbit, and that of the archbishop of Canterbury seems tailor-made to kill him. But to what purpose? I asked a senior executive with the Anglican Consultative Council if he could give an example of some way or other in which life in the Church of England had been influenced by anything done or said at the 1988 Lambeth Conference. 'I don't think I can,' he replied, 'without spending a lot of time thinking.' But he said he thought the Lambeth Conference was 'much more important to Churches overseas than to the Church of England. Regular meetings of bishops is a compensation for the loosening of relationships through missionary societies, and Desmond Tutu constantly testifies to the importance to a Church under siege of being able to belong to an international body, and for that body to make statements. Many are under that kind of pressure. Burma, for instance. There are constant pleas coming in to Lambeth Palace for Dr Carey to use his muscle and to intervene on their behalf. The Episcopal Church in the Sudan is being harassed. It's the same in Kenya. The Archbishop of Canterbury is automatically seen overseas as someone of international standing, and the Churches overseas are not remotely concerned about criticism of him at home. He is actually seen to represent the non-Roman Catholic Church worldwide, not just the 70 million Anglicans.'

This is a remarkable and humbling thought. And it reinforces the argument for the Church of England remaining established, an arrangement that provides links with the

Foreign Office so essential to the Church's dealings with governments overseas. Another argument against the presidency rotating is that no primate could attract publicity in the area he was visiting akin to that almost automatically focused on the person of the archbishop of Canterbury. The prestige of the office remains enormously high overseas, where, in his semi-official role as roving ambassador, Dr Carey, I was told, 'acts as a catalyst of good will in bringing warring factions together'. Because of access to theologians, theological colleges, universities and publishing houses, impoverished students and clergy from Brazil or Burundi, the Sudan or Tanzania who are able to study and research in England look upon England and its national Church with gratitude, and would find it incomprehensible if its senior archbishop did not continue to exercise a personal ministry within the Anglican Communion from a position of leadership. The cost of running the Lambeth Conference, however, is rising. 'The figure banded about for 1998,' I have been told, 'is about £1 million.' There is talk of laity attending, for it is fashionable now to try to find some role for the laity at every turn, and the danger is that as meetings of the Lambeth Conference continue to grow in size, so the mountain of paperwork will grow ever higher too, and the ideas and schemes engendered become ever more diffuse and ineffectual.

Since Randall Davidson's time, in other words, throughout the whole of this century, the ecumenical field has been another sphere of activity in which archbishops of Canterbury have been fully involved on top of their parochial work at home. But the failure of Anglican-Methodist reunion saw the ultimate ecumenical dream of inter-communion driven, for the foreseeable future, up a cul-de-sac. Nevertheless Robert Runcie maintained serious ecumenical dialogues; he was the first archbishop of Canterbury to meet with the pope more than once, and to sit down with Vatican officials and discuss in person a detailed agenda. Michael Ramsey had been quite happy with the idea of the pope at some stage assuming a position throughout the catholic world as first among equals, and this was a theme reiterated by Runcie when in Rome in 1989 he spoke of the pope enjoying 'the kind of primacy the bishop of Rome exercised within the Early

Church, "a presiding in love" for the sake of the unity of the Churches in the diversity of their mission'. The fact that this visit was consequently described as a debacle merely demonstrates the abyss of ignorance and stupidity into which, since Ramsey's time, the bulk of the press corps has fallen. Much of the vilification of the Runcies (Mrs Runcie was eventually driven to sue the *Daily Sketch* for libel) was motivated by editors of the right-wing gutter press desperate for honours, and instructed by their proprietors to dance to Mrs Thatcher's tune, as they conspicuously did in 1985 when they were encouraged by Downing Street to rubbish as 'pure Marxist theology' a highly competent and important 400-page report instigated by Dr Runcie, *Faith in the City*.

From almost every point of view, the ecclesiastical decade presided over by Robert Runcie will probably be regarded by future historians as a tragic one. *Faith in the City* was a rational critique of the Church's own performance in the inner cities along with a detailed examination of just those areas of human and social need the national Church and the state should be tackling together – job creation, child benefit, housing. To see this shredded in the press at the behest of Conservative MPs must have been a distressing and humiliating experience for Dr Runcie. The state had been shocked to discover that what it believed to be an unquestioning partner had dared to suggest that after six years of Conservative rule all was not perfection. Thanks to Mrs Thatcher's overzealous publicity machine, 80,000 copies of the report, possibly the most important single consequence of Dr Runcie's archiepiscopacy, were sold. A major watershed had been reached in relations between Church and state.

On 19 April 1991 George Leonard Carey, former bishop of Bath and Wells, picked up the burden of responsibility as archbishop of Canterbury when he was enthroned as the 103rd successor to St Augustine.[15] Inordinately proud of his working-class background and a bit of a bore on the subject of football, he was a totally unknown quantity. 'Dr Who?' people asked in astonishment when it was announced that he was to succeed Dr Runcie. 'He appeared out of the woodwork, really,' a dean told me. 'Even Coggan hadn't heard of him.' Indeed, although reporters sped to their *Who's Who* to pretend that *they* had known all along who Dr Carey was, and that his appointment had come as no surprise to *them*, nobody outside the Church had ever heard of him – and few within.[16] He had not been a bishop three years, and this implied that either he was another William Temple in the making, someone so outstanding that despite his lack of experience in almost every sphere in which an archbishop has to function from day one it was absolutely essential for the welfare of the Church that he should be catapulted into the highest office without delay, or else – and some people did believe this – the Church had taken leave of its collective senses. John Lyttle, Dr Runcie's secretary for public affairs, went round Lambeth Palace saying just that. As one of his obituarists tactfully put it (John Lyttle died on 27 April 1991), 'Lyttle was apprehensive about the likely consequences of the new regime at Lambeth.' 'The Church has gone totally mad,' a member of the House of Lords said to me. 'Barking mad.'

All that was known for certain was that Dr Carey was fifty-five, that he had been educated at a secondary modern school in Barking, east London, and at the London College of Divinity, and that he was an evangelical, having served a curacy at St Mary, Islington, London, before going on to lecture at Oak Hill Theological College and St John's College, Nottingham. While vicar of St Nicholas, Durham, Dr Carey had become attracted to charismatic worship, reviving, in the process, a parish once severely down in the dumps, and from there he had been appointed principal of Trinity Theological College, Bristol. It further emerged that he owned a Cavalier King Charles spaniel called the Duke of Buccleuch, as a result of which, in 1992, the RSPCA invited the archbishop to become its first ever vice-patron. (He was said, too, to use a word processor and to be 'computer literate'.)

So how, and why, did Dr Carey come to be the swiftly made choice of the Crown Appointments Commission, on to which Mrs Thatcher drafted as chairman for the occasion Viscount Caldecote, a 73-year-old Old Etonian, fellow of King's College, a businessman and engineer, a member of Pratt's and the Athenaeum, for five years a member of the old Church Assembly and, like the prime minister herself and her appointments secretary, of a Low Church persuasion? Many people felt there was a great deal at stake in the appointment, and politicking was rife. On this occasion, the wishes of the diocese, over which any archbishop of Canterbury inevitably exercises minimal episcopal influence, was going to be somewhere at the back of the Commission's mind. To the fore of their thoughts was the realisation that Mrs Thatcher was anticipating at least another five years in office and would not be best pleased if she was invited to rub along with another liberal in the mould of Dr Runcie. The danger of such an occurrence was, however, all too apparent when an unofficial ballot among General Synod members produced no fewer than fifty-four first preference votes for Dr Habgood of York. Just five had been cast for the Bishop of Bath and Wells.

Anyone who had ever propped up the bar of any West End watering hole frequented by Denis Thatcher would have been left in no doubt of Mrs Thatcher's dislike of Habgood. Partly this was a personal aversion to the sort of patrician figure cut by the Archbishop of York; public school cabinet colleagues of the same ilk she had found equally uncongenial. Upon this foundation of prejudice those churchmen with ecclesiastical objections to liberalism got to work. So seriously did right-wing politicians take the possibility of Dr Habgood being translated to Canterbury that some of them invited an eminent theologian to give a seminar criticising the archbishop's theology; he refused. Nevertheless, as a member of the cabinet John Gummer lost no opportunity, in private, of bending Mrs Thatcher's ear, and someone else who would hardly have been tempted to sit idly by was the head of her Policy Unit, Mr Brian Griffiths, an evangelical who had started life as a member of the Plymouth Brethren. (According to Hugo Young, writing in *One of Us*, Mr Griffiths's monetarism 'was seductively spiced with Christian morality'.) Meanwhile, in a more positive spirit of enquiry, Downing Street was sounding out a broad spectrum of people who perforce would have a particular interest in the outcome of the Commission's deliberations; senior bishops of the Anglican Communion overseas, the leaders of other Christian denominations at home. Anyone was free to send in nominations, but all the bishops, deans, provosts and archdeacons were specifically invited to submit suggestions – not necessarily for names but for guidance on the sort of person required to fill the post. In order to broaden their enquiries even further, representatives of the Commission met with the standing committee of the General Synod.

Meeting as usual in an atmosphere of prayer, the Crown Appointments Commission found they had roughly the same number of candidates' names in front of them as they would have had if they had been considering a normal diocesan appointment; that is to say, as many as fifteen. 'The decision to nominate George Carey was straightforward rather than quick,' a member of the Commission told me. The reason for this would have been that the Commission never had the slightest intention of considering seriously anyone who was not white, middle-aged, already a diocesan bishop – and an English diocesan at that. They almost certainly eliminated all those who did not fit this description, and started detailed deliberation with just four or five names in mind.

In order to clear the air even further, a fairly fundamental consideration would have been discussed: was it best for the Church to have a new long-term archbishop, with something like fifteen years ahead of him to devote to the job, or would a caretaker be acceptable? In normal times the answer to that question might ultimately have depended upon the credentials of the preferred candidates, but these were not normal times, they were critical times. The Commission knew there was a possibility that the General Synod would endorse the ordination of women to the priesthood in November 1992, and that the aftermath could be chaotic; it knew too that if in 1992 the Synod voted against the ordination of women, the arguments would continue with increasing bitterness for a further five years before fresh legislation was brought before the Synod to be debated and voted on yet again. Either way, what was clearly needed was an archbishop who was himself in favour of the ordination of women and would see it as his mission to steer the Church of England for a considerable time over dangerous rapids, and would in fact consider it an honour to take on such an awesome responsibility. Gifts of reconciliation he would need in abundance. Churchmanship would be a secondary but important consideration (except that a non-dogmatic evangelical might be thought best placed to appease evangelicals who were against the ordination of women). Another matter of importance would be the political element; in other words, the Downing Street factor.

Despite such strong arguments in favour of a long-term appointment, the Commission must have glanced at the claims of the Archbishop of York, the most senior bishop on the bench; at sixty-three he would have had at most seven years to devote to Canterbury, but along with the Bishops of Durham (too controversial), Chichester (too old) and Ely, he was one of the few experienced diocesans with real brains. But those brains, alas, had served him ill when it came to reacting to the Preface in *Crockford's*, and, despite the Synod's apparent endorsement of his qualifications, such an unpleasant aftertaste had been left in so many people's mouths that it seems odd he was ever touted as a serious candidate. Lord Caldecote has always maintained he had a free hand, having been told by Mrs Thatcher that she did not want to fetter the Commission in any way.[17] On the other hand, it is highly probable that she told her appointments secretary to keep an eye on the way things were going – and why not? – and if the Commission seemed to be veering towards Dr Habgood's name, to warn them it would be a waste of time sending it to Number 10 as their first preference. All Mrs Thatcher had ever had in common with Dr Runcie was that they were at Oxford together (and Oxford is a big place); one can just hear her saying to Mr Catford,[18] 'High Church if they must. But no liberals, thank you very much, we are very busy and we have no desire to have to send the names back and start all over again. Let's get it right first time, shall we.'

But the chances are that in the event Mr Catford had no need to utter. At the first session of the Commission's meeting those conservatives present made what has been described to me as 'a very strong pitch about the state of the Church, the disarray caused by liberal bishops. And they very quickly decided that none of the people in their sixties was a runner.' That being so, the Archbishop of York would have fallen at the first fence without any assistance from Mrs Thatcher. Quite apart from anything else, his allegiance to the catholic wing of the Church would have told against him – as it would have done against any other catholic bishop under discussion – because there is a strong tradition, amounting almost to a convention, for alternating at Canterbury. After Runcie, it was quite simply the evangelicals' turn. They had in any case climbed into the ascendant, their colleges were full, they deserved an archbishop. Having excluded on principle catholics, liberals and short-term appointments, all the Commission then had to do, irrespective of the inherent merits of the candidates in question, was to look at English evangelical diocesan bishops in their mid-fifties. In almost every respect, one of this tiny band, the Bishop of Bath and Wells, turned out to have impeccable credentials. He had held office for such a short time that he had no track record and hence had made no enemies. He was firmly in favour of the ultimately inevitable, the ordination of women to the priesthood. There was no evidence that on contentious matters like homosexuality he would charge up some embarrassingly liberal path. And Mr Catford could be relied upon to explain to Mrs Thatcher that the Bishop of Bath and Wells was just the sort of person she liked, a self-made man who was, in fact, One of Us. But just as it is inconceivable that Dr Habgood was not considered, if only briefly, so, once the Commission had settled, in principle, on an evangelical, it is almost certain they would have spared five minutes to mull over the possibility of recommending by far the most able and experienced evangelical bishop, David Sheppard of Liverpool. Against him might have been his age – sixty-two – but his name would have been dropped like a hot potato anyway after one warning glance from Mr Catford: too liberal. The final choice returned with a kind of fateful inevitability to George Carey who, believing he was God's choice (as would any evangelical worthy of the name), accepted with alacrity.

It was Robin Catford who broke the news to Dr Carey that the prime minister wanted to nominate him. 'We had a coffee together,' the archbishop told me. 'He had said he wanted to see me urgently, and I assumed either he wanted to find out if I was willing to let my name go forward or he was coming to ask me about someone else.' This was early in July. 'I had no reason to think they'd already made a decision. I assumed the Commission was going to meet a couple of times. So I was in fact quite astonished. I was fully expecting the process to go on to later in the year. It could easily have done so. And I was quite astonished to find that the letter he took out of his pocket was from the prime minister actually offering me the post.'

When Dr Carey took time off to have a coffee with Catford he was in the middle of a teaching mission in one of the deaneries. After Catford had left, he spoke to no one but his wife. 'My wife and I work very closely together,' he told me. 'Our policy is always to talk and pray over a particular thing together, and I wasn't going to make this an exception to a rule of life. So naturally we met up that day, talked it through over lunch, and I had to phone her later in the day because I was on this mission and couldn't go home.' It was during this telephone call that the decision was made.

Having been a bishop less than three years, Dr Carey had decided to accept the archbishopric of Canterbury after deliberating for about six hours. I asked if he had entertained any qualms. 'At the end of the day one has to say, I'm an unprofitable servant. I only did what it was my duty to do. And in all my ministry I have never run away from a challenge. But never once did I have a mitre at the bottom of my suitcase. I never believed that I would be asked to be a bishop, let alone archbishop of Canterbury.

'However, for those who think I may be a Johnny-come-lately I ought to point out that I've spent seventeen years in theological education, I'd been a member of the General Synod and chairman of its Faith and Order Advisory Group. I'd been in parish ministry. I just want to put it to you that all that actually gives me a very good background as archbishop of Canterbury at this particular time. So although I hadn't been very long as a diocesan bishop, it was long enough to get my feet under the table.'

On leaving the meeting which had alighted on Dr Carey's name, one member of the Commission was heard to exclaim, 'Good heavens, what on earth have we done!' They had surprised even themselves by the boldness of their decision, and they had certainly confounded the bookmakers, the punters and the ecclesiastical correspondents, one of whom, Clifford Longley, planted an article in *The Times* on 8 April

1991, just eleven days before Dr Carey's enthronement, an article described by Hector McLean – in a letter he felt constrained to write to *The Times* – as 'mischievous and idle speculation'. Longley said that Dr Carey's appointment had been met 'with a gasp of disbelief from the Church', and he went on to report a rumour (perhaps invented by himself) to the effect that the Commission had wanted Dr Habgood, and that in order to ensure that Habgood was chosen, although they realised he was regarded by 'the Tory Evangelical mafia' as too liberal, they had placed alongside his name that of someone (i.e. Dr Carey) 'not so lightweight that the Commission could be accused of not taking the exercise seriously, but weak enough to make it difficult for the prime minister to prefer him to the mighty Archbishop of York'. This somewhat convoluted plot is then supposed to have backfired, Mrs Thatcher presumably declaiming that Habgood would go to Canterbury over her dead body, and that whoever this George Carey was, his was the name she intended sending in a Red Box to the Queen. The balance of probability must remain, however, that George Carey's name emerged as the front runner without much difficulty, and that, contrary to Clifford Longley's 'mischievous' theory, Carey was the Commission's first preference. As a matter of courtesy and common sense – the Commission would have known there was no prospect of Mrs Thatcher reversing *this* decision! – the second name was probably that of John Habgood.

There were many who wished this was not so. 'I think a very great mistake was made in Habgood not being made archbishop of Canterbury,' a member of the General Synod told me. 'I believe he *was* the victim of a right-wing political assassination led by John Gummer. Hence a strong bandwagon rolled for a friendly evangelical, a nice, jolly, friendly evangelical, about whom no one could say anything nasty. Liverpool may have been number two. But Dr Carey came to metropolitan and national life with no experience at all. It is interesting that he went on television to address the nation in a brown cardigan. I asked a working-class East Ender in my parish what he thought of that, and he said, "A working-class man on television would wear a suit and look cool, a middle-class man would know he shouldn't wear a cardigan, and an upper-class man probably hasn't got a cardigan." I thought, why isn't *this* boy Archbishop of Canterbury! It's that lack of streetwiseness that worries me. Everyone was so fascinated by the cardigan that no one remembers what he said.'

Dr Carey's lack of experience of metropolitan or national life soon proved to be a formidable initial stumbling block. If he had been abroad it was only to Toronto. He knew nothing of the Anglican Communion, he had served in the General Synod only a very short time, he had never attended the House of Lords, he had probably met the Queen once, he had gained no ecumenical experience, and indeed his general view of the world was dictated by the limited horizons of three evangelical colleges. Did he realise how much of his blinkered progress through the real world he was giving away when on 5 March 1992 he told the *Daily Mail*, 'I've been ordained for thirty years and I've probably met only four or five homosexuals who are clergy. It's not as if they are an enormous proportion.' He thought there might be 'pockets of homosexual clergy' in London and Southwark, but 'in the evangelical tradition I come from, there has never been a great deal of homosexual activity'.

Unfortunately Dr Carey's most conspicuous characteristic, and the major reason for his being chosen as archbishop of Canterbury, his evangelicalism, has failed to keep pace with the expectations of many of his fellow evangelicals, from whose manly grasp he seems to be slipping. 'Carey now talks of evangelicals as "they", not "we",' Dr John Stott complained. 'I'm naturally sorry because I'm an evangelical and I wish he were too. But we don't burn our reformers nowadays, we make them bishops, and I suppose it would be very difficult for a committed evangelical to be archbishop of Canterbury. He would find himself in an impossible position. He has to be everybody's archbishop. I believe the reason he was invited to be archbishop was that he has a foot in all four Anglican streams. He was brought up within the evangelical fold, he had some kind of charismatic experience in Toronto, so that he associates with charismatics, he is euphoric about reunion with Rome and he is somewhat liberal in his attitude to the Bible. For example, his way of dealing with the ordination of women. One of the definitative tests for those who want to think scripturally is in the first letter of Paul to Timothy, in which he says he doesn't suffer a woman to exercise authority over a man. George Carey's way of dealing with that is to say it wasn't written by Paul and that therefore the text has no authority. My response would be that even if, for the sake of argument, you concede it wasn't written by Paul, and that's by no means proven, it's still in the canon of Scripture and has a certain authority for that reason. To disagree with what the New Testament plainly teaches is liberalism.'

Damian Thompson, religious affairs correspondent of the *Daily Telegraph* (he has become one of Dr Carey's *bêtes noires*), claims to have caught Dr Carey making the sign of the cross before celebrating a sung Eucharist at All Saints' Church in Rome.[19] 'The archbishop *comes* from an evangelical background,' his head of staff at Lambeth Palace, Bishop John Yates, reminded me, when I referred to the archbishop as being an evangelical. 'So what is he now?' I asked. 'Church of England,' the bishop replied.

It seems, from Jonathan Mantle's biography, that Dr Runcie was not even as a matter of courtesy informed who was to succeed him before the announcement was made, and that when he heard the news Runcie pulled himself together sufficiently to issue a dignified but minimal statement: 'George Carey is a teacher and a theologian, particularly qualified to lead the Church in a decade of evangelism. He commands respect and affection among us all in the House of Bishops.' No doubt he could think of nothing else to say. *Spitting Image* naturally fastened on the joyous image of an archbishop jangling tambourines. No previous appointment has elicited such a range of response, much of it pretty fatuous. 'I think I'm suspicious,' said an archdeacon. 'Arrogant and rude,' said a journalist, adding, 'but then, he hates the press.' 'Overpromoted.' 'Rather disappointing,' said a catholic cleric from the north. 'I thought someone who didn't come from the ordinary episcopal establishment would be rather different. He makes such a habit of putting his foot in it. He can't be a stupid man, exactly, he's quite learned. But he is very naive. He probably hasn't knocked around enough. That was the trouble with Coggan, he only knew a very narrow spectrum of the Church of England, and he never widened his horizons, so he never knew what catholics were talking about. Carey's not going to set anything on fire.'

Another journalist who writes on Church affairs told me he thought Carey had been 'the worst possible choice imaginable'. But 'a fast assimilator and learner' was the view of someone at the Anglican Consultative Council. 'But if you ask, has he an overall strategy, I think it is simply to fill the pews.' A catholic theologian said, 'In my few dealings with the archbishop I've been very impressed, really. There is someone there who is prepared to be a human being among human beings. I don't think it was a bad choice at all. When I heard the news, I just thought, Oh, poor chap. I wasn't surprised – and I certainly wasn't desolate.' An Anglo-Catholic lay woman went to Westminster Abbey expecting the worst and wrote to me afterwards, 'We were quite prepared to raise our hands and clap, but actually the archbishop preached an extremely good and acceptable sermon.' But an army chaplain just returned from the Gulf War, who attended a meeting for chaplains at Lambeth Palace, found the then bishop to the Forces, David Smith, 'enveloped us in warmth' whereas the archbishop was 'badly briefed and cold'.

'He's the only shilling article in a penny bazaar,' was one cynic's summing-up. 'It must be a real dilemma for the Crown Appointments Commission, having to produce two names. If you send two good names to Downing Street you may not get the person you really want. If you send one good name and one bad, you still may not get the person you want. I wouldn't buy a used clerical collar from George Carey, he's got no presence. I think it's going to turn out to be a disastrous archiepiscopate. He's got such a lot of lost ground to make up. I know it does sound awful, but it's his voice, his face and his clothes.'

It may be because the Church is so busy reflecting society that it fails to influence it. William Temple's dominance coincided with the rise of trade unionism; the postwar discovery of new theology related to the so-called permissive society; the rise in evangelicalism ran through the Thatcher years. The choice of an unspectacular, untried outsider like Dr Carey, born a working-class Tory, chimed in perfectly with the Tories' choice of Major, a politician who mirrors precisely the age of mediocrity. Someone at Lambeth Palace told me it was nice to see a great warmth between Dr Carey and Mr Major, but unlike Major, Carey was not even vouchsafed a honeymoon. The press immediately created him in its own image, and I was surprised when a suffragan bishop said to me, 'If it turns out he isn't a kind of gung-ho right-wing charismatic, which palpably he isn't, I think that George Carey will be turned on mercilessly.' It felt to me, and must have done to the archbishop, as if he had been turned on already.

In fact, there were individuals prepared to turn on the archbishop before ever the press got hold of the idea. 'He has become a joke,' a clergyman from Dr Carey's own diocese wrote to a friend in a heartfelt spate, 'even before he has taken up the job which he has largely brought upon himself by talking quite unnecessarily and far too much on every ecclesiastical hot potato in the oven.' It took the *Guardian* a year to echo these sentiments in a sarcastic trailer to one of numerous 'exclusive' interviews the archbishop was now busy giving: 'Since he's been Archbishop, more people have been praying. Praying he'd keep quiet.' There had been the famous gaffe, for instance, in the *Reader's Digest*, when the archbishop said that those who did not favour the ordination of women were heretics; this he retracted.[20] 'It is absolute nonsense to talk about him lacking sureness of touch,' his loyal former suffragan bishop of Maidstone (David Smith) told me. 'You cannot have that job sewn up within one minute of becoming archbishop.' On the other hand, if, as Dr Runcie averred, Dr Carey is a theologian, he should have had some idea what constitutes heresy. 'I've made gaffes, of course I have,' the archbishop admitted in the *Daily Mail*, giving 'exclusive' interviews on 5 March 1992 to both the *Mail* and *The Times*. 'Of course I have. No one is perfect.' 'It would take anybody time to get their feet under the table,' David Smith reminded me, echoing the archbishop's own sentiments. 'One of the things I rejoice about, and I think is good for the nation, is that we have someone like the archbishop who admits to making mistakes. For years we have had leading politicians who would never admit to any failures.'

Within ten months of the archbishop's enthronement, Ruth Gledhill was telling her *Times* readers that 'the criticism levelled against Dr George Carey from within the Church of England has been the most bitter faced by any Archbishop this century'. But this ignores a plot by what one provost has described as 'the Mafia', among whom he included two of the most senior laymen and one of the most senior bishops, to secure the resignation of Dr Runcie after Gareth Bennett's suicide.[21] In an article graced by a drawing of the archbishop wearing his episcopal ring on his left hand, Miss Gledhill accused the archbishop of self-pity, a pretty damning indictment of any man in public office. There is no question that a lot of the early criticism was unfair and unspecified. When Dr Carey blamed riots in Newcastle in September 1991 on 'social deprivation, poverty, poor housing and illiteracy' he was accused of condoning riots. A great deal of the Archbishop's first year was spent in damage limitation, and there were some shaky early appointments in the press office at Lambeth Palace which did not help. It does indeed take time to get your feet under the table in the sense of making full use of the best available advice if it seems that only yesterday you were doing the washing up in a vicarage. The archbishop's call for tolerance towards Muslim outrage over the wretched *Satanic Verses* was a perfect case in point; the archbishop was right as far as he went, but only a press officer who was not a halfwit would have allowed him to exclude from his remarks condemnation of the death sentence hanging over the author – assuming a press officer was consulted. It is also the greatest possible mistake for someone in such a high public position as the Archbishop of Canterbury to have his wife appear to be coming to his defence, as Mrs Carey did in the article by Ruth Gledhill. 'He is very, very able,' she told Miss Gledhill. No archbishop should require, or be given, such embarrassing domestic back-up. Equally distasteful is the archbishop's propensity for talking about the unimaginable possibility of being unfaithful to his wife: 'I couldn't live with myself and I wouldn't expect other people to have me as Archbishop.'

One of several interviews granted by Dr Carey to celebrate his first year in office appeared in the *Independent* during the general election campaign. Having just received a pay rise of 6.3 per cent, well above the level of inflation, he took the opportunity to attack 'massive individual pay rises' handed out to top executives during the recession. 'Carey tells greedy industrialists that God may curse them unless they help the poor and homeless,' a banner headline on the front page of the *Independent* warned. As was only to be expected, a Conservative MP said it was time for Dr Carey to return to his tambourine. He held a press conference the next day to urge people to read his comments in the context of the sermon in which they had been made, where, he said, he had gone out of his way to affirm wealth creation. Shocking though it is, few people these days read sermons; likewise, economics and the marketplace are a guaranteed minefield for the clergy, whose somewhat simplistic attitude to morality can even lead them to condemn the making of profits for shareholders, without whose investment in the first place industry would not exist. The archbishop was on firmer ground, although not necessarily safer, when at Easter he declared the bodily resurrection of Christ to be central to Christian belief. The ubiquitous John Gummer was at his heels again, demanding pay cuts for clergy who doubted the literal truth of the Resurrection. 'The Gospels,' Dr Carey said, 'do not explain the Resurrection; the Resurrection explains the Gospels.' Mr Gummer meanwhile was on the wireless hammering on about clergy who did not teach the fundamental doctrine of the Christian faith, which is that Jesus Christ rose from the dead; it was not possible, he said, for someone who denied the fact to be a priest. The BBC was guilty of heresy for interviewing such dissenters. Not for the first time, extremists from either wing of the Church were on collision course, and Dr Carey's evangelical brand was beginning to look a good deal more humane and conciliatory than Mr Gummer's.

The next bone of contention lying in Dr Carey's path was ecumenism. On the eve of a visit to Rome, to call informally on the Pope, Dr Carey made an attempt to regain some control over the ecumenical agenda – seen to have been set in recent years by the Vatican – by suggesting that Roman Catholic teaching on contraception was contributing to overpopulation. It was also a method of getting birth control discussed at the Earth Summit, about to meet in Brazil. Unfortunately, Dr Carey told the *Daily Telegraph* he had tried to understand the Roman Catholic position on birth control, but had failed.

It was perfectly obvious what Dr Carey meant: that he found himself unable to concur with *Humanae Vitae*, the papal encyclical of 1968, not that he was too stupid to comprehend it. Yet again, however, howls of derision went up. 'Glib' was how Andrew Brown of the *Independent* described Dr Carey's 'account of [the] Roman Catholic reasoning'. By this time Dr Carey may well have been recalling with nostalgia calmer days by the moat at Wells, contemplating the swans gliding by, days before he was expected to have every action rehearsed and every word off pat. Andrew Brown had managed to find two anonymous bishops who 'denounced Dr Carey's performance as "extraordinarily inept". One said: "It was an incredible thing for him to have said it now." Another "senior Anglican" asked whether Dr Carey's comments were "a calculated move to offend everyone".' He was defended, not too fluently, by Andrew Purkis, his secretary for public affairs, who told Mr Brown that Dr Carey was 'addressing, in a rather unique way, a nexus of issues and trends of concern to him'.

Having given an interview to the *Daily Telegraph*, Dr Carey was promptly ticked off by their leader writer. No wonder he soon came to distrust the press. The Pope and the Archbishop of Canterbury at loggerheads over sex was just the kind of controversy Fleet Street loves, and they ground into action, the *Guardian* giving a particularly well-informed and helpful lead: 'As the Pope is not in the habit of listening to his people, his bishops or his priests, why should he listen to a man rude enough to suggest that the Catholic Church's rule book might not be infallible?' it asked. Without a shred of evidence to support the theory, the *Daily Express* told its readers, 'Carey is set for clash.' The wind was taken out of their sails somewhat when the *Guardian*, updating its inside information, declared, 'Dr George Carey will not raise the subject of artificial birth-control when he meets the Pope today.' But the *Express* was determined to stick to its guns. 'Pope's veto on women priests shatters unity,' it announced. As Paul Handley wittily enquired in the *Church Times*, 'Which unity would that be, then?' Handley, who had spent a brief spell in the press office at Lambeth Palace, contributes by far the most readable regular column in the *Church Times*, and made fun in the same issue of an attempt by the *Guardian* to line up opinions of Dr Carey's performance so far. Philip Crowe, who had waxed lyrical about the appointment initially but was now understood to have reservations, remained loyal, but said, 'I don't think he's very astute politically. He's much more in the outspoken tradition of Becket and More, which is founded on personal integrity: say what you believe and let the consequences take care of themselves.' 'Yes,' Handley commented, 'but look what happened to Becket and More.' On the other side of the divide, David Holloway, a 'disappointed evangelical', said he was worried that the archbishop 'might stray into liberal, interfaith accommodation'. 'What,' asked the innocent Handley, 'Lambeth Palace not big enough?'

Back at home, Dr Carey found the terra no firma. In a bold decision not to retain his patronage of the Church's Ministry Among the Jews, on the grounds that he wished to remain free to act 'as the protector of the religious freedom of people of other faiths', he managed to get himself accused by a shameless fundamentalist, Tony Higton, founder of Action for Biblical Witness, of the twin sins of liberalism and abandoning evangelicalism. 'Many regarded him as the last hope for the Church of England nationally,' said Mr Higton, scourge of homosexuals and all who deviate from the true path of honesty and righteousness. 'Instead, he is leading us further down the road of interfaith compromise which, unless he corrects it, will seal the Church's fate.' Mr Higton must have fainted clean away when 'the last hope of the Church', in the form of the archbishop, went to Mirfield to preach at a Eucharist celebrating the centenary of the Community of the Resurrection.[22]

Having upset an assortment of Anglican bishops, fellow evangelicals, women against ordination, one or two cardinals and Damian Thompson of the *Daily Telegraph*, whose profile in the *Spectator* of 13 June 1992 was to accuse him of headline-grabbing, Dr Carey managed to get himself labelled in the letters column of the *Independent* 'smug, sanctimonious, patronising and pompous'. This time it was a lecture in the Church of St Lawrence Jewry that caused the outburst, in which the archbishop suggested that atheists did not fully understand the concept of goodness. Unfortunately, as an example of 'the pure goodness which atheists cannot explain', Dr Carey had cited Father Maximilian Kolbe, a Franciscan who, according to Dr Carey, had taken the place of another prisoner in a punishment detail at Auschwitz and been starved to death. The Catholic Media Office pointed out that Fr Kolbe had been killed by a lethal injection. What was bound to rile humanists was Dr Carey's assertion that even if atheists did indulge in 'truly selfless behaviour as exemplified by Mother Teresa, they acted as if they had faith, not as conscientious atheists'. Since Mother Teresa (constantly paraded by Christian apologists as some sort of icon) denies abortion to victims of rape, her name was perhaps another unfortunate choice with which to support his already dubious argument.

In June 1992 Walter Schwarz told readers of the *Guardian* that the archbishop's style and manner were 'unheroic to the point of banality'. Certainly the style in which he writes leaves a good deal to be desired (although I realise this is always a risky thing for one writer to allege of another), with its matey references to 'chaps' and 'kids'. People 'worm' their way into the life of the Church;[23] he uses hideous words like 'individuation', and expressions like 'mind-set' and 'the out-working of purpose'.[24] Asked in New York whether any decisions had been reached about the 1998 Lambeth Conference, he said, 'All is up for grabs at the moment.' This is scarcely the language of a theologian or an intellectual, but of someone who believes that if you popularise or even debase the coinage of communication you will somehow attract the common man. Yet if the *Reader's Digest* is to be believed – and their research is normally second to none – Carey, who as a boy was well and truly undereducated, leaving school at fifteen, has mastered Latin, Greek, Hebrew, French and German. It was at the London School of Divinity, again according to the *Reader's Digest*, 'that a superb mind came into its own'.[25] Carey has a doctorate in philosophy, and his academic achievements have indeed been impressive, but his mind still seems to lag behind his brain's potential. In his *Spectator* article, Damian Thompson pointed out 'the extreme contrast between his elegant sermons on abstruse philosophical matters (all his own work, he says) and the rambling worthiness of his live interviews'. Those words in brackets can be read as sarcasm.

Some of Dr Carey's analogies have certainly been inelegant. While still at Bath and Wells he referred to the Church of England as 'an elderly lady sitting in her corner muttering ancient platitudes through toothless gums'. He has also said some odd things, like 'homosexuality of clergy will always be a problem as long as sexuality is a problem.' Why? Is the same true of heterosexuality? 'The Church is more likely to die of intellectualism than of simplicity.' This remark is hard to grasp and at the same time sounds like a gratuituous swipe at intellectualism, of which, I should have thought, the Church could do with a great deal more.

Apart from having instant access to his own specialist staff, the Archbishop of Canterbury is free to call for advice on anyone he chooses, and it may be this wide-ranging freedom, so different even from anything an ordinary diocesan bishop experiences, that Dr Carey found almost embarrassing to deal with at first. The leap from office boy to Primate of All England is a remarkable one, and in some of the snide comments made about Dr Carey one should not discount the whiff of snobbery. But how professionally competent is the household at Lambeth, the permanent secretariat at the archbishop's daily disposal? 'I would have to say we are growingly professional,' the head of staff, Bishop John Yates, told me. 'We have plenty to learn. But we are understaffed compared with institutions to whom we have to relate, and we often reproach ourselves that we could be more professional by having more staff and smartening ourselves up.'

Bishop Yates, who was recruited by Dr Carey when he retired from the see of Gloucester, regards his title as too functional and would prefer a more pastoral designation; he is sometimes known as the Bishop at Lambeth. 'It's like being vicar of a very small parish,' he said. He regards part of his role as caring for the staff at Lambeth. 'We are a religious community although we don't run a religious test on anyone who works here. The other part of my job is a recognition that the actual demands that come upon the archbishop by way of correspondence are quite impossible for one man physically and mentally to fulfil. But some will benefit from being dealt with by someone with episcopal experience anyway. Authority figures in general in our society are perceived to be much more accessible than they used to be, which has added enormously to the workload. People are now able to write, telephone or fax to the Archbishop of Canterbury about things they are interested in or concerned about in a way that twenty or thirty years ago, never mind 100 years ago, was quite beyond their range. We also live in a world where paperwork is increasing all the time. And of course religion is more in the public eye than it has been for a long time. When Northern Ireland is reported, the words Catholic and Protestant are on everybody's lips.'

Since 1 January 1992 the archbishop's secretary for public affairs has been Andrew Purkis. He has an Oxford doctorate in philosophy. His task is to advise the archbishop on a wide range of political and social issues. There is a secretary for ecumenical affairs, Canon Stephen Platten, who deals with the Archbishop's personal ecumenical relations with other Church leaders, and a secretary for Anglican Communion affairs, Canon Roger Symon. A key figure for the first twenty months was the archbishop's Lambeth chaplain, Canon Graham James, a catholic who trained at Cuddesdon, whom Dr Carey wisely inherited from Dr Runcie. When, in 1992, Canon James was appointed Bishop of St Germans, an evangelical chaplain was appointed to replace him.[26] There is a press officer, a research officer, and a steward who supervises the house and gardens. The cleaners are part-time and the gatekeepers double up as gardeners. There is a chauffeur who drives a Ford Scorpio, a cook, a telephonist, librarians and some eight or nine secretaries.

Bishop Yates chairs a weekly staff meeting, sometimes attended by the archbishop. The bishop said, 'We are aware that a balance has to be struck between being pro-active and reactive. The archbishop is very conscious of the danger of doing nothing but react to events. The Lambeth staff is very much aware that they are the archbishop's staff. Episcopacy is a personal office, and our work is largely geared to his priorities. Contact between Lambeth Palace and the General Synod office is entirely a matter of conscious choice. There is no automatic arrangement whereby everything which emanates from Lambeth will be shared with Church House. Or vice versa. It is thought quite important that the archbishop is not to be identified with the General Synod, and that neither the archbishop nor the Synod is to be totally identified with the Church of England.'

Michael Ramsey never moved without a chaplain in tow, but Dr Carey was quite happy to go off to Italy leaving Canon James behind. He took with him his wife, his secretary for ecumenical affairs and the Suffragan Bishop of Grantham. 'It was a low-profile visit to Rome,' Bishop Yates explained. 'We are well aware of the need to economise so we don't go round in droves just to create a kind of court for the archbishop. In Rome, Canon Platten would have acted as chaplain. Any one of us would be competent to act as chaplain.' The sight of the former bishop of Gloucester carrying the archbishop's cross, or unpacking his suitcase, might raise eyebrows in certain quarters; it might even result in a whip-round to pay for an extra airline ticket.

At the Old Palace in Canterbury the archbishop has a second chaplain, concerned entirely with diocesan affairs. When in England the Archbishop spends most weekends in Canterbury, but authority for the day-to-day running of the diocese was handed over in 1980 to the suffragan bishop of Dover. Since May 1992 this has been Richard Llewellin, previously suffragan bishop of St Germans, who trained at Westcott House and will bring some catholic influence to balance that of Dr Carey's other new suffragan, the evangelical bishop of Maidstone, Gavin Reid. Dover is de facto a diocesan, and is sometimes even known as the Bishop in Canterbury. He offers livings, has pastoral care of the archdeaconry of Canterbury and chairs diocesan staff meetings. Dr Carey is known to miss the role of a diocesan bishop, which he greatly enjoyed at Bath and Wells. He realises there is no question of running the diocese full-time but he has been trying to meet the clergy and their wives in person, visiting three or four deaneries a year. There are fifteen. He should have got round his diocese by 1996.

According to Paul Handley, in his first year in office the Archbishop was called upon to preach, make a speech or present an address seventy times.[27] I am told he receives up to

2,000 'piffling' invitations a year, all of which are politely declined on his behalf. His chaplain sorts out the credible requests, the senior members of the household conduct a diary-planning session, and all final decisions are taken by the Archbishop himself. His instinct when asked to undertake an engagement or to meet someone is to say yes. His political instincts, I am told, are probably left of centre, his preference being 'for dialogue with people without firm and settled convictions but who might change their mind'. He early on learned how difficult it would be to protect his time and privacy; before his face became too well known he and Mrs Carey quite frequently went to the theatre, the Archbishop in collar and tie. Already, under the pressure of work and publicity, such outings are things of the past. What continues to amaze his staff is the amount of time he finds to devote to reading. 'He has no natural historical sense,' someone told me, 'but he has read himself into his office, devouring the lives of Tait, Temple and Davidson.' When he had the time, he used to review books. It is 'his ability to learn and the openness of his mind' that have most impressed one member of the household. These are attributes in any bishop not to be sneezed at. In an archbishop who has come to office with such limited previous experience of the episcopate, they are vital.

The aura of office does not in fact seem to have rubbed off on Dr Carey. It is difficult on a first acquaintance to say precisely why, but there seems to be no distinguishing hallmark, only a very cautious and measured approach. He has not the instantly recognisable donnish humour of Michael Ramsey or the wit yet basic profundity of Robert Runcie; nor indeed the rapier mind of Geoffrey Fisher. Of modern archbishops he approximates most closely to Donald Coggan, except that Lord Coggan has got two first-class degrees. Perhaps Dr Carey finds difficulty expressing, either in writing or verbally, the beliefs he holds, and certainly a hint of authoritarianism and impatience, allied with perhaps two serious flaws, a lack of originality and of humour, make one suspect he will always conscientiously do the very best he can, but that his best may not prove good enough.

One of his predecessors he admires most is Archibald Tait, originally a Scottish Presbyterian and born with a clubfoot.

He became archbishop in 1868, having paid his first visit to London at the age of nineteen. Asked why he had on that occasion taken a walk through Lambeth, Tait replied, 'I wanted to know how I shall like the place when I get there.' Dr Carey admires Tait because 'he was a very fine missionary, concerned about ordinary working-class people'. He himself comes, he likes to remind you, from 'a non-churchgoing working-class family, but the reality is that really the Church of England is a middle-class Church'. Looking ahead to the next decade he told me, 'I do hope that we might find ways of really reaching to those people like my mother and father, my family, who felt they were Anglican but didn't feel comfortable going to church. If at the end of my time we are a compassionate, comprehensive Church – and that comprehensiveness is deeply important to me – I shall be well satisfied. The presence of women in the priesthood will make us comprehensive, and more "catholic" than we were before.

'I would be very sad if I were assessed in ten or fifteen years' time as an archbishop who was afraid to take risks, because I believe that living the Christian faith is risk-taking. It means to entertain very seriously the possibility of falling flat on your face.'

ELEVEN

Sidetracked by Sex

THE bishop who was asked what he thought about sin and replied that on the whole he was against it probably had sex on his mind, for by and large the Church these days seems to equate sin only with sex, perhaps because by comparison with sex, most other transgressions are fairly easy for moralisers to cope with. They don't upset the equilibrium of society in the way sex can – as a political force, for instance. Sex can break down barriers between rich and poor, between classes and between races. It is because sex is so closely related to love that the Church finds it so difficult to come to terms with; in the idealised religious state, love is represented as some sort of perfection. God is said, among other things, to be love, but no one can cope with Him sexually, which is why His son was born immaculately and never married. Sex, for the Church, is a real problem. In the Good Old Days it used to be contained; sex was what married people did, preferably in the missionary position, and anything else was taboo. But certain sections of the Church are slowly waking up to the realisation that love and the sexual expression of love are not the sole prerogative of married couples.

Half of those who ask for a church wedding are already living together, and there are some evangelical clergy who have spotted in this development a golden opportunity for a spot of public breast-beating; they insist that the couple should give them permission to disclose their previous reprehensible conduct to the congregation and to explain that they have asked for God's forgiveness. Can anything more prurient be imagined? But moral confusion is rife. In one recent Synod debate a bishop-designate said cohabitation was a sin against the community, an archdeacon admitted he did not know what Christian marriage was, and a lay woman from Derby pleaded with the bishops not to give moral guidance to the nation; it was, she said, a 'very outdated idea'.

When it was mooted that the Mothers' Union should debate proposals for legalising brothels, a former vice-president, Dr Margaret White, opposed the holding of such a debate and lamented that 'for many years the Mothers' Union has been shedding its principles like leaves on the trees in autumn'. She claimed that Christ had taught that if we found someone in the gutter 'we should help them get out of it, not get down into it and wallow in the mud with them'. One of the 'principles' Dr White mourns was shed in 1970 when divorcées were allowed to join the Mothers' Union – founded in 1876 'to be specially concerned with all that strengthens and preserves marriage and Christian family life'.

Many of those who get divorced are the clergy themselves. Numbers fluctuate, and there is no identifiable group of separated or divorced clergy, but the wives are better organised. In 1983 Frank Field, the MP for Birkenhead, brought together a support group of about ten clergy wives whose marriages had come adrift and who were having problems over things like pensions. He is now honorary chairman of Broken Rites, which currently numbers some 240 women, almost all Anglicans. The membership is fluid, and gives no true indication of the total number of divorces or separations over, say, a decade. 'After receiving support there comes a time when it is right for them to move on,' I was told. 'Some of the early members have remarried, and then they felt it appropriate to discontinue membership.' And of course there are casualties of marriage breakdown who have never even heard of Broken Rites.

The reasons behind the failure of clergy marriages are various, but certain patterns seem to recur. Both the clergy and their wives often find having their home in constant use by other people a strain. Unlike a doctor or a dentist, a priest works at home, and people are in and out all the time. Clergy themselves say that 'having to satisfy the expectations of others all day long' is a particular burden, especially in a job where there is an absolute minimum of supervision. One result of the clergy's perception of themselves as an icon in society is that their wives say they never get to know the man behind the clerical collar; they just see their husband playing out a role. Allied to this is an apparently notorious inability on the part of many clergy to admit to failings or to seek help. Many members of Broken Rites have reported a lack of any social life outside the ranks of their husband's calling – rather as police officers never seem to integrate with the community. 'My husband always insisted on never making friends in the parish' is a typical comment, but one which some of the divorced wives have found ironic when they recall it was their husband's 'friendship' with a female parishioner that brought their marriage to grief.

Although for administrative purposes Broken Rites is located in Durham, it is odd that the treasurer, the editor of the newsletter and the press officer, Maureen Dodd, all live in the diocese of Chichester. 'You could say there are more people on the south coast who have heard of Broken Rites and therefore have joined,' says Mrs Dodd, 'but I don't believe that is so. I believe there are more members in Chichester than in any other diocese because of the lack of pastoral care of the clergy in Chichester.

'You've got a couple whose marriage is rocky: if they are to contact the bishop, the archdeacon or the rural dean they are immediately contacting a member of the hierarchy, on whom their job depends. If, as very frequently happens, the marriage is in trouble because the clergyman is having an affair with somebody, he is putting his job on the line if he confesses to any of the hierarchy. So the initial problem is who to contact. Some dioceses are now building up a network of counsellors, but there is seldom enough support until things have got absolutely critical. The idea is that the clergy should support each other within their deaneries, but how often does that happen? In my experience, very, very rarely. Clergy do not talk to their brother priests. They are very, very reluctant to admit they are under pressure and cannot cope.

'The clergy are expected to be wonderful preachers, marvellous counsellors, and they are supposed to be able to do a vast range of jobs equally well, and an awful lot of clergy feel very vulnerable about admitting inadequacy in any area at all.'

Mrs Dodd has recently encountered clergy couples whose marriage has broken up after a considerable period of time. One woman who contacted Broken Rites had been married fifty years. 'Her husband had just told her to get out because he wanted to marry somebody else. Marriages ending after thirty or forty years are not uncommon. I have not spoken to a single wife who, even at the time of the divorce, did not think that for her, divorce was unthinkable. It is something they do extremely reluctantly. Marriage break-up is something that anyone married to a clergyman finds incredibly hard to deal with. I know couples who have had a nervous breakdown because the decision was such a hard one to come to. Whatever the underlying tensions, adultery accounts for more breakdowns than any other cause.'

Jean Matthews (not her real name) was married in 1977, has been divorced since 1986 and is now a science teacher. She has two daughters. She met her husband, David, when they were both at university, got married while he was still training for the priesthood, and they lived in married accommodation at his theological college. He was ordained when he was twenty-four, so theirs was a youthful marriage, and although he had undertaken various social enterprises, her husband was fairly inexperienced in the ways of the world.

Jean told me, 'The ordination service stressed that the families of married clergy were a reflection of the family of Christ, so expectations of clergy families are much greater even than those of, say, a doctor. They are expected to be perfect. Clergy children cannot do anything wrong.

'A lot of the features of my marriage breakdown I have heard over and over again. The first parish we were in, where my husband was curate, was great. It was really supportive. Then we moved to a parish in a New Town, where the pressures were considerably greater. We stayed there for six years and we went through absolute hell. There was one occasion when the entire PCC resigned en masse, because they wanted to force the bishop to sack David. The church wardens said, "You do a wonderful marriage service, you do marvellous funerals, you do terrific baptisms, but you are not a priest, you're a social worker." There was always conflict in that parish. They expected someone to be on hand in the clergy house twenty-four hours a day. There was a very small congregation and they bitched incessantly. And there was always the anxiety that you weren't getting enough people into the church, that you weren't being a success.

'But the greatest part of our time had to be spent outside the Church – and yes, to a certain extent David was a glorified social worker. It put enormous pressures on him, to the extent that he considered giving up the job. We were living in a council house where there wasn't a proper room to hold meetings. Every time there was a meeting the children had to be pushed out. Money was pretty tight as well. We saw an advertisement for a sewage worker – for three times the pay that David was getting!

'Soon he started knocking the image. People outside the Church have a more conservative image of the clergy than those within and he tried to be one of the lads with people in the parish. It was partly through disillusionment, I think. And also at that time he was doing an awful lot of visiting of women on their own, when their husbands were out at work, and I don't know for certain, but I have been given to understand by a number of other people that at that time he started sleeping around, partly because there were a fair number of women throwing themselves at him, partly because it was effectively the only support and caring he was getting.

'It was just a very, very difficult time for all of us. My health was not fantastic, but we grimly decided we were going to stick it out, come what may. Then David was asked to be a youth officer, and we moved to a small country parish. It was then he was asked to organise a trek across Africa, and he took a woman leader with him. They started an affair as soon as they got across the Channel.

'When he came back it was all "The trip was sheer hell . . . I needed the support of someone". There were excuses and justifications but the affair continued. She left her husband and moved into the rectory. He claimed it was because he was weak and couldn't live up to my expectations or the expectations of the Church. He said he felt a failure . . . she was the only one who could understand what he had been through in the desert, etc. To a large extent I think he was not able to withstand the pressures that he felt himself to be under as a parish priest. He found it impossible to talk to anybody else. He had no close friends in any of the parishes we were in. He used to say that it wasn't a good idea to get too close to people, and he made it abundantly clear right from the start that the Church came first and I came second.

'David went off regularly to clergy retreats, but I couldn't go on a clergy wives' retreat because he wasn't prepared to look after the children. There is minimal support for clergy wives. When I realised things were going wrong I contacted the suffragan bishop, who had been very supportive when the PCC resigned. I wanted him to talk to David to try to get him to give up this woman. He asked David to go and see him, and said that he would find some way of talking to him while retaining my confidentiality. He agreed to deal with the whole thing in strict confidence, and said it was not going to be a disciplinary matter. David came back saying the bishop obviously suspected something but had told him it was all right as long as there wasn't any scandal. I believe this is what David wanted to hear. I don't believe it's what the bishop said.

'When things really came to a head I rang the bishop again, although by then we were out of his patch, but he was the only person I could think of to contact. I said I needed help. I told David what I had done and he said his prospects of promotion were now at an end and he resigned his living.

'Then he married the other woman. By this time he was a school chaplain, and the school said they would help him find another job as long as there was no scandal. The bishop said he would endorse David's application to be a teacher but not a priest, and then gave him a limited licence. There is just no uniformity. I know of several cases where an adulterous priest has persuaded his wife to have a divorce on some other grounds, and has then managed to continue in the parish. I feel this is altogether wrong. I don't consider my husband ought to be a priest. The affair was one of many he had as a result of pressures he was under in the parish and I don't see that he is any more capable of withstanding those pressures now than he was at the time.

'The response of the parish we were in was that I had been the cause of the break-up and all their sympathy was with

David. It is automatically assumed that clergymen can't be in the wrong. Later I plucked up courage to go back to the parish, and a number of people came up to me and said "How nice to see you" and gave me a hug. By then they had heard what had actually been happening.

'My children are totally disillusioned. They are now very anti-Church. It might have happened anyway in adolescence, but they really have become anti-clergy.

'When we were divorced I saw the bishop and he was very supportive. He gave me some money to tide me over to meet immediate bills, which was the best practical help I could have got at that time. One of the problems is that if a wife sues for divorce on the grounds of adultery she makes it impossible for her husband to continue in a job and hence support her and her children. Divorced clergy wives are an embarrassment to the Church. They don't know what to do with us.

'The bishop told David he knew there was an organisation supporting ex-clergy wives but they were a load of interfering women and he wouldn't give him their name and address. I only found out about Broken Rites because a friend of mine heard their name mentioned on *Woman's Hour*. It has been a long slow struggle in my diocese to get Broken Rites accepted. Some time ago I asked if details could be published in the diocesan handbook and I was told that to do so would be seen as condoning marriage breakdown![1]

'Adultery is widespread. My sister-in-law was divorced and immediately she was propositioned by four clergy because they seemed to think that now she was on her own she obviously needed a man to go to bed with. And these were clergy she had known and respected for some time. There's often a conspiracy of silence within the family itself. When my husband was having an affair I couldn't cope with it and he said, "If you blow the lid off this and tell anybody about it it means I lose my job, we lose our home, the children will have to move from their school, the whole fabric of our lives will totally fall apart." So what are your options?

'Talking to other wives in my position you hear the same personality characteristics of the adulterous clergyman coming out again and again. They are enormously manipulative. There are a number of us who are beginning to wonder just how effective the selection boards are in choosing the right ordinands. Perhaps it is time the Church started using some sort of personality test.

'When my marriage broke up, one of the things I desperately wanted to do was talk to a priest and sort out where my belief was. And I could not find anyone who was prepared to do it with me. The archdeacons in my diocese seem to feel that as long as the material needs are met you don't need any other support. But it is the emotional pain that takes time to sort out. That's not recognised enough.'

In the sphere of sex generally the Church of England often behaves at its most inhumane and incompetent. The Christian Church was founded as a radical institution, the very reverse of an Established Church, intended to challenge the world and its secular values, not to uphold the status quo. Jesus exhorted his disciples to leave their homes and to follow him. The woman, the child and the non-aggressive celibate man became its original ideals, all three of whom have for centuries been marginalised by the mainstream churches, where women are tolerated if they stick to flower arranging, children if they keep quiet, and homosexuals if they live in monasteries. Ordained women, on the other hand, are commonplace in Nonconformist churches, and homosexuals have never been ostracised by the Quakers or the United Reformed Church. But while they glory in the erotic art that Christianity has inspired, the mainstream churches have developed a fear of sex that is pathological. The problem is not that the Church has been run for centuries by heterosexual men; it has been run by men deeply ambivalent about their sexuality, whatever its orientation. They have behaved like footballers who hug and kiss on the pitch and later engage in verbal queerbashing in the pub. 'Why,' asked Don Cupitt in a *Guardian* article, 'are women and gays disproportionately attracted to a Church that is so relentlessly determined to give them as bad a time as it knows how? Why haven't they left?'[2]

Had they done so, the Church would have collapsed. Women form the backbone of almost every congregation and they constitute by far the largest number of members of religious orders; without gay clergy in the parishes and monasteries, nothing like 13,000 parishes could be maintained. Until the rise of evangelical fundamentalism these facts were tacitly admitted. The bishops were trusted to take pastoral responsibility for their clergy, and by and large people minded their own business. If the clergy caused a scandal, it had to be dealt with; otherwise what they did in the privacy of their own homes was between them and God. 'Not even apostolic succession confers upon a bishop the right to spy through bedroom keyholes,' as Mervyn Stockwood wrote in his autobiography.[3] Back in 1964 Ian Ramsey remarked during a seminar on natural law, 'The Church has always been opposed to homosexuality. I don't know why.'

Anxious to speak to an 'active' homosexual cleric, I spotted an advertisement in *Gay Times* from someone who was obviously ordained and appeared to be seeking a discreet partner. I wrote asking for a non-attributable interview, and received the following reply: 'I would like to assist you but honestly feel that being aware of the current homophobic climate within the Church of England it would be most unwise for me to do so.' So what has happened to make someone so nervous as even to decline an interview with an assurance of anonymity?

While advocating, for purely pragmatic reasons, the legalising of homosexual conduct in private between consenting men over twenty-one (which came about in 1967), Michael Ramsey felt obliged, no matter what his true feelings, to cover his tracks in the House of Lords by declaring, as had his predecessor, Geoffrey Fisher, that all homosexual relationships were sinful. But when even the Church of Rome recognised the validity of sexual pleasure for its own sake within marriage – that is to say, it ceased to hold that procreation was the sole or prime purpose of sex – it became almost impossible for theologians not to begin to ponder the theological position of people like homosexuals for whom marriage was not an option but who had no vocation to celibacy. That there were no theological objections per se to homosexual conduct had been concluded by the Quakers as early as 1963, and the Methodist Church caught up in 1979. Hence for the past decade or so the Church of England has been inching its way towards a theology of sex that takes into account the homosexual as well as the heterosexual condition. A decision by the 1978 Lambeth Conference to give the question of homosexuality 'deep and dispassionate study' prompted the Church of England's Board for Social Responsibility to set up a working party; its 1981 report, *Homosexual Relations: A Contribution to Discussion*, took thirteen authors, just two of whom were homosexual, three years to produce, the signatories admitting they knew 'very little about the majority of homosexual men and women'.[4] Its other farcical failing, for which it was much derided and ridiculed, was its suggestion that clergy who wished to live in a homosexual relationship should offer their resignation to their bishop, hastily explaining that of course there was no compulsion upon the bishop to accept it. It was, said Richard Kirker, administrative secretary of what was then known as the Gay Christian Movement, 'wicked and naive of them to have posed this dilemma.' And indeed, it is hard to think of any other employer who, after taking on staff following an interview, and perhaps having extracted twenty years' loyal service from them, would invite them to resign with a vague hint that their resignation might not be accepted, and with no offer of compensation if it was. But such is the cloud-cuckoo land in which the Church resides when it comes to sex. There were at the time an estimated 3,000 homosexual clergy out of a total workforce of about 14,000. Between one-third and a half of all the ordinands in training at St Stephen's House, Salisbury, Chichester and Cuddesdon were said to be gay.

This half-baked report was debated in the General Synod on 27 February 1981. The contribution made by the archbishop of Canterbury, Robert Runcie, was less than inspired, and showed how little serious thought even intelligent people had given to the subject. He said his rule of thumb for not ordaining a homosexual would be 'if a man was so obsessive a campaigner on this subject that it made his ministry unavailable to the majority of Church people. Then I would see no justification in ordaining him.' The message to ordinands was clear: keep your mouth shut until after ordination. And by 'unavailable' the archbishop surely meant 'unacceptable', a very different thing indeed. Having condemned the 'casual contempt and unthinking mockery' of homosexuality which, said Dr Runcie, so often passed for discussion, he went on to ask whether it was possible to believe that 'all those hairy old toughs of centurions in Tacitus, clinging to one another and begging for last kisses when the Legion was breaking up,' were 'all pansies'. He concluded by expressing the view that homosexuality was neither sin nor sickness, but a 'handicap', and his considered advice to the Church was, 'I do not believe it is possible for anyone to be loyal to the Christian tradition and to see homosexual and heterosexual relations as having equal validity.' This was to clothe 'Christian tradition' in some sort of eternal mystique, but even Christian traditions have proved capable of being jettisoned. The Church no longer burns heretics. Neither does it any longer advocate slavery. As for the 'tradition' that only men can be priests, that too has gone by the board.

The bishop of London, Graham Leonard, did acknowledge the Church's guilt for its share of hostility towards homosexuals, but promptly added, 'In saying this, I am not implying that we must necessarily take homosexuals at their own valuation, especially bearing in mind that some of them have explicitly said that they want acceptance as embodying normal variants of sexuality and not compassion or cure.' What that sentence meant, translated into normal English, was: 'Unless you are prepared to be patronised or cured, do not expect to be accepted.' Dr Leonard later singled out for special commendation the most unpleasant speech of the day, made by a gay evangelical cleric, Robert Lewis, a former chaplain to Donald Coggan, in which he described homosexuality as 'a cheat' and the position from which he viewed himself as 'a dung hill'. This was received with prolonged and wildly enthusiastic applause. It was just what the Synod wanted to hear: a self-confessed homosexual in an attitude of abject abasement and self-disgust. But ignorance and prejudice were having a field day. One speaker fell back on 'the transforming power of the gospel'; the director of the Festival of Light assured the Synod it was not possible to produce any definition of sin that did not include 'male homosexual pseudo-copulation' (presumably mutual masturbation and fellatio were all right); a young doctor launched into a lecture on hormones; a nun commended celibacy (the least she could do); and one old boy seriously suggested that a man's sexual orientation might be swayed up to the age of forty-five.

In the 1980s permission for queerbashing, both of a physical and discriminatory nature, was granted by two sources: the Thatcher government passed legislation preventing local authorities from 'promoting' homosexuality, which not only forbade intelligent discussion of the subject in schools but cut out essential counselling, and the gutter press labelled AIDS a 'gay plague'. This created a right-wing climate in the country which was seized upon by Christians with a fascist mentality to reassert mindless fundamentalism with great effect. On 11 November 1987 (no armistice day for the Church of England) the General Synod debated a private motion tabled by the Rev Tony Higton, rector of Hawkwell in Essex. The damage Mr Higton did cannot be calculated.[5] In one fell swoop he asked the Synod to 'reaffirm' that sexual intercourse should be restricted to marriage, that in 'all circumstances' fornication, adultery and homosexual acts were sinful, that as a condition of being appointed to or remaining in office 'Christian leaders' should be 'exemplary' in all spheres of morality, including sexual morality, and that the ministry of healing should be offered to all who suffered physically or emotionally as a 'result of such sin'.

As soon as he stood up he disclosed his hand. 'Today,' he said, 'the nation and the world are going to make a decision, *not about sexual morality* [my italics] but about the credibility of the General Synod and of the Church of England. Whatever decision we take will send out a powerful message, either that the Church is courageously true to its biblical and traditional foundations or that it is not.'

The debate was to be about fundamentalism. However, sex was not exactly left on the sidelines, for what Mr Higton had on his mind in particular was homosexuality and its practitioners. What sort of example, he wanted to know, was it to the young and those outside the Church when it was 'common knowledge' that gay clerics were 'frequently' seen in bars and gay clubs? He hastened to assure the Synod he did not suffer from homophobia, nor was he calling for a witch-hunt; it was just that the Church should teach that 'all homosexual practice is an abomination and a perversion'. Those who refused to repent should face discipline.

Warming to the true purpose of his motion, Higton admitted that his main concern was with 'immoral practices among the clergy' and only secondarily with 'immorality amongst Church members'. Presumably this was because 'Church members' are more amorphous and thus less easy to target.

There followed what Mr Higton said he knew to be 'thoroughly reliable evidence', although it sounded more like hearsay: a lurid catalogue of seductions at theological colleges, 'priests convicted of child molestation' (trying to link homosexuals with paedophiles is a well-known homophobic trick), the pursuit of the laity by sex-crazed clergy, and distraught wives on the telephone begging Mr Higton to tell the Synod about their husband's homosexual affairs, 'so that we could do something to help'.

What, he asked, *could* the Synod do? He wanted only those 'upholding biblical and traditional morality' (whatever that might be) ordained. The bishops should 'investigate situations concerning clergy brought to their attention, and practise correction and Church discipline'. And, he said, 'we can affirm the gospel of God's free grace in Christ' and the fact that 'Christ can transform human beings, including those facing homosexual tendencies'. Those who called themselves 'gay Christians' were undermining the central message of the Christian gospel – the message that lives could be changed through the power of the Holy Spirit. 'We must,' he concluded, 'help them to see the error of their ways and unashamedly proclaim biblical beliefs and morals.'

It was left to a gay clergyman, Malcolm Johnson, then still rector of St Botolph's, Aldgate, to explain to the Synod that the motion 'hit the single parent with condemnation and calumny', that it injured the divorced and maimed the remarried, 'for in biblical terms they are adulterers'. How, he asked, when many in the Synod had fought hard to recognise second marriages, could they now say that adultery was sinful in all circumstances? He thought the motion a 'negative piece of work, lacking in faith, lacking in hope and lacking in love'. He recalled that many gay clergy were ministering effectively in inner-city areas and they owed their stability to 'deep, good relationships'. He had recently conducted the funeral of a man who had been with his lover twenty-seven years. 'Should I have faced his partner at the crematorium,' he asked, 'and told him that we judge his friendship by his genital acts? Should I have told him that he has sinned for twenty-seven years, that his love "falls short" and that he needs forgiveness?' And he poured scorn on the idea that ministers might remain in office only if they led exemplary lives. 'There are seven deadly sins,' Father Johnson reminded the Synod, 'not just one: lust, pride, sloth, gluttony, covetousness, envy, anger. If we have to leave after committing these, the Church will be very short-staffed indeed,' a state of affairs underlined by the Bishop of Chester, who said, 'If we pass the main motion today, all the bishops and clergy would need to resign tomorrow morning.'

The archbishop of Canterbury, Dr Runcie, made amends for his insensitivity in 1981. 'I want to insist,' he said, 'that to be a homosexual by nature is to be a full human being, that homosexuals have human rights like the rest of us. We need to listen to what such homosexuals say about their situation.' He said the House of Bishops had given particular thought to homosexual clergy, and he did not believe more legislation was needed. 'Rather, I believe that clergy behaviour is best left to their fathers-in-God within the present terms of the law.'

As Peter Selby has stated in his book *BeLonging*, the situation of gay clergy

> has been rendered extremely perilous by the November 1987 debate. A few speakers, including one or two bishops, complained about the tone of the proposition and its supporters' collusion with the gutter press; but there was no corporate dissociation of themselves by the Church's chief pastors from the stream of lurid tales of homosexual immorality which amounted to a public and general attack on a whole group of clergy who had in those circumstances no means of defending themselves.

The result, says Bishop Selby, could have been predicted. 'Honesty has been the first and immediate casualty; the pressure is there on all homosexual people to deceive themselves, and certainly not to reveal their self-knowledge to those whose task, in theory, is to care for them.' Who can count, the bishop asks,

> the invisible multitude of the dismayed, those who thought that the gospel of Jesus Christ might have something to say to people who have found their own sexuality, for all its not having been chosen, something gracious and life-giving not just for themselves but for others?
>
> The evidence of the Synod debate is that their experience is not worth listening to, that they are guilty by association with abusers and paedophiles, that they are not welcome if they are not celibate and likely to be suspected if they are.

Bishop Selby felt great concern not just for Christian homosexuals but for 'homosexual people generally', as did his wife, Jan Selby, who wrote to the *Church Times* to say she thought the outcome of the debate would confirm to those with whom she worked – children excluded from school for bad behaviour and other problems – that the Church had nothing to offer them. The great majority came from broken homes where there had been little love or care, and few had ever witnessed stable and loving relationships. Hence for them to form a committed relationship for six months represented a major breakthrough. She recalled a former pupil, a gay teenager, who had attempted suicide, and despite most of the arguments she had heard at the Synod she remained convinced 'it is right to hope that this young man will be able to find a permanent, committed and loving relationship with another man'.

We could all tell stories, Mrs Selby wrote, about homosexual clergy, but she doubted if they would be of a kind cited in the debate. 'Rather, they would have to do with receiving sensitive pastoral care and wise spiritual counsel; of warm and generous hospitality and friendship which reaches out to welcome those ill at ease with many conventional Church gatherings, acting as a corrective to the view that the nuclear family is the be-all and end-all of community living.' Her letter was not published.

In June 1992 the Bishop of Toronto, Terence Finlay, told the Anglican Church of Canada, 'My heart aches for gays and lesbians trying to live monogamous lives and stay in the

Church.' It is interesting that there was no condemnation by Mr Higton, or even mention, of lesbians who live together. Perhaps he was unable to unearth any 'biblical tradition' with which to belabour them. Or perhaps because they are congenitally incapable of the sin of Onan – they have no seed to waste – they pose less of a threat to the perpetuation of the human race, which is what really lies, back in Judaistic tribal tradition, behind irrational hostility towards male homosexuals. Be that as it may, no English diocesan has yet had the courage to say anything so straightforward, but some seem to be edging towards it, despite the continuing fallout from what has come to be known as the Higton debate. Encouraged by the regurgitated balderdash about changing people's sexual orientation, self-appointed counsellors, all evangelicals, set to work to persuade homosexuals they were heterosexual. The vicar of St Peter's at Littleover in Derbyshire told Diana Hinds of the *Independent* he wanted to learn more from the Living Waters Sexual Redemption in Christ Programme, imported from America by St Michael's, Chester Square. Clergy, who themselves are almost always untrained in psycho-sexual counselling, are permitting totally unqualified lay members of their congregation to dabble in it. Canon Michael Cole of Woodford Green in Essex told Miss Hinds the laity in his church who offered 'sexual wholeness counselling for homosexuals' were trained 'mainly on the job', perhaps a slightly unfortunate choice of phrase in the circumstances.[6]

But when it comes to homosexuality, the Church of England moves in any number of mysterious ways. The bishops commissioned an advisory report, known as the Osborne Report,[7] which, like an earlier report on homosexuality, was never published. The bishops read it (in 1989) and promptly hid it under the carpet. One of the seven compilers was Malcolm Johnson, who told me, 'The bishops said it was too contentious to publish, but I can't think why. We felt it was very even-handed.' What it did was recommend that the Church should 'affirm the values and richness of same-sex friendships and consider ways in which support and structures can be provided'. Sensibly, it made no distinction between the laity and the clergy. But this was too frightening for the bishops, so in December 1991 they decided to spread further alarm, despondency and uncertainty by publishing their own statement, *Issues in Human Sexuality*; its most contentious conclusion was that while homosexual relationships might be 'tolerated' among the laity they were not acceptable for the clergy.

Significantly, the statement carried a preface by the Archbishop of Canterbury, acknowledging that it did not pretend to be the last word on the subject, but there were those, among them the former bishop of Lincoln, Simon Phipps, who were not prepared to sit idly by while the House of Bishops took another decade or so to decide what that last word was to be, or indeed to catch up with the pioneering work undertaken in serious studies thirty years ago by Douglas Rhymes, Donald West, Gordon Westwood and many others.[8] Bishop Phipps argued that the House of Bishops was wrong to insist that liberty for clergy to enter into 'sexually active homophile relationships' would be seen as placing that way of life 'in all respects on a par with heterosexual marriage', and that to make the distinction between clergy and laity in this respect was pastorally and therefore theologically untenable. Having made these points in a letter to the *Independent*, he then produced a paper for the Association of Pastoral Care and Counselling, of which he is president, in which he wrote that some homosexuals

> have felt that the Gospel has called them into a stable commitment to a partner of their own sex in an ongoing, faithful, tender relationship resourced by Christian faith. They see this as a living of the Gospel in the context of their particular sexuality and sexual orientation.
>
> The commitment in such relationships, the costly love, the human warmth, the mutual fulfilment, the conscious dependence on God for all his graces, is no different, nor any less, to that in stable Christian marriages. Indeed, the patient and courageous endurance of much misunderstanding, which often attends upon such relationships, may make for an even deeper 'living of the Gospel'.

The bishop concluded by quoting from the statement: 'There is such a thing as the mind of the Church on matters of faith and life. Those who disagree with that mind are free to argue for change.' And then he lunged at his fellow prelates by adding, 'The Bishops have not numbered themselves among them, and thereby have abrogated their vocation to prophecy.'

'The bishops get full marks for trying,' the rector of St Mary-Le-Bow, Cheapside, London, Victor Stock, told me, 'but until the Church can offer adult homosexual people an ethic to live by as Christians it hasn't got much useful to say. Because whatever the Church says officially, human beings will want to share their lives with someone else and base their whole life upon that partnership. It is a basic human need, and I think this focusing on sexual activity all the time is a kind of reactive muddle the bishops get into. I wonder if the gay bishops were asked to give any evidence?' He thought there were three or four.

Father Johnson said, 'The Church has got to look at the whole spectrum of sexuality, and I would hope that in every deanery there would be some way of setting up at least a discussion. We shall disagree, but then in the Church of England we disagree about everything. And if a deanery or diocese is looking at homosexuality I feel very strongly there must be an openly gay or lesbian person present. You can't keep talking about "these people" or "them". The diocese of Chester set up a working party to look into homosexuality and they wrote to me to ask what I thought. I asked if they had got a gay man or a lesbian on the group? No, they hadn't. It hadn't occurred to them!'

As far as *Issues in Human Sexuality* is concerned, Fr Johnson says it is the bishops' insensitivity about their relationship with their clergy he finds most disturbing. 'I suspect few of them have any knowledge of committed gay relationships. Don't they realise the tenuous relationships they now have with their homosexual clergy will be even further weakened by this statement? I counsel and talk with homosexual clergy and ordinands every day, and this statement has forced me to advise them to lie to the very men who should be offering them support and care. But a growing number of parishes, particularly in urban areas, now accept that their parish priest is living in a discreet homosexual relationship, and I think it may be time for the laity to educate and reassure their bishops. The bishops are terrified of the subject, and terrified that if they openly come out in support of homosexual clergy they will be picked off one by one by the gutter press. They could prevent this if they spoke with one voice.'

The next major rumpus over sex blew up in March 1992: the aborted publication of a prayer book for gays, *Daring to Speak Love's Name*. This had been commissioned by the Society for Promoting Christian Knowledge, an eminently respectable publishing house with a governing body packed with establishment figures, and had been vetted by six readers, including the Bishops of Edinburgh and Crediton. In a most ill-advised move, the Archbishop of Canterbury guaranteed maximum publicity for the book. He is ex officio president of SPCK, but it is stretching credulity too far to suppose that such a busy man in a purely honorary role reads every manuscript before publication. Yet he was sent the manuscript of this book, and concluded it was regrettable that prayers relating to AIDS should appear alongside those concerned with people 'celebrating same-sex relationships', because 'this could reinforce the myth that AIDS was only a problem for the homosexual community'. He informed the editorial director, Judith Longman,'If a divergence between me as president and SPCK's editorial policy were frequently repeated then I would have to consider whether to remain in the role.' This, as a child of ten could have foretold, was taken as a threat to resign over publication of a book for and about gays. 'Archbishop halts gay prayer book' was only one of many inevitable headlines. If Dr Carey did not appreciate the kind of pressure under which a letter such as his would place SPCK, many of whose donations are induced by his name and that of the Queen on its letterheading, then he still had a lot to learn about the office of an archbishop. It was under such pressure that the publication committee took the cowardly decision to break their contract with the author.

Dr Carey had complained that the contents of the prayer book did not conform with the bishops' recent statement, but why should they? The book had been compiled ecumenically (the author, a lecturer in theology, was a Roman Catholic), SPCK is not an official Church of England publisher, and the book specifically stated it was not a Church of England publication. As a leading article in the *Independent* concluded,

Dr Carey emerged from this episode 'looking intolerant, heavy-handed and homophobic'.

In a letter to the *Church Times*, the Bishop of Edinburgh, the Bishop of St Andrews, the Dean of Winchester and the writer Monica Furlong asked the governing body of SPCK to reverse the publication committee's decision, but this it declined to do, and the book was then snapped up by Hamish Hamilton. 'Yet again,' the Rev Michael Vasey, tutor in liturgy at St John's College, Durham, wrote to the *Church Times*, 'gay Christians have to find in Jesus and the Cross the resources to forgive and love a rejecting, blind and unrepentant Church.'

One of the guests at a service of blessing for a gay couple held at St Luke with Holy Trinity, Charlton, Southwark, turned afterwards to the rector, Tony Crowe, and said, 'I wish I'd had a wedding service like that.' Mr Crowe, who is himself married, has now held some twenty services of blessing for gay couples, both men and women, and he is one of a growing number of clergy prepared to do this in defiance of a Church whose liturgy in any case is practically a free-for-all. 'The Higton debate,' he told me, 'did dreadful damage. It made the bishops very frightened, and they feel that as well as the press they have the evangelicals breathing down their necks. Individually, except for Chester and Ripon, who says he has never ordained a homosexual, they are fairly liberal. But there is so much deceit. The pastoral havoc that debate created is that gays feel very marginalised, as though they are not part of the Church of England.

'The sooner the ordination of women and the situation of gays is sorted out and is out of the way, the better. The real problems we should be dealing with are homelessness and poverty. The mission of the Church has been sidetracked by sex.'

Mr Crowe's PCC debated whether he should hold services of blessing, and gave him the go-ahead in 1980. Some twenty years ago, a handful of clergy would have conducted a short improvised service in private on their own initiative, but although services are still not exactly advertised, and are usually conducted fairly privately, if possible in a chapel, service sheets are printed and there is a defined liturgical structure. In no way, however, do they ape the marriage service. And not every couple who applies for a blessing is given one. Tony Crowe has turned down two couples, including a lesbian couple, one of whom wanted to turn up dressed as a man. Some of the couples whose union he blesses have been referred to him by Gay Switchboard; some have been Roman Catholics, driven to the Church of England on the assumption that their own parish priest would deny them his blessing. About half are committed to the Church – a rather higher proportion than in the case of heterosexuals seeking a church wedding. Mr Crowe claims that a proposed move to another parish was blocked on Dr Runcie's instruction when it became known that he conducts these services, and now he has given up all hope of a transfer. He hardly goes out of his way to ingratiate himself with the establishment, permitting women priests from overseas to celebrate in his church as well.

Tony Crowe sees far more lesbian couples than he does gay men, and thinks this is because women are more religious and tend to be homemakers. His first assumption is almost certainly true; nearly twice as many girls as boys are confirmed. Three-quarters of the women have children, who usually accompany their mothers to the service. 'I am,' Crowe said, 'always moved by the commitment they have. In fact, I take more care and time over blessings than I do over weddings. I think it is very important for the couple to choose the prayers, the readings and the promises. I try to maintain a balance between informality and reverence. Most of the congregation are gay and it is essential for them to feel accepted and welcome. I was terrified before my first blessing, of two men, but by actually doing it I became convinced it was absolutely right and that my conscience was clear. We may feel that we are pioneering new forms of ministry, yet the sense of Christ's presence is very much with us on these occasions.'

Michael Peet is the team rector of Holy Trinity and All Hallows in Bow, east London. He told me, 'Wherever I work in future it will be somewhere where the openness of being gay will be important. All the way through my ministry my being gay and my attitudes to the Church have been tangled up together. There are umpteen gay clergy who are very happily conservative, nay reactionary, and are happy to live a very quiet life. They don't rock any boats or see that they have any political role. So being gay per se doesn't make you active or radical or whatever. At the same time, I think, in my own personal journey, that such radicalisation as has taken place in my life – having come from a very conventional Tory working-class background – has been partly because I am gay. The fact that I was gay tended to make me more left-wingish in the Church.

'When I was ordained, the fact that I was gay was totally unthought-through. I went to King's College, London, in 1964 and was selected for ordination training when I was nineteen. I knew I was homosexual but I didn't have a clue what to do about it. There was certainly no idea about celibacy in the Church. I didn't come from that tradition at all. The clergy got on quietly with their lives and some had partners. There were those who sublimated, I suppose, and were celibate, and there were those who were promiscuous, I suppose, and hung about the bars or whatever. I sailed through college and selection conference without anyone asking me. The subject wasn't raised. I went to see the dean of King's[9] in my third year and said, "I think I've got homosexual tendencies," and this was because I'd fallen in love with another student, so he sent me to a psychiatrist! Someone else told me to go to the chapel every time I felt temptation and pray. Which was equally helpful!

'I went through a very unhappy time during my year as a deacon. It was a disaster in all sorts of ways. I was disastrously misplaced and I am very angry with the Church for dumping me in a very bad parish in Battersea, with a vicar who was about to go off his head. He was on the turn from being very Anglo-Catholic to very Pentecostal and ended up taking to drink. He was a very unstable person and there was me in this rotten parish. I was too young and innocent to know what was going on, and pastoral care wasn't very good. Being unhappy in this parish and not being far from Chelsea across the river, it didn't take me long to work out where the gay bars were, so I had encounters and affairs which were rather miserable and unhappy. I told the vicar and he laid it down in no uncertain terms that it was a sin and that I must repent and change my ways. So I went to see Mervyn Stockwood, who was my bishop, and said I can't be priested. He was very good and told me to take a couple of years out, so I did a post-graduate teacher training course, and then went back into parish work.

'Such ministry as I have to gay people has only developed in the last few years. I started off by feeling accepted by God and having a very positive view of myself as being gay. Obviously this was not a blank cheque for doing anything that came along, but basically it was a feeling that it was OK in the eyes of God to be gay. And it was what you did with it, like anything else, that was the important thing. I've lived with my partner now for seventeen years and that's given me a stability, a strength and an insight into relationships. A lot of the work I do with marriage preparation and counselling is informed by my own relationship. The echo is there. In each parish where I have worked, everyone has known. When I came here it was a job that was advertised, and the job description said the parish was non-racist, non-sexist and non-heterosexist. Very trendy. So in my application I mentioned Raymond and that I'd been involved in gay groups, so I came openly to the parish here. I'm not a callow youth any more. I've been in this diocese fifteen years. They can't boss me about any more. I've got allies and supporters, and although it's true I am defying the bishops by living with another man, I think I've pulled it off.

'The new bishop, David Hope, has been very pastoral and has chatted to me for an hour, about the issues rather than about me. And when I came away I thought, whoopee, I've bucked the system. But that's the bishops' problem.

'For two clergy living together, mobility can be very difficult, if one is moved. For a priest living with a layman it's no different to the sort of problems faced by married clergy. Raymond is a bookseller, and has no difficulty commuting to work. I think if we had a real difficulty over moving house he would think my job would take priority. We had our relationship blessed by a priest in London after six years, with the church doors closed but plenty of friends present. My team rector and the rest of the staff came. It was not a marriage, it was a thanksgiving for six years and a pledge to each other to carry on. Which we have done!

'I give other couples a blessing. There is no set form. We construct together what people want to do. Without exception they all have only a nominal Christian faith, which is slightly disappointing because I have fantasies of working together with a really committed group of gay Christians, so it's never quite as exciting as you think it's going to be. I've never had a couple who have thought through the theology of their promises. They tend to be the sort of couples you get for weddings in the East End. My criteria are the same as for weddings and baptisms round here. If you're too highfalutin it isn't pastorally very apt.

'For a blessing, it's got to be a relationship that has been going for a while, something like six months to a year at least. I'm not interested in people saying, "I met this wonderful guy last Friday." I make it slightly difficult for people. I won't say yes over the telephone. I let them go through a couple of little hoops, like "Come and talk to me, but I'm sorry, I can't make it for the next fortnight." And when we have talked about it, I tell them to go away and think about it. And one or two haven't come back. I had a phone call a couple of weeks ago from a chap who said he wanted a blessing quickly, and became a bit shirty when I said I wanted to discuss it first, and I never heard from him again. But if they say they want God's blessing I'm not going to give them a theological examination.'

Father Peet was ordained in 1968 and met Raymond in 1975. 'It's been very nice to have someone to love and support me, encourage me and look after me. It's given me, under God, a stability. And as far as being gay is concerned, it has absolutely reinforced my feelings about the goodness of gay relationships, and the strength and ordinariness of them. It makes me more and more angry about the people who condemn and abuse such relationships. Over the years I wonder how many gay people I failed to help pastorally because they never thought to come and see me. Who knows how many young people in previous parishes would have been helped if I'd been a bit more open years ago? Maybe there are youngsters in this parish who know I am gay and will be helped directly or indirectly by that.

'But I'm getting a bit weary now, I must confess. It isn't an issue round here. Then you have archbishops and reports all making it an issue. What are these people talking about? Are they talking about me and my friends? Why are they getting in such a tizz about it? In the age of AIDS a good model of gay life is even more essential. I believe in monogamy and all the very boring, old-fashioned virtues.

'I used to think there was a premium against being honest and having a committed relationship, with pressure on you to lead a promiscuous life. As a young man, the message I got was that to nip down to Brighton for a dirty weekend and then to keep quiet about it was all right, but to live with a partner was not on, because this would be a cause of scandal and offence. There's still an undertow of that. The Church can't face up to stable relationships. There's no other area in life where the double standard pertains. Theft is taboo for all. There are lots of things Christians disagree about fundamentally. We disagree about war and peace, and economic policies, and yet we live together. We can be polite. But the nearer it gets to sexual things, the ordination of women, abortion, homosexuality, the passions really tear us apart. You don't hear Higton denouncing usury, do you? Or militarism?'

TWELVE

The Women's Vote

THE decision to ordain women to the priesthood has divided the Church of England just as it divided many of those provinces and dioceses of the Anglican Communion – fifteen by 1993 – who had taken the plunge and decided to ordain women before the Church of England got around to it. But it has also united members of the Church of England across party, gender and sexual lines in ways which suggest the complexity of the issues at stake. Both men and women were for and against; homosexuals came out on both sides of the argument; so did evangelicals and catholics, laity, clergy and bishops. The arguments against the ordination of women got polarised – in the catholic camp – as an affront to catholic order, the Church of England, it was said, having no authority to ordain unilaterally, without the concurrence of Rome and the Orthodox Churches; and – among evangelical opponents – as unscriptural, women apparently having no business to be in authority over men (the 'headship' argument). Likewise, among catholics there was objection to women usurping the iconic role at the Eucharist. What, on the other hand, united so many apparently disparate representatives of the body of Christ was a realisation of the inevitable, a desire to appear credible to society, a wish to create 'equality' and 'justice', and a genuine inability to discern any theological objections.

The 'social' arguments in favour of women priests were put to the General Synod by Dr Carey, when he said, 'We are in danger of not being heard if women are exercising leadership in every area of our society's life save the ordained priesthood,' and by the Bishop of Southwark, who declared, 'I cannot with any degree of integrity challenge the injustices of society and turn a blind eye to the apparent injustice in the Church which prevents women from testing their vocation to the priesthood.' Knowing how close the vote would be, they presumably agreed with the *Independent* that it was 'better that women priests should be ordained into a divided Church than that they should not be ordained at all'. And presumably they believed, too, that the time for finely tuned theological debate was over. To what extent, all along, theological arguments had in fact masked unspoken fears of change in general, had been used as an excuse for misogyny, and had allowed a distaste for feminism in its more extreme manifestations to form a general judgement about women, it is quite impossible to say, but obviously some theological objections were at least tinged with cultural and sexual attitudes.

Those simply unable to stomach a women priest will have to hope their parish has both ordained men and women on its staff, or they will have to shop around for a sympathetic parish that retains male clergy; Anglican laity are quite accustomed to this exercise already, seeking out Series B or the Prayer Book, High Mass or no candles. Those who believe the ordination of women to be invalid, despite the sanction of the General Synod, have far greater problems; they will either have to act as if the women are not really ordained at all or seek solace elsewhere.

Between 1975 and 1987 the timetable in England went as follows: by a majority of seventy-five, the General Synod of the Church of England passed a motion in 1975 decreeing there were 'no fundamental objections' (whatever that meant) to the ordination of women to the priesthood, and then promptly rejected a motion to remove legal 'and other' barriers. But nine years later the Synod changed its mind and agreed to bring forward legislation to ordain women, passing a motion a year later, in 1985, to ordain women deacons. Having set in train a course of events almost bound to result in women being ordained priests one day, in 1986 the Synod rejected a call to allow ordained women from Churches overseas in communion with Canterbury to officiate in England, a ruling eventually ignored by a good many clergy, who saw it as not only bad manners but the denial of valid orders. The following year the first women deacons were ordained.

On 11 November 1992 the General Synod decided by the closest of squeaks to legislate for women to be ordained to the priesthood. For once the word 'historic' is justified; say what you will about the Synod mustering an overall majority of 215, just two votes in favour in the House of Laity changed the face of the Church of England for ever. A two-thirds majority was required in each house. The House of Bishops voted 39 in favour, 13 against, a majority of 75 per cent; the Clergy 176 for, 74 against, a majority of 70.4 per cent; and the House of Laity, in which a decision in favour of the ordination of women had always been most problematical, 169 in favour and 82 against, thus scraping home with a majority of 67.3 per cent – a mere 0.47 per cent above the required two-thirds.

A shift of opinion in the Synod in favour of women being ordained had actually occurred during the last frantic months of campaigning, a shift no one had predicted. A sort of trial run at the summer meeting of the Synod in York had resulted in 70.45 per cent of the Bishops declaring themselves in favour, 68.91 per cent of the Clergy and only 61.41 per cent of the Laity. Those against women priests immediately began to talk about the Church regarding women already ordained as members of a permanent diaconate; those who were in favour said they would carry on praying. Presumably it was their prayers God answered, but like Waterloo, it still remained a close-run thing. A woman in the House of Laity who would undoubtedly have voted in favour died just three days before the final vote, and had death or a puncture overtaken one or two more of her like-minded colleagues, things would have been very different.

So far as one can judge from previous diocesan and deanery voting (votes taken with no mandate for action) and from opinion polls, about two-thirds of the Church at grass roots had also, by November 1982, come round in favour of the ordination of women, so in the end the Synod's decision reflected the Church's views pretty accurately. A consensus was later claimed, but this of course is an exaggeration. Two-thirds in all three houses of the Synod is generally regarded on crucial issues as acceptable, but such a figure is only a democratic majority, not a consensus. What it did on this occasion, after a quarter of a century of heated debate on the most contentious issue to face the Church of England in 400 years, was to leave, both in the Synod and the pews, one-third of the Church behind; and one-third is a very large minority. That third includes, most embarrassingly of all, at least thirteen bishops. We do not know how many suffragans not in the Synod are opposed.

I asked the Archbishop of Canterbury afterwards if he thought a two-thirds majority represented a consensus. 'Oh yes, quite definitely,' he said. 'Quite definitely. How does the Church make any decision? We are not simply a hierarchical Church. We have chosen this form of government and we ought to abide by the decision the Synod has made. I cannot think of one contentious issue which has resulted in the Church being totally united in going forward together. There have always been splits. There has always been division. And we have to live with that very human tragedy. If you take the First Vatican Council, of 1870, which led to the proclamation of papal infallibility, some of the Old Catholics split from the Roman Catholic Church. The Second Vatican Council led to Archbishop Lefebvre and the Tridentine Church not being in communion with the Church of Rome. We're not alone in struggling with issues of change.'

While it is easy to ridicule what seemed like pretty hollow theological arguments against the ordination of women, it needs to be recognised that it is possible to hold theology as deep in one's heart as in one's head. Threadbare though most of the arguments became, all contained the ring of genuine concern for a Church fated to have to decide between two seemingly irreconcilable courses of action. What people like Dr Carey are gambling on, and probably with good reason, is that the groundswell for change, slow and far from decisive though it has been, will continue to gain momentum, a view expressed to me by the Archbishop in unequivocal terms. 'I believe,' he said, 'that in ten years' time there will be even more people who will change their mind and see that God's will is to be perceived in women being ordained.'

In view of so much venom previously engendered by the issue, the final debate was conducted with surprising decorum and quite a lot of humour. The outcome was largely a pragmatic one; the ordination of women was an event whose time had come, no matter what the perils, and if the Synod did not say yes in 1992, fresh legislation, almost bound to be passed, would be brought in after another five years. Better, the argument went, to get on with it now. As befitted the occasion, it also proved to be one coloured by drama. No sooner had the Archdeacon of Leicester got launched on his opening speech against the legislation than the alarm bell rang, and the debating chamber had to be evacuated. Microphones went down like ninepins, the jovial Bishop of Sheffield seemed about to pen his resignation there and then, the Bishop of Durham was so driven by pent-up passion he could scarce hold back his tears. The best performance, however, was reserved for the vote, when the Bishop of Gloucester, having decided to abstain, remained in his seat enfolded in his monastic habit and deep in prayer, and a lay woman, quite unable to decide what to do, remained sobbing in hers. But no one could be spared to comfort her. Their votes were too precious.

To say that some of the bishops sounded like worried men would be an understatement. Portsmouth thought the debate one of the most difficult and distressing events of his life, for he found his heart and his head in conflict; he wanted to see women ordained but he could not vote for the legislation because he did not believe the Synod knew the will of God. London warned that if the legislation was passed, life would become intolerable for the bishops, with those opposed to women priests 'marginalised and ignored'. A measure of the sense of last-minute desperation on both sides can be gauged from the fact that even at this late stage 200 members of the Synod wanted to speak. Few had anything new to say, only 43 were called, and only one, the Rev Peter Geldard, chairman of the Catholic Group in the Synod, managed to speak without notes.

'A disappointingly lacklustre speech' was how *The Times* described the Bishop of Guildford's contribution; he had been deputed to open the debate commending the legislation. Dealing with the qualms of those who saw in tradition no evidence for women clergy, he came up with a novel definition of 'tradition' – a living and organic truth; in other words, tradition is not a matter of following precedent but of changing the rules if you feel like it. The Archbishop of Canterbury wisely led from the front, speaking fifth, so that no one could later accuse him of failing to offer leadership; *his* speech was described by the *Daily Telegraph* as 'unexpectedly partisan'.

Whichever way the vote had gone, the newspapers would have been able to print many of the same headlines: 'Signs of rift that could split the Church', 'Turmoil over Synod vote', 'Divided Church moves to civil war'. But because the vote had gone in favour, by 16 November Radio Four was referring to those opposed to ordination as 'Church rebels'. Only the Vatican proved to be equally off course, weighing in within minutes with a prepared statement describing the Synod's decision as 'a new and grave obstacle to reconciliation'. This was pretty rich, coming from a Church which does not even acknowledge the validity of Anglican orders, and served only to reinforce Dr Carey's view that ecumenical objections were not overriding. It also masked the belief, widely shared by many Roman Catholics and Anglicans alike, that after the present pope's demise, the Roman Church too will have married secular clergy, and eventually women priests. They are already happy to ordain married Anglican converts, although the great stampede of Anglo-Catholic clergy to Rome, prophesied in the event of a Yes vote, was almost instantly stopped in its tracks by warnings from Rome that objection to the ordination of women was not a good enough reason to become an instant convert.

One of the most unexpected outcomes of the debate was the unearthly calm that descended. There was no triumphalism among those who had 'won', and leaders of organisations that had campaigned against the ordination of women counselled against precipitate action, by which they meant any sudden mass defections to Rome; the figure banded about had always been a possible 1,000 clergy, and the wildest guess for laity a possible 500,000, with whole parishes supposedly seeking Roman Catholic oversight. When finally faced with a *fait accompli*, it may have dawned on catholic clergy in particular that to submit to Rome because of disillusion with one facet of Anglican Church life would call for a renunciation too great to make. If you cease to believe in the Anglican apostolic succession you may, most reluctantly, have to admit that your own priestly ministry has all along been invalid, but that is a terrible thing to have to face, and this is what Rome demands that you must confess. No priest can lightly say that every Mass he has celebrated and every absolution he has granted has been a waste of time and effort, a meaningless charade. But Rome thinks it is. One requires very positive reasons for such a conversion at the present time, and numbers of Anglicans who had threatened to go over to Rome over the ordination of women soon saw that the issue at stake was not a primary one.

Indeed, with his usual succinct turns of phrase, Kenneth Leech put the matter in a nutshell in a letter to the *Church Times* on 4 December 1992:

> There is an illogicality about the 'threats' of some Anglicans to become Roman Catholics at some unspecified future date, which puzzles me. If they are convinced that the Roman claims (including the crucial claim to universal ordinary jurisdiction) are true, then surely it is their duty to submit today (tomorrow at the latest) irrespective of what the Church of England does about women priests or indeed anything else. If, on the other hand, the Roman claims are not true, then it would surely be immoral to submit until they are convinced otherwise. To 'threaten' or 'promise' to submit in the future is neither here nor there.

I asked the Archbishop of Canterbury in what way he thought the ordination of women would actually change the Church of England, and he said, 'I don't think it will alter the Church of England fundamentally at all. I view the ordination of women as being an element of Church order rather than a fundamental shift in faith. I hear the phrase "a new orthodoxy" and I get impatient with that. There's no new orthodoxy about it. I've long been a student of ecclesiology and I'm sure that issues of ministerial order are secondary matters. They don't belong to the deposit of faith found in the creeds, so with the ordination of women there will be no constitutional alterations of the Church of England's faith.'

If the Archbishop is right, there will be no need for anyone to go anywhere. This is not to minimise the problems remaining for both catholic and evangelical opponents. 'Theological confusion and pastoral mayhem' have been predicted by the Archdeacon of Leicester, who believes the legislation will drive a wedge between the episcopate and the priesthood. If clergy go so far as to refuse to recognise the validity of women priests, they effectively cease to be in communion with any bishop who ordains women – and of course with the women themselves. Those bishops currently in office and opposed to women priests will not be obliged to ordain, and this may mean that some dozen dioceses will, for the time being, have no women priests. But within six months of taking office, any new bishop must ordain women – or so the legislation decrees. Within weeks there was talk of suffragans ordaining instead. What kind of pastoral relationship would a diocesan bishop have with women he had refused to ordain but had deputed a suffragan to ordain for him? And how could a diocesan authorise a suffragan to ordain women whose orders he would not accept as valid? One might say that it was an opportunity for a greater sharing of episcopal oversight, but in effect some clergy would be in communion with some bishops but not with all. What kind of a Church would that be?

It is impossible to discern or quantify any way in which life will change just because women as well as men are priests. All that will change for the women themselves is that they will be able to celebrate holy communion and give absolution. These are the priestly functions for which they have been fighting. Of course, there is a whole range of pastoral opportunities open to a parish priest, and what remains to be seen is whether, in the future, vocations to the priesthood increase because women are attracted, in a caring, motherly role, to the ordained ministry rather than, as before, in a more restricted and contemplative role, as religious.

The Church has been living with muddle ever since, in 1985, it agreed to the ordination of women deacons while denying them ordination to the priesthood, thus at a stroke creating an entirely new, second-class diaconate, inferior to that for men, practically all of whom automatically go forward to ordination as priests a year after being ordained deacons. Now, legislation for the ordaining of women to the priesthood specifically excludes legislation enabling women to be consecrated to the episcopate – once again creating a second-class order, this time of priesthood. Hence the fight for women to become bishops will have to be fought as the third round in a battle that has already made a mockery of the Church's professed adherence to its traditional ministry and to its professed desire to update that tradition.

Cynics will tell you that restricting the present legislation to the priesthood was an attempt to capture a few more votes for women priests than would have been cast if some doubters did not indeed believe they could live to fight another day; women clergy were just about palatable while women bishops would be completely beyond the pale. One argument for originally accepting women as deacons was put to me by a catholic member of the Synod who was opposed to women priests. 'There is nothing,' he said, 'that a deacon can do which in principle a lay person cannot do. A deacon may do things like baptising and burying which the laity may be restricted from doing by Church discipline, but nothing that a deacon does has any sacramental content. On the other hand, it is common ground that you must be a priest to consecrate the Eucharist and pronounce absolution, so it matters who a priest is whereas it doesn't really matter much who a deacon is. But once you have women ordained to the priesthood, episcopal certainty has gone, because a large number of people will either say, "I am certain she is not a priest because she cannot be ordained", or "she may be a priest, she may not, and I haven't enough knowledge to know". And from such a person you can't expect to receive the sacraments.'

Legislation framed so as to ban women from the episcopate, first introduced in 1988, was voted against by Robert Runcie on the grounds that it would 'institutionalise schism', and there is a perfectly plausible theory that many of its convoluted provisions were drawn up by opponents of the ordination of women because the last thing they wanted was for the legislation to work. And to a very large extent it was in fact the legislation itself rather than the principle of ordination that exercised the minds of speakers during the final debate. A bishop at present in office may not only refuse to ordain women, he can block the appointment of a woman priest ordained elsewhere to a benefice in his own diocese, and refuse her a licence to officiate, despite the fact that one of his parishes might be desperate to have a woman priest. Those bishops in favour of the ordination of women will at the same time lose full control of their diocese, because a parochial church council can veto the appointment of a woman. A parish denied a woman incumbent may well threaten to withhold payment of its quota to the diocese, and lawyers must already be rubbing their hands in glee at the prospect of court cases being fought up and down the land between dioceses and parishes.

On top of all this there is generous financial provision for clergy who in conscience cannot remain in the ministry, and decide to resign. No one yet knows – and a final figure may not emerge for several years – how many clergy will leave, not necessarily to take up a post in another Church but to enjoy early retirement, but it has been estimated by the Church Commissioners that the bill will come to £4.6 million per 100 men, spread over twenty years, although some £2 million would be offset against savings in reduced stipends. If the oft-quoted guess of 1,000 resignations materialises, the expense will be enormous.

The cost, both emotionally and financially, of the Yes vote may yet prove out of proportion to the benefits, but many people believe that threats of disruptive action on the part of parishes denied a woman priest will be nothing compared to the chaos that would have resulted from a No vote. At least one theological college principal had promised to resign, male deacons were going to be asked to refuse ordination to the priesthood, women deacons were confidently expected to fly to the United States for ordination, returning to celebrate holy communion in England without permission, and an even more serious possibility was the unlawful ordination of women by English bishops impatient with delay. It was under the shadow of threats of pastoral and legal havoc whatever the outcome that the Synod had to decide what to do. 'Massive support' for English bishops who did ordain illegally had been urged by the sub-dean of Lincoln. 'If the legislation fails,' Bishop Selby told me before the debate, 'the level of devastation will be nearly beyond control. There will be women deacons who will resign. And there are congregations that will go bonkers – in my patch, anyway.' Selby was at that time suffragan bishop of Kingston. 'If it doesn't go through there will be a total perplexity that will sweep through congregation after congregation. Most lay people don't understand how there can be an argument against women priests, and the arguments get worse and worse and worse.'

Those who objected to the Church of England taking a unilateral decision out of step with the universal Church, by which opponents of ordination meant the Orthodox and Roman Churches, lost sight of the fact that Canterbury was a good many years behind the rest of the Anglican Communion. Although the ordination to the priesthood of Florence Tim Oi Li was not made regular until 1970, and for many years she ceased to officiate, she had in fact been priested in 1944 by Ronald Hall, bishop of Hong Kong, entirely on his own initiative in circumstances of wartime desperation and in order that she could celebrate as a priest rather than as a deaconess, which – again in extraordinary circumstances – she had already been authorised to do. By the time this courageous and self-effacing woman died at the age of eighty-four, in Toronto in 1992, she had lived to see hundreds of other women throughout the Anglican Communion canonically ordained as priests, and two of them become bishops. Canada ordained women in 1976, New Zealand and the USA in 1977, Uganda in 1983. Ireland, Kenya, Burundi, West Africa, the Philippines, Brazil, South Africa, Bangladesh, Western Australia and New South Wales have all followed suit. Exact figures have never been possible to come by, and obviously they increase all the time, but by the time the Church of England emerged from its relative isolation and voted for legislation to ordain there were at least 1,400 women priests throughout the Anglican Communion, and perhaps 2,000 women deacons. In some provinces, individual dioceses have acted on their own, and the numbers of women priests are minuscule in certain areas (two in Burundi, one in Kenya) but overwhelming in the United States, where by 1992 there were over 1,000 women priests. It was in the Episcopal Church in the United States that in 1989 the first woman bishop was consecrated – amidst scenes of both joy and regret, for Barbara Harris, Suffragan Bishop of Massachusetts, is perhaps an unfortunately strident voice by which to judge the calibre or otherwise of future Lilly Liverpools or Bessy Birminghams. The first woman diocesan followed only nine months later, when Penelope Jamieson, born in Britain, was elected Bishop of Dunedin in New Zealand, and a second American female suffragan, Jane Dixon of Washington, has also been consecrated. There is no doubt that the Church of England's decision to ordain women will stiffen the resolve of those Churches overseas who have been waiting for a green light from Canterbury, and an ever increasing tide of opinion in favour of women priests will now sweep across the continents. This will at least have the effect of repairing the Anglican Communion's 'impaired communion', for once women are licensed to officiate in the Church of England there can be no impediment to women clergy from overseas being permitted to do so while resident in England.

The blazing of the trail overseas was not without distress, dissent and, in the United States, a demonstrable falling-away of lay participation in worship – uncomfortable truths played down as far as possible by the Movement for the Ordination of Women but inevitably highlighted by their opponents. Even as the Church of England was voting for women priests, the Dean of Adelaide was denouncing the ordination of Australia's first women priests as 'contrary to Scripture, apostolic order and Catholic tradition', and at the service of ordination a lay woman pronounced a curse on 'man who ordains woman to the priesthood'. What effect this may have on the Archbishop of Adeliade remains to be seen, but half the clergy in the diocese of Ballarat immediately announced they would not accept as their bishop anyone consecrated by the Archbishop of Melbourne 'or any other bishop who has purported to ordain women to the priesthood'. They have also signed a petition rejecting as invalid all ordinations and sacramental acts celebrated by bishops who ordain women. The Dean of Ballarat personally announced that he was no longer in communion either with his own archbishop or with Canterbury. There is only one word for such a tragic development as that: schism.

Susan Mackay (not her real name) was at college when the legislation for women deacons went through and she found herself a member of the last generation of women to have the choice of being a deaconess or a deacon. She told me, 'There was one girl at college with me who wanted to be a deaconess and she found she was being pressured by bishops to be ordained.' A Scottish Presbyterian by birth, Susan, who was in her mid-twenties when I met her, had flirted with the Church of Rome before being confirmed in the Church of England, and was accepted for training as a deacon in 1986. In trying to describe her sense of vocation she said, 'It was triggered by a visit to Walsingham, but started with no definite end in view. It was just a kind of itch that wouldn't go away.' At her selection conference she was one of six women out of sixteen candidates, and received a letter from her suffragan bishop to say she had been turned down. 'Apart from dented pride I was highly relieved, actually, because I didn't really want to be ordained. There were a lot of things I didn't want to get involved with. But the examining chaplain wasn't happy with the board's decision, and eventually it was overruled by the bishop. There were three candidates from my diocese on that selection conference; all three were turned down, and the bishop overruled for two of us.'

So Susan ended up training for the diaconate at St Stephen's House, where she was one of five women out of sixty students. 'I found problems I hadn't expected. For the first time in my life I came up against a very small group – not more than half a dozen – who I would say embodied the least attractive elements of Anglo-Catholicism. They had a very definite party line. They almost seemed to tick off points, and if you hadn't got the right number of points you were not considered sound. I remember when for the first time a female deacon was due to give a lecture, someone rubbed out "The Reverend" before her name because he didn't believe she was validly ordained.

'But for the most part, knowing I was not to be priested was not a problem. When lecturers said, "When you are a priest . . ." most of the men would correct them and say, "There are women here, remember."

'Have I a vocation to the priesthood now? I would like to be tested. I think a number of women do quite genuinely have a vocation to the priesthood, but I don't think the diaconate has yet been fully explored. I have an idea there are men who would like to remain deacons but they are in this sausage machine, and out they come as priests. I would like the Church of England to make the diaconate open to everyone as a permanent order.'

Having been ordained deacon, Susan went to a parish that had never had an assistant curate before, let alone an ordained woman on its staff. 'I have ended up,' she said, 'having to answer to almost everything. I'm called deaconess, sister, the parish deacon, the curate and even sometimes the vicar, because anyone who wears a dog collar is thought to be a vicar. Most people know what a curate is but they don't know what a deacon is. I know one High Church deacon who is called Mother in her parish. I'm not sure if the PCC was consulted about my appointment, to be honest. By and large my reception was good, but there was one family who left. The parish had had a woman reader, and they had had a woman administering the chalice, but this family just couldn't cope with the notion of a woman in a dog collar, who was entitled to be called Reverend. The family's leaving probably worked out to my advantage, because a lot of other people were highly embarrassed and so they were especially kind to me.

'People have refused the chalice from me. But there are Anglo-Catholics who won't accept the chalice from anyone but a priest. They won't take it from a lay person of either gender. I know why they feel like that, but I don't see that it makes any difference who's holding the chalice. It's not the person administering the chalice that's important, it's what's in the chalice that matters. If my bishop refuses to ordain women priests [which he almost certainly will] I may stay here, because if everyone moved out you would be creating a no-go area.'

For Susan, the ordination of women has always been about the incarnation. 'If you pursue to its logical conclusion the idea that only a man can be a priest, you are back in the early Church arguments about whether women can be saved. If the important thing about the incarnation is not its humanity but its gender, that raises questions of salvation. When people say to me, "I'm in favour of women priests because we've got women doctors," I agree with the conclusions but I'm not happy about the reasons for getting there. It is a secular analogy. On the other hand, you could argue that there is no reason why, in trying to open up the Church, God cannot use the secular world. It is arrogance to assume God does not make known His will outside the Church.

'Sometimes I am asked to take a funeral because people think a woman is more sympathetic than a man, but I'm not sure that's true. There are lots of men I would consider extremely sensitive. Whether women will be used for certain tasks more in future may depend not on whether they are a woman but on whether they are married. People often think a single woman knows nothing about babies. I think in pastoral matters we shall now be able to offer people much wider choice.'

One reason the arguments about the ordination of women became so stale and trivialised was that they had gone on so long – ever since 1930, in fact, when the Anglican Group for the Ordination of Woman was founded. In 1976 it was confidently being predicted that the Church of England would have women priests within five years (there were at that time just 83 women anxious to be ordained); the Congregationalist Elsie Chamberlain was complaining that these women were being turned into religious suffragettes; and Father John Coventry, who was then a member of the Roman Catholic Ecumenical Commission, and for many years had been an observer at the British Council of Churches, was quoted as saying, 'It's only a matter of time before we have married clergy, and then presumably we, too, will be on the way to women clergy. It is unrealistic to say that ordaining women would make reunion harder. We have got to move towards a diversity we have never experienced before, and what Anglicans who object to women clergy are doing is projecting their own disagreements on to Rome, which I think is rather unfair.'[1]

Progress was far slower than many commentators imagined it was going to be. Eventually the battle lines were drawn up with the Movement for the Ordination of Women on one side and an assortment of mainly High Church organisations, notably the Cost of Conscience and Women Against the Ordination of Women, on the other. By no means every catholic was opposed. Speaking at York Minster in 1988, the Archbishop of York stated his position in the following terms: 'I believe women ought to be ordained to the priesthood . . . for the fundamental reason summed up in the idea of Christ's inclusive humanity. I believe that truths which were there from the beginning in the Christian faith can lie dormant until the social and psychological conditions are right for them to be perceived. And I affirm that the time has come to express this truth in the life of the Church, and that is not going to go away.'

A prominent member of the Synod and of Women Against the Ordination of Women, Mrs Christine Cavenaugh-Mainwaring, had no doubt who was to blame for setting the ball rolling. 'If,' she wrote in an advertising feature, 'the Church of England hadn't been cursed with a handful of bishops who a generation ago began to seriously undermine the faith, authority and beliefs of the Church I doubt if we would be facing the crisis which the campaign for the ordination of women to the priesthood precipitated.' I thought the guilty men should be exposed, so I wrote to Mrs Cavenaugh-Mainwaring to ask for names. She told me:

> The bishops in particular who I had in mind, although there are many, are Bishop Barnes of Birmingham. Really a bit before my time but he began the public questioning of the Scriptures. Bishop John Robinson of Woolwich with his book *Honest to God*. The Dean of Canterbury (not a bishop but a man in authority), Dr Hewlitt Johnson. My brothers were pupils at the King's School, Canterbury, and the Headmaster, Canon Shirley, would not allow the boys to take Communion from the Dean. Bishop Hugh Montefiore of Birmingham who as, I think, Dean of Gonville and Caius, Cambridge, preached a sermon on Christ as a homosexual.[2] The present Bishop of Durham. I feel that it is wrong for men in authority within the Church to air their doubts. And for a bishop to undermine the faith of his flock is unforgivable.[3]

In order to raise funds to counter-charge, the Movement for the Ordination of Women were busy flogging car stickers that read 'In 1992 Go For Women Priests', very reasonably priced at £1 for five. More upmarket were 'large golf umbrellas in three colour combinations', described as 'just the thing for MOW vigils'. Mrs Caroline Davis, executive secretary of the Movement, was remarkably accurate in her predictions for the outcome of the vote. She had told me during the summer of 1992 that 70 per cent of the bishops would vote in favour (the figure was 75 per cent) and that the Bishop of London, who all along had appeared to be hedging his bets, would vote against, which he did. But what I really wanted to know was whether she was satisfied that the issues had been debated theologically.

'I would say so, among those people who want to debate theology, but your average person in the pew doesn't. Being a Christian doesn't necessarily mean being theologically literate. I'm sure you would find most Christians don't particularly want to be. They know they believe in God and they know they go to church and they worship God and Christ was the Son of God and that's enough, thank you very much. That's an adequate way of going about things. To force people into theological debate seems to me unnecessary.'

She thought some 80 per cent of women deacons would want to be priested. Some would now be too old to go forward. Why, I asked, had the Movement not fought for women priests from the start so that the deacons could have been priested automatically after a year? 'Because those in the General Synod who run the Church of England made a political decision to do it step by step. At it's worst it is saying, "Let them be deacons, and see how it goes. See how good they are, whether they are worthy to be priests. Let them prove themselves." ' Of her defeated opponents she had this to say: 'I suppose I shall feel sorry if they feel obliged to leave. But I can't feel sorry that the life of the Church is moving forward. I don't think you can for ever accommodate people, because that accommodation will mean backsliding for the Church. I think there comes a time when you have to say, "Well, I'm sorry you feel you have to leave but goodbye and good luck, I hope you'll find something else you want to do." '

Perhaps the voice heard least was that of the catholic priest in favour of the ordination of women. Many felt there had been an unfortunate polarization. 'If you are a catholic and in favour of the ordination of women you are no longer regarded by your fellow catholics as a catholic,' Victor Stock of St Mary-Le-Bow told me. 'But it is intrinsic to the nature of catholicism for it to develop and grow, and I cannot see that the Church can be weakened and its message made less effective by the eucharistic presidency in the twentieth century in a country like England being held by women as well as by men. To believe otherwise seems to me to reduce Christ as the embodiment and revelation of God to a matter of genital representation. Christians aren't called to represent the genitals of Christ, they are called to represent the love, compassion and self-giving. So the idea that because a women has a different set of genitalia to a man invalidates her iconically from presiding over the Eucharist seems to me to be a misunderstanding of a rather childish kind.'

Was Father Stock prepared to face up to the possible departure of fellow catholics? 'Well, I must, obviously. But it won't be the first time in history it has happened. It will also, in the event, be less dreadful than it seems now. I always thought it would be better for the legislation to pass no matter how narrow the majority so that we could settle down into the new world, which of course will be precisely the same as the old world. Having women priests isn't going to make a ha'pence of difference to most human beings. A lot of the shrillness against ordination was because the arguments against were so weak. The Church of England exists because it decided to break with Rome. The ecumenical movement is as dead as a doornail. It will remain in cold storage for twenty or thirty years, while local initiatives and friendships go on growing, and people will go on breaking the rules about intercommunion, as almost all young people do. It no longer matters what the official line is because people will take no more notice of prohibitions against Christian fellowship than RCs do about birth control.'

The precisely opposite point of view was put to me by a married catholic parish priest, Alan Sharpe of St Patrick's, Hove. 'I think the ordination of women is very wrong. I believe that Jesus expresses the fatherhood of God, just as motherhood is expressed through Our Lady. I believe very profoundly in the fatherhood of God. If women are ordained priest I dread to think what my position will be. I believe it to be very wrong, yet I don't want to join strange groups. I think I shall stand and fight. But there doesn't seem to be any way to fight.'

But those who were against the ordination of women can, at any rate with the benefit of hindsight, be seen to have been swimming against the tide. 'I believe that the Movement for the Ordination of Women has had its day,' Mrs Elizabeth Mills, a member of the executive committee of Women Against the Ordination of Women, told me over a hospitable drink at Church House early in 1992. 'If the legislation goes through in November I shall be amazed.' Echoing Archbishop Runcie, it was, she said, 'legislation for schism'. She told me, 'I cannot help but have sympathy for those women who feel they are called to be ordained. I have sympathy with anyone who feels they have a calling to something that has not been satisfied. Frustrated vocations are a problem, but then I guess being on the cross was fairly uncomfortable too. Just because one feels oneself to have a vocation is not to say that vocation exists.'

She thought one of the justifications for the ordination of women had been a lack of vocations among men. 'But the reason we haven't enough men is not a lack of men wishing to be ordained, it's lack of money to pay them. What we need is more money, not more people.'

Mrs Mills, who resigned from the Synod's panel of chairmen immediately after the vote, reserved her best quote for the *Independent on Sunday*. She told Martin Wroe, their religious affairs correspondent, 'I personally feel as if I have been given the boot by a rather beloved boyfriend whom I have known extremely well, but now that I have been chucked I have seen that there is a boy next door who seems to be very nice.' She declined to reveal the name of the boy next door, but added, 'If you have been told that your husband is going to commit adultery in eighteen months' time it is not yet grounds for divorce. But when he does commit adultery it is right to make sure you get the settlement you are entitled to.'

Mrs Mills's organisation had mustered some 6,500 lay members; the Association for the Apostolic Ministry about the same, both lay and clerical; and the Cost of Conscience perhaps 3,500. Forty per cent of the clergy in Chichester are said to support the Cost of Conscience, with figures for Exeter, Gloucester, Peterborough and Truro dioceses scarcely smaller. Cost of Conscience was masterminded by Geoffrey Kirk from the vicarage of St Stephen's, Lewisham, south London. Their major achievement was to produce a blueprint for Alternative Episcopal Oversight, involving 'a firm move away from the authority of the bishops who ordained women, into looser associations under the leadership of bishops opposed to it – with all the messy legal and financial problems that such a move would entail'. That is Father Kirk's own description of the scheme. He first listened to the arguments in favour of the ordination of women as presented by his former bishop, Ronald Bowlby. 'I thought, this isn't about the ordination of women, these people actually want to change a good deal of the fundamental basis of the Church of England in order to rewrite the title deeds of the institution,' he told me. 'What feminists in favour of the ordination of women object to is not the Church's failure to give equal opportunities to women but, at heart, it is the incarnation itself. What is wrong for them is the injustice of God being born as a male, and their notion is that some sort of adjustment to that can be made in the psychopathology of the worshipper if there is a female minister. What is wrong, in their view, about Christianity is its christology. It's the maleness of Jesus they are after. Bowlby said he took it as axiomatic that the risen and ascended Christ had no gender. What they are after is the doctrine of the incarnation.'

As to the immediate future, Fr Kirk told me, 'The question is, can you run an institution making a major change of this sort when one-third of the people for whom you are catering are in disagreement with what you are doing? Those bishops in favour will have to decide how many people they are prepared to lose – to the Roman Church, the Orthodox or the golf club. Then there remains the competence of the General Synod. Constitutionally, the General Synod is a sub-committee of the House of Commons. And it seems to me an absurd proposition that a sub-committee of the House of Commons can determine doctrine.'

Fr Kirk told me he thought 800 clergy might leave, but despite the possible price to be paid for a Yes vote, he ought to be glad of the decision for he also told me he thought that if the legislation had failed it might have come back not as a fresh proposal for the ordination of women but as plans to allow the laity to celebrate. 'It's not a long step from saying it's not a male priesthood to saying it isn't a priesthood at all. If you really want an egalitarian society you get rid of hierarchies, including the orders. I don't think it will happen in the immediate future, but eight years ago I didn't think the ordination of women was possible.

'But I'm really not sure what they are capable of next. There is a movement in the spirit of the age which has entered the Church, and there are people in the Church of England whose attitudes are inimical to the very nature of the Christian religion. The Church is becoming more and more secularised. We are constantly told there is no liberal agenda, no shopping list of changes, but people who are in favour of one liberal change don't realise it logically obliges them to be in favour of the next. They are in favour of the ordination of women because they think it's about being fair, and I entirely sympathise with them. I see how you can be misguided in that way. And I can see how justice and fairness are very important things, and how the Church must stand for them, but I can also see that if you commit yourself to certain attitudes it leads to abolition of the priesthood, and I don't think they realise the direction in which things are going.'

Father Geldard, whose Synod Catholic Group numbers 184, does not predict such a large loss of clergy as does Fr Kirk; he believes that, over a period of time, perhaps 250 will leave, but he emphasises they will almost all be catholics, and will not necessarily be replaced by catholic women. 'The Anglo-Catholics will plod on. The younger ones will wrestle hard over a period of time to decide where their home is to be. Some people who are disgruntled about the Church of England may suddenly have qualms about the ordination of women, leave and take compensation – full salary for the first year, three-quarters of your stipend for the second year, and for the next eight years two-thirds of your stipend. Plus pension rights. Plus housing. Plus a block grant when you leave. Plus a discretionary training grant! Someone of fifty-six who's fed up with his rural dean may very well be tempted to have qualms! I would put the true figure of those with serious conscientious difficulties at about 500.

'But in fact I think catholicism has been hit below the waterline. It's a tragedy for the Church of England. It will wither. The stuffing will have been knocked out of catholic worship. For me, it will be hard to convert people to a Church I think is flawed. You may think that *your* parish is all right, but late at night you begin to think, what am I actually asking them to join? Slowly the water will come in.

'For the dynamic charismatic evangelical, Church order is irrelevant. And once the Church of England believes it is free to alter its historic ministry it will take on board whatever is going. All its points of reference will disappear. Liturgical life will suffer because there will be great pressure for an open-ended liturgy.' And he shared with Fr Kirk the fear that 'there will even be pressure for a lay celebration.'

For people like himself he saw three unpalatable options. 'For better or worse you realise you were wrong, and accept the decision. Or you plod on as you are, depressed, isolated, congregationalist, and just pretend the world hasn't changed. Or you realise that the Church of England which you loved has changed, and is no longer able to make the claims she used to make about herself, so my home must be elsewhere. Each option is painful. I could not go along with continuing churches and schismatic bodies. I want to be in a Church which is spiritually alive and renewed, that I can hand on to another generation, which has a future where it's not fighting negative battles. You just could not have a schismatic church alongside the Church of England. People will have to accept women priests and bear it or move on somewhere else.'

One reason the Scheme for Anglican-Methodist Reunion foundered was that a majority of Anglican clergy could not accept the validity of non-episcopal Methodist orders. Nevertheless the Church of England enjoys courteous relations with the Methodist Church. One way forward for opponents of the ordination of women may be for them frankly and openly to deny the validity of female priestly orders but nevertheless extend the hand of fellowship to the women themselves, in the way that Rome acknowledges the legality if not the canonical validity of Anglican clergy. Yet one sees the difficulty of such a course of action for many; these women, after all, will have had hands laid upon them by diocesan bishops with whom the opponents of the ordination of women are supposed to be in communion. Nevertheless, 'the November vote need not be a cataclysm,' the *Church Times* predicted on 3 July 1992. 'The landscape will look very much the same afterwards. There need be no great divide, no pressure to conform, no sanctions against nonconformism.' And it reminded its readers that the 1990s were not the 1640s, when 2,000 incumbents who had sided with Charles I and Archbishop Laud were turned out by the Long Parliament, nor yet the 1660s, when 1,000 incumbents opposed to Charles II and the new prayer book were similarly ejected. 'If the November vote were to go in favour of the priesting of women,' the paper said, 'the Church of England would not become a different Church: it would be a Church in which the balance of opinion on one disputed point – the nature of priesthood – had shifted. That would be something for opponents of the change to take seriously, but not tragically.'

Within days of the vote, an Anglo-Catholic priest in a staunchly Anglo-Catholic diocese, Chichester, the Rev Frederick Jackson of St Michael and All Angels, Brighton, whose bishop had remained in office well beyond the call of duty to vote as his conscience dictated, issued a printed statement to his parish.

> We prayed and offered Mass that God's will might be done, and that is the only thing that matters. And so we must accept the outcome. You cannot pray for something and then only accept a reply that you agree with . . . Personally, like my bishop, I cannot accept the ministrations of a woman priest – and there is provision made for those who cannot. We can agree to disagree and be courteous to each other.
>
> Nor is it my intention to leave the Church of England. It would be ironic if one left the Church of England for the Church of Rome because of this particular issue and then

> in twenty years' time or so had to go through the whole thing again.
> The only thing that matters is that eventually God's will is done and in Jesus Christ He is praised. Let us now get on with praising Him.

By John Stott I was told, 'Although I do not have facts and figures to present to you, I believe that the evangelical opposition to the ordination of women is a small minority within our constituency, and that very few if any will leave the Church of England if the legislation is passed.'[4]

It may come as a surprise and relief to the bishops to discover, in a critical hour, just how loyal to the Church of England many of its members are. Another catholic priest opposed to the ordination of women said to me some weeks before the vote, 'If it happens, I may be persuaded that I am wrong. There is no belief so strong that it can't be changed.' An elderly retired Anglo-Catholic said to me just a week after the vote, 'I wouldn't in the least mind making my confession to a woman. As one gets older one tends to fuss less!'

But even as support emerges from unlikely quarters, women will still have sexual prejudice to contend with, as they have in commerce or the police force. A remarkably blinkered letter appeared in the *Church Times* from a Manchester cleric immediately after the vote, referring to a plea made during the debate by a woman deacon to have her vocation to the priesthood tested. He thought the likelihood was that 'most, if not all, of the Church of England's women deacons will automatically be ordained priest in 1994, without their vocations to the priesthood being tested'. Like male priests, however, they will have been to a selection conference and will have studied in a theological college; but, unlike men, they will not have had to wait a mere twelve months to be priested. In many cases, they will have waited six years. How many men would have stayed at all as second-class deacons, with no guarantee of ever being priested, seeing friends with whom they trained being inducted as vicars and team rectors? How much more testing do they have to go through?

Organisations opposed to the ordination of women amalgamated within weeks to form a single body called Forward in

Faith, claiming some 3,400 priests as members. No one kept a tally on the numbers of laity actively opposed, and it soon began to seem likely that in relatively larger numbers than the clergy, those laity unhappy with the outcome of the November vote would simply bite on the bullet and get on with their parish activities. Talk of entire congregations, split in any case as most congregations were, seeking some sort of Roman Catholic umbrella began to melt away, and the former bishop of London, Graham Leonard, who emerged from retirement to rush into print with proposals for a scheme whereby Anglicans who wished to defect could retain their Anglican identity while enjoying communion with Rome, soon found himself ignored. It just had the ring of impracticality.

Those serving bishops trying to resolve the problems likely to result from the legislation were helped more constructively by Forward in Faith, who told them they were pledged not to cause further division but to cooperate 'in seeking a just solution to this unhappy situation'. The solution the House of Bishops came up with, in January 1993, was to propose the appointment of two bishops for the Canterbury province and one for York to care specifically for the opponents of women priests. Forward in Faith had said there would need to be an assured succession of bishops who did not ordain women to the priesthood or recognise them as priests, and the bishops' general idea of permitting roving bishops to officiate, with permission, in other people's dioceses was an attempt to cobble together some kind of compromise and a semblance of unity. Nine diocesan bishops who had voted against the legislation described the proposals as 'a realistic framework for enabling those opposed to the ordination of women to remain within the Church of England'.

But the idea of bishops moving in and out of the dioceses is a very short-term solution to new issues of Church order and discipline, and it is quite impossible to see how for any foreseeable length of time clergy and bishops opposed to women priests can seriously rub along with bishops they believe are acting illegally by ordaining women and with women whose claims to orders they do not acknowledge. Either every member of the Church of England is in full communion with every other member of the Church of England, or there is schism. Equally impossible to conceive is how any schismatic Church that came out in its true colours, by becoming some sort of Church within a Church, could survive financially. All Church property belongs to the Church of England; none of it would be surrendered. The laity has no experience of financing their local church. What will probably happen is that individual parishes at present opposed to women priests will continue in communion with Canterbury but in ever increasing isolation from neighbouring parishes, and that every now and then some catholic cleric will tentatively invite a female priest to visit, just as thirty years ago a Methodist was invited to preach. And just as the ecumenical movement snowballed at grass-roots level once the ice had been broken, so more and more parishes at present opposed to women clergy will gradually assimilate the new ethos, and come to wonder what all the fuss was about.

On the assumption that in the summer of 1993 the Synod legislation is approved by both Houses of Parliament,[5] in all probability the necessary canon to permit the ordination of women to the priesthood will be promulgated in July 1994, and not long after that the Archbishop of Canterbury will ordain the first women into the Church of England as priests. No doubt the proceedings will be attended by demonstrations of protest outside the cathedral or parish church chosen for the occasion, and inside by exuberant clapping. And it may be at this last moment that a symbolic number of opponents will resign from the Church of England. But all the signs since November 1992 have been that the majority of opponents want, somehow, to find a way of remaining Anglicans.

In view of the paucity of accommodation for the debate on women priests it would be advisable to book your seat now for the consecration of the first woman bishop. Legislation will have to be drafted and introduced into the Synod, debated and no doubt amended, debated yet again, and voted on. I cannot see the process beginning for at least five or six years. But neither can I envisage inordinate delay. Normally a man would expect to have been in priest's orders at least fifteen or twenty years before becoming a bishop, perhaps twenty-five, depending how young he was when he was ordained, but as so many women have been in deacon's orders five years or more, perhaps the first woman bishop will be chosen within ten years of her ordination to the priesthood.[6] Assuming she is ordained in 1994, and that legislation for women bishops goes through in about the year 2000, we are talking about a woman bishop by 2005, not necessarily nominated by the Crown Appointments Commission but quite possibly hand-picked by a trendy diocesan as his suffragan. There may even ensue something of a race among diocesans to grab the laurels, if more than one suffragan see becomes vacant.

By the year 2005 there could be a new archbishop of Canterbury. Always assuming the first woman bishop is appointed to the southern province, and assuming also that Dr Carey retires at sixty-five, my guess is – although my guesses have been known to backfire before now – that the man who will eventually consecrate the first woman bishop in the Church of England will be the present Suffragen Bishop of Stepney, Richard Chartres.

An Epilogue

No one is indifferent to religion, for *Homo sapiens* is inherently a 'religious' animal. He is aware of history; hence he knows that he will die. And he would quite like to know why he lives and what, if anything, will happen afterwards. So, although my basic intention was always to interview and allow other people to speak for themselves, thus attempting to present a self-portrait of the Church of England, it would be cowardly to dodge presenting a very brief summary of my own conclusions. They are as follows:

By no stretch of the imagination can the Church of England any longer be regarded as a broad or comprehensive Church. In the way that over the past decade society at large, at the mercy of a catastrophic political ideology, has become intemperate, uncaring and dogmatic, so the Church of England, ever a slave to fashion, has ceased to reflect that pragmatic liberalism, tolerance and receptivity to new ideas often said to have been characteristic of the British people. Those who are frightened of change and so insecure they cannot acknowledge past mistakes always cling to the apron strings of fundamentalism, and in the Church of England evangelical fundamentalism is swamping the broad, liberal tradition. Whatever moribund spiritual needs are being met, evangelical fundamentalists are in fact pandering to the lowest common denominator. Their services lack intellectual credibility, spiritual challenge or concern for the world; they are inward-looking, smug and basically fascist, denying as they do all uncertainty; in particular, they deny that most valuable of all spiritual gifts, Christian agnosticism. No Church with any faith in its future can afford to foster the fascist mentality, and for the health of the

Church and the nation it serves, a revival of undogmatic Anglo-Catholicism, that carefully worked-out amalgam of humility, faith and doubt, together with healthy, non-fundamentalist evangelicalism, is imperative. With his abandonment of charismatic worship and his evident desire to be the broad leader of a broad Church, the present archbishop of Canterbury is ideally positioned to draw the Church of England back to its central path, the path it knows best and treads most surely.

However, if the Archbishop of Canterbury is to devote a proper amount of time and thought to the Church of which he is senior primate, he will have to relinquish a great deal of his globe-trotting. It is not enough for Church people in this country to encounter the Archbishop occasionally through the distorted medium of their newspapers. He needs to spend more time in parishes outside his own diocese, in theological colleges, in synods other than his own, fostering vocations to the ministry and above all encouraging struggling clergy and young ordinands. The Church *will* respond to charismatic leadership of a personal kind on the ground. If, on the other hand, the Archbishop is fully persuaded that the international Anglican Communion will fall apart unless he pays it constant visits, he might be well advised to abdicate in all but name and hand over the running of the Church of England to the incumbent archbishop of York, who holds a post that has always been underemployed. The archbishop of Canterbury cannot continue to lead both the Church of England and the Anglican Communion.

So far as the ordination of women to the priesthood, and eventually the episcopate, is concerned, I take no sides. I am not sufficiently involved. If you believe, as I do, that this development was inevitable, two possible conclusions follow. One, that it was better to get on with it than postpone it; two, that despite the pain and confusion (or perhaps because of them), it was the will of God. He does, after all, move in mysterious ways. In any case all the pain expressed and experienced pales into insignificance compared to the dilemmas that have faced Anglicans in the past and have even led to torture and death. No one owns the Church of England; perhaps it is up to those who disapprove of the ordination of women to question whether they were wrong. Both parties cannot be right. Of one thing I am absolutely certain; the ordaining of women priests by the Church of England, whatever else it may do, will affect the ecumenical movement not one iota.

If in future the laity want a full-time priest in their parish, they will have to wake up to the fact that the legacies of the dead, on which they have blithely depended for centuries, can no longer support the bills for stipends, housing and pensions. This means that parishes must become self-supporting. If they do that, they will discover – many for the first time – the real purpose of their existence: to be Christian cells within a secular society, proud to exist through their own missionary efforts. While they are about it, they should start choosing from among their congregation a priest to administer the sacraments who will be licensed to serve that parish and nowhere else. How can a parish ever become a real community if every five years or so they have to go through the rigmarole of finding a new parish priest? The mobility of this nation is one of its gravest problems, and the sooner the clergy learn to sit tight and care for one parish for life, the sooner parishes will become ideal communities for other units – families, for example – to copy.

At present the Church of England is in thrall to secular values. That is why it is racist and persecutes homosexuals. The remedy for both these aberrations is too obvious to bother spelling out.

Compared to the 1960s, when there were two organisations dedicated to radical reform riding high, Parish and People and the Keble Conference Group, seminal books on morality and theology being written and read, discussion and debate widespread, and detailed and realistic plans for structural reform being drawn up, the present climate in the Church of England strikes me as pretty dismal. What remains unquestionably true is that the Church does not lack individual men and women of heroic quality, who will always stagger on despite the ineptitude of the Church's leaders. For such people I retain great respect and admiration. I only wish for all our sakes that at the evangelical end they were not saddled with a liturgy that has become a travesty of Anglican worship and a betrayal of the faith that created martyrs. For a Church to be worth preserving it needs to practise a religion that is extremely tough; it needs to make spiritual and intellectual demands. Drawing now upon the often neglected heritage bequeathed by a long line of women divines, a new generation of women clergy have been given the chance they have fought and prayed for to show their mettle. It would be a hard-hearted man who did not at this stage in the Church's life recall the endearing, and enduring, words from her *Revelations of Divine Love* of one of those divines, Dame Julian of Norwich, adding the hope that they may, if only at the last trump, prove true: 'Sin is behovely, but all shall be well and all shall be well and all manner of thing shall be well.'

Notes

Introduction

1 (Church Information Office, 1985).

Chapter One: Roughly Knowing What to Do

1 The blessed Sacrament is reserved, that is to say, kept on permanent display, often in what is called a tabernacle, to provide inspiration for private prayer, to take out and display at the service of benediction or for immediate administration to the sick or dying.

Chapter Two: By Law Established

1 The modern diocese of Lincoln dates from 1072. The diocese of Sodor and Man on the Isle of Wight, now part of the Province of Canterbury, predates the diocese of Canterbury by 150 years, having been established in 447. The diocese of London is older still, dating from 314, and its present bishop is the 131st. The diocese of St Albans was not created until 1877.

2 In the national Table of Precedence the archbishop of Canterbury ranks immediately after the sovereign's cousins, and the archbishop of York two paces behind him, after the Lord Chancellor, but ecclesiastically it is a fallacy to imagine that the archbishop of York is in some way inferior, or subservient, to the archbishop of Canterbury; he consecrates bishops to the northern province, both archbishops chair their own Convocation (these two elected bodies of clergy together form the House of Clergy of the General Synod), and no provincial decision of the archbishop of Canterbury has any binding effect on the province of York.

3 There is a semantic difference of opinion as to whether Henry VIII sought a divorce or an annulment, but the ecclesiastical consequences of his separation from his first wife would have been the same in either event.

4 Thomas Cranmer was burned, William Laud was beheaded and two archbishops of Canterbury have been murdered. Retirement for the

clergy being a modern innovation, so far 92 out of 103 archbishops have died in office, many after a very short time indeed. Infirmity and disease carried off Anglo-Saxon archbishops at an alarming rate, and Matthew Hutton, who died in 1758, did not even make it to Lambeth Palace, expiring after a hearty dinner which 'aggravated his gout and inflamed his bowel'.

5 The Queen is frequently but inaccurately referred to as 'head of the Church of England'. There is no head of the Church of England.
6 *Counsel and Consent.*
7 *Church and State.*
8 SPCK.
9 *A History of the Church of England: 1945–1980* (Oxford University Press, 1984).
10 Plans for bypassing the prime minister in the case of suffragan bishops and deans, but retaining a prerogative for the sovereign, have been made in a working party report on Senior Church Appointments, discussed in Chapter Three. In the event of disestablishment these too would necessarily fall.
11 Marriages contracted in the eighteenth and nineteenth centuries by the Prince of Wales, his brother the Duke of Sussex and his nephew the Duke of Cambridge are sometimes mistakenly cited as morganatic; they were quite simply illegal and hence invalid. The semi-morganatic marriage foisted on the Duke of Windsor in 1937 by Letters Patent is generally regarded as having been a constitutional blunder.
12 'I confess to entertaining the gloomiest apprehensions as to the future of the Church of England,' the prime minister Arthur Balfour wrote to Edward Talbot, bishop of Rochester, in 1903. Similar pessimistic sentiments could be quoted through the ages.
13 Published by Davis-Poynter.
14 'For Christ's Sake', 24 October 1991.
15 The mania for producing statistical evidence has led to the Rev Leslie Francis, professor of pastoral theology at St David's University College, Lampeter, taking four years to discover that 50 per cent of children interviewed between the ages of twelve and sixteen find church services boring. The wonder, surely, is that the other 50 per cent don't. (*The Teenage Soul*, to be published in 1993.)
16 *Britain 1992: An Official Handbook* (HMSO, 1992).
17 Between 1836 and 1888 eight new dioceses came into existence: Ripon, Manchester, Truro, St Albans, Liverpool, Newcastle, Southwell and Wakefield.
18 Michael De-la-Noy, *Michael Ramsey: A Portrait* (Collins, 1990).
19 Because the Queen was in residence at Windsor, George Carey did homage on his appointment to Canterbury in the Throne Room at Windsor Castle.

Chapter Three: The Making of a Bishop

1 From 787 to 803, Lichfield also briefly ranked as an archbishopric.
2 Honorary canons and prebendaries of cathedrals are appointed for life. A retired dean may sometimes be created dean emeritus.
3 It is permissible to serve as an assistant bishop in more than one

diocese. Simon Phipps, a former bishop of Lincoln, is an assistant in both Chichester and Southwark dioceses.

4 In 1993 there were sixty-three suffragan bishops in English dioceses and four full-time assistant bishops.

5 From this proposal Mr Frank Field MP dissented.

6 Strictly speaking, praemunire is the offence against the English Crown of asserting that the pope has supremacy in England.

7 The 'bench of bishops' properly refers to those bishops who sit on the bishops' bench in the House of Lords, who number only twenty-six out of forty-four. It is, however, used as a general term of reference for all the diocesan bishops, two of whom, Sodor and Man and Gibraltar in Europe, are not eligible to sit in the House of Lords anyway. When the term 'bench of bishops' was first coined, there were far fewer diocesan bishops than now.

8 An exception is Graham James, appointed suffragan bishop of St Germans in 1992 at the age of forty-one. (He was consecrated in 1993.)

9 On the other hand, there have been people like Ambrose Reeves – expelled from the diocese of Johannesburg because of his opposition to apartheid and refused an English see by the prime minister although favoured by the archbishop of Canterbury – who might fare better today with the Commission.

10 By John Robinson, bishop of Woolwich (SCM, 1963). *Honest to God* sold one million copies, and caused a furore.

11 After the resignation in March 1993 of Peter Ball, a monk and bishop of Gloucester, following allegations of homosexual misconduct, it can safely be assumed that the Crown Appointments Commission will look more nervously than ever at the marital status and known or assumed sexual orientation of potential diocesan bishops, and that the chances of a homosexual priest or suffragan receiving preferment will correspondingly diminish.

12 *Chantonbury Ring* (Hodder & Stoughton, 1982).

13 Quoted in *Michael Ramsey: A Portrait*, op. cit.

14 Leslie Paul, *A Church by Daylight* (Geoffrey Chapman, 1973).

15 In 1993 John Major made John Holroyd prime minister's appointments secretary to succeed Sir Robin Catford, appointed in 1982 by Mrs Thatcher.

16 Vacancy-in-See Committees predate the Crown Appointments Commission by a decade.

17 If the vacancy is in the southern province, the archbishop of Canterbury will take the chair; if in the northern province, the archbishop of York.

18 For a detailed analysis of the controversy, see Bernard Palmer, *High and Mitred* (SPCK, 1992), pp. 290–92.

19 *One of Us* (Macmillan, 1989).

20 The dean of Windsor is one of only three people with direct access to the Queen. The other two are the Lord Chamberlain and her private secretary. In 1909, against the wishes of Asquith, Edward VII was directly responsible for the appointment of Bertram Pollock to the see of Norwich. In 1959 Archbishop Fisher was so concerned for the Queen's peace of mind that he wrote to tell her the names of three possible candidates for Norwich he had suggested to Macmillan.

21 For a full account of the foundation of all the cathedrals and their status, see Welsby, *How the Church of England Works*, op. cit.
22 In 1990 the government made a total grant of £11.5 million over three years. At the end of 1992 the government promised English Heritage a further £8 million over two years to help with restoration work both on Anglican and Roman Catholic cathedrals.
23 In 1943 Dean Selwyn was short-listed for the bishopric of Bath and Wells but Churchill appointed William Wand, archbishop of Brisbane. On Wand's translation to London two years later, Archbishop Fisher tried to get Attlee to appoint Selwyn to Bath and Wells, and failed. In 1952 Archbishop Garbett of York suggested Selwyn for Durham, but the see went to Michael Ramsey, and Dean Selwyn was finally lost to the episcopate for ever.
24 And from whom the author is collaterally descended.

Chapter Four: Money Matters

1 *Christian Statesman*, Summer 1987.
2 SPCK, 1991.
3 *A History of the Church of England*, op. cit.
4 'The General Synod: 1975 version', *Crucible*, October-December 1976.
5 In October 1992 the Archbishop of Canterbury appointed the Bishop of Chelmsford chairman of an inquiry into the administration of the Church Commissioners following specific allegations that a loss of £500 million had resulted from property speculation.
6 This was Sir Douglas Lovelock, who retired in March 1993. He was succeeded, at the age of sixty-four, by Sir Michael Coleman, who makes mustard.

Chapter Five: Training for the Next Century

1 In 1991 Sir Derek Pattinson, on his retirement as secretary-general of the General Synod, was ordained deacon by Graham Leonard, bishop of London, without being obliged to attend a bishops' selection conference, and the next year likewise was ordained priest by Dr Leonard's successor, David Hope. An almost total lack of formal training has not prevented Michael Ball from becoming bishop of Truro.
2 *ACCM Occasional Paper* No. 12, revised August 1990.
3 *The Times*, 4 May 1992.
4 *ACCM Occasional Paper* No. 12, op. cit.
5 'For Christ's Sake', op. cit.
6 In 1992, twelve serving diocesan bishops and ten suffragans had trained at Cuddesdon (now Ripon), fifteen bishops, all told, at Westcott House, and twelve at Ridley Hall. St Stephen's House had produced seven bishops, Wycliffe six, Wells, Lincoln and Mirfield four each and The Queen's College and Cranmer Hall two each.
7 Church House Publishing, 1992.
8 The Jubilee Group, 1991.

9 *Issues in Human Sexuality: A Statement by the House of Bishops*, 1991, discussed in Chapter Eleven.
10 Chichester Theological College *Newsletter* No. 1, Lent 1992.

Chapter Six: Head-Hunting for Patrons

1 Judith Judd, 'A learning experience that's beyond belief', the *Independent*, 6 August 1992.
2 Immediately after the General Synod voted on 11 November 1992 to legislate for the ordination of women to the priesthood, Father Flatman announced that he would be seeking reception into the Roman Catholic Church.
3 Peter Selby was in 1993 appointed William Leech professorial fellow in applied Christian theology at Durham University.
4 The person appointed was a Franciscan, Brother Colin Wilfred.
5 Malcolm Johnson was being unduly pessimistic. In 1992 the Queen appointed him master of a Royal Peculiar, the Royal Foundation of St Katherine in Ratcliffe, Butcher Row, Stepney, east London. A Royal Peculiar is an appointment in the gift of the Queen. The others are Westminster Abbey, St George's Chapel, Windsor, the Chapels Royal, the Royal Memorial Chapel at Sandhurst, the Queen's Chapel of the Savoy, and All Saints, Windsor Great Park.

Chapter Seven: The Lambeth Way

1 For an interesting critique of Parish and People, and its merger in 1963 with the Keble Conference Group, see Trevor Beeson's essay 'Reform or removal?' in *God's Truth* (SCM, 1988).
2 *The Anglo-Catholic Social Conscience* (Jubilee Group, 1991).
3 Reviewing *The Billy Graham Story* by William Martin (Hutchinson) in the *Church Times* of 11 September 1992, the Bishop of Edinburgh wrote, 'Billy Graham has become less fundamentalist down the years, but he is still essentially a biblical literalist who reads scripture as though it were a fax sent from God this very morning.'
4 *A History of the Church of England*, op. cit.
5 Thomas Butler, Bishop of Leicester.
6 *Me and My Girl*, 1937.
7 Before the bread and wine are placed on the altar to be consecrated, the celebrant says, 'Let us offer one another a sign of peace.' The intention is that the clergy, and then the congregation, should exchange the traditional kiss of peace, but many English people funk it with a handshake.
8 A Protestant religious community in the Burgundian village of Taizé, founded in 1948 by a Franco-Swiss, Roger Schutz. Within only a very few years its spiritual atmosphere and mode of worship had exerted an influence internationally not experienced since the times of Benedict and Ignatius.
9 Michael Joseph, 1990.
10 Denis Shepheard, who died in 1992, an evangelical whose conversion at

Billy Graham's 1954 Crusade led to ordination, claimed to have been cured of marrow cancer in his left ankle after he had been anointed.
11 St Nicholas, where the Archbishop was vicar from 1975 to 1982.

Chapter Eight: Bars and Bombs

1 Edward Holland.
2 A few weeks after my visit a prisoner of twenty-three, on remand charged with murder, did commit suicide, the third suicide at this prison in ten years.
3 By December 1992 Father Riggs had worked for four and a half years at Open Door, and resigned in order to have a period of rest and to consider his future. The work continues under the Rev Peter Browne.
4 By mid–1992, heterosexual intercourse was already the most common cause of HIV infection in Scotland.

Chapter Nine: The Religious in Retreat

1 Originally known as Cardinal's College.
2 Anyone who wishes to read in detail about monasticism should consult Geoffrey Moorhouse, *Against All Reason* (Weidenfeld & Nicolson, 1969).
3 *The Vision*, 24 South Audley Street, London W1, lists 160 retreat houses.
4 It can be done. The author has personally known a monk, now dead, who was seldom if ever sober.
5 Information about religious communities can be obtained by sending a stamped addressed envelope to the Administrative Secretary, The Communities Consultative Council, 9 Stafford Road, Eccleshall, Staffordshire ST21 6JP.

Chapter Ten: Dr Who?

1 *Cantaur: The Archbishops in their Office* (Cassell, 1971).
2 *A History of the Church of England*, op. cit.
3 Temple's book *Christianity and Social Order*, published in 1942, sold 139,000 copies, and has even been credited with contributing to the election three years later of a Labour government. He shared with Oscar Wilde the gift of a photographic memory. His biographer, F. A. Iremonger, believed that no other bishop 'possessed in equal measure his many qualifications'.
4 Perhaps even more reprehensibly, in 1945 Churchill declined to appoint Bell to London, contenting himself with Brendan Bracken's nominee, Wand of Bath and Wells.
5 *A History of the Church of England*, op. cit.
6 Gordon Savage, bishop of Southwell, who died in 1990.
7 Sinclair-Stevenson, 1991.
8 The *Independent Magazine*, 11 July 1992.

9 *The Crockford's File: Gareth Bennett and the Death of the Anglican Mind* (Hamish Hamilton).
10 SPCK, 1988.
11 Undated letter from Lord Runcie to the author, postmarked 29 June 1992.
12 Credence to the story about Lord Runcie trying to telephone Dr Bennett was first given by William Oddie in *The Crockford's File*, where it was dramatically described as 'a heart-stopping event'.
13 The other biography to which Lord Runcie would have been referring is *Robert Runcie* by Adrian Hastings (Mowbray, 1991), not so racy as Mantle's but a reliable and well-researched read. An official biography of Lord Runcie has been commissioned from Humphrey Carpenter, whose father was at one time bishop of Oxford.
14 Between 1979 and 1993 the primates met in Ely, Cambridgeshire; Washington, DC; Limuru, Kenya; Toronto, Canada; and Cyprus.
15 He actually became archbishop at a ceremony at St Mary-Le-Bow, Cheapside, London, on 27 March 1991, when he was declared to be 'a man both prudent and discreet, deservedly laudable for his life and conversation'. From 1290 the election of all bishops in the Province of Canterbury was confirmed at St Mary-Le-Bow – an ancient custom now discontinued by Dr Carey, who has transferred the ceremony to Lambeth Palace.
16 The editor of the 1992 *Church of England Year Book* remained so thrown off balance that he listed the new archbishop as the Rt Rev, not the Most Rev.
17 Private information.
18 Knighted by the Queen personally (he was made a KCVO) in the 1993 New Year Honours List.
19 *The Spectator*, 13 June 1992.
20 But the remark came back to haunt him in a *Times* leader the day after the General Synod voted for the ordination of women to the priesthood. There are some errors of judgement, it seems, that can never be forgotten.
21 Private information.
22 It is unlikely Mr Higton's reputation will ever fully recover from his assertion, made in the *Christian Herald*, that the fire at Windsor Castle in November 1992 was a warning from God to repent for the practice of 'multi-faith worship'.
23 *The Church in the Market Place* (Kingsway Publications, 1984).
24 *The Great God Robbery* (Fount, 1989).
25 March 1991.
26 Chaplains to Archbishop Ramsey, Archbishop Runcie and Archbishop Carey have now all been made suffragan bishops.
27 *Church Times*, 13 March 1992.

Chapter Eleven: Sidetracked by Sex

1 Broken Rites are listed in the *Church of England Year Book*. Their address is 30 Stevenson Street, Bowburn, Durham DH6 5BA.
2 14 April 1992.
3 *Chantonbury Ring*, op. cit.

4 A previous report, circulated privately to the bishops, was never even published.
5 'Holy homos escape ban' (the *Star*) and 'Pulpit poofs can stay: Church votes not to kick them out' (the *Sun*) were just two of the inflammatory newspaper headlines for which he was ultimately responsible.
6 25 April 1992.
7 The chairman was the Rev June Osborne.
8 Rhymes, *No New Morality* (1964), West, *Homosexuality* (1960), Westwood, *Society and the Homosexual* (1952).
9 The late Sydney Evans.

Chapter Twelve: The Women's Vote

1 'Could you accept a woman vicar?', *Good Housekeeping*, 1976.
2 In 1977 Montefiore's preferment from the suffragan bishopric of Kingston to the see of Birmingham was a result of the first recommendation to be made by the new Crown Appointments Commission.
3 Letter to the author dated 20 July 1992.
4 Letter to the author dated 25 June 1992.
5 This part of the timetable was being put into operation as this book was going to press. In the event of either House voting against the legislation, the General Synod would have had the right to present the legislation a second time.
6 In America it took twelve years for a woman to become a bishop, but she had to be elected. So long as English diocesans are free to choose suffragan bishops, it is likely that the Church of England will have more women bishops more quickly than Churches overseas.

Index